Understanding Organized Crime

Second Edition

Understanding
Organized
Crime

Second Edition

Stephen L. Mallory, PhD

Professor, Chair
Legal Studies Department

University of Mississippi
University, Mississippi

JONES & BARTLETT

World Headquarters

Jones & Bartlett Learning	Jones & Bartlett Learning Canada	Jones & Bartlett Learning International
40 Tall Pine Drive	6339 Ormindale Way	Barb House, Barb Mews
Sudbury, MA 01776	Mississauga, Ontario L5V 1J2	London W6 7PA
978-443-5000	Canada	United Kingdom
info@jblearning.com		
www.jblearning.com		

Jones & Bartlett Learning books and products are available through most bookstores and online booksellers. To contact Jones & Bartlett Learning directly, call 800-832-0034, fax 978-443-8000, or visit our website, www.jblearning.com.

Production Credits

Publisher, Higher Education: Cathleen Sether
Acquisitions Editor: Sean Connelly
Editorial Assistant: Caitlin Murphy
Associate Production Editor: Lisa Cerrone
Associate Marketing Manager: Lindsay White
Manufacturing and Inventory Control Supervisor: Amy Bacus
Composition: Laserwords Private Limited, Chennai, India
Cover Design: Scott Moden
Photo Researcher: Sarah Cebulski
Permissions and Photo Researcher: Amy Mendosa
Cover Image: © Bliznetsov/ShutterStock, Inc.
Printing and Binding: Malloy, Inc.
Cover Printing: Malloy, Inc.

Library of Congress Cataloging-in-Publication Data

Mallory, Stephen L.
  Understanding organized crime / Stephen L. Mallory. — 2nd ed.
    p. cm.
  Includes bibliographical references and index.
  ISBN 978-1-4496-2257-2 (pbk.)
  1. Organized crime. I. Title.
  HV6441.M38 2012
  364.106—dc23
                                        2011018473

6048

Printed in the United States of America
15 14 13 12 11   10 9 8 7 6 5 4 3 2 1

Dedicated to the men and women who are engaged in the battle against
organized crime and terrorism.

Brief Contents

Chapter 1 An Introduction to Organized Crime 1

Chapter 2 Evolution of Organized Crime and the Impact on Investigative
Strategies and Law Enforcement 15

Chapter 3 Theories on the Continued Existence of Organized Crime 33

Chapter 4 Colombian Drug Cartels 51

Chapter 5 Mexican Drug Trafficking Organizations 67

Chapter 6 The Russian Mafia 89

Chapter 7 The Italian American Mafia 109

Chapter 8 The Yakuza 139

Chapter 9 Triads and Tongs 159

Chapter 10 American Outlaw Motorcycle Gangs 179

Chapter 11 Hispanic and African American Gangs 207

Chapter 12 Major Statutes, Legislation, and Methods of Organized
Crime Investigations 223

Chapter 13 The Intelligence Function in Organized Crime Investigations 243

Chapter 14 The Nexus of Transnational Organized Crime and Terrorism 257

Chapter 15 Where Do We Go from Here? 279

TABLE OF CONTENTS

Preface xvii
Acknowledgements xxi

Chapter 1	**An Introduction to Organized Crime**	**1**

Objectives 1
Defining Organized Crime as Part of the Process of Investigation 1
  A Working Definition for Organized Crime 2
  Definitions of Organized Crime 3
Investigation Definitions 4
Organized Crime as Defined by Laws, Agencies, and Governments 5
  International Perspective 6
  United States Federal Definitions 7
  A Synthesis of Definitions 9
  Other Approaches to Defining Organized Crime 10
Conclusions 11
References 12

Chapter 2	**Evolution of Organized Crime and the Impact on Investigative Strategies and Law Enforcement**	**15**

Objectives 15
Introduction 15
Origins of Organized Crime in the United States 17
  Colonial Piracy 17
  Rise of Robber Barons and Crime Families 18
  Immigrant Crime Groups and Political Machines 19
New Impetus for Expansion of Organized Crime in the United States 21
  Anti-crime Legislation and the Growth of Organized Criminal Groups 22

Development of Organized Crime in the South	23
Illegal Whiskey	24
Modern Development	27
Commissions and Task Forces	27
Corporate and Political Corruption: The Major Contribution	
to Organized Crime Growth and Power	28
Future Impact on Law Enforcement Efforts	29
References	31

Chapter 3 Theories on the Continued Existence of Organized Crime — **33**

Objectives	33
Introduction	33
Theories of Organized Crime	35
Alien Conspiracy Theory	35
Social Control Theory	36
Albanese's Theory of Typologies	36
Sutherland's Theory of Differential Association	37
Durkheim and Merton's Strain Theory and Anomie	38
Beccaria's and Lombroso's Classical Theories	38
Biological Theories	39
Summary of the Theoretical Approaches	39
Theories Related to Law Enforcement Efforts	40
Enterprise Theory	40
Hierarchical and Local-Ethnic Models	42
Deterrence Theory	42
Other Models	43
Beyond Theory	43
Combining Theory and Other Explanations	45
Conclusions	47
References	49

Chapter 4 Colombian Drug Cartels — **51**

Objectives	51
Introduction	51
Historical Perspective	52
The Medellín Cartel	54
Operations	55
The Cali Cartel	55
Operations	56
Decline of the Major Cartels	59
Current Activities	60
"Baby" Cartels	61
FARC	61
Paramilitary Groups	61
Plan Colombia	62

*Assessment of the Current Threat from Colombian
Cartels*   63
Conclusions   63
References   65

| Chapter 5 | **Mexican Drug Trafficking Organizations** | **67** |

Objectives   67
Historical Perspective   67
Development and Expansion   69
Mexican Drug Violence and DTO Competition   71
The Four Major Cartels   73
  Tijuana Cartel (Arellano Felix Organization)   74
  Gulf Cartel   75
  Sinaloa Cartel   76
  Juárez Cartel   76
  Subsidiary and Emerging Organizations   78
Current Activity   81
Drug Policies: Impact and Consequences   83
Conclusions   84
References   85

| Chapter 6 | **The Russian Mafia** | **89** |

Objectives   89
Historical Perspective   89
Structure and Organization   93
Activities and Methods of Operation   95
  Theft, Kidnapping, and Murder   95
  Cybercrime   96
  Extending Their Reach   97
Investigative Strategies   104
Conclusions   106
References   107

| Chapter 7 | **The Italian American Mafia** | **109** |

Objectives   109
Introduction   109
Historical Perspective   110
Overview   110
  Immigration Years: The Black Hand   111
  Violation of Omerta   113
  The FBI and the Mafia   114
The New York Mafia   114
  Arnold Rothstein   114
  Charles "Lucky" Luciano   115

The Commission	*116*
The Five Families of New York	*118*
Other Mafia Groups	*120*
Chicago	*120*
Las Vegas and Sam Giancana	*120*
Philadelphia and Atlantic City	*121*
New Orleans	*122*
The American Mafia Today	*123*
Structure and Organization	*125*
Membership	*127*
Initiation	*128*
Activities and Methods of Operation	*129*
Provision of Illicit Services and Goods	*129*
Gambling	*129*
Labor Racketeering	*130*
New Partnerships	*131*
Investigative Strategies	*132*
Exposure: Informants and Witnesses	*132*
Sting Operations	*133*
Government Oversight	*134*
Grand Juries and Legislation	*134*
Conclusions	*135*
References	*136*

Chapter 8	The Yakuza	**139**

Objectives	*139*
Introduction	*139*
Historical Perspective	*140*
Early Criminal Groups	*140*
The Industrial Age Through the Post–World War II Era	*141*
Yamaguchi-Gumi Crime Group	*142*
Yakuza Today	*144*
Structure and Organization	*146*
Membership	*146*
Code of Conduct and Oaths	*147*
Activities and Methods of Operation	*150*
Business Acquisition	*150*
Protection and Extortion	*150*
Gambling	*150*
Narcotics Trafficking	*151*
Pornography	*152*
Weapons and Smuggling	*152*
Money Laundering	*152*
Investigative Strategies	*153*
Laws and Statutes	*153*

Special Task Forces	*154*
Follow the Money	*155*
Conclusions	*156*
References	*158*

Chapter 9	**Triads and Tongs**	**159**

Objectives	*159*
Introduction	*159*
Historical Perspective	*160*
The Fighting Shaolin Monks	*162*
Chinese Rebellions Through the Revolution	*163*
Global Dispersal of the Triads	*163*
Structure	*164*
Triad Membership	*164*
Tongs	*167*
Investigating Triads and Tongs Based on Structural Considerations	*168*
Activities and Methods of Operations	*169*
Triad Activities	*170*
Tong Activities	*171*
Chinese Gang Activities	*172*
Violence and Intimidation	*173*
Human Smuggling	*174*
Business Investments	*174*
Investigative Strategies	*174*
Cultural and Language Barriers	*175*
Surveillance and Sting Operations	*176*
Conclusions	*176*
References	*178*

Chapter 10	**American Outlaw Motorcycle Gangs**	**179**

Objectives	*179*
Introduction	*179*
Historical Perspective	*180*
The Post–World War II Era	*180*
1970 to Today	*183*
The Big Four	*184*
Hells Angels	*184*
Outlaws	*185*
Bandidos	*186*
Pagans	*186*
Other OMGs	*191*
Grim Reapers	*191*
Mongols	*192*

Structure	*194*
Membership	*194*
Retirement Bylaws	*199*
Activities and Methods of Operation	*199*
Networks	*200*
Investigative Strategies	*201*
Intelligence	*201*
Laws and Statutes	*202*
Grand Juries	*203*
Conclusions	*204*
References	*205*

Chapter 11 Hispanic and African American Gangs — **207**

Objectives	*207*
Introduction	*207*
Historical Perspective	*208*
Hispanic/Latino Gangs	*209*
Gang Communication: Language, Graffiti, Hand Signals, and Dress	*209*
Clicas	*210*
Gang Culture	*210*
Gang Structure	*211*
Members	*211*
Major Gangs	*212*
Bloods and Crips	*212*
Jeff Fort and the Black P. Stone Nation	*214*
Larry Hoover and the Gangster Disciples	*214*
Historical Black Figures of Organized Crime	*216*
Frank Lucas	*216*
Frank Matthews	*216*
Leroy Barnes	*217*
Charles Lucas	*217*
Other Black Criminal Organizations	*217*
Nigerian Organized Crime	*217*
Jamaican Organized Crime	*217*
Prison Gangs	*218*
Investigative Strategies and Laws	*220*
Conclusions	*221*
References	*221*

Chapter 12 Major Statutes, Legislation, and Methods of Organized Crime Investigations — **223**

Objectives	*223*
Introduction	*223*
The Hobbs Act and Extortion	*224*

RICO   225
Property Forfeiture   227
Violations of the Internal Revenue Code   228
Money Laundering Laws   229
    The Money Laundering Cycle   231
Controlled Substances Acts   232
Conspiracy Statutes   233
    Conspiracy Case Development   235
    Continuing Criminal Enterprise Statute   236
    The Kingpin Act   236
    Regulation and Monitoring of Business and Labor   236
    Electronic Surveillance   237
    Investigative Grand Juries   239
Other Statutes Frequently Used During Organized Crime Investigations   239
Conclusions   240
References   241

Chapter 13   The Intelligence Function in Organized Crime Investigations   243

Objectives   243
Introduction   243
Current Assessment of Organized Crime in the United States   244
    Organized Crime's Connection to Terrorist Groups   244
    Legislation   245
Intelligence   245
    Historical Perspective   246
    Evaluation of Information   248
    Sources of Intelligence   249
    Application of Analytical Models to Organized Crime Investigations   250
Conclusions   254
References   255
Suggested Reading   256

Chapter 14   The Nexus of Transnational Organized Crime and Terrorism   257

Objectives   257
Introduction   257
Comparing Terrorism and Transnational Organized Crime   258
Comparison of the Structure of Terrorist Groups and Transnational
    Organized Crime   261
Early History of Networking and Common Criminal Activity by Organized
    Crime and Terrorists   264
Types, Links, and Methods of Cooperation Between Organized Crime and Terrorists 267
Recent Developments in Networking and Criminal Activity of Terrorists
    and Transnational Crime   271
Conclusions   274
References   275

Chapter 15	Where Do We Go from Here?	279
	Law Enforcement Response to Organized Crime	279

Author Index   287

Subject Index   291

Photo Credits   303

PREFACE

With the current emphasis on terrorism, it is apparent that the assets of the U.S. Federal Government are being shifted to the enforcement efforts of antiterrorism and counterterrorism measures. This effort is placing more of the burden of the investigation of organized crime on state and local law enforcement. Although this emphasis on terrorism is both necessary and important, the enormous negative impact of organized crime on our society will not diminish, and the current trend of alliances between these criminal syndicates and the evolvement of new transnational organized crime groups will demand innovative strategies and increased investigative efforts and resources. This book addresses the concept of organized crime and the various types of knowledge that students who wish to become criminal investigators need to effectively cope with the organizations that dominate the criminal world.

An investigation of an organized or syndicated crime group is perhaps the most complex and time-consuming effort an investigator is likely to encounter during his or her career. Facing an organization that is located in numerous jurisdictions, states, and/or countries and commands unlimited resources and large memberships, the task of case development is very difficult at best. When the element of corruption is added to the equation, the investigation is often compromised in situations that become both frustrating and dangerous for the witnesses, informants, victims, and officers involved in the case.

The second edition of *Understanding Organized Crime* reflects the dynamic nature of transnational organized crime. The world is changing and the criminal syndicates are adapting and emerging to meet the illegal needs and services demanded by the global community. Methods and techniques of criminal investigation of organized crime that have been successful in the past are still effective against members of organized crime. However, advancing technology has been a double-edged sword for criminal investigators. Criminal organizations have not suffered from limited budgets and economic crises; law enforcement and governments have.

The recent eruption of violence in Mexico and along the southwest border of the United States has demonstrated the rise and power of the Mexican cartels. Chapter 5 of this text reveals the escalation of violence by the cartels and the impact on crime in America. These cartels are now considered the most serious threat posed by organized crime to the security of our country and that of Mexico. The struggle for power among the cartels has resulted in the loss of over 7000 lives in the past two years and is now a major topic of debate among leadership and law enforcement in both the United States and Mexico. The most recent violent event of using car bombs to kill police in Juárez is evidence of a problem that will require extraordinary methods and resources to address. Chapter 5 discusses the rise of new players and organizations such as Los Zetas and La Familia Michoacana, among others. New alliances and wars over territories and smuggling routes between established cartels and emerging organizations are outlined and discussed in this revised chapter, along with policies and intervention efforts to address this escalating problem.

Chapter 14 was added to address the increasing nexus between terrorist groups and transnational organized crime. The increased cooperation and networking between these major threats is now evident and will likely become more of a challenge for governments and law enforcement. The chapter identifies these alliances and examines the modern terrorist or "hybrid" organizations and compares them to methods and activities common to organized crime. Comparing terrorist and organized crime as to motive, methods of operation, and activities is a section that is paramount to understanding why these organizations have increased their cooperation. The chapter outlines the structure of terrorist groups and compares it to the structure of organized crime groups. The involvement of terrorists in criminal activity such as drug and human trafficking is not new, but it has become a major source of funding for terrorist operations due to a decline in state-sponsored terrorism. The examination of both terrorist and organized crime structures and current activities gives the reader a better understanding of why these organizations have moved into networking, which has resulted in both groups' growth in power and the ability to achieve their goals. Dangerous levels of violence and corruption are now common to both groups and have added to the challenge of law enforcement.

While emerging alliances between organized crime groups and terrorists is a major concern, activities such as the age-old crime of piracy have not gone away. Recent events have been added to this Second Edition outlining the new age of piracy that has resulted in the creation of task forces that focus on areas around the Gulf of Aden off the coast of Somalia. Recent information has been added to Chapter 4 regarding the modern assessment of the remaining threat of the Columbian cartels. Additional and updated information is included in the chapters on outlaw bikers (Chapter 10), the Russian mafia (Chapter 6), the Italian American mafia (Chapter 7), and the Yakuza (Chapter 8). Recent events concerning each of these organizations reveal their continued existence and how they remain a threat to governments and law enforcement. The recent arrest of over 300 members of organized crime in Italy, the Yakuza, and gangs such as the Mongols motorcycle group are indications that these organizations will remain a problem for law enforcement for some time.

The Second Edition emphasizes the need to understand who the players and leaders are, how they are financed, how they recruit, methods of operations and activities, and what new alliances are forming, and gives examples of gangs that are now considered organized crime. With this information, effective investigative strategy, policies, and laws can be established and employed to address this growing threat to the global community. Today, the world is facing an increasing impact from established organized crime, emerging transnational organized crime, and gangs that requires more understanding of who and what these organizations are and how they achieve their goals. Given the dynamic nature of organized crime, no text can ever be complete, but the Second Edition of *Understanding Organized Crime* is an attempt to give the reader a better understanding of how and why these criminal groups continue to dominate the world of crime and what law enforcement must do to address this threat.

Investigative techniques that have been effective in the past can be applied to each criminal enterprise with some success. Certainly, there are unique characteristics of each criminal organization that may call for specific enforcement techniques, but the majority of enforcement measures will be effective strategies to combat most of these groups and their activities. Law enforcement must continue to develop innovative tactics to address this type of criminal activity as well as build international cooperation to meet the challenge of global alliances and the growing complexity these organizations present.

The theme of corruption is paramount. Clearly, these criminal organizations cannot exist without corruption of not only police, but of many government officials and a variety of private citizens and businesses. The abilities of organized crime members to take advantage of financial systems that are cloaked in secrecy, supply the public's demand for illicit goods and services, and continue to create criminal opportunities that are extremely profitable are three common traits that serve to describe the organized crime groups.

Some organized groups originated as people forming alliances for good causes, such as protection and security from powerful foes. However, as with many enterprises, greed and power became the prime motivators fueling the formation of criminal syndicates. Although many writers and academics point to prohibitions of narcotics and alcohol as the origins of organized crime, it is my experience that power and greed are the root causes of this type of criminal behavior, with prohibitions only serving as the impetus for their growth and success. Many of these groups have existed for decades and continue to evolve into more complex and diverse organizations. Leaders and bosses of these organizations typically began their careers as petty criminals who escalated into the positions of authority because of their greed, cunning, ruthlessness, and lust for power. They are street smart and are often intelligent. But in the end, it is the public's demand for illicit goods and services, corruption, and black markets that support the existence of these groups. Effective investigation can and does deter organized crime activity, but it will continue to exist as long as public support and market demand remain.

This book was written in an effort to increase the success of tomorrow's criminal investigators and those who will be involved in the profession of criminal justice. It is the informed criminal investigator who can apply the evolution, theories, structure, methods of operation, law, and investigative techniques to develop effective strategies to minimize the impact of these criminal groups or eliminate the criminal enterprises themselves. Students will gain a better understanding of today's transnational organized crime groups as well as insight into their thought processes and operations. *Understanding Organized Crime* provides tools for the student whose goal is to become an organized crime investigator and to develop critical thinking skills essential to deal with these powerful and continually evolving adversaries of the rule of law.

This textbook is accompanied by a series of valuable supplements. Microsoft® PowerPoint® slides, organized by chapter, are available to assist instructors in effectively teaching courses on organized crime. Additionally, a TestBank containing discussion questions and practical exercises is provided to stimulate the critical thinking skills of students.

Students will benefit from the companion website designed exclusively for this text. The website features a variety of interactive study tools, including a glossary, interactive flashcards, practice exercises, and more!

ACKNOWLEDGEMENTS

Thank you to the following reviewers for their contributions to this text:

Joseph D. Alkus, Temple University

Hasan T. Arslan, University of New Haven

Earl Ballou Jr., Duquesne University

Thomas Barker, Eastern Kentucky University

Stephen Brodt, Ball State University

Lisa A. Eargle, Francis Marion University

Michael Freeman, Mountain View Community College

Patrick D. Walsh, Loyola University New Orleans

Chapter 1

An Introduction to Organized Crime

Objectives

After completing this chapter, readers should be able to:

- Describe the differences between organized and disorganized crime.
- Explain why defining organized crime is important to law enforcement.
- Compare the United States' definitions of organized crime with those of other countries.
- Discuss state and federal legislation that address organized crime.

Defining Organized Crime as Part of the Process of Investigation

What is organized or syndicated crime? Why is it important for the criminal investigator to identify a target as organized crime? These questions must be answered before successful strategies, laws, and techniques can be developed for use in any successful investigation of a group of individuals engaged in criminal activity.

During the years when J. Edgar Hoover was the Director of the Federal Bureau of Investigation (FBI; 1924–1972), Americans debated whether organized crime actually existed. Later, organized crime became synonymous with the American Mafia. But the true nature and scope of organized crime is the insidious dynamic between those using ruthless methods (including corruption and murder) to increase their profits and an insatiable public hungry to purchase illegal goods and services.

Organized crime can be defined by the members and the activities of a group. Although organized crime might potentially be involved in many crimes, what separates individual crime from crimes committed by groups of people is the term *organized* or *organization*. Organization has been described as a group of people who cooperate to accomplish objectives or goals. Max Weber, known as the "father of sociology," examined the elements of an organization. Weber (1947) lists rules, specialization and specialized training, a division of labor, a hierarchy of authority, and continuity or routinization as the parts of a structure necessary for the efficient function of bureaucracies.

Organized crime has incorporated many successful principles utilized by legitimate business organizations:

- A unit of command: a superior to whom one is directly responsible
- The principle of definition: clearly defining authority and responsibility
- The span of control: a limited number of people controlled by a supervisor
- The principle of objective: defining the purpose of the organization or the business that is undertaken (i.e., drugs, murder for hire, extortion, gambling)
- Insulation and the need-to-know principle: personnel have contact only with their immediate boss and peers
- A pyramidal structure: orders flow down the hierarchical chart and important decisions are made at the top
- The principle of specialization: members of organized crime are experts in a single job function
- Rules: omerta (vow of silence, never talking to police) and the process of becoming a member of an organized crime group

As with legitimate organizations, no two organized crime groups are exactly alike. Each group evolves in its own manner. Crime organizations require supervision and management to implement strategies that accomplish the goal of profit. Personnel administration is critical to organized crime, just as it is to legitimate business organizations. Crime organizations remain bureaucratic, with an autocratic leadership that employs punishment for failure, and monetary reward and promotion for success. Many organized crime members also are motivated by a need for esteem, power, and recognition.

A Working Definition for Organized Crime

The 1986 President's Commission on Organized Crime concluded that a working definition must contain characteristics of both the activities and the group. Many countries and states include the structure of the group in their definition. The term *working definition* is useful to the investigator. Many police departments as well as state and federal agencies have dedicated resources to the investigation of organized crime. For the investigator, these resources are essential to the success of an organized crime investigation.

Resources such as personnel, money, equipment, and time are major considerations in an organized crime investigation. Classifying, identifying, or defining a group as a crime organization usually requires an extensive investment by the agency or department—a task often made more difficult by a scarcity of resources. Once a group is declared to be engaging in organized crime by a law enforcement entity, multi-agency and federal support is likely to become available. The original case officer or agent may lose much control over the direction of the case or even be directed to go back to his or her normal duties, and allow the major case squad or agency to take charge of the case. Ideally, the supervisors would allow the originating officer or agent to be a part of the investigative team. Because special equipment and technology (such as electronic eavesdropping, remote sensing, and night or low-light vision equipment) are very expensive, however, use of these resources will most likely be handled by major case squads or federal or state agencies. Money is certainly the major factor in informant development, overtime pay, and use of special vehicles. These investigations may continue for years and require large numbers of officers and staff. It is easy to understand why organized crime investigations are not small support unit operations with limited resources. Therefore, the investigator must understand thoroughly and meticulously articulate why a group meets the organized crime definition to obtain the resources needed for a successful investigation.

Definitions of Organized Crime

The definition of organized crime varies from agency to agency, from federal to state, and from state to state. An investigator must be sure to use the same definition employed by the jurisdiction or agency in which the case is worked. Each element of the statute or definition must be articulated clearly to ensure the necessary resources and investigative support from the proper agencies are obtained. Defining organized crime accurately also will help in determining solutions for unique problems arising from a long-term and complex investigation. These cases often require long-sitting grand juries, informant protection, special prosecutors, extensive undercover operations, and extraordinary surveillance techniques.

It is important for investigators and resource allocators to agree upon a definition of organized crime when distinguishing it from other criminal activity. A well-defined problem can link an initial investigation to the current evolution of organized crime. The group in question may be a transnational or even international criminal organization requiring international cooperation and assistance. The proper definition refers to acts that are both *mala in se* and *mala prohibita*, and includes detailed information about how these activities became organized. The investigator must have an understanding of not only the academic definitions of these issues, but also the legal definitions.

Finding a comprehensive definition of organized crime is difficult and requires the investigator to synthesize definitions from both academia and the legal community.

There are also differences in world perceptions of organized crime (Albanese, Das, & Verma, 2003). If investigations are conducted outside the United States, knowing the other country's legal and academic definitions of organized crime is essential for obtaining assistance from the foreign government.

The advantages of synthesizing definitions of organized crime are as follows:

- Develops strategies and techniques for effective investigation
- Gains appropriate resource allocation to complete a long-term investigation
- Obtains cooperation and assistance regionally, nationally, and internationally
- Increases the investigator's understanding of the particular criminal group
- Prepares the investigator to address the sophistication, activities, and structures of organized crime
- Increases the understanding of the motivations that drive those involved in both case strategy and the judicial process
- Copes with the ever-present aspect of corruption
- Develops proactive solutions to prevent organized crime from becoming involved or controlling legal enterprises
- Predicts future organized crime trends and activities

Definitions provide understanding and often lead to effective solutions to problems that arise during the investigation. The investigator who can synthesize numerous and diverse definitions becomes more effective because of the deep knowledge of the magnitude and complexity of the target: organized crime.

Investigation Definitions

The investigator can use a variety of terms to define organized crime. While these terms are similar in some respects, each provides a different insight into what it means to the investigator.

Consortium has been defined as "the union of fortunes, or the joining of several persons as parties to one action" (*Black's Law Dictionary*, 1990). A broader definition is "an agreement among or the combination of groups to undertake an enterprise beyond the resources of any one member" (*Webster's Ninth New Collegiate Dictionary*, 1983).

Cartel is "a combination of producers to control, monopolize, and restrict competition of the sale and price of a particular product or service" (*Black's Law Dictionary*, 1990).

Syndicate refers to an association of individuals who wish to carry out a business transaction, usually financial in nature. The risk of any single investor is diminished because of this partnership.

Organization also refers to two or more persons forming an association to conduct business. Individuals organize to function as a whole to become more effective and efficient.

A **gang** is "a company of persons who act in concert for criminal purposes" (*Black's Law Dictionary*, 1990). Gangs are organized entrepreneurs who reinvest profits into the gang. These structured organizations market their illicit goods and services to make huge profits (Taylor, 1990). Other authors view gangs as disorganized individuals who form alliances to make money for each member (Fagan, Kelly, & Chin, 1989). Gangs have been described by law enforcement as organized groups with a recognized leader and a less powerful under-command. Their activities are viewed as criminal and a threat to society. Street-gang mentality includes what is often referred to as the "three R's": reputation, respect, and retaliation. (Note that the three R's are characteristics found in almost all organized crime groups.) The Texas penal code defines a gang as follows: "Three or more persons having a common identifying sign or symbol or an identifiable leadership who continually or regularly associate in the commission of criminal activities" ("Texas Statutes and Codes Annotated," 2003). Some street gangs have reached a level where they could be classified as engaging in organized crime, but this classification is debated even today.

Complex criminal groups may be classified as organized crime, syndicated crime, cartel, consortium, or gangs. How each group is classified remains the subject of debate. One author may refer to the "Bloods" or the "Disciple Nation" as a gang, while another refers to them as organized crime. The most important point for the criminal investigator to know is the specific definition that the resource allocators employ to make their decisions.

Organized Crime as Defined by Laws, Agencies, and Governments

Organized crime is defined differently depending on the perspectives of the legal profession, academia, government commissions, and other writers. Although some definitions are similar, there is no consensus of what defines a group as an organized crime group. In fact, there is no agreement that organized crime can be fully defined at all. Attempts by the legal community include the following:

> Organized crime means the unlawful activities of the members of a highly organized, disciplined association engaged in supplying illegal goods and services including, but not limited to, gambling, prostitution, loan-sharking, narcotics, labor racketeering and other activities of members of organizations. (Omnibus Crime Control and Safe Streets Act of 1968)

The FBI describes organized crime as a continuing criminal conspiracy with an organized structure that is successful because of its use of fear, corruption, and violence. The motivation behind this conspiracy is greed (Bill McMath, FBI, personal communication, August 2, 2001). This definition is very similar to that given by the President's Commission on Organized Crime in 1986. The FBI considers the following groups to be organized crime, and they are top priority targets for FBI agents:

1. La Cosa Nostra
2. The Russian Mafia

3. The Mexican drug cartels

4. The South American drug cartels

5. Asian organized crime groups

6. Major national gangs ("Bloods," "Crips," biker gangs, and so on)

The Racketeering Influenced and Corrupt Organizations (RICO) statute describes acts of organized crime as "acquiring or receiving income from a pattern of racketeering through a criminal enterprise" (18 U.S.C. 1961). Federal and state RICO statutes include both civil and criminal remedies for these acts. Congress passed the federal RICO statute in 1970 as Title IX of the Organized Crime Control Act of 1970 (Public Law 91-452).

Conspiracy to violate RICO is included in both the federal statute and many state statutes. *Conspiracy*, which may be defined as the agreement between two or more people to commit a criminal violation, helps to describe the operation of criminal groups such as organized crime. Investigators must understand the concept of conspiracy and be able to apply the conspiracy statutes to effectively address organized crime.

Two other laws that help to define organized crime activities are the Continuing Criminal Enterprise (CCE) statute and the Money Laundering Control Act of 1986 (U.S. Codes 21 and 18). The CCE statute was part of the Comprehensive Drug Abuse Prevention and Control Act of 1970, and is directed at any person who "occupies a position of organizer, supervisor, or any other position of management" in a narcotic-producing or distribution enterprise such as organized crime. The Money Laundering Control Act created two new offenses that are common to organized crime during attempts to conceal the origin of illicit funds; these offenses were codified in 18 U.S.C. 1956 and 1957. Any investigator who wants to define organized crime must have a clear understanding of the activities described in both the CCE statute and the Money Laundering Control Act. These tools are discussed in the law enforcement strategies section for each of the criminal groups in Chapters 4 through 11.

International Perspective

Authors such as Albanese, Das, and Verma (2003) discuss the consensus of international perspective on the common features of organized crime. These features include the following:

- Planned criminal activity for profit
- A conspiracy of a continuing enterprise formed around social, ethnic, or business relationships, or around a certain product or opportunity
- Use of violence, threats, and intimidation to achieve goals
- The use of corruption to protect its interest and avoid arrest and prosecution

These features help investigators to recognize organized crime, and are a common bond and starting place for international cooperation.

The Treaty of Mutual Assistance in Criminal Matters of 1973 illustrates an international definition of organized crime. This treaty refers to organized crime as "an association of individuals for periods of time for profit by both illegal and legal means." Although the word *corruption* is not used in the treaty, protection from prosecution is mentioned. The method of operation is described as being methodical and systematic.

Louise Shelley (1995), director of the Transnational Crime and Corruption Center (TraCCC) at the American University's School of International Service in Washington, D.C., includes three characteristics to define transnational organized crime groups:

- Based in one state

- Commit crimes in several countries when opportunities arise

- Conduct illicit activities with low risk of arrest or detection

In describing organized crime, Shelley refers to the mobility and versatility of these groups and writes that there is no prototypical crime cartel. Although their activities and structures vary, all have engaged in money laundering to conceal their enormous profits. Shelley views the corrupting influence of these organizations over both law enforcement and governments to be a threat to the stability of governments and nations.

United States Federal Definitions

Many investigations in the United States use the definitions provided in both state and federal RICO statutes (1970). G. Robert Blakey, known as "the father of RICO," has described "organized crime" as a political term. Organized crime is characteristic of an enterprise with a continuing criminal conspiracy that is motivated by profit from illicit activities demanded by the public. Violence, threats, and corruption ensure its continual existence.

Academics, law enforcement personnel, and state governments often replace the term "organized crime" with *illegal enterprise*. The California Penal Code defines organized crime as "a crime of conspiratorial nature that seeks to supply illegal goods." It describes organized crime as an activity of planning and coordination of individual efforts of illegal activities for profits, and includes crime committed by criminal street gangs ("Deering's California Codes Annotated," 2003). Maryland and Arizona also refer to "organized crime" in their statutes ("Annotated Code of Maryland," 2003; "Arizona Revised Statutes," 2003). Delaware provides funding to combat organized crime under its Special Law Enforcement Assistance Fund ("Delaware Code Annotated," 2003). Maryland lists characteristics that define organized crime as follows:

- Criminal activity for significant income

- Combination or conspiracy

- Violating criminal laws relating to prostitution, drugs, corruption, extortion, counterfeiting, loan sharking, and gambling ("Annotated Code of Maryland," 2003)

New Mexico statutes describe organized crime as supplying illegal goods and services for a profit by members of a structured and disciplined organization ("New Mexico Statutes Annotated," 2003).

The New York legislature recognized the difficulty in precisely defining organized crime, but still passed the Organized Crime Control Act, which includes a charge of enterprise corruption. New York also created a statewide organized crime task force to conduct investigations and to prosecute organized activities. Its statute defines organized crime and gives officials the power to issue subpoenas, obtain warrants, and investigate organized crime activity. New York describes organized crime as follows:

> An efficient and disciplined organizational structure that is very complex and diversified in its activity. It uses corruption as a means to protect and expand its operations. Organized crime consists of intricate statewide and nationwide conspiracies that have extended life spans. Organized crime must be addressed by a concerted, concentrated investigative, and prosecutorial effort to break the structure and power. ("New York Consolidated Law Service," 2003).

By creating the task force and addressing organized crime by statute, New York has brought together considerable resources to address this type of criminal activity.

The Texas statutes and codes contain language concerning organized crime in the state's Penal Code Title 11, Chapter 71. The code requires a person or persons who intend to establish, maintain, or participate in a combination of or gain profits from a combination of a variety of illegal activities such as gambling, promotion of prostitution, sale of a controlled substance, murder, arson, and robbery, among others, to be characterized as organized crime ("Texas Statutes and Codes Annotated," 2003).

One attempt to measure organized crime in Western Europe reached a consensus that 11 characteristics were common to organized crime. To meet the criteria of being defined as organized crime, the group had to exhibit at least six of the 11 characteristics. Conspiracy, serious criminal acts, and the motivation of profit and/or power were considered to be essential factors for a group to be classified as organized crime. Other characteristics include the following (Van der Heijden, 1996):

- Influence on politics, public administration, the judiciary, and the media (corruption)
- Money laundering activity
- Business-like structure
- Use of violence and intimidation
- International activity
- Specialization
- Continuity
- Employing discipline and control

Dobovšek (1996) concluded that creating a definition of organized crime was impossible, but noted that characteristics that describe organized crime activity were useful. Organized crime, according to this author, may be described as "quick development and changing of the forms" in response to the environment. Dobovšek specified the traits of organized crime as professionalism, organization, unlimited financial means, and enormous corruption potential. Organized crime varies from country to country because of differences in geographic, economic, and social factors of each country. The variety of definitions by each country leads to problems with measuring organized crime activity and obtaining international cooperation.

Donald Cressey (1969), a consultant to the 1967 President's Commission Task Force on Organized Crime, wrote that the positions of corruptor, corrupted, and enforcer were essential to the activities of organized crime. He used such terms as "division of labor," "coordinated activities," and "rules involved in criminal operation" in describing these positions. Other U.S. government committees and commissions have also contributed to defining organized crime and its activities and players.

The Kefauver Committee identified the syndicated nature of organized crime and described an organized hierarchy with centralized direction and use of violence and corruption to achieve organized goals of profit. The Committee described the Mafia as a secret conspiracy that was ruthless and very successful. The President's Task Force on Crime of 1967 and 1976 and the 1986 President's Commission on Organized Crime expanded the definition and knowledge of organized crime as well.

A Synthesis of Definitions

Definitions incorporate a range from five to more than 10 characteristics. Kenny and Finckenauer (1995) list 12 characteristics that represent a synthesis of the features identified in studies of Hagan (1983) and Maltz (1976, 1985). Albanese (1996) lists 11 characteristics similar to those of Kenny and Finckenauer. Howard Abadinsky (1985) proposed two different models of organized crime: the bureaucratic/corporate model and the patrimonial/patron–client model. There are six to eight attributes of organized crime according to Abadinsky's work.

The characteristics of organized crime described in these scholarly works also can be found in the reports of U.S. government and European task forces, committees, commissions, and a variety of organizations. These attributes include the following:

- Has non-ideological motives
- Exhibits continuity over long periods of time; is perpetual in nature
- Uses tactical and strategic or long-term planning to reach the goals of organized crime
- Governed by rules and codes of secrecy
- Seeks to monopolize products and services

- Has an organized hierarchy
- Uses force and intimidation
- Restricts membership
- Provides illegal goods and services as demanded by the public
- Obtains enormous profits by criminal means
- Employs corruption for immunity and control
- Creates a division of labor with job specialization
- Engages in money laundering
- Invests profits in legal enterprises and seeks to control these businesses
- Exhibits an ability to adapt to changes in supply and demand, law enforcement, and competition
- Operates internationally
- Engages in more than one illicit activity (diversity in business)
- Uses legal businesses as fronts for illegal activity

Other Approaches to Defining Organized Crime

When examining the numerous definitions of organized crime, it becomes apparent that some countries divide organized crime groups into traditional organized crime (e.g., Italian Mafia, American La Cosa Nostra, Yakuza), drug-specific organized crime (e.g., South American cartels), and entrepreneurial organized crime (e.g., Russian, Ukrainian, West African, and other groups). Other types of classifications include the terms "transnational," "international," and "amalgamation." *Amalgamation* is based on factors such as geography or territory, ethnicity, product, or service as a commodity or a sociopolitical cause.

Another approach to the classification of major criminal groups is to view them as *organizing* crime rather than *organized* crime. This concept, which was developed by Brodeur (1996), views these organizations as continuously changing or fluid rather than as a single bureaucratic enterprise. Such groups are constantly evolving around a variety of activities and alliances. These alliances are dependent on a symbiotic relationship with society and—if unchecked—form a global threat.

Organized crime has become both transnational and international because of its ability to be opportunistic with products and services as well as alliances with other criminal and noncriminal groups. Prohibition of drugs has made organized crime the most powerful criminal groups in history. Santino (1988) defines the Mafia as "a financial Mafia employing the tactic of investing in legitimate markets and institutions to gain enormous wealth and power." International rules ensure secrecy and tax havens, which allow money to be circulated through trust companies, stocks, and other financial innovations.

The President's Commission on Organized Crime reached the same conclusion as Santino's conception of organized crime. It reported that drug trafficking was the major source of income for such groups and required complex money laundering operations. The Commission concluded that organized crime consists of three essential components:

- Criminal groups that are structured using corruption, violence, and intimidation to gain wealth and power

- Corrupt public officials and businesspeople who act as protectors ensuring continuity and insulating the group from civil and criminal action by the government

- Social support including use of illegal services and products and specialists who facilitate organized crime activity

Unlike its predecessors, this Commission identified a number of organized entities in addition to La Cosa Nostra, including the Colombian cartels, Yakuza, Russian Mafia, and outlaw motorcycle gangs, among others. The Commission viewed these entities as emerging groups that met the definition of organized crime. History has proven both Santino's and the Commission's concepts to be correct. Organized crime evolves and continues to form alliances and new groups to expand their control over the market of a product or service.

Conclusions

Clearly, there is much debate about what organized crime means. Many different types of organized crime are possible, just as organized crime groups are not limited to La Cosa Nostra. Investigators of these and other criminal groups must understand and be capable of presenting the elements that are used by both the prosecutor of the case and the agency or department that can supply the needed resources for a successful investigation. In defining organized crime primarily as a criminal conspiracy, the investigator has only to include the legal requirements of a criminal conspiracy in the definition. This practice allows for La Cosa Nostra, Yakuza, the Russian Mafia, militant groups, Triads, and other specified groups to be legally declared a criminal organization. Membership in one of these groups would mean that the person is guilty of a criminal conspiracy simply by belonging to the group. La Cosa Nostra has been classified as a racketeering enterprise; thus all of its members are guilty of RICO violations. Declaring a group to be a criminal enterprise establishes a *prima facia* case for the existence of a conspiracy. It allows all members to be prosecuted for the crimes of all involved in the conspiracy, and it allows the prosecutor to employ rules of evidence and testimony such as hearsay in the trial. This is a very innovative strategy to prosecute every member of an entire organization.

As discussed in this chapter, the criteria needed to classify an organization or group as organized crime vary not only between jurisdictions, but also between agencies, states, and countries. Some countries have yet to define organized crime. Definitions are crucial because they provide information needed for effective laws, investigations, and prosecutions.

In addition, these definitions enhance efforts to prevent the formation of new organized crime groups and the unholy alliances formed between numerous organized crime groups worldwide. The creation of measures used against organized crime must begin with an understanding of what organized crime is and how it functions.

Sun Tzu, the 5th-century Chinese general and author of *The Art of War*, had this to say about an enemy and victory:

> If you know the enemy and know yourself, you need not fear the result of a hundred battles. If you know yourself but not the enemy, for every victory gained you will also suffer a defeat. If you know neither the enemy nor yourself, you will succumb in every battle.

In our case, the enemy is organized crime. You as a potentially successful investigator must first define the problem before attempting to address a phenomenon as complex and constantly evolving as organized crime.

Discussion Questions

1. How would you define organized crime? What distinguishes it from disorganized crime?

2. Why is defining organized crime important to law enforcement? Prosecutors?

3. Discuss United States Commissions' findings with regard to organized crime.

4. Of the 18 characteristics discussed in this chapter, which do you consider the most important? Why?

5. How do the United States' definitions of organized crime and those of other countries differ, and how are they alike?

6. List and discuss state and federal legislation that address definitions of organized crime (e.g.,. conspiracy laws, RICO, money laundering).

References

Abadinsky, H. (1985). *Organized Crime* (2nd ed.). Chicago: Nelson-Hall.

Albanese, J. (1996). *Organized Crime in America* (3rd ed.). Cincinnati, OH: Anderson.

Albanese, J. S., Das, D. K., & Verma, A. (Eds.). (2003). *Organized Crime: World Perspectives*. Upper Saddle River, NJ: Prentice Hall.

Annotated Code of Maryland. Retrieved July 22, 2003, from http://www.lib.umd.edu/guides/MDAnnCodes.html

Arizona Revised Statutes. Retrieved July 22, 2003, from LexisNexis Academic: http://lynx.lib.usm.edu:2147/universe/printdoc

Black's Law Dictionary. (1990). St. Paul, MN: West.

Brodeur, J. P. (1996, September). *Organized Crime: Trends in the Literature*. Paper presented at the meeting of The Forum on Organized Crime, Ottawa, Canada.

Cressey, D. (1969). *Theft of a Nation: The Structure and Operations of Organized Crime in America*. New York: Harper.

Deering's California Codes Annotated. Retrieved July 22, 2003, from LexisNexis Academic: http://lynx.lib.usm.edu:2147/universe/printdoc

Delaware Code Annotated. Retrieved July 22, 2003, from LexisNexis Academic: http://lynx.lib.usm.edu:2147/universe/printdoc

Dobovšek, B. (1996). Organized Crime: Can We Unify the Definition. In: *Policing in Central and Eastern Europe: Comparing Firsthand Knowledge with Experience from the West*. Retrieved June 3, 2006, from http://www.ncjrs.org/policing/org323.htm

Fagan, J., Kelly, R., & Chin, K. L. (1989). *Patterns of Organized Crime Activities in Asian Businesses in the New York Area*. Newark, NJ: Rutgers University School of Criminal Justice.

Hagan, F. (1983). The Organized Crime Continuum: A Further Specification of a New Conceptual Model. *Criminal Justice Review, 8,* 52–57.

Kenny, D., & Finckenauer, J. (1995). *Organized Crime in America*. Belmont, CA: Wadsworth.

Maltz, M. (1976). On Defining Organized Crime. *Crime and Delinquency, 22,* 338–346.

Maltz, M. (1985). Toward Defining Organized Crime. In: H. Alexander & G. Caiden (Eds.), *The Politics and Economics of Organized Crime*. Lexington, MA: Lexington Books.

Money Laundering Control Act of 1986 (Pub. L. 99-570).

New Mexico Statutes Annotated. Retrieved July 22, 2003, from LexisNexis Academic: http://lynx.lib.usm.edu:2147/universe/printdoc

New York Consolidated Law Service. Retrieved July 22, 2003, from LexisNexis Academic: http://lynx.lib.usm.edu:2147/universe/printdoc

Omnibus Crime Control and Safe Streets Act of 1968 (Pub. L. 42 U.S.C. §3789d).

Organized Crime Control Act of 1970 (Pub. L. 91-452, Stat. 922).

Racketeer Influenced Corrupt Organizations Act of 1970 (Pub. L. 91-452, Stat. 922).

Santino, U. (1988). The Financial Mafia: The Illegal Accumulation of Wealth and the Financial-Industrial Complex. *Contemporary Crises, 12*(3), 203–243.

Shelley, L. I. (1995). Transnational Organized Crime. *Journal of International Affairs, 48*(2), 485.

Taylor, C. (1990). *Dangerous Society*. East Lansing: Michigan State University Press.

Texas Statutes and Codes Annotated. Retrieved July 22, 2003, from LexisNexis Academic: http://lynx.lib.usm.edu:2147/universe/printdoc

United States Code 18 U.S.C. 1956.

United States Code 18 U.S.C. 1957.

United States Code 18 U.S.C. 1961.

United States Code 18 U.S.C. 1961–1965.

United States Code 18 U.S.C. 1962.

United States Code 18 U.S.C. 1963.

United States Code 18 U.S.C. 1964.

United States Code 18 U.S.C. 1965.

United States Code 18 U.S.C. 2510–2520.

United States Code 21 U.S.C. 846.

United States Code 21 U.S.C. 848.

Van der Heijden, T. (1996). Measuring Organized Crime in Western Europe. In: *Policing in Central and Eastern Europe: Comparing Firsthand Knowledge with Experience from the West*. Retrieved June 3, 2006, from http://www.ncjrs.org/policing/mea313.htm

Weber, M. (1947). *The Theory of Social and Economic Organization* (A. M. Henderson & T. Parsons, Trans.). New York: Oxford University Press.

Webster's Ninth New Collegiate Dictionary. (1983). Springfield, MA: Merriam Webster.

Chapter 2

Evolution of Organized Crime and the Impact on Investigative Strategies and Law Enforcement

Choose as a guide one who you will admire more when you see him act than when you hear him speak.

—Lociuc Annaeus Seneca, philosopher (3 BCE–AD 65)

Objectives

After completing this chapter, readers should be able to:

- Recognize how American organized crime has become more transnational.
- Discuss the impetus to evolution of organized crime in the United States and identify the first organized crime groups in America.
- Understand the common threads between early organized crime in America and current organized crime groups.
- Discuss the impact of organized crime on the U.S. government, society, U.S. business, and law enforcement.

Introduction

The origins of organized crime in America continue to be debated among academics, law enforcement professionals, and historians. Many believe that organized crime in America began with pirates (Kenny & Finckenauer, 1995). Others point to the New York and Chicago gangs of the 1920s as the beginning of organized crime in the United States (Albanese, 1996; Peterson, 1952). Abadinsky (2003) writes about the "Robber Barons" who were replaced by the Irish, Jewish, and Italian criminal gangs. Currently, these enterprises are being replaced with "nontraditional enterprises" of Asians, Russians, Africans, Hispanics, outlaw biker gangs, and other emerging groups.

Regardless of the origin of organized crime, its impact on U.S. law enforcement has been substantial. A major downside of their operations is the extensive capability of these organizations to corrupt law enforcement, making corruption an integral characteristic of organized crime. Upsides include the trend of modernizing law enforcement in terms of training, selection, technology, and the ability to network internationally and globally.

Today, nearly all of the approximately 200 nations of the world are experiencing some form of organized crime, which is evolving toward transnational crime as operational links between these groups strengthen. Shadow governments control much of the businesses and economy of the developed and most powerful nations, including the United States. One example is the Japanese group, the Yakuza, whose members were estimated to reap rewards of $10 billion in 1988 through smuggling American guns into Japan, controlling the crystal methamphetamine market in Hawaii and the mainland, and making heavy inroads in the lucrative pornography and prostitution industries.

Law enforcement and governments have been threatened by organized crime activity. In response, the United Nations sponsored the Convention Against Transnational Organized Crime in 2000. International measures were developed, signed by 147 countries, and ratified by 40 countries. These documents represent a commitment by nations to adopt a number of measures against organized crime, such as money laundering statutes, extradition laws, mutual legal assistance, and some standards for the law enforcement effort. The United Nations is providing assistance to countries to help them develop measures to combat organized crime.

In the post–September 11, 2001, terrorist attack era in the United States, the highest political priority of Congress and the President has been to address the threats of terrorism from groups such as Al Qaeda. Another priority has been corporate (or *white collar*) crime, best illustrated by the 2001 Enron and 2002 WorldCom scandals. While these forms of criminal activity justify a considerable effort and expenditure of resources, many in law enforcement voice concerns that the issue of organized crime is now taking a back seat in terms of resources and investigative activity. Nevertheless, some data indicate that enforcement activities against both terrorism and white-collar crime also have an effect on organized crime activity. A hardening of borders prevents some smuggling activity, financial investigations have uncovered organized crime activity, and law enforcement have discovered weapons trafficking by organized crime groups that has a connection to terrorism.

Efforts against terrorism may evolve into an offensive against organized crime groups as well. Alliances between terrorist and organized crime groups are a trend predicted by some in the U.S. intelligence community to escalate for two reasons: greed of the organized crime groups and the need for weapons by terrorist groups. Although there has been much distrust and competition between the major organized crime groups such as La Cosa Nostra (LCN; American Mafia), Yakuza, and Russian Mafia, these factors have not prevented alliances between these groups as they seek to reap huge profits from drugs, arms trafficking, and other criminal activities.

Origins of Organized Crime in the United States

Colonial Piracy

Organized crime in the United States did not begin during the Prohibition era of the 1920s, but rather with the pirates of the colonial period (Browning & Gerassi, 1980). If the characteristics of organized crime explained in Chapter 1 are compared to the actions and character of the pirates of colonial America (hierarchy and structure, non-ideological, violent, restricted membership, huge profits from criminal activity, continuity and supplying public demand, and above all, corruption), then pirates indeed can be considered the earliest form of organized crime in America.

Piracy was the result of the British rulers employing a number of seafaring buccaneers to attack and disrupt Spanish shipping in an attempt to defend the American colonies. Perhaps not surprisingly, the pirates, who were referred to as *privateers* (because their pay came from the plunder and goods of the Spanish ships they captured), soon began to attack ships other than Spanish and form alliances with corrupt governors of the colonies. Many pirates became famous; Captain William Kidd, Bartholomew Roberts ("Black Bart"), and Edward Teach ("Blackbeard") are a few. These pirates established rules of conduct and recruited men with skills needed to carry out their attacks on shipping.

Pirates were initially perceived by the colonists as gentlemen or Robin Hood–type bandits. As such, privateers were honored guests of the colonists and governors with whom they traded. Colonists bought goods from the pirates and offered them refuge and protection. Pirates sold the luxury items to the colonists at a fraction of their cost, much like "hot goods" are purchased by the public today from "fences" or other criminals. Like later criminals such as Al Capone in Chicago and Pablo Escobar in South America, pirates ingratiated themselves with the colonists and government officials. At the peak of piracy in America, around 1720, an estimated 2000 pirates controlled many of the shipping lanes off the eastern seaboard.

Piracy, like the illicit drug trade today, flourished because of the demand by the colonists. Pirates became the best customers of the colonists' goods and services. The colonists, for their part, did not seem to care if the pirates were bringing stolen goods and corrupting their new government. When the colonists began to export their goods, however, they also became victims of attacks on shipping. Soon they withdrew their support from the pirates. In addition, colonists replaced corrupt officials with those who could not be corrupted. America had become more commercial, with a number of industries thriving in the New World. When piracy began to die, another enterprise began to flourish: smuggling.

Smuggling survives today as an influx of arms, drugs, humans, and body parts. Pirates used corruption and mercantile demand to support their illegal activities. This trend of American organized crime was set in early colonial America through the cooperation of the pirates with the public, government, and legitimate business enterprises, and it forms the future vector of organized criminal activities.

Although piracy has ended along the U.S. coastlines, modern piracy remains common today off the coasts of Southeast Asia and Africa (Gallant, 1999). Like the pirates in colonial America, corruption continues to play a role in the success of modern piracy. The modern pirate networks obtain shipping routes and schedules from corrupt sources to plan their action. They are extremely successful and highly violent, often disposing of their bounty through other organized crime groups. Losses to legitimate companies and nations from such piracy amount to millions of dollars and an ever-increasing number of deaths of crewmembers. In addition, environmental damage to the seas and coastlines often results from abandonment of ships that were carrying hazardous material.

Piracy has been given a priority by the U.S. Navy, which has created a specialized unit, the Combined Task Force 151, to battle pirates attacking shipping around the Gulf of Aden off the coast of Somalia. This unit is part of an existing force that deals with security issues such as drug smuggling and arms trafficking in addition to piracy. The United States is among 20 countries that are combating piracy in the region. The Navy unit became necessary because of the human and economic cost of piracy and the value of the ships that were being held for ransom, including luxury yachts and supertankers. In 2008, more than 100 vessels were hijacked or attacked by pirates—more than 40 of these in the waters off the coast of Somalia. Some of the pirates are now operating 80 miles out into international waters. Merchant mariners have added security measures to address this rise in piracy. These measures have reduced the frequency of piracy, but not stopped the attacks (Sterling, 2009). It seems that the more things change, the more things remain the same.

Rise of Robber Barons and Crime Families

As the piracy era ended in America, criminal groups remained disorganized for a few years, during which time disproportionate wealth became the trend. By the mid-1700s, crime had become a major problem in major cities. Before the 1920s (when the LCN became powerful), a number of powerful business entrepreneurs and their families began to monopolize the American economy by violent and corrupt means. The Vanderbilts, Rockefellers, Carnegies, Standfords, and others used the law, private police, military, and even the National Guard to gain financial and political control. These groups of ruthless business owners in the Industrial Age were collectively referred to as *Robber Barons* (Browning & Gerassi, 1980; Klepper et al., 1998).

The Robber Barons' cut-throat business activity was very similar to the newly discovered corporate crime the United States has been experiencing in the 21st century (such as the Enron and WorldCom scandals). In writing about corporate corruption, Clinard

(1990) concluded that organized criminals and corporate criminals are very similar in that both influence law and employ corruption to achieve power and profits. Clinard's examples include the 1986 Union Carbide disaster in Bhopal, India; the selling of illegal pharmaceuticals, pesticides, and medical devices to low- and middle-income countries; exploitation of land for agribusiness and lumbering operations in underdeveloped countries; and exploitation of workers to produce products for these corporations. Much of what these corporations are doing in those countries would be illegal in the United States. As Sutherland and Cressey (1960) pointed out, a large number of violations by corporations are actually a type of organized crime. Until recently, most of these corporate criminals were neither identified nor prosecuted, and they remained in their powerful positions despite their offenses. Thus the Robber Barons of the early 20th century in America were the quasi-forerunners to the enterprises of LCN and the present nontraditional groups such as the Russian, Mexican, and Colombian drug-trafficking organizations (**Figure 2-1**).

Immigrant Crime Groups and Political Machines

By the 19th century, major population growth had occurred in cities such as New Orleans, New York, and Chicago. Although the evolution of organized crime had many similarities in both urban and rural areas, north and south, and east and west in the United States, each area had some unique characteristics in terms of the development of particular organized crime entities.

Even before the legal prohibitions of alcohol and illicit drugs, organized crime had begun to develop in America. Rapid and massive immigration into cities such as New York resulted in tremendous overcrowding and unemployment. To survive, the unemployed began to commit criminal acts and then form gangs for power and profits. Politics became the means to obtain power and money for many immigrants. The vote became a commodity that could be controlled by the alliance of gangs and political organizations. These so-called *political machines* gained control of not only the gangs, but also the police, courts, prosecutors, and government. Immigrant groups such as the Irish, the Jews, and the Italians became involved in organized crime, as did non-immigrants such as African Americans (Joselit, 1983).

The first massive immigrant group to come to the United States was the Irish, who were enticed by the economic opportunities that America offered in the early 1700s. Most were farmers who settled in eastern and midwestern cities. Living in poverty and denied access to education, their first jobs were as laborers. During the potato famine in Ireland of the 1840s, more than 250,000 Irish Catholics entered the United States, and by the 1950s the number of Irish immigrants approached nearly 2 million. The Irish established their own neighborhoods and with their large ethnic vote established the corrupt political machine, which allowed them to control both the legal and illegal enterprises of the cities where they settled in large numbers.

Two of the most notorious of these political machines were the Tammany Hall Machine in New York and the Pendergast Machine in Kansas City. The Tammany Hall Machine

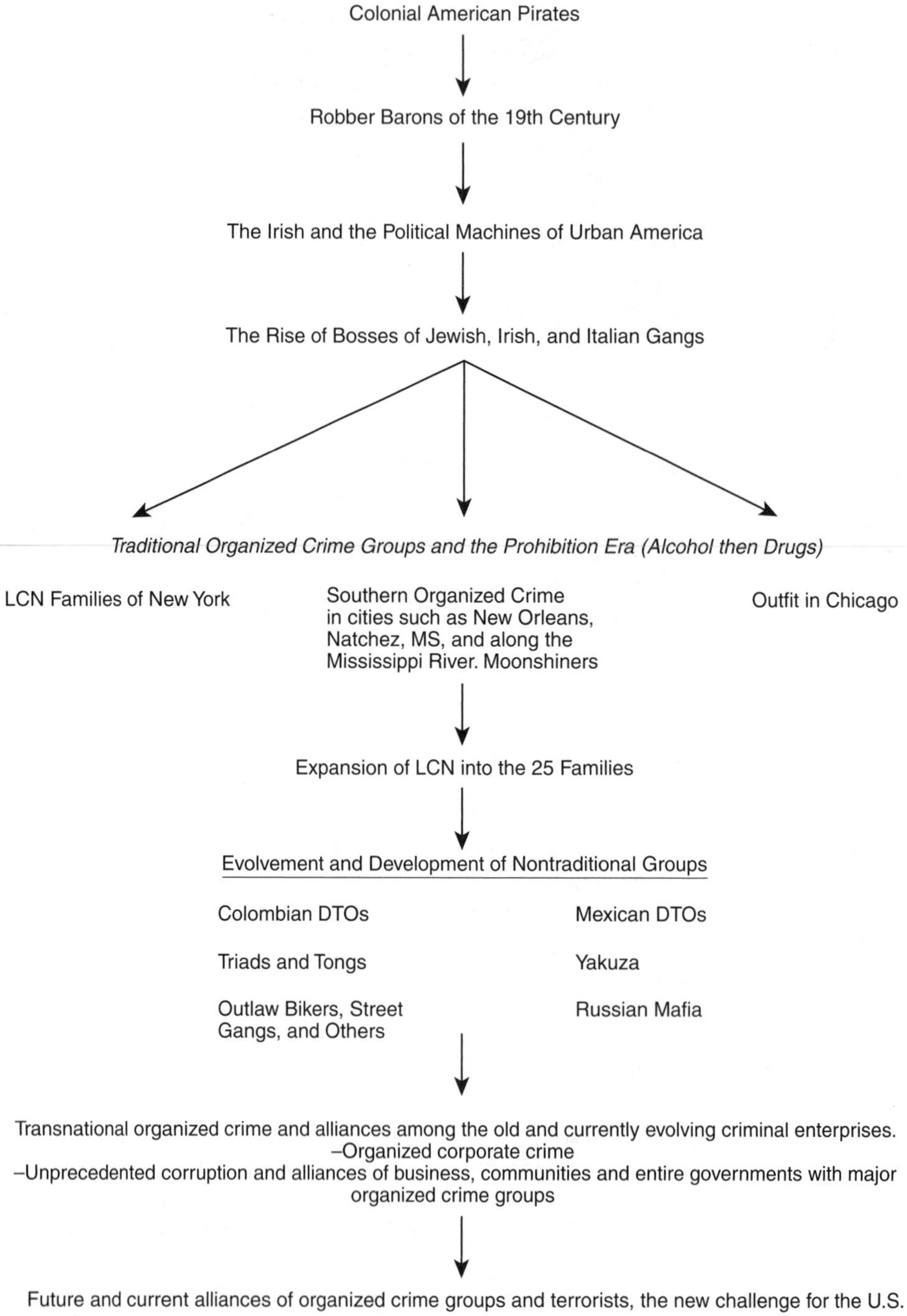

Colonial American Pirates

↓

Robber Barons of the 19th Century

↓

The Irish and the Political Machines of Urban America

↓

The Rise of Bosses of Jewish, Irish, and Italian Gangs

Traditional Organized Crime Groups and the Prohibition Era (Alcohol then Drugs)

LCN Families of New York

Southern Organized Crime
in cities such as New Orleans,
Natchez, MS, and along the
Mississippi River. Moonshiners

Outfit in Chicago

↓

Expansion of LCN into the 25 Families

↓

Evolvement and Development of Nontraditional Groups

Colombian DTOs   Mexican DTOs

Triads and Tongs   Yakuza

Outlaw Bikers, Street   Russian Mafia
Gangs, and Others

↓

Transnational organized crime and alliances among the old and currently evolving criminal enterprises.
–Organized corporate crime
–Unprecedented corruption and alliances of business, communities and entire governments with major
organized crime groups

↓

Future and current alliances of organized crime groups and terrorists, the new challenge for the U.S.

Figure 2-1 Historical evolution of organized crime in the United States.

controlled the gangs, jobs, and gamblers of New York. This alliance between the politicians, gangs, and gamblers led to the rise of such characters as William March Tweed ("Boss Tweed"). Tweed and other bosses who followed him (such as "Big Tim" Sullivan) stole millions from the city and government through fraud, bid-rigging, overpricing goods and services, and kickbacks. Municipal graft was a way of life for the people who ran these powerful organization. The machines operated "wide open" cities where gambling and vice were protected and encouraged and relationships between the criminals and machine bosses were highly symbiotic. Gang violence ensured the vote went in favor of the machine's candidates, and in turn gang members were protected by the corrupt government controlled by the machines. In Kansas City, Thomas Pendergast ran the political machine and employed gangsters to ensure survival of the machine, just as Tweed did in New York.

Gang leaders became wealthy and powerful men in early America, and many became powerful bosses of the LCN in a number of cities. Al Capone, for example, was a member of the Five Points gang in New York before he moved to Chicago. Gangs performed legal and illegal activities for the political machines, including distributing campaign material, encouraging repeat voters, and assaulting rival campaign workers. The politicians controlled the police and courts, which allowed for protection of the gang members who helped the politicians stay in office.

During the 1800s, gangs in major cities of the United States became more organized and entrenched in politics. The Five Points and Eastman gangs of New York, the Purple Gang of Detroit, and the gamblers of Chicago were the beginning of the criminal organizations such as LCN in the United States (Browning & Gerassi, 1980; Peterson, 1952).

New Impetus for Expansion of Organized Crime in the United States

As criminal groups became large organizations allied with the political machines, the stimulus for growth was market driven. These huge markets required an extensive infrastructure able to import, distribute, protect, and monopolize the organization's products and services. Gambling, prostitution, labor racketeering, and loan sharking had contributed to the growth of organized crime in the early years. Now, in the 20th century, two new prohibitions would be the impetus to unprecedented growth of these criminal groups.

The Harrison Narcotics Act of 1914 was the first major step in U.S. drug enforcement. It established a tax and regulations for the manufacture and distribution of narcotics as well as licenses for pharmacists and physicians who prescribed them. At the time, patent medicines—many of which contained opium and/or hard liquor and herbs—were unregulated "cures" for a variety of ailments and were marketed especially for women who would never dream of drinking an alcoholic beverage. With more than 500,000 opiate addicts in the United States, a huge market opportunity for organized crime existed. The U.S. drug rings suddenly became nationally organized crime groups. (These drug rings preceded the gangs associated with the alcohol-Prohibition era.) There were reports of corruption of large police departments because of the enormous profits from drug operations. Before the 1920s, large drug rings existed that were both highly organized and international. Not only were opiates a major product of organized crime profits, but cocaine was a highly profitable product as well. (Until the 1920s, it was an ingredient of the soft drink Coca-Cola.) As profits soared from the illicit drug trade, the corruption of politicians, law enforcement, and businesspeople grew as well.

The prohibition of alcohol era from 1920 to 1933 provided yet another market opportunity for expansion of organized crime in the United States. In New York, the early gang era was ending and the political machines were evolving into the next phase of the alliance of politicians, gamblers, gangs, and the criminal world.

Men like Arnold Rothstein brought about a Jewish influence into organized crime. In fact, Rothstein is credited with creating the modern bureaucratic structure of an organized crime group. He was an effective administrator from 1914 until 1928, and transformed criminal activity by using specialization, administrative hierarchy, and methods of operation that were similar to those of a successful legitimate business. Rothstein is known as the original "Don," reflecting the fact that he brought bootlegging and narcotics trafficking into the modern era of organized crime. Much of his illegal profits were invested into legitimate enterprises. Rothstein engaged in labor racketeering as well as a variety of legal business ventures (such as real estate, the garment industry, securities, insurance, and bail bonding) and illegal businesses (such as smuggling, bootlegging, gambling, narcotics trafficking, and strikebreaking for hire). Rothstein was the role model for organized crime bosses in other ethnic groups, including the Italian LCN. Also like many organized crime bosses throughout history, Rothstein was shot and killed by an unidentified assailant. The organized crime figures who followed him continued to expand organized crime activity in New York (Joselit, 1983).

Other cities, such as Chicago, were also experiencing an evolution in organized crime. After Big Michael McDonald came characters such as Mont Tennes, James Colosimo, and Johnny Terrio, who was an original New York Five Pointer. Eventually, the infamous Al Capone, also a New York Five Pointer, became the boss of organized crime in Chicago, known as the "Outfit."

Anti-crime Legislation and the Growth of Organized Criminal Groups

Another impetus to the continued growth and expansion of organized crime in the United States was the proliferation of drug control legislation. After the Harrison Narcotics Act, public opinion changed to reflect a perceived threat from drug addiction, particularly for the youth of America. A fear of dangerous Chinese and African American drug addicts added to public support for drug laws (King, 1972). When repeal of prohibition of alcohol in 1933 left the LCN and other criminal enterprises without the profits of bootlegging they had counted on for growth, drug trafficking became a more important source of income for organized crime. Organized crime bosses such as Meyer Lansky, Lucky Luciano, and Arnold Rothstein became heavily involved in the illicit heroin market. Because other LCN bosses such as Joseph Bonanno, Tony Accardo, and Frank Costello were initially opposed to involvement in drug trafficking, their hesitation allowed for the new faces of organized crime to begin their own rise to power.

The Great Depression, the Korean Conflict and Vietnam War, and the 1960s' more liberal social climate produced ideal conditions for traffickers of illicit drugs. In turn, Albert Anastasia, Vito Genovese, and many others became wealthy as a result of drug trafficking. More recently, a new generation of organized crime groups, such as the Mexican drug trafficking organizations (DTOs), Colombian DTOs, Tongs and Triads, among others, have become major players in the world of criminal enterprises because of their ability to supply illicit drugs to America and the world. Heroin from Mexico, the Golden Triangle (Burma, Thailand, and Laos), and the Golden Crescent (Pakistan, Iran, and Afghanistan) arrived on American shores, providing enormous profits to LCN and other organized crime enterprises. Cocaine from Colombia, Peru, and Bolivia produced new billionaires and a new generation of organized crime organizations. Marijuana, clandestine drugs such as Ecstasy (3,4-methylenedioxymethamphetamine), PCP (phencyclidine), and LSD (lysergic acid diethylamide), and diverted pharmaceutical drugs became a lucrative money market for organized crime as well.

The government responded to these trends with a variety of legislation. The Uniform Narcotic Drug Act of 1932 was passed by the U.S. Congress as a complement to the Harrison Narcotics Act and became a model for later statutes in the United States. Other acts, such as the 1937 Marijuana Tax, were passed to stop the illegal use of marijuana. By 1951, penalties began to be more severe for violations of drug laws. Today, the federal government and all states have a Controlled Substance Act that lists drugs subject to penalties for their sale, possession, and delivery, and a variety of laws regarding conspiracy and assets forfeiture for violation of drug laws. With these laws in place, the price of illicit drugs has soared—and, correspondingly, the profits for organized crime.

The latest organized crime organization to enter the drug trafficking business is probably the Russian Mafia. Partnering with Colombian DTOs, its members have established operations in areas such as Miami, Florida, to smuggle cocaine from South America to Russia. For example, Oleg Kirillov, a leader of a Russian group, has been identified as having a number of operations in the United States that are involved in the cocaine smuggling business.

Some would argue that we should deal with drug prohibition the same way we dealt with alcohol prohibition (Nadelmann, 1989). However, America currently has drugs that are restricted and legal. Pharmaceuticals account for more than 40% of addictions and are still providing profits for organized crime groups. According to estimates, if some drugs were legalized, the number of addicts would increase as much as 20-fold. Given the correlation between drug use and crime, the results would be devastating for our society.

Development of Organized Crime in the South

Southern organized crime often is described as the *Dixie Mafia*. The question of whether a Dixie Mafia exists and if it is defined as organized crime is debatable. Nevertheless, it is clear that some form of criminal organization and planning involving corruption has operated in a number of southern states, especially on the Mississippi Gulf Coast. This network of individuals has been, and continues to be, involved in numerous crimes.

The impact of this activity on law enforcement has been mixed. The public image of government is tarnished when a sheriff and former mayor are found guilty of criminal activity. In response, the public may become more apathetic on the one hand and more demanding of action against corruption on the other hand. More oversight by federal authority of local law enforcement has been instituted, but corruption is difficult to discover and requires lengthy investigations and expenditure of resources that should be directed at criminals who do not wear badges. Unfortunately, the enormous profits of drug trafficking have proved too tempting for many in law enforcement, whose salaries cannot come close to matching that of "the bad guys." Although law enforcement has become more professional and high tech, corruption remains an avenue for organized crime to continue to operate in the south.

Unlike the LCN, which is a structured organization with a hierarchal command, the Dixie Mafia appears to have developed as a loose-knit group of professional or traveling criminals who formed partnerships based on enterprises or geographic location to execute a variety of criminal activities. Traditionally, this group has been active in Texas, Mississippi, Louisiana, Tennessee, Arkansas, and Kentucky, and possibly in some other states. The group has no central bosses or commission (as does the American Mafia), but rather forms subgroups as needed to carry out specific crimes or operations. The most powerful criminals know who to contact to contract a murder, arson, transport of guns or dope, or any specialty operation required to achieve the objective of the criminal activity. Members are involved in a variety of criminal activities, including gambling, bootlegging, prostitution, drug trafficking, murder, arson, theft, and fraud. Each member frequently specializes in one criminal activity.

Some of the organized crime in southern states—specifically prostitution, gambling, and drug distribution—has been assisted by corrupt law enforcement officials. Much of this activity traditionally took place in coastal bars and gambling halls (*joints*) that operated 24 hours a day in violation of numerous statutes and regulations.

Intelligence indicates that the Mississippi Gulf Coast has been wide open to a variety of criminal activity, somewhat like Chicago and New York during the Prohibition era. In many cases, local officials did little to quell the criminal activity by members of the Dixie Mafia. A recent example of the exploits of the Dixie Mafia came to light in the trial of the former mayor of Biloxi, Pete Halat, in 1997. Halat and members of the Dixie Mafia were involved in an extortion scam operated from Angola Prison in Louisiana. Members of the group were convicted in the murder of Biloxi Circuit Court Judge Vincent Sherry and his wife Margaret. Mike Gillich, Jr., and a number of alleged members of the Dixie Mafia were convicted on a variety of charges surrounding the murder of the Sherrys.

Illegal Whiskey

Although many in academia attribute the development of organized crime to the Prohibition era, the smuggling and production of illegal whiskey in this country actually began during colonial America. Known by many names (such as *shine, hooch, rock gut, white lightning,* and *corn liquor*), illegal whiskey has existed in America since the founding of the country. For example, John Hancock—famous for his signature on the Declaration of Independence—was the owner of a sloop named *Liberty* that was seized by British customs agents in 1768 for smuggling rum and spirits to avoid taxes owed to the British government.

To pay off the debts incurred in the American Revolution, the fledgling U.S. government placed a tax on whiskey and other distilled spirits, and the American moonshiner was born. Scotch-Irish farmers were among the first to produce illegal whiskey in the northeastern states. The whiskey riots of 1794 in Pittsburgh, Pennsylvania, marked America's first resistance to taxes and began its tradition of rebellion to federal authority or oversight. President George Washington led a militia to stop the rebellion, a feat that was achieved with little bloodshed. However, because of this political pressure, moonshiners began to migrate to the southern states and western areas such as Kentucky and the Appalachian Mountain region, which shortly became the capital of American moonshine (Miller, 1991).

The first prohibition of alcohol was not the 18th Amendment. Rather, prohibition first occurred in Georgia in 1733, where it continued for nine years. The results were illegal alcohol stills and smuggling of illegal whiskey by boats (similar to methods used in the 1980s to smuggle drugs into the United States). Moonshiners manufactured whiskey and bootleggers sold their product. The second prohibition appears to have occurred in 1851, where whiskey consumption had reached 5 gallons per capita per year.

Over the years, crime associated with alcohol soared and included abuse of spouses and children. The price for alcohol rose to $5.00 per gallon. By 1917, approximately half of all U.S. states had enacted prohibition laws. Then in 1920, the 18th Amendment was passed, nationally banning the manufacture, sale, and transport of alcohol. Many citizens became lawbreakers for the first time. Fishermen became smugglers. Farmers operated stills that percolated homemade hooch. Hip flasks and semi-secret bars known as *speakeasies* became normalized among the citizenry. Criminals and gang members, for their part, did not lose out on the opportunities for gaining enormous profits from this illicit business.

While national prohibition did reduce overall alcohol consumption, it also sparked the growth of corruption of law enforcement, business, and politicians, along with the establishment of powerful organized crime families. During the era of national prohibition, 800 million gallons of illegal whiskey entered the U.S. market every year. Almost anyone could make $500 per day in the illegal business, although this enterprise was certainly risky. Many deaths were attributed to poisonous whiskey produced or smuggled into the United States because of a lack of quality control and inspection. In 1920, there were 1,000 deaths from the consumption of illegal whiskey.

Smugglers became very innovative in developing routes and methods that avoided detection by law enforcement. Boat builders became part of the business, as they built fast boats with secret compartments that were suitable for smuggling illegal alcohol. Even a World War I German U-boat was used to deliver the product to American shores. People were willing to risk jail or even death to enjoy the profits, adventure, and excitement produced by this dangerous game. On the law enforcement side of the equation, the U.S. Coast Guard sought to stymie the smugglers with frequent gun battles and chases.

Perhaps the most serious impact of prohibition was the formation of organized crime groups such as the Purple Gang of Detroit, Michigan. Cooperation between gang members resulted in organized crime. When Canada legalized the production of whiskey for importation, a massive amount of smuggling across the Detroit River into Michigan began. The use of airplanes, boats, and vehicles and the development of sophisticated secret compartments were two notable results of the smuggling phenomenon. Not satisfied with their individual profits, criminal groups began to monopolize the illegal alcohol market by hijacking other smugglers' loads and engaging in violent takeovers of the transportation and distilleries. The Purple Gang, for its part, supplied liquor to such organized crime figures as Chicago's Al Capone. Prohibition bankrolled organized crime and became the impetus to its growth.

Even with the repeal of the 18th Amendment by ratification of the 21st Amendment, the U.S. Congress continued to tax liquor. This practice produced—and continues to produce—moonshiners such as Junior Johnson, who later became a famous racecar driver. In fact, the creation of the National Association for Stock Car Auto Racing (NASCAR) in 1947 is attributed to the so-called ridge runners and blockaders who developed fast cars to outrun the revenuers who were trying to arrest them for hauling illegal whiskey. Family operations had stills and produced spirits, which were then transported to distribution sites in vehicles with supercharged engines and large load capacity. These drivers became legends in U.S. history.

Whiskey organizations included those who financed the operation, transportation specialists, distillers, distribution, and security. The 18th Amendment had resulted in a huge market for moonshine and—like the LCN—moonshiners in the south used corruption and sometimes violence to ensure their operations continued to profit after the repeal of Prohibition. From 1950 to 1965, the U.S. government reported the production of more than 1 billion gallons of illegal whiskey, which led to a loss of $12 billion in federal and state taxes (Miller, 1991; Woodiwiss, 1988).

Illegal distillers were especially common in Mississippi, Tennessee, Georgia, Kentucky, Missouri, Arkansas, Alabama, North Carolina, South Carolina, and West Virginia. The Appalachian region became infamous for its production of illegal whiskey and selling whiskey without a license. The average still produced around 80 gallons each week, which meant an income of approximately $100 per week. It was common knowledge when a sheriff or chief mostly overlooked the illegal alcohol trade. Some law enforcement personnel also took payoffs to allow the whiskey operations to do business.

Moonshining was usually a family business that traditionally was passed down from one generation to the next. In most southern towns, the public knew where to buy illegal whiskey and knew who was producing it. Both white and black people were involved in the manufacture and selling of whiskey.

From the perspective of the blockaders of the mountains of the south and their counterparts in rural towns and big cities like New Orleans or Atlanta, moonshining is an organized activity that is part of the historical development of crime in the south. Like illegal drugs, it was an impetus to the growth and expansion of organized crime activity. Today's moonshiners may operate stills capable of producing up to $40,000 per month in profits. Despite the fact that Department of Alcohol, Tobacco, and Firearms (ATF) agents often find illegal whiskies that contain poisons that can be very dangerous for human consumption, there is a large public demand for the product.

Modern Development

Organized crime engages in many activities that contribute to its growth and expansion in addition to drug trafficking and bootlegging. Such groups have derived much power and profit from business racketeering, gambling, labor racketeering, and a variety of white-collar and fraud crimes. Meanwhile, LCN remains a major player in the evolution of organized crime in America. It learned much from its Jewish and Irish gang predecessors, and improved the concepts of diversity, corruption, and integration of the group's illegal operations into legitimate business.

The rise of the American Mafia, or La Cosa Nostra, is discussed in depth in Chapter 7. Powerful families in New York (such as the Luciano, Columbo, Gambino, Luchesse, and Bonnano families), Chicago (headed by Al Capone, Sam Giancana, John Torrio, and Joseph Aiuppa), New Orleans (Carlos Marcello), and at least 22 other major cities established the American Mafia as a lasting presence in American organized crime. The rise of LCN covers much of the history of organized crime in America up until nontraditional groups began their rise to power in the 1970s.

Commissions and Task Forces

Much of what is known about organized crime in America comes from a number of governmental commissions that investigated organized crime in the United States. As early as 1915, the Chicago Commission made inquiries into what was called *institutional crime*. Later, the Wickersham Committee of 1931 examined the impact of Prohibition on organized crime growth and power.

In 1950, the Kefauver Committee concluded that a nationwide syndicate known as the Mafia controlled much of lucrative crime in major cities. Described as "muscle and murder," the Mafia was involved in criminal interstate commerce. The McClellan Committee recorded the testimony of Joseph Valachi (a low-level organized crime "made" man who gave questionable testimony before Congress in 1963; he was the first member of the LCN to confirm its existence). The Oyster Bay Conferences from 1965 to 1966 assembled a number of experts to examine organized crime as a criminal enterprise. President Lyndon Johnson established the President's Commission on Law Enforcement and Administration of Justice in 1965. It examined the activities of organized crime, including how the groups were organized, and identified some members of these organized crime groups. Influenced by the Kefauver and McClellan hearings, the 1967 President's Committee concluded that organized crime was a national threat motivated by money and power, and the result of intricate conspiracies. In 1976, the National Task Force on Organized Crime recognized a lack of knowledge and understanding of organized crime, and added groups other than LCN to the list of organized crime activity.

In 1983, President Ronald Reagan created yet another commission to analyze organized crime on a regional basis to determine the extent of LCN and emerging organized crime groups. His President's Commission on Organized Crime classified other groups as organized crime and concluded that drug trafficking was the largest source of income for organized crime in the United States. Groups identified as organized crime included outlaw biker gangs, a number of prison gangs, Colombian cartels, Cuban Marielitos, Russian groups, and the Japanese Yakuza. Although the Yakuza was considered the largest group by this commission and other organized crime groups posed a serious threat during the period of 20 years (1966–1986) covered by Reagan's Commission, LCN remained the most powerful and extensive group operating in the United States. LCN recognized the importance of corruption in its ability to continue to extend its power and influence while amassing large profits. Some states such as New York, Pennsylvania, and Florida have examined organized crime activity over the past century and determined that organized crime is dynamic, and that corruption plays a vital role in the existence of these criminal enterprises.

Corporate and Political Corruption: The Major Contribution to Organized Crime Growth and Power

Corruption is not confined to organized groups. Corporate scandals, the Robber Barons' methods, and political corruption all share one similarity with organized crime: their common use of corruption. From price fixing, toxic waste dumping, and illegal campaign contributions to criminal violations by executives in companies such as Enron and WorldCom, corporate corruption may have been an impetus to methods employed by modern organized crime.

The connection between the underworld (organized crime and others) and the upperworld (corporate America and politicians) has a long history, beginning with the pirates and continuing with the political machines of the 1860s and today's complex political system. This symbiotic relationship between organized crime and the political system is well documented. Beginning in the 1960s, organized crime members have contributed $2 billion annually to a variety of public officials (King, 1969). This practice is not unique to the United States, however. The Japanese government and the Yakuza are almost indistinguishable, as are the Cali cartel and the Colombian president, Ernesto Samper; Mexican presidents and Mexican DTOs; and the Russian Mafia and government officials in Moscow and other major cities in the former Soviet Union countries.

In the United States, senators, mayors, police chiefs, governors, and prosecutors are prime targets for corruption by organized crime. Such relationships can be found in both yesterday's and today's headlines.

Some U.S. presidents have reported connections to LCN as well. Richard Nixon's campaign manager in his race for the California Congress, Murray Choitner, was a well-known Mob lawyer. Nixon had friends who were friends of Meyer Lansky, and Nixon obtained the endorsement of the teamsters (Moldea, 1978, 1982). Even the administration of the popular President Ronald Reagan had connections to organized crime members. For example, Reagan's friends Senator Paul Laxalt, Jackie Presser (Teamsters Union president), and Raymond Donovan (Reagan-appointed Secretary of Labor) all had connections to known LCN figures. Many of Reagan's appointments were also determined to have connections to organized crime (Moldea, 1978, 1982).

The executive levels of the governor's office in some states have been reported to have Mob connections. Two governors of Louisiana were convicted of felonies and had alleged connections to Carlos Marcello. Louisiana political boss Huey P. Long was alleged to have approved and accepted money for allowing Frank Costello, a New York Mob boss, to bring slot machines to New Orleans.

LCN is not the only organized crime group that employs corruption as a means to an end. Mexican DTOs, Colombian DTOs, outlaw bikers, and most all organized crime groups have corrupted politicians, law enforcement, and legitimate businesses to maintain and protect their lucrative enterprises. Without exception, when organized crime activity has been detected in any jurisdiction or area, political or corporate corruption has been revealed. The connection to licit business allows organized crime members to safely invest their illegal proceeds and form symbiotic relationships similar to those between organized crime and politicians.

Organized crime has become transnational and international, as groups form alliances wherever or with whoever they need to achieve power and wealth. It has become a global enterprise and is so intermingled in the socioeconomic and political process that it is difficult to separate these entities. This evolution presents a formable challenge for U.S. law enforcement.

Future Impact on Law Enforcement Efforts

The growing disparity between organized crime and law enforcement resources has put law enforcement at a distinct disadvantage. The enormous profits and power of organized crime allows members of these groups to employ the finest support. Attorneys, financial advisors, and experts in technology and methodology allow organized crime to maintain highly effective and efficient operations. The expansion of the size and number of organized crime groups now operating in the United States has stretched law enforcement resources to the point of limited success.

Add to this mix the threat of terrorism, which demands resources for its prevention and detection, thereby diverting investigators and agencies away from their focus on organized crime, and it becomes clear that fewer resources exist to combat this growing threat. Many agencies have begun to connect terrorism to drug trafficking, as this activity may be the major source of income for terrorists and is a definitive organized crime mainstay. In turn, some agencies have received additional resources so that they can battle both terrorism and organized crime simultaneously. Despite this trend, however, it is apparent that homeland security has become the political and economic priority for U.S. law enforcement.

The threat of corruption has resulted in a lack of sharing information between many law enforcement entities, out of fear of compromising major cases and putting informants and law enforcement personnel in danger. Federal agencies were not sharing information after the terrorist events of September 11, 2001, for example. Task forces have been reluctant to provide or share information with local or state members who might be represented on, or assigned to, these federal task forces. Corruption scandals also have required extensive scrutiny and resources dedicated to internal investigations at the state, local, and federal levels of employees of these agencies who themselves investigate organized crime activity and are watching the people who are watching members of organized crime. Temptation combined with greed has compromised a number of organized crime investigations.

There is an upside to these otherwise problematic trends. The growth and evolution of organized crime have led to improved intelligence gathering, enforcement techniques, and strategies. Law enforcement strategies are extending intelligence-gathering capabilities and are becoming more proactive. The creation of task and strike forces focused on organized crime activity has resulted in the arrest and conviction of many traditional and nontraditional organized crime members.

Another positive impact has been the creation of more effective crime control legislation, both at state and federal levels. RICO, money laundering acts, chemical diversion acts, asset forfeiture, improved physical and electronic surveillance, conspiracy and Continuing Criminal Enterprise statutes, drug control legislation, and most recently the Patriot Act have allowed law enforcement actions to become a serious threat to organized crime activity.

The recent creation of multi-jurisdictional task and strike forces has resulted in increased cooperation between agencies and all levels of law enforcement. Task forces offer advanced training and additional resources dedicated to law enforcement. These resources are not limited to money. In turn, the technology and equipment provided to these task forces have led to increased efficiency and effectiveness of law enforcement in general. The techniques and technology applied by the task forces often carry over to member agencies that employ these advanced technology and strategies to develop other criminal investigations.

The overall impact on law enforcement of the growth and evolution of organized crime in the United States has been the development of strategies, technology, training, education, and improved law and statutes to address the dynamic phenomenon that is organized crime. Such efforts have resulted in a more professional and effective law enforcement community at the local, state, and federal levels.

Although cooperation among state, local, and federal agencies has increased in recent years, law enforcement has not arrived at the level of cooperation needed to reverse the growth of organized crime activity that is affecting the United States so profoundly. Additional resources, along with highly experienced, educated, and trained personnel, are required to check the deeply integrated growth of organized crime into the political and economic structures of this country.

Organized crime is continuing to evolve, and its growth or demise will depend on how the United States, as a culture and a people, along with the law enforcement efforts, choose to deal with this threat. Examining the evolution of organized crime and recognizing the mistakes and successes of the past may result in more effective legislation and better efforts to address the growing complexity of organized crime. History is a great teacher.

Discussion Questions

1. How has American organized crime become more transnational? Which strategies are needed to address this trend?

2. What do you believe was the impetus for the evolution of organized crime in the United States? What were the first organized crime groups in America?

3. What are the common threads between early organized crime in America and the current organized crime groups?

4. What parts did Lansky, Rothstein, Luciano, and Marcello play in the development of organized crime in America?

5. Is there or was there a "Dixie Mafia"? Who are or were these people?

6. Discuss the impact of organized crime on the U.S. government, society, U.S. business, and law enforcement.

7. What can be learned from past efforts, including enforcement and legislation, that might improve modern efforts to address organized crime?

References

Abadinsky, H. (2003). *Organized Crime.* Belmont, CA: Wadsworth/Thompson Learning.
Albanase, J. (1996). *Organized Crime in America.* Cincinnati, OH: Anderson.
Browning, F., & Gerassi, J. (1980). *The American Way of Crime.* New York: G. P. Putnam and Sons.
Clinard, M. (1990). *Corporate Corruption: The Abuse of Power.* New York: Praeger.
Gallant, T. W. (1999). Brigandage, Piracy, Capitalism, and State Formation: Transnational Crime from a Historical World Systems Perspective. In: J. McC Heymand (Ed.), *From States and Illegal Practices.* New York: Berg.

Joselit, J. (1983). *Our Gang: Jewish Crime and the New York Community, 1900–1940.* Bloomington: Indiana University Press.

Kenny, D., & Finckenauer, J. (1995). *Organized Crime in America.* Belmont, CA: Wadsworth.

King, R. (1969). *Gambling and Organized Crime.* Washington, DC: Public Affairs Press.

King, R. (1972). *The Drug Hang-Up: America's Fifty Year Folly.* Springfield, IL: Charles C. Thomas.

Klepper, M., Gunther, R., Baik, J., Barth, L., & Gibson, C. (1998, October). The American Heritage 40. *American Heritage,* 56–60.

Miller, W. R. (1991). *Revenuers and Moonshiners.* Chapel Hill University of North Carolina Press.

Moldea, D. E. (1978). *The Hoffa Wars: Teamsters, Rebels, Politicians, and the Mob.* New York: Paddington.

Moldea, D. E. (1982, February). Reagan Administration Officials Closely Linked with Organized Crime. *Organized Crime Digest,* 6–10.

Nadelmann, E. (1989). Drug Prohibition in the United States: Cost, Consequences and Alternatives. *Science, 245,* 939–947.

Peterson, V. F. (1952). *Barbarians in Our Midst: A History of Chicago Crime and Politics.* Boston: Little, Brown.

Sterling, J. (2009, January 8). Navy Creates Force Devoted to Fighting Piracy. Retrieved June 25, 2010, from http://www.cnn.com/2009/WORLD/africa/01/08/piracy.task.force/index.html?iref=newssearch

Sutherland, E., & Cressey, D. (1960). *Principles of Criminology* (6th ed.). New York: Lippincott.

Woodiwiss, M. (1988). *Crime, Crusades and Corruption: Prohibition in the United States, 1900–1987.* Totowa, NJ: Barnes and Noble Books.

Chapter 3

Theories on the Continued Existence of Organized Crime

The first to present his cure seems right, till another comes forward and questions him.

—Proverbs 18:17

Objectives

After completing this chapter, readers should be able to:

- Recognize the impact of globalization on organized crime.
- Explain specific theories or explanations that apply to the different organized crime groups.
- Understand why some law enforcement professionals believe that enterprise theory is the most valuable contribution made by the explanations of organized crime.
- Discuss how public demand for illegal products and services can be reduced and how illegal markets can be disrupted.

Introduction

Many criminal investigators have not been enthusiastic about studying and understanding theory. What they want is concrete application and a discussion of what works. In reality, application of theories can assist the investigation. Theory provides a systematic view of a phenomenon and helps to explain that phenomenon (Kerlinger & Lee, 2000). Theories describe all that is known about a concept (such as organized crime) and, therefore, suggest what can be done to control its activities.

One of the purposes of research is to predict future events and developments. As past events and behaviors are analyzed, they become strong predictors of future actions. A theory consists of certain sets of interrelated concepts that define the problem and specify a means of measurement. In the case of organized crime, these elements focus on measuring the types of crimes of organized groups that are interrelated. These measurements stimulate further research and planning, help to distinguish between organized and disorganized crime, and suggest strategies for complex investigations that will deter the existence and expansion of organized criminal activities.

From a practitioner approach, the continuity of organized crime should be examined in a social context. Organized crime groups operate in complex economic markets and are affected by the legal system, politics, and community environment where they do business. The investigator must not only target criminal activity, but also focus on the institutionalization of organized crime—that is, its integration into the political and economic fabric of society. Corruption and the politics of big business are, therefore, targets for effective enforcement of organized crime activity. Investigators must develop an understanding of how organized crime groups emerge, determine the cycle of profit from their activities, and learn how they survive in the face of law enforcement efforts.

Not only do investigators need to understand the motivation of individuals to become members of organized crime groups, but they also need extensive knowledge of corporate crime as well as political and economic corruption. They need to focus on market assessments, production, and conditions in society that spawn organized criminal activity. Law enforcement's lack of strong alliances with regulatory agencies and inadequate funding of these agencies have allowed organized crime to continue to form relationships with legitimate business partners, which then allow banks, corporations, and other business entities to assist these criminals in creating fortunes. Through those fortunes, organized crime groups gain power in society, the business world, and even government. These groups tend to grow when prohibitions are implemented. There will always be prohibitions in society, and organized crime groups capitalize on them by supplying black-market goods and services demanded by the public and unavailable in legitimate markets. Increased oversight and public education about these issues would likely result in market disruption of these criminal organizations. Thus supply and demand of illegal services must be priorities of strategies for reducing the growth of organized crime. A focus on white-collar criminal activity is necessary before the connection between organized crime and political and business entities can be reduced or eliminated entirely.

Another practical approach involves examining the specific characteristics of criminal operations as well as those who depend on them for their survival. The number of safe havens—areas where organized crime members are protected because of corruption and collusion with governments—is growing. The large number of locations throughout the world where money can be laundered also contributes to the growth and continuity of organized crime. Alliances between organized crime groups facilitate their survival, as do the lack of accurate and timely intelligence and the non-cooperation of international law enforcement.

The level of sophistication of major organized crime groups is the most important factor in their ability to continue to dominate both criminal and noncriminal enterprises. Organized crime groups have an uncanny ability to adapt to changing markets and new technologies. All too often, law enforcement is playing catch-up when it comes to resources, technology, and inter-agency cooperation.

Many of the major organized crime groups rely on some form of *guanxi*, a concept that has existed for generations. This concept requires a binding and reciprocal obligation between members of organized crime groups that creates an enterprise that protects itself through trust and a code of silence. This code of silence is also termed *omerta* by La Cosa Nostra (LCN, the American Mafia).

Theories of Organized Crime

Bell (1953) uses the term "queer ladder of mobility" to explain organized crime as a means of finding wealth and power through expedient means such as gambling and provision of illicit goods and services. This theory does not attribute organized crime membership to frustration or blocked opportunity, but rather to greed.

Ianni's (1973) view on organized crime casts it in the light of ethnic succession. According to this author, every new immigrant population in the United States encounters blocked opportunities and obstacles in achieving respect, power, and wealth. In response, many immigrants resort to organized crime activity to achieve their dreams or goals. This theory helps explain the ever-changing face of organized crime in America: With each new wave of immigrants, new organized crime groups emerge to present a challenge for law enforcement.

Most criminological theories deal with characteristics of individual behavior and some connection to social problems. Are causes of organized crime different from causes of individual or disorganized crime? After reviewing a number of theories, it becomes clear that no single theory can explain the existence of all the various organized crime groups. At the same time, each theory provides insight on why organized crime exists. As discussed in Chapter 1, corruption, political involvement, illegal markets, and influx of new cultures and immigrants all contribute to the existence and the extent of the growth and stability of organized crime groups.

Alien Conspiracy Theory

One of the most common theories found in many texts is the *alien conspiracy theory*. Many authors who cite this theory refer to the members of the Sicilian Mafia who transplanted their criminal culture when they migrated to the United States. More recently, this theory has been cited to explain the methods used by the Russian Mafia as they established operations in the United States after the breakup of the former Soviet Union. There is also evidence that many organized crime groups organized themselves around the ethnic backgrounds of their members (Abadinsky, 1985). However, as explained in Chapter 2, organized crime in America began with the pirates and profiteers, and continued with the Jews and Irish long before other ethnic groups immigrated (Kenny and Finckenauer, 1995). Certainly, while the alien conspiracy theory has some merit, it falls short of explaining the rise of other groups, such as outlaw motorcycle groups and the rise of black organized crime groups.

The question also remains: Why do most individuals choose *not* to become organized crime criminals?

Social Control Theory

Social control theory proposes that the community, family, and bond with society collectively act to prevent most individuals' entry into a life of crime. According to this theory, fear of punishment, shame or embarrassment, and psychological restraints such as conscience (described as the "superego" in Freudian theory) are a few reasons why not everyone who has the opportunity to do so will engage in criminal activity.

Wilson and Herrnstein (1985) illustrated this personal decision by considering both the rewards and the punishment as a result of committing a crime. Becoming a member of a criminal group creates more opportunity for rewards, and the group encourages the type of criminal behavior that requires structure or organization to reap as many rewards as possible. The group then seeks low risk with many of these reward activities and, therefore, moves toward syndicated criminal activity.

Gottfredson and Hirschi (1990) believe that self-control is an underlying cause of criminal activity. According to these authors, the criminal is opportunistic and impulsive, as the result of poor family monitoring and correction. Greed, anger, lust, and peer pressure are common characteristics of many organized crime members.

Albanese's Theory of Typologies

Albanese (1996) explains crime and organized crime in terms of the typologies of positivism, classicism, structuralism, and ethics. The positive approach explains organized crime as caused by a variety of social and economic factors—for example, poor neighborhoods and role models, lack of opportunity to achieve the "American Dream," dysfunctional families, and even genetics. The positivist sees change in the conditions as a means to prevent criminal behavior.

The classical view highlights the tendency of people to consider pleasure and pain as guides to their decision to commit criminal acts. According to this perspective, individuals choose to become organized crime members because this path offers maximum pleasure and short-term gratification with little risk of apprehension and punishment. The classical school suggests that the certainty of arrest and other painful consequences will prevent individuals from becoming members of organized crime.

The structural approach focuses on the political and economic conditions of society, suggesting that individual gain is the most important goal and that success equals assets and money. Structuralists believe that arbitrary laws create criminal activity; thus what is needed to prevent criminal activity is equitable distribution of power and wealth. In this perspective, criminal activity is attributed to class conflict. Capitalism both creates the desire to obtain success and blocks opportunities to achieve that success. In other words, members of the ruling class create laws and policies to simultaneously protect themselves and control the working class so as to maintain the status quo. Conflicts between the upper and lower classes result in more prohibitions and acts that are forbidden, which in turn creates more crime. A different theory focusing on this aspect of the structural view suggests that many organized crime groups emerged to protect themselves from the upper or ruling class and governments (e.g., Triads, Yakuza, Sicilian Mafia). Organized crime has developed in countries with both weak and strong governments, after all, but not all people take advantage of prohibitions and commit criminal acts for profit and power.

The ethical perspective views crime as a moral failure, where self-interest is the driving force of existence. Proponents of the ethical view ask two questions: (1) Why are most people not criminals? and (2) What deters them from belonging to an organized crime enterprise? Their response to these questions is that values or virtues of morality prevent most people from harming other people. The protection of human dignity and human rights is important to good people. Most people are taught right from wrong and have a method for making ethical decisions.

Sutherland's Theory of Differential Association

When a group of people share common values and associate in a common environment, behavior is learned. This behavior can be criminal when the group to which a person belongs has a tradition of organized crime activity. Sutherland (1973) has described criminal behavior as part of the knowledge passed on during intimate personal group contact, such as occurs in gangs or cliques. The group rationalizes criminal behavior and develops a lack of respect for law and law enforcement. This type of association can vary in intensity and duration, and it results in a criminal lifestyle that may produce a member of an organized crime group. This theory has been referred to as *differential association* and *cultural transmission* (Sutherland & Cressey, 1960). Sutherland and Cressey propose that the development and recruitment of organized crime members occurs frequently when three conditions are met: (1) the environment has considerable crime; (2) there is frequent contact between upcoming youth and organized crime members who are role models and mentors; and (3) the community has little respect for the law. Cultural transmission involves passing down criminal values from generation to generation.

This ecological explanation of criminal behavior is similar to today's "hotspot" theory, which suggests that most crimes occur in the same location and are perpetrated by the same people (i.e., repeat offenders). According to this theory, the proximity of wealthy "targets" to those living in lower-income areas produces feelings of anger and frustration in poor youths who are deprived of opportunities for success, so the targets become a means for them to obtain wealth.

Durkheim and Merton's Strain Theory and Anomie

Both Durkheim (1964) and Merton (1964) wrote about an American society and culture that produced strain. These authors described the "American Dream" as obtaining wealth and power, which equates to success. When groups or individuals cannot obtain this success by legal means, however, they may resort to illegal means. *Differential opportunity* occurs when this type of strain is produced by socioeconomic stratification of people into lower, middle, and upper classes (Abadinsky, 2003). This *anomie* occurs when people cannot obtain the "American Dream" of success because they do not have equal opportunities to climb the ladder of success. To succeed in this milieu, organized crime members act with what Merton (1957) refers to as *innovation*, which is defined as success by organized, planned, and strategic activity—that is, by employing the characteristics discussed in Chapter 1.

The concepts of anomie, cultural transmission, and cultural conflict add to the theoretical understanding of why organized crime exists. Cultures and subcultures (alien conspiracy and ethnic succession) may be brought to America by immigrants or originate here (e.g., outlaw biker groups). Sellin (1938) described *culture conflict* in which crime is the result of different cultures having different norms about what to believe or value. Because the United States is home to people from many different cultures with many different values, many conflicts are inevitable. Activities and products that may have been acceptable in a person's country of origin, for example, may not be legal or culturally acceptable in the immigrant's new homeland. In an effort to obtain these now illegal services and goods, people may become involved in organized crime activity.

Beccaria's and Lombroso's Classical Theories

Most of the theories described so far in this chapter were developed from the classical school linked to Marchese de Beccaria (1735–1794) (Beccaria, 1819) and the positive school associated with Cesare Lombroso (1836–1909).

The classical theory often is referred to as *rational choice*, as it posits that people are free to make choices based on their values and logic. Public embrace of this theory resulted in harsh and immediate punishment of offenders—a strategy viewed as dissuading offenders from making a choice to commit criminal activity again. The motto of classical school advocates was that "The punishment should fit the crime." According to this view, before committing a crime, people weigh the risks of getting caught and being punished against the rewards of getting away with the crime. Members of organized crime groups, however, believe that the organization itself can prevent them from being caught or can use corruption to reduce the risk of apprehension and punishment. In contrast, Jeremy Bentham (1748–1832), a supporter of positive theory, measured the degree of good or bad of an act by proportion to affect the greatest happiness for the greatest number (Ferm, 1956).

Lombroso placed more emphasis on individual and environmental influences on behavior. Thus positivism examined criminal behavior in terms of the internal and external influences driving it. The poor economy, bad associates, poor family supervision, lack of positive role models, peer pressure, unequal opportunities such as inability to attend college or find a good job—all are factors that positivists cite as contributing to the propensity toward criminal activity. Although blocked opportunity and criminal association do explain much of criminal activity, most people who are exposed to all of the previously described conditions manage to rise above criminal activity and become successful noncriminals. For their part, *utilitarians* assumed that people exercised free will in seeking pleasure and avoiding pain.

Biological Theories

Another group of individuals proposed explanations for criminal behavior that are based on biology. Factors cited in such theories range from endocrinology, physical, and physiological characteristics (e.g., redheaded men), to mental deficiency, to morphological characteristics. This approach has drawn much criticism, however (Hooten, 1939).

Summary of the Theoretical Approaches

Three major theoretical approaches have been used to explain criminal activities: environmental, individualistic, and genetics/biological. Much of what today is termed *profiling* originated from psychoanalytical theories that conceptualized mental deficiency as an additional explanation of criminal activity. Goddard (1923) , for example, suggested that at least half of all criminals suffer from some form of mental deficiency. The Freudian explanation for criminal behavior is that the superego, id, and ego are the unconscious world of inner feelings that become the source of mental conflict and result in criminal activity. Certainly, the study of psychoanalytic theory can help the investigator "get into the mind" of a criminal and help develop a plan for intervention and arrest.

Some theorists believe that organized crime exists solely because of prohibitions, such as those focusing on drugs, prostitution, and gambling. Although illicit drugs are certainly major sources of income for most organized crime groups, many continue to profit from legal enterprises, such as waste management, the garment industry, and labor racketeering. Russian gangs, Chinese gangs, and the Yakuza, for example, extort millions from companies and individuals in legitimate businesses.

Organized crime will find a means to obtain enormous profits and power no matter what is decriminalized, made illegal, or legalized. Organized criminal groups are a part of the political and economic systems of every nation and, as such, will continue to develop schemes to take advantage of their political and economic relationships. As long as the risks are acceptable and the profits large, organized crime will continue to exist in our complex global environment. Removing the criminal statutes for drug trafficking and other crimes will not eliminate organized crime activity.

Theories Related to Law Enforcement Efforts

Albanese (1996) believes that organized crime should be defined by its activities. His typology of organized crime includes both the activity or provision of illicit goods and services (e.g., gambling, sex, drugs, and human trafficking) and the infiltration or abuse of legitimate business (Albanese). According to Albanese, three kinds of factors explain the existence of organized crime: opportunity factors, the criminal environment, and special access or skills.

Opportunity factors include economic, governmental, law enforcement, and social or technological changes. Economic factors include poverty, poor standards of living, or demand for an illicit product for which an adequate supply is available. Government conditions include weak governments that cannot effectively address organized crime and those that have inadequate laws or regulations to deal with the complex nature of organized crime. Law enforcement factors include the level of training, corruption, and the degree of government interference. Poor internal control of law enforcement agencies, for example, may lead to weaknesses that include the failure to monitor an agent's activity or evaluate training. The level of professionalism exhibited by law enforcement may contribute to either the ability or the inability of organized crime to corrupt these personnel. Social and technological changes such as globalization (travel and unlimited communication) also affect organized crime activity. For example, the ability to supervise an organized crime group's operations from a long distance or to easily transfer money allows organized crime to flourish.

For organized crime groups, special skills may be needed to exploit recognized opportunities. Computer expertise, smuggling expertise, management skills, and other technological abilities—all permit organized crime to grow and become more efficient and effective, in much the same way that legitimate enterprises expand and advance their operations. Thus countries with high levels of education and training offer organized crime the skills and knowledge needed to succeed and evolve over the long term.

Criminal environment issues include whether organized black markets exist in the country, the prior existence of organized groups, and the presence of gangs. If the country or jurisdiction has a history of frequent and serious criminal activity, then the presence of organized crime is more likely.

Albanese developed a risk assessment tool based on the preceding explanations of organized crime. In this tool, 17 factors (among them, risk factors of economic, government, law enforcement, criminal history, social and technology changes, and harm) and measurement methods are used to determine specific illicit activities in a particular locality and to predict the existence and extent of organized crime activity (Finckenauer & Schrock, 2004).

Enterprise Theory

Enterprise theory is probably of high interest to the organized crime investigator for its practicality. This theory explains organized crime activity as the result of unfilled public demand for goods and services. For example, when the number of people who use illegal drugs in the United States is examined, it is evident that a huge market for these substances exists. The Office of Drug Control Policy has estimated that approximately 3% of the U.S. population (about 4.5 million persons) is dependent on illicit drugs. The same sort of demand exists for gambling, prostitution, and stolen goods. The passage of the Prohibition amendment and the Controlled Substance Act produced a market whereby large profits could be made by providing illegal services and goods that had once been legal, and that were now in high demand. The law of supply and demand results in an enterprise that uses corruption, violence, planning, and organization, combined with the other characteristics of organized crime described in Chapter 1, to control and expand the market for these illicit goods and services. Such a single supplier can control the price and reap huge profits. Even today, organized crime and transnational criminal organizations continue to evolve through networking between organized crime groups and development of structures that are adapted to the ongoing globalization of markets.

Although drug trafficking remains a mainstay activity of organized crime groups, new markets for illicit goods and services are emerging. Among these growing criminal enterprises are trafficking in human body parts, trafficking in biological and nuclear materials, trafficking of women and children for the sex industry, smuggling of humans, cybercrime, and a wide variety of crimes of fraud.

Enterprise theory describes organized crime activity as being well planned and executed with the primary objective of attaining profit and other goals, such as power and political influence. The organized crime group involves itself in both licit and illicit activities to meet demands of willing consumers. Enterprise theory suggests that, to adapt to the dynamic nature of these demands, the structure of organized crime groups is flexible and often features a decentralized leadership or leadership by a cartel or committee.

McFeely (2001) concluded that enterprise theory can serve as a valid basis for a proactive investigative strategy focused on destroying an organized crime group. The enterprise theory of investigation (ETI) is effective against various types of organized crime groups, which are highly diverse in their criminal activities. Organized crime groups do consistently one characteristic, however: They nearly always invest their profits into legitimate businesses that serve as fronts for such activities as money laundering, fencing operations, and warehouses for contraband. The ETI approach seeks to identify all members of an organized crime group and develop prosecutable cases on all members. The primary target is the money trail or financial operations of the group. By seizing the money and assets of the group, investigators destroy its ability to continue operating. In addition, seizure of legitimate businesses of organized crime groups cripples their ability to develop corruption opportunities targeted at both government officials and business executives, which are fundamental for the expansion of their criminal enterprises.

Because organized crime has an identified leadership structure, the application of conspiracy statutes is very effective when prosecuting these individuals. Enterprise theory describes organized crime members as members of a group whose structure and membership are identified and who pose an internal threat to a country. The integration of illegal funds into legitimate business amounts to a national threat, as it can enable organized crime to control large corporations and the political process.

Hierarchical and Local-Ethnic Models

Albanese (1996) presented three models (paradigms) of organized crime, but admitted that, due to the dynamic nature of this type of crime, their use is limited to understanding the activities of organized crime. The hierarchical model describes the structure of organized crime as a family whose ranks are ordered from boss to soldiers, where the boss supervises the activities and is in control of the group members' behavior. A commission of bosses exists that handles disputes between "families" and that approves certain aspects of the organized crime organization of families. The American Mafia exemplifies this model.

In the local or ethnic model of organized crime, group members are bound together by cultural or ethnic ties. Activities are controlled by individuals rather than by a single boss. Partnerships form around choices to work on a particular project or in a specific area. This model suggests that there is no national commission that oversees all organized crime groups. Thus the major difference between the hierarchical model and the ethnic/local models lies in how the individual relationships are structured.

As previously discussed, the enterprise model defines economic relationships rather than personal relationships as the basis for the organized activity and structure. These activities are similar to those carried out in legitimate businesses, are not ethnically exclusive or violent, and center on market opportunities. Albanese (1996) gives the example of cooperation between Italian, Greek, Irish, Jewish, and African American criminal groups. A more recent example involves the cooperation between Colombian drug cartels and Mexican drug cartels and among black, Dominican, and Jamaican criminal groups or gangs.

All three of these models suggest strategies for law enforcement efforts directed against organized crime. The hierarchical and local/ethnic models describe how organized crime groups are structured. The enterprise model provides insight into how groups' activities are organized and carried out. The primary goal of organized crime is power and profit, and according to the enterprise model, all criminal groups share these goals.

Deterrence Theory

The assumption that organized crime groups and members consider the risk of arrest and punishment before engaging in crime gives rise to the deterrence theory. This theory suggests that crime can be prevented by the threat of punishment. Wilson (1975), however, noted that most crimes are committed by a small number of people who are habitual offenders. Like many members of the law enforcement profession, Wilson views the severity and surety of punishment as elements not considered by organized crime members because of the leniency of the courts and the ongoing lack of resources needed to investigate and arrest major violators.

Other Models

Abadinsky (2003) offers two models to describe the structure of organized crime groups. The first is the *bureaucratic/corporate model*, in which efficiency is seen as the prime factor driving the establishment of large-scale operations or activities; this model adheres to the characteristics of Weber's and Taylor's models described in Chapter 1. When activities continue to expand, development of a bureaucratic structure becomes necessary to control the enterprise, including the creation of rules, hierarchy, specialization, and means of communication. Colombian cartels and the outlaw biker groups are examples of this type of structure.

The *patrimonial/patron–client model* is based on bonds that tie the organization together. In this paradigm, the patron provides aid and protection, while the client becomes a loyal member who is respected. The emphasis is on traditions such as rituals and personal relationships. Such a model offers the advantage of continuity when the leader is incapacitated, as a patron will assume the position. The patron–client model is less centralized and features less control over subordinates than the bureaucratic model. Albini (1971) and Abadinsky (2003) characterize the American Mafia as a patron–client group whose structure is hierarchical and bureaucratic, but whose activities follow the patron–client model in that members operate in an entrepreneurial fashion, as independent crews. The Mafia's goal is to conduct criminal activity for profit; in contrast, while the outlaw biker gangs' goal is to promote their lifestyle, which includes criminal activity.

Investigating an organization that adheres to the patron–client model requires a more complex law enforcement effort because of the group's decentralized activities and the large number of social networks whose members are not connected to one another. The bureaucratic model is more vulnerable to law enforcement investigation because of its rigid chain of command, communication structure, and heavy involvement of the leaders in the criminal activity; that is, the leaders give orders and oversee operations directly. In the patron–client model, the patron is often uninvolved in the actual criminal activity and simply provides information on targets for the client to rob or steal.

Beyond Theory

Organized crime will continue to exist because these organizations are extremely dynamic and resilient, and they can re-form even after effective law enforcement and intervention strategies succeed in temporarily breaking them up. For example, LCN is not finished in the United States despite the arrest of most of the crime family bosses. These organizations are network based, which allows them to ally with both powerful political and economic structures and other powerful organized crime groups, thereby continuing to survive and prosper. Organized crime remains part of the local culture, and its ongoing existence depends on corruption and market demand. Members of such groups have taken advantage of technological advances and thrived in the new era of global trade and communication. Their current connection to multinational business and corporations is unprecedented and provides additional evidence of their resiliency. Their durable nature derives from their many years of experience with violence, corruption, and successful recruitment, which have led to the survival—not the demise—of organized crime.

The increased emphasis on fighting terrorism and decreased emphasis on organized crime investigation can only help organized crime in the United States. Funding task forces, research, regulatory agencies, and intelligence operations is crucial to plan successful strategic and tactical interventions. The U.S. government can never hope to provide the entire breadth of employment, security, and goods and services demanded by the public. Thus the enormous profits earned by organized crime groups will continue to be a driving motivator for criminal enterprises. These profits are invested into both the political arena and the economy, which gives organized crime groups more power and influence than the government, even allowing them to become "shadow governments."

The sincerity of international cooperation on this front remains questionable. Are organized crime groups too powerful and too politically connected to allow governments to fully cooperate and aggressively pursue strategies for dealing with or even eliminating these groups? If not, then organized crime groups are certain to attempt to extend their activity and become even more powerful. Will countries forcefully address the problem of corruption, or will governments continue to allow bribery and apathy to continue? If corruption is necessary for organized crime's ongoing existence, then these questions have already been answered, because organized crime activity is expanding and becoming more embedded into our society.

Globalization, along with increased economic interdependence on an international scale, is yet another reason why organized crime has expanded. Agreements such as the North American Free Trade Agreement (NAFTA), liberal immigration policies, and growing transnational networks have provided organized crime with opportunities that are equal to those associated with drug and alcohol prohibitions. The emergence of international banking systems that are subjected to little oversight or control has allowed organized crime to move money undetected to and from anywhere in the world instantaneously. Extensive advances in technology have given rise to communication systems that enable organized crime members and leaders to communicate without detection from any location around the world.

Increases in rural crime now present organized crime groups with new opportunities and markets, in addition to their traditional footholds in the large urban areas. Because rural areas often do not have access to the same levels of resources and enforcement as major urban areas, professional law enforcement in rural America is not prepared to deal with the sophistication of organized crime activity.

The world is becoming smaller through the advent of globalization and networking, and many benefits are certainly resulting from this process. At the same time, this interdependence is counterbalanced by the rapid growth and increased longevity of organized crime.

Combining Theory and Other Explanations

Smith (1980) has written that *conspiracy* is the only way that people engage in organized crime. Conspiracy answers the question of how the activity is planned and executed. None of the theories or models put forth by criminologists and theorists fully explains organized crime. Thus a comprehensive theory is needed that contains elements of all those theories and models discussed in this chapter.

In today's society, immediate gratification is a sought-after quantity. Nevertheless, society will always be characterized by a condition of anomie—there will always be "haves" and "have-nots." Society's preoccupation with success (power and wealth) is a potent force that drives some people to criminal activity when they are deprived of what they saw as their deserved rewards. Albini (1971) found that criminal patrons exchange information and are connected with corrupt government officials, and noted that these networks are in a constant state of flux, with the roles of patrons and clients changing rapidly. Such networks exist because of a demand by society. Society has accepted and embraced this relationship with organized crime groups, prohibition, the drug trade, gambling, and prostitution.

Theorists and law enforcement officials alike readily acknowledge the reality of environmental and role-model influences in driving organized crime. For example, youths may begin their criminal career as specialists in theft, drug trafficking, or arson, and later become a member of an organized crime group due to their expertise. Flashy cars, expensive jewelry, and large rolls of money help organized crime members appear as success stories, which in turn helps in recruiting young people into their organization (Cressy, 1969).

Ethnicity serves as a variable in this environment, but is only part of the equation. Membership in the American Mafia, Yakuza, and certain black gangs is linked to certain ethnic backgrounds, for example. Kenny and Finckenauer (1995) summarize the factors that combine to produce organized crime by stating that conspiracy is the *how*, ethnicity is often the *who*, and illicit enterprise to supply demand is the *what*. Ethnic succession may affect the evolution of such crime, too. For instance, Irish gangs were replaced by Italian groups in U.S. organized crime; according to some law enforcement sources, the latter groups are now being replaced by African American, Russian, Hispanic, and Asian groups.

These emerging groups operate in an American environment where the last few decades have seen reduction of major industries, resulting in fewer good-paying jobs for low-skilled and uneducated workers. The disappearance of this type of employment has resulted in a growth of the lower class; in the case of gang members, these individuals may turn to the criminal world to make a living. Examples of this new breed of organized crime groups include Disciple Nation, the Crips, Vice Lord Nation, and the Bloods, among many others. In addition, Nigerian criminal groups have evolved as major drug suppliers to many of these street gangs.

Crime has become a way of life for many of these Americans, and the socialization function helps explain their acceptance within the community in many localities. Indeed, studies by researchers such as Albanese (1996), Potter and Lyman (2004), and Abadinsky (2003) have reported a criminal–community relationship in which criminal groups are not considered very different from legitimate enterprises. This relationship leads to successful recruitment and support for organized crime groups.

Of course, the great majority of people with a low income do not become members of organized crime, despite their poverty, limited opportunities, and lower socioeconomic backgrounds. Merton's (1964) and Durkheim's (1964) anomie concept provides some clarity on this matter. Merton (1957) and Abadinsky (2003) conclude that organized crime is an adaptation to anomie based on innovation (illegal means to obtain the American dream of success), such as long-term strategic planning and other characteristics of organized crime activity. Durkheim's research reached the same conclusion.

Nevertheless, this theory fails on another front: It does not explain why wealthy people become members of criminal groups. Many members of organized crime groups explain that they are just providing what the public desires and demands. This attitude is summarized in their beliefs that "only suckers work" and that laws are made to control the working class.

What is the relevance of all this theory? If an explanation of why organized crime exists can be developed, then a comprehensive plan of action by the government and law enforcement can also be developed.

Yet another approach would be to determine why most people do not enter criminal organizations. Certainly, most people fear the threat of apprehension and punishment. Social control theory also helps explain why most individuals do not choose criminal careers. Many who do choose criminal careers could be diagnosed with antisocial personality disorder or possess psychological traits that predispose them to criminal careers (i.e., sociopathic personality disorder). Criminologists believe that crime is the result of the combination of individual personality and social conditions or social disorganization. Organized crime, then, might be described more as criminal cooperation with the "legitimate" world than as groups or individuals engaged in criminal activities. Conspiracy is an accurate description of organized crime activity; the co-conspirators of these criminals are the people who demand the goods and services provided by organized crime. Put simply, there does not appear to be any real possibility of completely removing organized crime from the world, or more specifically from the United States, because its existence is demanded by human weaknesses.

Perhaps a deeper understanding of these theories may provide a better explanation of organized crime activity and answer the question of why individuals become organized crime members. Meanwhile, the enterprise theory gives the investigator more suggestions for investigative techniques that may be applied to such groups.

Although there have been successful law enforcement efforts, such as those leading to the demise of the Cali and Medellín cartels and the arrests of many LCN and other members of organized crime groups, the removal of large groups or bosses has not eliminated organized crime in any country. Other groups or bosses always spring up to replace the ones who have been removed.

Market demand remains a determining factor in the continued existence of organized crime. The failure to effectively address corruption, develop accurate and timely intelligence, and reduce public demand for illicit goods and services ensures the survival of organized crime. Unless governments can disrupt the relationship that organized crime has with the political and economic elements of society, organized crime groups will continue to expand into new markets and governments, thereby ensuring their ongoing existence. Criminal intelligence in part consists of identifying members, structures, methods of recruitment, retention, methods of operations, motives, areas of activity, types of services and goods provided by the group, and ways that money and assets are handled.

Theories help with assimilating this information and can help make predictions about the future growth and development of organized crime. Immediate gratification, greed, and power are clearly motives that make organized crime both successful and vulnerable. Organized crime is a career pattern that offers many opportunities for tracing its participants' activities and assets. The investigator must understand that the activities of organized crime groups are flexible networks that change with market demands and opportunity. Organized crime groups are often loosely structured and fragmented, with no single group exercising complete control over activities such as drug trafficking, gambling, or prostitution. This flexible nature does not make them any less a threat and often results in conflicts that produce extraordinary crime rates in categories such as murder. Ianni's (1972) view was that organized crime groups are ethnic social systems. Haller (1990) described organized crime groups as small-scale business partnerships. Again, there is no consensus on how to best characterize their organization.

What is evident from the many different studies is that organized crime requires public participation and corruption to achieve either enterprise status or power. Block (1983) defined enterprise syndicates as forming to distribute large amounts of illicit goods and services whose acquisition and delivery require a large number of members, hierarchy, centralization, and division of labor. In the past, power syndicates were involved in extreme violence to control other enterprise syndicates. These power syndicates often had no division of labor and were loosely structured, flexible associations. Such associations did not last for any long periods of time, in contrast to enterprise groups that were long-lived organizations.

Conclusions

When addressing organized crime, investigators must identify the groups operating in their jurisdictions and determine which of the theories do not apply. Perhaps a comprehensive theory could be developed for an individual organized crime group, but to date no "one theory fits all" approach has proved valid. Understanding and prediction should be the investigator's goals when examining theory and organized crime. Both theories and common sense help explain why organized crime activity exists and why individuals choose to belong to these groups. So far, enforcement and policies have failed to eliminate the profitability of organized crime activity. It appears that some people choose to join organized crime groups for myriad reasons: because of their better assurance of success and power, to gain extraordinary wealth, as a result of peer pressure, because of role-model influences, and owing to the recruitment efforts of these criminal enterprises.

The investigator can benefit from examining the "why" of organized crime groups so as to better develop plans of intervention, market disruption, arrest, and prosecution. Individuals who belong to organized crime groups tend to support one another and maintain the group's purposes, just as bureaucracies tend to support bureaucratic characteristics. These actions and mindsets tend to keep the members doing what the group has always done to continue its organized activity.

Organized crime's survival depends on two elements: corruption and public demand. Although structure, individual motive, and conspiracy are important elements of organized crime, it is the exploitation of human weakness and weak governments that ensures the long-lived continuity of organized crime groups. Arrest and prosecution of members of organized crime groups will not eliminate these criminal enterprises, because there will always be an ambitious recruit or member waiting to take the place of the arrested leader. These organizations are too dynamic to be destroyed by law enforcement efforts alone. Instead, it must be recognized that public demand drives the illicit markets on which organized crime groups depend for their profits.

Groups such as the Yakuza and Triads have existed for hundreds of years and will continue to exist because they are not only shadow governments, but also necessary to supply the public's insatiable desire for illicit goods and services. The trend for organized crime groups to invest in legitimate companies and businesses gives them both political power and control of corporations that are an integral part of society or part of the political economic system. There is a high probability that businesses benefiting from partnerships with organized crime groups will continue to resist measures that would lead to effective enforcement of laws against these groups. Strict regulation and monitoring of corporate America may be difficult to implement due to the many benefits, including power and profit, that these business and corporate entities receive from organized crime activity and partnerships. These explanations may say more about why organized crime will continue to exist than do the traditional theories of crime. Certainly, there is a need for additional research about why organized crime exists and continues to be a national threat to society.

Discussion Questions

1. Why are theories important in addressing organized crime?
2. Which particular theories do you think best explain organized crime, and why?
3. What has been the impact of globalization on organized crime?
4. Which specific theories or explanations apply to the different types of organized crime groups, and why?
5. Why do people become members of organized crime?

6. Why do some members of law enforcement believe that enterprise theory is the most valuable contribution of the explanations of organized crime?

7. How can public demand for illegal products and services be reduced? How can these illegal markets be disrupted?

References

Abadinsky, H. (1985). *Organized Crime.* Belmont, GA: Wadsworth/Thompson Learning.

Abadinsky, H. (2003). *Organized Crime* (2nd ed.). Chicago: Nelson-Hall.

Albanese, J. (1996). *Organized Crime in America* (2nd ed.). Cincinnati, OH: Anderson.

Albini, J. L. (1971). *The American Mafia: Genesis of a Legend.* New York: Appleton-Century-Crofts.

Beccaria, C. (1819). *An Essay on Crime and Punishment.* Philadelphia: P. H. Nicklin.

Bell, D. (1953, Summer). Crime as an American Way of Life. *Antioch Review, 13,* 130–150.

Block, A. (1983). *East Side–West Side: Organizing Crime in New York, 1930–1950.* New Brunswick, NJ: Transaction.

Cressy, D. (1969). *Theft of a Nation: The Structure and Operations of Organized Crime.* New York: Harper and Row.

Durkheim, E. (1964). *The Rules of Sociological Method.* New York: Harper and Row.

Ferm, B. (Ed.). (1956). *Encyclopedia of Morals.* New York: Philosophical Library.

Finckenauer, J. O., & Schrock, J. L. (2004). *The Prediction and Control of Organized Crime: The Experience of Post-Soviet Ukraine.* New Brunswick, NJ: Transaction.

Goddard, H. H. (1923). *Feeblemindedness: Its Causes and Consequences.* New York: MacMillan.

Gottfredson, M., & Hirschi, T. (1990). *A General Theory of Crime.* Stanford, CA: Stanford University Press.

Haller, M. (1990). Illegal Enterprise: A Theoretical and Historical Interpretation. *Criminology, 28*(2), 207–236.

Hooten, E. (1939). *The American Criminal: An Anthropological Study.* Cambridge, MA: Harvard University Press.

Ianni, F. (1972). *A Family Business.* New York: Russell Sage Foundation.

Ianni, F. A. (1973). *Ethnic Succession in Organized Crime.* Washington, DC: U.S. Government Printing Office.

Kenny, D., & Finckenauer, J. (1995). *Organized Crime in America.* Belmont, CA: Wadsworth.

Kerlinger, F., & Lee, H. (2000). *Foundations of Behavioral Research* (4th ed.). New York: Harcourt College.

McFeely, R. A. (2001, May 19). Enterprise Theory of Investigation. *FBI Law Enforcement Bulletin.*

Merton, R. K. (1957). *Social Theory and Social Structure.* Glencoe, IL: Free Press.

Merton, R. (1964). *Anomie and Deviant Behavior* (Ed. by M. Clinard). New York: Free Press.

Potter, W., & Lyman, M. (2004). *Organized Crime* (3rd ed.). Upper Saddle River, NJ: Prentice Hall.

Sellin, T. (1938). *Culture, Conflict and Crime.* New York: Social Science Research Council.

Smith, D. (1980). Paragons, Pariahs, and Privateers: A Spectrum-Based Theory of Enterprise. *Crime and Delinquency, 26*(3), 375.

Sutherland, E. H. (1973). *Edwin H. Sutherland: On Analyzing Crime* (Ed. by K. Schnessler). Chicago: University of Chicago Press.

Sutherland, E., & Cressey, D. (1960). *Principles of Criminology* (6th ed.). New York: Lippincott.

Wilson, J. Q. (1975). *Thinking About Crime.* New York: Basic Books.

Wilson, J., & Herrnstein, R. (1985). *Crime and Human Nature.* New York: Simon & Schuster.

Chapter 4
Colombian Drug Cartels

Example moves the world more than doctrine.

—Henry Miller, author (1891–1980)

Objectives

After completing this chapter, readers should be able to:

- Describe the major drug trafficking organizations of Colombia.
- Discuss the organization and growth of the Medellín and Cali cartels and their methods of operation.
- Describe how the efforts of law enforcement led to the decline of the Medellín and Cali cartels.
- Explain the significant aspects of the U.S. policy, "Plan Colombia."

Introduction

During the last two decades of the 20th century, drug trafficking became a staple of organized crime in the Americas. As profits from the smuggling of marijuana, heroin, and, subsequently, cocaine across national borders multiplied, organizations devoted to meeting the demand for these substances grew in size, scope, and sophistication. Until recently, the primary destination for smuggled drugs was the United States. The major players in this process were the Medellín and Cali cartels of Colombia and a variety of Mexican drug trafficking groups who eventually became partners with the Colombians and have now become powerful in their own right. The U.S. Drug Enforcement Administration (DEA) estimates that more than 300 drug trafficking organization operate in South America and now pose a challenge to governments and law enforcement. Organizations such as the Norte del Valle cartel have taken up where the Cali and Medellín cartels left off.

Historical Perspective

Colombia's role in the international proliferation of drugs is rooted in its politics, and the policies designed to minimize drug production and distribution within and across its borders (Ramirez et al., 2005). In the middle of the 20th century, the civil war known as La Violenca (1947–1953) created divisions that have had an impact until the present time. A key force that emerged from this internal conflict was leftist guerillas. U.S. Presidents John Kennedy and Lyndon Johnson feared that this group would set in motion the type of upheaval that had occurred in Cuba, which resulted in a communist state. With this possibility in mind, support for the military and subsequently for paramilitary groups became part of U.S. policy toward Colombia in the 1960s.

The threat posed by leftist guerillas has been a constant concern of U.S. policy makers during subsequent presidential administrations. The control that these groups have exerted over prime coca-producing territory has enabled the United States to link drug control issues to the counter-insurgency campaign. This point was important because it provided a rationale for the support of "Plan Colombia," a formal policy still supported financially by the United States. Under this plan, success in combating the drug traffickers would have to be limited to a by-product of anti-guerilla efforts. One significant aspect of Plan Colombia is that the Colombian military now receives more money than the police, a change from prior years and an indication that the balance of power is shifting.

As the 1970s began, Colombian drug entrepreneurs had made marijuana their drug of choice. Elsewhere, heroin attracted the lion's share of law enforcement activity. In 2003, according to freelance journalist Ron Chepesiuk, this policy caused the DEA to neglect the emerging popularity of cocaine, which was becoming associated with a glamorous lifestyle. Colombians were able to capitalize on cocaine's comeback because they had been shadowing Cuban criminals, learning the cocaine production process (Chepesiuk, 2003).

As the 1970s turned into the 1980s, Colombia became, in the words of Chepesiuk (2003), "the linchpin of the Latin American drug trade." Several factors contributed to this newfound prominence. Initially, access to coca leaves was provided by Colombia's neighbors, Peru and Bolivia, where large quantities of the plants or bushes were grown. By the 1990s, however, Colombia had become the "premier coca-cultivating country in the world, producing more coca leaf than both Peru and Bolivia combined" (Bagley, 2001, p. 1). The last half of the decade was a period of dramatic increase in the amount of land devoted to coca leaf cultivation.

With the ample supply of coca leaves available, Colombia solidified its position as the world's major refiner and supplier of cocaine hydrochloride. Clandestine laboratories in Peru, Bolivia, and Colombia produced hundreds of tons of pure cocaine.

Smuggling the finished product into the United States was facilitated by Colombia's proximity to the U.S. border and the fact that Colombia has both Caribbean and Pacific coasts (**Figure 4-1**). Colombia's historical affinity for smuggling provided an atmosphere that was conducive to making drug trafficking just another facet of a national tradition (Chepesiuk, 2003). In addition, the money to be made in trafficking drugs was very attractive in a country experiencing a high poverty rate and an unstable economy. Initially, the Colombians did their own smuggling using the Caribbean as the main route and the United States as the primary destination.

Figure 4-1   The Caribbean and Pacific coasts of Colombia.

Necessary changes in trafficking patterns were brought about by the U.S. government's move to stem the flow of drugs into the country (Chepesiuk, 2003). Central America and Mexico became logistical destinations for the airlift of drugs destined for U.S. drug customers. Shipments were transported to northern Mexico and then flown across the southwestern border of the United States. Mexican traffickers became more directly involved in the business and by the early 1990s were major players. Cocaine was added to the list of drugs finding their way along the so-called *Mexican drug highway*. Entrance across the United States border has been facilitated by driven vehicles and couriers, called *mules*, who transport small quantities. In addition, passage of the North American Free Trade Agreement (NAFTA) has increased border traffic, making detection of illicit drugs far more difficult. Commercial vehicles of all types, including tractor-trailer units, are now used to haul drugs in large quantities.

During the 1990s, as the Mexican drug groups became increasingly involved in the diversified cocaine trade, the Colombian cartels switched their focus to heroin trafficking. Home-grown opium is processed locally and then transformed from opium gum into morphine and then into heroin. Movement of heroin to the United States is directed by smaller cartels and syndicates, which have replaced the larger, more notorious groups that were formerly synonymous with Colombian drug dealing. Discussion of the participants in the Colombian drug scene from the 1970s to the present follows.

The Medellín Cartel

The Medellín cartel was the first of the major Colombian drug groups to emerge. This organization was the most powerful cartel for more than 12 years, and its power transcended national boundaries. It employed producers, murderers, chemists, attorneys, government officials, accountants, transportation experts, and a variety of distributors throughout the world. Cartel leaders became major landowners with powerful political influence. In addition, the Medellín cartel increased its efficiency by forging alliances with such groups as the traditional American La Cosa Nostra.

This loosely knit group of drug dealers joined forces for the purpose of achieving common goals with fewer liabilities than were associated with operating individually. The leaders of this tough group became known as the Hoodlums ("Los Hampones") and included Pablo Escobar, Carlos Lehder, the Ochoa brothers, and Jose Gacha.

As the boss of the Medellín cartel, Escobar was considered by many to be the "godfather of cocaine." The son of a schoolteacher and a farmer, he chose the criminal life. He ingratiated himself not only with the people of his native country, but also with officials of the governments of both the United States and Colombia while building his cocaine empire. He built schools, churches, and housing, while simultaneously corrupting government officials with bribes and intimidating them with threats of violence.

Escobar began as a petty thief, became a gang member, excelled as a paid murderer, and rose to become boss of a major organization with a personal net worth estimated at between $2 billion and $4 billion. While building his empire, he established a large following among Colombians because of his physical and financial support of Colombian soccer. Escobar was so politically powerful that when the Colombian government, under U.S. pressure, finally agreed to deal with him, he was able to dictate his own terms of incarceration. He continued to run his enterprises while imprisoned.

Although Escobar captured more headlines because of his public persona and violent style, Lehder was perhaps more important to the success of the Medellín group. Lehder established an airlift that involved flying cocaine shipments from Colombia to an island in the Bahamas, where refueling took place before the planes continued to the United States. This process served as a model for other similar operations during the 1970s and 1980s.

Operations

The Medellín group's backgrounds were reflected in the way they conducted their drug business (Chepesiuk, 2003). Violence was the primary tool for dealing with discord. Much of this activity was engineered by Escobar. During the 1980s, the cartel planted bombs that killed 63 people in one incident. In 1989, the cartel blew up a commercial aircraft, killing a large number of people because they believed an informant/witness was aboard. They killed 30 of Colombia's judges, a state police officer, a presidential candidate, and a minister of justice as well as hundreds of police officers and innocent bystanders. Bounties were placed on police officers and hundreds were killed. Innocent bystanders in the wrong place at the wrong time routinely paid for their mistake with their lives. The violence intimidated the government to such extremes that Colombian officials gave in to the cartels, refusing for years to extradite members to the United States for trial. Members of the cartel lived in fortified homes protected by armed guards and elaborate surveillance equipment.

For a time, Medellín leaders even attempted to become a part of Colombia's political system. This effort had limited success before they reverted to the most extreme form of narco-terrorism: the murder of anyone who stood in their way.

The Cali Cartel

The second cartel to have an impact on the international drug scene, the Cali cartel developed a stronger presence than the Medellín group. Its founders were the Rodríguez brothers, Gilberto and Miguel, and Jose Santacruz. Ron Chepesiuk, author of the definitive work about this group, *Drug Lords: The Rise and Fall of the Cali Cartel*, states that the backgrounds of these individuals remain unclear (Chepesiuk, 2003, p. 22). Whatever their origins, the skills of the three men blended together to create an effective and powerful organization. The fourth member of the directorate was Pacho Herrera, whose initial focus was the New York market and who would later become the major player in establishing alliances with Mexican traffickers.

Operations

The approach taken by the Cali leaders was in stark contrast to the flamboyant style of Escobar and his Medellín partners. Avoiding media and legal attention and promoting a professional image were preferable to the violent stance adopted by the notorious Medellín group. However, Cali members were ruthless when murder served their purpose.

Despite their different philosophies, the two cartels were able to coexist well into the mid-1980s. This lack of friction was due at least in part to the rapidly expanding drug market and the enormous profits that came from supplying this demand.

The Cali cartel took numerous steps to ensure that its operations could continue without legal interruption. Security and intelligence were given high priority. Telephone calls were monitored and taxi drivers kept track of visitors (Chepesiuk, 2003).

The city of Cali quickly became the cartel's town. Chepesiuk (2003) likens the leaders' control to that of feudal barons controlling large estates in medieval times. As was the policy under earlier drug leaders, economic development was launched in a variety of areas, which created jobs, provided a way to launder drug money, and led to acceptance of Cali members by the local populace.

The cartel's control also extended to the media. Their lawyers threatened lawsuits when anything negative appeared in the press. Media employees were paid to generate favorable publicity.

Chepesiuk states unequivocally that the Cali cartel was solidly entrenched by the mid-1980s: "Its members felt untouchable; they were untouchable" (2003, p. 71). This growth was aided by the preoccupation of Colombian authorities with the Medellín cartel, which they perceived as being more dangerous.

The Cali cartel grew into a multinational corporation by the early 1990s and became the model for multinational crime. Both the size of the marketplace and the number of personnel who served it expanded in a dramatic fashion. Perhaps the most important step that the Cali cartel took in the early 1990s was to develop operations in a number of Latin American and Caribbean countries. Ties forged with Mexican traffickers would prove to be the most significant alliance, which represented a highly profitable arrangement for both parties. The most notorious of these partnerships was formed with Amando Carrillo Fuentes, the "Lord of the Skies" who originated the concept of using jets to fly cocaine from Colombia to Mexico (Chepesiuk, 2003).

After ties between Mexican traffickers and the Cali group were established, Colombian cocaine increasingly came into the United States via the Mexican pipeline while the Caribbean connection became less important. Mexican cartels would become major operatives in the Cali's Mexican presence. In the late 1990s, because of U.S. interdiction along the U.S.–Mexican border, the Caribbean countries returned to prominence as links in the drug trade (Bagley, 2001). More recently, as the Mexican cartels have grown stronger, trafficking across the U.S. border has regained its prominence.

Markets in the other parts of the world would eventually be established by the cartel. A Mafia–Cali alliance developed, for example. The possibilities for further European business were heightened by the collapse of communism, dissolution of the Soviet Union, and the elimination of European trade barriers. In the face of these changes, organized crime syndicates wasted no time making international contacts.

The success of the Cali cartel can be attributed to a variety of factors, but the scale and attention to detail of the organization were perhaps most important (Chepesiuk, 2003). Operations were directed from the "home office" in Cali, which approved all customers before a drug sale occurred. Cells operating within specific geographic areas were responsive to policies and decisions made in Cali. Cell managers supervised 25 to 50 employees whose duties reflected a division of labor that included transportation, distribution, support, and accounting. Cell managers were responsible to regional managers, who in turn reported to the Cali office. **Figure 4-2** shows the organization chart of the Cali cartel.

This network of managerial and support personnel numbered in the thousands. Their operations were strictly wholesale, however. Cali members were not involved in retail sales, as those were handled by street traffickers.

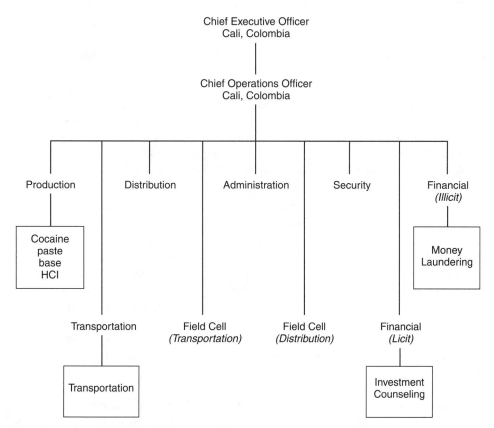

Figure 4-2 Cali cartel organization chart.

Actually, the management model developed by the cartel resembled that found in fast-food chains (Chepesiuk, 2003). Vacations and financial incentives were provided to maintain commitment to the organization. U.S. workers were transferred between cities and were expected to maintain the daily routines of typical Americans. Discipline for misbehavior was reinforced by potential threats of violence to family and relatives.

The major difference between Cali units and fast-food franchises was the isolation of cells. This organization was not dealt a major blow when individual cells were shut down by the criminal justice system.

Movement of cocaine inside U.S. borders was facilitated by trains, vehicles, planes, and the postal service. In addition, a variety of boats, including cargo ships, fishing vessels, and cigarette boats, were used to carry the drug.

As a result of these smoothly running operations, the Cali cartel became a major player in the U.S. drug market during the 1980s. The income generated in the Unites States was "dirty money," however, and by necessity had to be "laundered" so that it could be used to finance the many operations of the trafficking business back in Colombia. *Money laundering* is a process whereby money earned illegally is made to appear to have a legitimate origin. While laundering is a useful tool for many organized crime activities, it is particularly valuable for drug traffickers given the large amounts of cash involved. The purpose of this action is to avoid prosecution and a number of other legal consequences such as taxation.

Over the course of its operations, the Cali cartel graduated from the simple laundering methods used in the 1970s to a series of more sophisticated techniques in the 1980s—an evolution that became necessary as financial restrictions were tightened. Wiring money directly to Colombia, using businesses as fronts, became more difficult, as all transactions of $10,000 or more were required to be documented with the U.S. government. Subsequently, "smurfs," or innocent-looking individuals, were used to purchase money orders for less than $10,000 that were then either deposited into several bank accounts or wired out of the country. When this system proved to be unsatisfactory, the same large planes that transported cocaine to the United States were called upon to return to Colombia with large amounts of cash on board.

The cartel constantly looked for ways to improve its laundering techniques so as to keep out of the reach of law enforcement. One of the most notable and innovative of these strategies was the black market peso exchange initiated in the mid-1980s. In this alternative to the traditional financial system, brokers used a variety of methods to convert dollars to pesos. This practice enabled the Cali group to steer clear of legitimate financial institutions. Billions of dollars were laundered every year by the Cali group and other drug traffickers (Chepesiuk, 2003). This system still exists and has become an important element of the Colombian economy.

Despite the Cali cartel's success in "washing" large amounts of money, international law enforcement began to adopt measures that significantly affected the money laundering system (Chepesiuk, 2003). These included the "kingpin strategy," which targeted higher-echelon traffickers. The DEA created "Operation Green Ice" under the kingpin program, a successful sting program that enticed traffickers to launder money through a company created by the agency. Another successful venture, Dinero, used a full-service bank established specifically for Cali leaders to clean their money.

Decline of the Major Cartels

Although the Medellín and Cali cartels coexisted somewhat peacefully for several years, their relationship eventually began to sour for several reasons. By 1990, the Cali cartel had become the dominant force in the U.S. cocaine market, a situation that did not please Pablo Escobar. Escobar had been at war with the Colombian government since at least 1986, and became convinced that governmental agencies were in collusion with the Cali cartel. His forces engaged in a variety of terrorist acts designed to solidify his position. Some of these activities were directed at politicians, while others targeted members of the Cali group. The Cali group responded in kind, and kidnappings, bombings, and shootings became common.

After several more rounds of bloodshed, Escobar surrendered in June 1991 as the Ochoa brothers had done before him. He did so because he was promised that he would not be extradited to the United States. Escobar was allowed to build his own jail, dubbed "The Cathedral," a facility that cost $5 million. Amid luxurious surroundings, he continued to run his cocaine empire. His jailors allowed him to leave and return at will and to have an unlimited number of visitors. He waged a terror campaign against those he believed did not adequately support him. During this period, Escobar allegedly killed two of his employees whom he believed had cheated him.

During his stay at The Cathedral, Escobar's enemies attacked his associates relentlessly. Escobar eventually feared for his safety and sneaked out of his fortress estate in July 1993. His escape embarrassed the Colombia government, and a manhunt was undertaken for the purpose of putting him in a real penal facility. It was spearheaded by the vigilante group, "Los Pepes" (those persecuted by Pablo Escobar). Information supplied at least partly by the Cali cartel led to Escobar's being shot and killed on December 2, 1993, after an 18-month search. He was only 44 years old. The Cali group members were immediately crowned as the "New Kings of Cocaine," a somewhat misleading title because they had already been the "kings" for several years at this point.

During the time that law enforcement officials were focused on Escobar, attention was still being paid to the Cali cartel. Despite its earlier international successes, the cartel would find that the ensuing years would be difficult. As discussed earlier, its money laundering activities were coming under increasing scrutiny from the DEA and other agencies. The structure of the organization and its chain of command were proving to be problematic. Because the home office in Cali made most of the decisions, dependence on electronic communication was a necessity. Micro-management from afar was prone to the technological and legal advances that the DEA and other agencies were making with tapping into transactions and conversations (Chepesiuk, 2003).

The other major problem that developed for the Cali group was one of its own making. As the organization grew, it relied on the same methods for sending its product to market (Chepesiuk, 2003). For example, the vehicles of preference were large boats and frequently cocaine was hidden in shipments of coffee, frozen vegetables, and other products. The Cali group also preferred to use a transfer point rather than shipping drugs directly from Colombia to the United States or some other destination.

After years of frustration and hard work, the efforts of law enforcement began to produce significant results. The combination of improved investigative techniques, luck, and Cali greed would prove to be the end of Colombia's slide toward "narco-democracy." The proverbial "nails in the coffin" were the sanctions applied by the Office of Foreign Assets Control (OFAC). This agency used information gathered by the DEA, FBI, and other law enforcement agencies to create a stranglehold that squeezed the economic life out of the cartel.

Because of the slowly turning wheels of justice, the end came gradually for the leaders of the Cali cartel. A series of arrests and subsequent imprisonments occurred during 1995 and 1996. A brief respite for Gilberto Rodríguez occurred in November 2002, when he was released from a Colombian prison by a judge who cited his participation in a work-study program. Eventually, however, Gilberto and his brother Miguel were extradited to the United States and pleaded guilty to drug trafficking and money laundering charges. On September 26, 2006, the brothers were sentenced and imprisoned, forfeiting several billion dollars in fines, businesses, and assets. U.S. Attorney General Alberto Gonzales commented on the sentencing, stating that it was "the final fatal blow to the powerful Cali cartel" (Eggen, 2006, p. A08).

Current Activities

The takedown of the Cali cartel was perhaps the DEA's finest hour (Chepesiuk, 2003). Defeat of the multinational monolith left a giant hole in the Colombian drug scene. However, demand for illegal drugs did not disappear. In fact, even before the "last hurrah" of the Cali godfathers, a multitude of trafficking organizations were jockeying for position in the contest to see which ones would become primary suppliers for the world's drug cravings.

The Norte del Valle cartel reputedly has been the most powerful drug coalition of any size in years following the demise of the Medellín–Cali cartels. One of its leaders, Diego Montoya Sanchez, is currently on the FBI's "Ten Most Wanted Fugitives" list, alongside Osama bin Laden. This drug gang had ties to the Cali group and has operated in Cali territory. In 2004, violent infighting among factions occurred and hundreds were killed. The conflict produced three divisions, reflecting discord within the cartel. These three syndicates now operate separately from one another. Arrests of several major figures since 2004 have weakened these groups and their future is now less viable given the uncertainties of the drug trade (*El Espectador*, 2004). The remaining elements rely on Mexican syndicates to handle cocaine smuggling and wholesaling.

"Baby" Cartels

Another development in the post-Cali era has been the emergence of baby cartels, known as "cartelitos" or "traquetos." These smaller groups do not have the problems of scale that plagued the Cali group (Chepesiuk, 2003). They use the latest technology, alliances formed during the Cali reign, and face-to-face meetings to further their interests. They have also become a force in the trafficking of heroin derived from the central area of Colombia, where the climate and terrain are ideal for growing opium (Chepesiuk). Colombian heroin has dominated the East Coast market in the United States for the past several years.

There is now agreement among authorities that Mexican groups are playing a major role in the Colombian drug trade. According to John Walters, Director of the White House Office of National Drug Control Policy ("Drug Czar"), "The Mexicans have taken over and are running the organized crime, and getting the bulk of the money" (Harman, 2005, p. 1). Carlos Medina, deputy director of the National Narcotics Directorate, said emphatically that "the Colombians have a weak position with respect to the power of the Mexican mafias" (Notimex News Agency, 2006b, p. 1). Production is still in the hands of the Colombians but Mexicans are now moving into control of transport to the United States and subsequent distribution (Harman, 2005, p. 1).

FARC

Two groups that have emerged as players in the post-Cali period have histories that reflect their contrasting orientations. The older and larger of the two, the Revolutionary Armed Forces of Colombia (FARC), developed largely as a reaction to exclusion from the political process. It is the principal guerilla organization in Colombia and still engages in violent activity against the Colombian government. FARC has profited from the drug business by taxing coca growers and

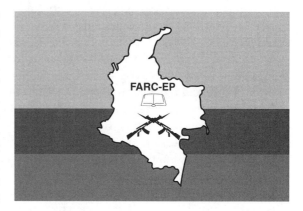

The FARC flag.

performing various services for traffickers such as protecting crops, laboratories, and air ships. FARC also earns a sizable amount of money from "traditional" guerilla pursuits such as kidnapping and extortion (Bagley, 2001).

Paramilitary Groups

The second drug-dealing groups to emerge in the wake of the Cali cartel's demise are paramilitary groups that formed in opposition to the leftist, anti-government FARC. These organizations were originally created to support the military's anti-guerilla campaign and were compatible with U.S. policy (Ramirez et al., 2005). In the 1980s, they grew quickly in response to guerilla activity that forced landowners to relinquish their estates. Drug traffickers obtained this land and partnered with the military and gentry to form private armies. These paramilitary units were the antidote to fears about marginalization harbored by the military and local elites.

By the mid-1990s, the fortunes of the paramilitary groups had improved (Ramirez et. al., 2005). First, they united under the banner of the United Self-Defense Forces of Colombia (Autodefensas Unidas de Colombia [AUC]). Second, they began to compete with FARC for control of coca-producing regions. Subsequently, they began to tax the drug trade and now earn a substantial part of their income in this manner.

Plan Colombia

Ties among the military, paramilitary groups, the police, and drug traffickers have become a routine part of the narco-political atmosphere. Recent U.S. aid to Colombia largely has been earmarked for the military to strengthen anti-guerilla activities (Bagley, 2001). In 2000, U.S. officials stipulated that much of that year's aid appropriation was to be used in southern Colombia, which is FARC territory (Bagley). This direction suggests that U.S. policy continues to revolve around the political objective of controlling leftist elements, with anti-narcotic strategy being a secondary consideration.

Since its creation, Plan Colombia has received funding of $4.7 billion from the United States (Harman, 2006a). It has recently achieved some measure of success, as Colombia is now freer from the civil disorder that has plagued its recent past. Tensions between leftist and rightist groups seem to be easing. Large-scale coalitions no longer dominate the drug market. Growth of coca and production of cocaine have been hampered in some areas, and many drug traffickers have been caught and either imprisoned or extradited to the United States.

Despite these achievements, Colombia remains the top producer of cocaine in the world, with its production amounting to 776 metric tons in 2005 (National Narcotics Directorate data, as quoted in Harman, 2006b). The flow of product continues northward, conveyed by the remnants of the Norte del Valle coalition and the cartelitos. The failure of a fumigation campaign, directed by U.S. government agencies, illustrates the frustration associated with finding effective strategies to combat the drug production. Aerial eradication using U.S. pilots to spray coca leaves with a variation of the herbicide Roundup resulted in a record-breaking number of acres of coca being destroyed in 2005 (Harman, 2006b). Despite this destruction, coca cultivation actually increased by 8% according to a United Nations agency (Harman, 2006b). Improved growing techniques and the spread of cultivation to two-thirds of the country's provinces have produced more coca leaves. This geographical expansion also has led to more agencies interfacing with drugs, creating an increased potential for corruption (Harman, 2006b).

As early as the 1920s, it was evident that conventional law enforcement efforts were no match for the complexity of organized crime. Although undercover operations and physical surveillance continue to be used today, it is increasingly difficult to place an agent in an organization at a level where he or she can gather direct evidence on the top management. Cartel leaders, such as regional directors or family heads, do not personally conduct drug transactions, nor do they get involved in the actual operation of the enterprise. However, informants offer an avenue that is much more effective and efficient. Informants may be cartel members or close associates who can offer information or testimony on the structure, membership, and operation of the organization. When high-ranking members of the cartels and knowledgeable associates provide information, their testimony can lead to convictions of major cartel leaders.

Assessment of the Current Threat from Colombian Cartels

Colombian groups continue to maintain significant control over South American cocaine and heroin smuggling and distribution in the eastern United States, although their role has diminished with rise of the Mexican drug trafficking organizations (U.S. Department of Justice, 2006). The Mexican government has stated that the Colombians continue to control drug trafficking in Mexico. The DEA, however, has argued that Mexican cartels have both command and control over drug trafficking and are becoming organized into cells with subordinate cells that operate throughout the United States and are the major launderers of drug money in the United States (Cook, 2007). Colombian cartels still produce the bulk of the cocaine that supplies the world. In addition, Mexico's drug wars have their origins in Colombia.

The government of Colombia, with help from the U.S. government, almost destroyed the Cali and Medellín cartels in the 1990s, but hundreds of smaller organizations that were more difficult to address soon sprang up to replace them. The Cali cartel's tool of ownership of many legitimate businesses enabled members of this group to become firmly entrenched in the country's economy. Corruption was widespread during this cartel's heyday and remains so today. In response, the government of Colombia has passed powerful laws to address drug trafficking and corruption, and hundreds of police and military have been discharged or prosecuted (Kellner & Pipitone, 2010). Moreover, since the end of the Cali cartel, guerilla and paramilitary (narco-terrorist) groups such as FARC, Ejercito de Liberacion Nacional (ELN), and AUC have emerged as major suppliers of heroin and cocaine and are now considered major traffickers as well as ruthless terrorists.

The situation in Colombia remains critical, with drug trafficking being a major industry in that country as well as in the rest of South America. Of course, as in any other country, the Colombian public must demand change for the problem to be solved.

Conclusions

The gains and losses associated with Plan Colombia suggest that its future and the future of Colombia itself are uncertain. The social fabric of the country is stretched dangerously thin by the social phenomena linked to drug trafficking and the battle against it. Violence, corruption, and displacement of rural residents by both FARC and paramilitaries remain major problems despite the infusion of U.S. aid.

The primary role played by the military is problematic and raises renewed questions about its loyalties. On May 22, 2006, 11 members of an elite Colombian police narcotics unit trained by the DEA were massacred by Colombian soldiers in Jamundí, a city in the middle of Norte del Valle territory. An Army spokesman described the incident as a tragic case of "friendly fire." Others alleged that the soldiers "were doing the bidding of a drug trafficker" (Harman, 2006a). Electronic evidence supports the latter conclusion. According to Bruce Bagley, a leading expert on Colombian politics and drug trafficking, "Jamundí is the tip of the iceberg" (Harman, 2006a). He asserts that this event is indicative of the failure to develop a professional military in Colombia and the tendency to ignore questions about corruption and the realities of failed policies.

In September 2006, the U.S. Senate Appropriations Committee refused to approve that year's funding earmarked for Plan Colombia by the State Department. The agency took this action three days after the Jamundí massacre without mentioning the incident. Senate approval was dependent on receiving satisfactory explanations for Jamundí and other questionable events.

The re-election of President Alvano Uribe, the U.S.'s conservative ally, in May 2006 suggested that more intrigue of the type surrounding Jamundí may be forthcoming. The central role of the military in the U.S.-supported Plan Colombia promises an even stronger military presence and fewer pretenses about human rights. In addition, the hand-in-glove relationship between the military, the police, and drug traffickers discussed earlier remains a debilitating element in Colombia's experiment in democracy and its failure to mount an effective anti-narcotic strategy.

One sign of a more positive future was the 2005 action of 2000 members of the paramilitary group, United Self-Defense Forces. These individuals turned in their weapons and were granted amnesty and given a monthly stipend by the Colombian government.

In a less hopeful note, Brazilian police reported in April 2005 that FARC had established a drug trafficking network on the Brazilian–Colombian border (Notimex News Agency, 2006a). This operation is thought to be critical to the achievement of FARC's ultimate ambition: the creation of New Colombia, a political entity independent of the present-day state. A supply line has transported a variety of items into Brazilian territory including portable x-ray machines, food, tool kits, and insecticide equipment. Stolen explosives and the presence of cocaine laboratories reflect FARC activity in the border area and other remote locations. Notably, Red Command, a Brazilian criminal organization, has sold weapons to FARC. Investigations indicate that purchases of arms and ammunition also have been made from Paraguayan cartels. Cocaine is the currency used in these transactions. Cocaine is still produced in Colombia and South America, and groups from this region of the world will continue to be powerful transnational organized crime players and pose a major challenge for law enforcement worldwide.

If these movements and transactions are a valid indicator of trafficking activity in these and adjoining areas, then the adage "The more things change, the more they remain the same" applies to the Colombian drug scene. Shifts in location, changes in group structure and dynamics, and rearrangement of the players have all taken place during the past 15 years. What has remained steadfast is the world's demand for cocaine and other drugs and the quest by various groups to supply that demand.

Discussion Questions

1. How and why did the cartels of Colombia begin? What has led to their success?

2. Explain the typical structure of Colombian cartels. How have these cartels changed since the fall of the Medellín and Cali cartels?

3. What have been the most effective efforts against drug cartels?

4. If you were appointed Director of the DEA, which changes would you make to improve the law enforcement response against drug trafficking organizations?

References

Bagley, B. (2001). *Drug Trafficking, Political Violence, and U.S. Policy in Colombia in the 1990's.* Unpublished paper provided to the author.

Chepesiuk, R. (2003). *Drug Lords: The Rise and Fall of the Cali Cartel.* Wrea Green, UK: Milo Books.

Cook, C. W. (Ed.). (2007, October 16). Mexico Drug Cartels. CRS Report for Congress, Congressional Research Service. Retrieved March 11, 2010, from Congressional Research Service Digital Database.

Eggen, D. (2006, September 27). With Guilty Pleas, Cali Cartel Finished, U.S. Says. *The Washington Post.* Retrieved September 27, 2006, from http://www.washingtonpost.com

El Espectador. (2004, July 11). Colombian Drug Lord's Arrest Could Mark End of Norte del Valle Turf War—Weekly. Retrieved October 9, 2006, from http://infoweb.newsbank.com

Harman, D. (2005, August 16). Mexicans Take Over Drug Trade to U.S. *Christian Science Monitor.* Retrieved October 9, 2006, from http://www.csmonitor.com

Harman, D. (2006a, September 27). The War on Drugs: Ambushed in Jamundí. *Christian Science Monitor.* Retrieved October 9, 2006, from http://www.csmonitor.com

Harman, D. (2006b, September 28). Plan Colombia: Big Gains, But Cocaine Still Flows. *Christian Science Monitor.* Retrieved October 9, 2006, from http://www.csmonitor.com

Kellner, T., & Pipitone, F. (2010, April 8). The Forever Drug War: Inside the Mexican Drug Wars Quickly Consuming a Nation. Retrieved June 25, 2010, from http://www.huffingtonpost.com/tomas-kellner/the-forever-drug-war-insi_b_531005.html?v

Notimex News Agency. (2006a, May 16). Colombian Drug Trafficking Networks Expanding Operations in Brazil. Retrieved October 23, 2006, from http://infoweb.newsbank.com

Notimex News Agency. (2006b, July 16). Mexican Drug Gangs Funding Colombian Mafias, Says Colombian Official. Retrieved October 17, 2006, from http://infoweb.newsbank.com

Ramirez, L., Clemencia, M., Stanton, K., & Walsh, J. (2005). Colombia: A Vicious Circle of Drugs and War. In: C. Youngers and E. Rosen (Eds.), *Drugs and Democracy in Latin America: Its Impact on Latin America and the Caribbean* (pp. 99–142). Boulder, CO: Lynne Rienner.

U.S. Department of Justice, National Drug Intelligence Center. (2006, October). *National Drug Threat Assessment 2007.*

Chapter 5

Mexican Drug Trafficking Organizations

Leaders make things possible. Exceptional leaders make them inevitable.

—Lance Morrow, Boston area journalist and author of *Evil: An Investigation*

Objectives

After completing this chapter, readers should be able to:

- Describe the current major drug trafficking organizations (DTOs) and explain why they are so successful.
- Understand the basic structure of the Mexican DTOs.
- Discuss the Mexican DTOs' activities and methods of operation.
- Describe the current status of DTO and terrorist cooperation.

Historical Perspective

The evolution of Mexican drug cartels dates back to the early years of smuggling whiskey into the United States. By the turn of the 19th century, the southwestern U.S. border was a major site for illegal smuggling. During the 1930s, marijuana replaced alcohol as the smuggler's product of choice. Around the time of World War II, heroin became a major smuggling enterprise.

After the war, the major route for bringing heroin into the United States was the "French Connection" from Turkey to France and then to the East Coast. As law enforcement applied pressure to this enterprise, part of the U.S. market began to be supplied by the Herrera family, whose home ground was the state of Durango, Mexico. The Herreras were a family unit who operated as low-profile traffickers smuggling "Mexican brown" heroin across the border to Chicago and then to the East Coast.

In the 1980s, the United States' "War on Drugs" would provide Mexican groups with more opportunities in the drug market. Law enforcement focus on the Caribbean and Florida—major routes for transport of Colombian cocaine—led the Cali cartel to seek new avenues through Mexico to the United States. Mexico had a long tradition of production and trafficking of marijuana and heroin (Freeman & Sierra, 2005). Crops grown in the southwestern and southern areas were routed into the United States along well-established networks. These networks became more sophisticated as Mexican groups added cocaine and methamphetamines (meth) to their wares and became major players in the U.S. drug market.

In 2001. the DEA listed six Mexican drug trafficking organizations (DTOs) as major suppliers of illicit drugs to the United States:

- The Carrillo-Fuentes or Juárez cartel
- The Arellano-Felix or Tijuana cartel
- The Garcia-Abrego/Cardenas-Guillen or Gulf cartel
- The Caro-Quintero or Sonora cartel
- The Amezcua-Contreras or Colima cartel
- The Herrera or Durango cartel

As with all organized crime groups, these organizations and their leadership must evolve or become extinct due to a variety of reasons. The most significant change in recent years has been the Mexican cartels' policy of employing groups of enforcers, known as sicarios, who have in some cases evolved into significant cartels or powerful groups themselves. From January 2000 through September 2006, the Mexican government arrested more than 300 sicarios from the following seven cartels:

- 134 enforcers from the Gulf cartel
- 107 enforcers from the Tijuana cartel
- 98 enforcers from the Sinaloa cartel
- 66 enforcers from the Juárez cartel
- 15 enforcers from the Millennium cartel
- 6 enforcers from the Oaxaca cartel
- 2 enforcers from the Colima cartel (Cook, 2007)

As is evident from these statistics, the number and power of the Mexican cartels have grown and will likely continue to change in the future, along with leadership of these groups. After the fall of the Cali and Medellín drug cartels, the Guadalajara cartel in Mexico, led by Miguel ("El Padrino") Angel Felix Gallardo and his successors, began to seize control of the massive and lucrative North American drug trade. Eventually, the Guadalajara cartel dissolved when Gallarado was arrested and the Colombian cartels were put under intensive investigation. The Arellano Felix organization (AFO; also known as the Tijuana cartel) and the Sinaloa cartel emerged from the Guadalajara cartel in a bid to fill the power vacuum. This type of change has traditionally created a period of violence and tension for a period of time followed by a return to normal business. However, the current discord in Mexico between the cartels has now continued for more than 10 years and has become increasingly violent, with no apparent end in sight (Stewart, 2010).

The rise of the Mexican cartels is due in part to the success of the U.S. and Colombian war on the Cali and Medellín drug cartels. During their heyday, the Colombian cartels paid the Mexican DTOs as much as $2000 per kilogram of cocaine for delivery of these drugs to U.S. destinations where Colombians would distribute the product. Today, the transportation and distribution are controlled by the Mexican DTOs by means of business alliances with U.S. Mexican gangs. The Barrio Azteca, for example, is tied to the Juárez cartel. Prison gangs are reported by the U.S. Justice Department to operate in all 50 states and are increasing their influence over drug trafficking. These street and prison gangs include La Eme, Raza Unida, MS-13, Latin Kings and a number of others (National Drug Intelligence Center, 2009; Stewart, 2010).

Today, the Gulf, Sinaloa, Tijuana, and Juárez cartels operate in most of the Mexican states. The Sinaloa cartel has a presence in 17 states, the Gulf cartel in 13 states, the Juárez cartel in 21 states, and the Tijuana cartel in 15 states. Alliances are routinely formed and dissolved by these groups. For example, several cartels have formed an alliance known as the "the Federation," which is led by members of the Sinaloa cartel (also known as the Pacific cartel and the Golden Triangle), Juárez, and Valencia cartels who work together, even though the groups remain independent organizations (Cook, 2007).

According to the U.S. National Drug Intelligence Center, in 2009 Mexican and Colombian DTOs generated as much as $38 billion in gross wholesale proceeds from drug sales in the United States. As their profits soared, so did the violence and struggle for "turf" and control of the ports of entry from Mexico into the United States. Control of places such as significant highways, border crossings, airstrips, and ports allows a cartel to reap enormous profits in the drug trade. Such places are often referred to as "plazas" by the DTOs. If the DTO does not control a plaza, it must pay the DTO that has control of it to use the corridor. The violence that has occurred as groups struggle to control these areas has claimed more than 20,000 lives to date, and the current president of Mexico, Felipe Calderón, has deployed approximately 45,000 troops to address the war between the cartels.

Development and Expansion

Mexican drug trafficking is driven by the demand for drugs in the United States and other countries of the world. According to a United Nations estimate, the U.S. market alone is worth $142 billion per year (Harman, 2005). Freeman (2006) suggests that the Mexican drug scene is a product of two intertwined segments of U.S. policy. The first is U.S. prohibition of drugs (heroin, cocaine, marijuana) for which there is a strong demand. The resultant black market generates violence as a by-product and encourages the corruption of agencies and institutions that bear responsibility for enforcing the law. The second segment of U.S. policy that is problematic because of drug prohibition is the failure by the U.S. government to shrink the demand for the banned substances. As an example, cocaine use has recently risen in the United States (Freeman).

Since 1999, Mexican drug trafficking has undergone some major changes and, concurrently, has expanded at a significant rate. These developments can be attributed to several factors. First, Mexico's 2000-mile-long porous border with the United States, traditionally a magnet for drug trafficking, became even more susceptible to smuggling contraband because of economic priorities. Passage of the North American Free Trade Agreement (NAFTA) was designed to promote free trade. It has succeeded in one sense, as Mexico is now the second largest U.S. trading partner (Freeman & Sierra, 2005). However, because the United States also seeks to prevent the flow of illicit drugs, this country is simultaneously and paradoxically trying to create what is in effect "a borderless economy and a barricaded border" (Freeman & Sierra, p. 265). The odds of achieving the latter have been reduced by the escalation of commercial vehicle traffic, with the potential of actually finding contraband becoming the proverbial "needle in the haystack" (Library of Congress, 2003).

Second, Mexican DTOs became an even more important element in the transport of Colombian cocaine to the United States. The decline in Colombian dominance over the process and subsequent change in the balance of power has led to Mexican DTOs financing the Colombian "cartelitos" that formed in the absence of the Medellín and Cali cartels (Nortimex, 2006).

Third, the election of Vicente Fox as Mexican president in 2000 created a hostile political atmosphere for drug trafficking. Previous administrations had benefited from the DTOs' bribes and had protected smuggling operations. Having run on a "war without mercy" political platform against organized crime, Fox's anticrime directives resulted in the killing or jailing of numerous drug kingpins and interrupted the normal routines that had corrupted agencies at every level of government (Library of Congress, 2003). These actions, while productive in one sense, were also unsettling because they "altered the balance of power among Mexico's four major drug trafficking organizations" (Freeman, 2006, p. 2). In turn, this uncertainty has set off a particularly violent phase in Mexico's drug war, as a brutal struggle of "each against all" has ensued that is reminiscent of the battle between bootlegging factions in Chicago during the Prohibition era. The goal of each drug group is to attain dominance over its rivals so as to control trafficking through the most desirable smuggling routes.

By virtue of its attack on the kingpins of Mexican drug trafficking, the Fox administration created opportunities for what the president called "second-level players."

Bruce Bagley, a noted expert on drug trafficking, states that the drug industry has been "restructured, [so that] new, smaller groups now fight over turf that used to be dominated by the big boys" (Hall, 2006). As Mexico is now more democratic, so is the drug trade.

In June 2007, President Felipe Calderón, in addition to mounting a major military campaign against the Mexican DTOs, purged Mexican law enforcement of 284 federal police commanders, including commanders of all 31 states and the federal district. The 700-member Nuevo Laredo police was suspended under corruption investigations. The Mexican federal government has conducted purges in Apatzingan, Michoacan, and Tijuana, Baja California, as well. The deployment of 800 Federal Protective Police and 300 federal officers to Nuevo Laredo demonstrates the extraordinary measures taken by President Calderón to address corruption and the Mexican DTOs (Cook, 2007).

The level of violence in areas such as Nuevo Laredo, Guerrero, and Michoacan has resulted in discussion of Mexico as a failed state. A failed state is one in which the government has lost control over large areas of its country and the state is unable to function. The drug cartels claim that they have an army of 100,000 soldiers and that their enterprise of drug trafficking is the largest source of income in Mexico. Despite the efforts of both the U.S. and Mexican governments, heroin availability production increased to 38 pure metric tons in 2008, methamphetamine availability has increased, and both marijuana and MDMA production has grown in Mexico, according to the 2010 National Drug Assessment by the National Drug Intelligence Center.

The National Drug Intelligence Center also reported that the Mexican DTOs represent the single greatest drug trafficking threat to the United States. While Colombian DTOs' strength in the U.S. East Coast drug markets is diminishing, the Mexican DTOs are gaining strength as the predominant wholesale suppliers in the United States. The Mexican DTOs are now operating in every region of this country. As part of their expansion, they have increased their cooperation with U.S.-based street and prison gangs, which comprise more than 900,000 gang members in 20,000 street gangs in more than 2500 U.S. cities. The economic impact, according to the National Drug Intelligence Center's 2010 report, is nearly $215 billion annually. The prediction is that this threat will not diminish in the future. The alliances between U.S. criminal gangs and Mexican DTOs are creating a major challenge for law enforcement agencies (U.S. Department of Justice, 2010).

Mexican Drug Violence and DTO Competition

The war on and about drugs reached new heights in 2005 and 2006. More than 2000 drug-related murders have occurred since the beginning of 2005, most of them unsolved (Freeman, 2006). In Mexico, drug trade violence has spread to tourist areas such as Acapulco and Cancun, as well as to remote areas far removed from traditional smuggling routes.

A substantial amount of the current epidemic of violence can be attributed to the struggle among DTOs to gain control of key trafficking routes. Grisly murders, decapitations, and mummified corpses haunt the front pages of Mexico's newspapers. Nowhere is the violence more intense than in Nuevo Laredo, sister city to Laredo, Texas. The competition in this area is especially fierce because Nuevo Laredo is "the most important launching point for illegal drugs entering the United States" (Freeman, 2006, p. 3). An estimated 6000 trucks cross the border into Laredo, Texas, each day and carry 40% of all Mexican imports bound for the United States (Freeman). Drug smugglers then use the interstate system to bring their goods to the rest of the United States. During the height of the drug wars in 2005 and early 2006, Nuevo Laredo became the murder capital of Mexico (Freeman).

The Gulf and Sinaloa cartels have clashed over control of trafficking through Nuevo Laredo for several years. Both groups have used special enforcer units to spearhead their activities. Intimidation, murder, bribery, and manipulation of press coverage are among the variety of tactics employed by these deadly rivals.

The atmosphere in Nuevo Laredo has steadily deteriorated during recent years. "Paralyzed by fear" aptly describes the demeanor of public officials (Freeman, 2006). Murders of journalists and policemen, shootouts on city streets, and the ineffectiveness of federal troops and police have created an aura of helplessness in the populace. As many as 40 U.S. citizens have disappeared in and around the city (Freeman). In August 2005, the U.S. Consulate in Nuevo Laredo was closed for a week after a downtown skirmish between rival traffickers who used bazookas, high-powered rifles, rocket-propelled grenades, ground to air missiles, armored Humvees, cluster grenades, and chemical protective suits (Harman, 2005).

Groups such as Los Zetas—the enforcement arm of the Gulf cartel, which now may be a separate cartel of its own—have burned rivals alive, boiled them in large drums filled with diesel, and beheaded both police and rivals. However, as the violence rages, there are reports by some news organizations that the Sinaloa and Gulf cartels may be negotiating a truce. This development may be the outgrowth of the same conclusion that La Cosa Nostra reached in the United States: War and violence are bad for business. Nevertheless, similar to the history established by La Cosa Nostra, if a truce is reached by the Mexican cartels, it will probably be short-lived. It is more likely that what started in the 1990s will continue, as the cartels in Mexico grow more independent and fight for more control of the territories and corridors into the United States.

The violence associated with the Mexican DTOs has escalated in recent years. For example, on February 15, 2007, in an event labeled by the media as "Black Thursday," a local police commander and three of his officers were killed while investigating a vehicle crash. The vehicle, which was occupied by members of a drug gang in Aguascalientes, Mexico, was loaded with AK-47 assault rifles and police uniforms. In addition, the latest attacks have not been confined to Mexico. A U.S. soldier was paid to kill a lieutenant in the Juárez drug cartel in his El Paso home; the soldier shot his victim eight times. The lieutenant was believed by the Juárez cartel leadership to be an informant ("Army Soldier Charged," 2009). In areas experiencing turf wars, such as in Michoacan where the Juárez, Gulf, Millennium, and Colima cartels are all fighting for control, events such as those described previously will likely continue (Cook, 2007). The Mexican newspaper *Reforma* reported that there were 6587 drug-related murders in 2009 in Mexico. After the Mexican Navy Special Forces killed "El Barbas" Beltrand Leyva in a raid, the one Navy man who was killed in the raid was hailed as a hero by President Calderón. However, only hours after the Navy man's funeral, the hero's family—including his mother, two sisters, brother, and aunt—were killed by the drug cartel in their family home (Kellner, 2010).

The Four Major Cartels

Currently, there are four major drug cartels in Mexico. Although each has a base of operation, their tentacles reach over the whole of Mexico from the northern border with the United States to the remote hamlets bordering Central America.

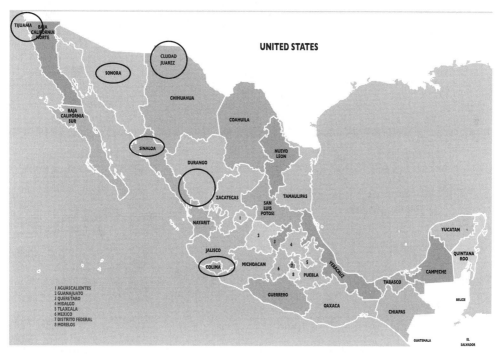

Major strongholds of operations of Mexican cartels.

Source: Modified from Cook, C. (2007). CRS Report for Congress Mexico's Drug Cartels, p. 6.

Mexican cartel areas of influence.

Tijuana Cartel (Arellano Felix Organization)

The Tijuana cartel (Arellano Felix organization [AFO]) has been a major trafficking network since the mid-1980s. Using fees and tolls to permit other Mexican groups to operate in its territory during the 1990s, the AFO developed ties to organized crime groups in South America and to Russian organized crime. It developed a unique internal security mechanism consisting of electronic monitoring of all members and calls from DEA and government sources, surveillance of members, and mail and trash monitoring, in addition to corrupt contacts in utilities and government to guard against possible disloyalty within AFO and its business partners. Serious setbacks because of murders and arrests occurred in 2002 and again in 2006 when Javier

Arellano Felix wanted poster.

Arellano Felix was captured. In addition, Francisco Rafael Arellano Felix was extradited to the United States in September 2005, the first major drug lord to be sent north. Although most of the seven Arellano Felix brothers have been arrested or killed, the organization still transports cocaine and marijuana into the United States (Carl, 2006). The Tijuana cartel has a presence in 15 states of Mexico.

The Tijuana and Juárez cartels have both reemerged as players in the drug wars in Mexico since the truce established by "El Chapo" Guzman of the Sinaloa cartel between the Sinaloa, Tijuana, and Juárez cartels has dissolved. In addition, a struggle has emerged between factions within the Tijuana cartel.

The Tijuana cartel was the first to bring in hired help—that is, its own police force known as La Linea—to carry out enforcement and security operations. The organization used active and current police officers and youth gangs as enforcers. These actions began a trend of the cartels hiring enforcers that has continued and has led to the escalation of the current level of violence between the cartels (Stewart, 2010).

Gulf Cartel

The Gulf cartel is based in two northern Mexico states (primarily in the northeastern border state of Tamaulipas, along the Gulf of Mexico), but has operations in 13 states including the cities of Nuevo Laredo, Miguel Aleman, Reynosa, Matamoros, Monterrey in Nuevo Leon, and Morelia in Michoacan. The leader of the cartel, Osiel Cardenas Guillen, was arrested in 2003 and sentenced to 25 years in prison by a U.S. court in 2010, yet still manages to run the organization from inside prison walls.

The Gulf cartel grew dramatically during the 1990s when it moved from smuggling into direct sales of drugs. This brought group members into conflict with "El Chapo" Guzman of the Sinaloa cartel. In 2002, Cardenas persuaded a group of federal soldiers to leave the military and become his "enforcers" and security detail. These individuals were "likely trained at Fort Bragg and Fort Benning in the mid-to-late 1990s as part of a U.S. program to train and equip Mexican soldiers for antidrug operations" (Freeman, 2006, p. 3). This training has enabled Los Zetas, as they are known, to operate with a high degree of efficiency on behalf of Cardenas. Notably, he has used Los Zetas to gain control of the drug trade in many Mexican cities. Los Zetas have begun to branch off from the cartel and build their own drug trade and criminal enterprise that includes kidnapping, extortion, and murder for hire in addition to their drug trade.

The Gulf cartel is also recruiting MS-13 gang members and Guatemalan Kaibiles (former Guatemalan Special Forces). Los Zetas has now approximately 1200 to 4000 members, and has connections or a presence in U.S. cities including Dallas, Laredo, and Houston, Texas. There is some debate about who runs the Gulf cartel today; however, Los Zetas may have considerable influence. Other reports indicate that Los Zetas has become powerful enough to split from the Gulf cartel and there is conflict between the Gulf cartel and Los Zetas in northeastern Mexico. At one time Los Zetas formed an alliance with the Beltran Leyva organization (BLO). This alliance included elements of the AFO and Juárez cartels. Elements of the Nueva Federacion (New Federation), Los Zetas, the Gulf cartel, and the BLO have attempted to establish a truce to increase profits and fight the government (Jones, 2008). Currently, the Gulf cartel appears to have separated from Los Zetas and formed an alliance with the Sinaloa cartel and Guzman and the La Familia Michoacan organization against Los Zetas (Rodriguez, 2010).

Sinaloa Cartel

The state of Sinaloa traditionally has been associated with the production of opium and marijuana, and has produced a number of Mexico's most celebrated drug lords. The Sinaloa cartel has experienced a recent resurgence after being weakened by a battle with the Tijuana cartel. It has maintained ties with the Juarez cartel (also known as the Carrillo Fuentes organization [CFO]) over the years.

Sinaloa's current leader is Joaquin Guzman Loera, known as "El Chapo." He escaped from a Mexican federal prison in 2001 and remains at large while directing the cartel. This group has waged war against the Gulf cartel for supremacy in Nuevo Laredo. In particular, it has developed a Zetas-like group of enforcers, the Negros, to specifically counter the activities of Los Zetas (Freeman, 2006). The Negros, which are led by Guzman's associate Edgar "La Barbie" Valdes Villarreal, are believed to have been responsible for the attack against police officers in Nuevo Laredo, which represented an attempt to take control of the police away from Los Zetas. The enforcement arm of the Sinaloa cartel also includes the Pelones.

The Sinaloa cartel is now the leader of the Federation, Mexico's largest alliance of DTOs. Guzman, the leader of the Sinaloa cartel, has an estimated fortune of $1 billion (according to *Forbes* magazine's list of the world's richest people) and there is a $5 million reward out for his capture. Guzman is currently allied with Ismael Zambada Garcia, and the two are considered Mexico's top drug kingpins by the DEA.

Like the Gulf cartel, the Sinaloa cartel has formed alliances that have later dissolved. The Juárez cartel, which was once part of the Sinaloa-led Federation, separated from this organization in 2004. The Beltran Leyva organization was also once allied with the Sinaloa cartel. The Gulf and Sinaloa cartels have now joined forces with La Familia Michoacan (LFM) in what is called the New Federation to fight against Los Zetas, the Juárez cartel, and BLO, all of which also broke away from the Sinaloa cartel. The violence continues in this turf battle in the Mexican cities of Reynosa, Nuevo Laredo, Ciudad Juárez, and Tijuana. The Sinaloa cartel continues to show aggressiveness in taking control of plazas and drug trafficking territory from other cartels. However, the battle continues with Los Zetas and its allies rallying to stay in the fight (Cook, 2007, 2009).

Juárez Cartel

Discussion of the Juárez cartel and, for that matter, Mexican DTOs in their entirety would be incomplete without elaborating on the saga of Amado Carrillo Fuentes, whose personal story parallels the rise and growth of Mexican drug organizations. Carrillo grew up in the 1950s in Sinaloa, a state known as "Jurassic Park" because of its "monster" drug dealers and operations. He learned the drug trade from his uncle, who was a veteran drug trafficker. Carrillo's experience included membership in the Federal Police where he earned the title of Director of Federal Security.

In the mid-1980s, the Cali cartel responded to the U.S.-declared "War on Drugs" by initiating relationships with Mexican drug trafficking organizations. When the Caribbean route to the United States became problematic, the U.S.–Mexican border emerged as a useful alternative. Mexico offered a "2000 mile expanse of the border that offered unlimited smuggling possibilities, experienced smugglers eager to collaborate, and a ready-made infrastructure to meet its needs" (Chepesiuk, 2003).

One of the first Colombian–Mexican partnerships involved Carrillo and Albert Ochoa-Soto. The pair worked together in an early Carrillo venture that took place in Ojinaga, a rural town near the U.S. border that offered undetected crossings (Chepesiuk, 2003). They maintained close ties as Carrillo gradually became a major player in the Mexican drug scene.

Carrillo took advantage of the opportunities that arose, eventually becoming the prime connection between the Cali cartel and the Mexican DTOs. Miguel Rodríguez became a business associate of Carrillo's and employed him to transport cocaine into the United States.

Carrillo took charge of the Juárez cartel by ordering the murder of his predecessor. He was able to sustain his position by three methods: (1) keeping a variety of officials on his payroll; (2) building an image as an Escobar-like community benefactor; and (3) orchestrating the murder of hundreds of enemies and opponents. His low profile kept Carrillo out of the public eye, perhaps providing him with whatever protection anonymity enables.

Carrillo used whatever technology was developed, such as pagers, fax machines, and night-vision equipment, to make his organization ever more efficient. Counter-surveillance methods were employed to monitor the activities of U.S. agents. Innovation and versatility marked Carrillo's reign. The essence of his management style is captured by veteran journalist Tracey Eaton: "He ran his operation much like a corporation and got into profit sharing before it became fashionable. He bribed Mexican police chiefs and politicians. He also has the touch of Tony Soprano of the TV series, *The Sopranos,* in that he could go from polite gentleman to ruthless thug in a minute" (cited in Chepesiuk, 2003, p. 109).

As 1997 approached, Carrillo began to sense that law enforcement was closing in, and his enemies both within and outside his cartel were becoming bolder. In July 1997, in the midst of surgery to alter his appearance, he died. Speculation about the cause, either a heart attack or drug overdose, persists; the Mexican government ruled that it was homicide.

In the wake of Carrillo's death, a deadly struggle developed over the control of the Juárez cartel. Amando's brother Vicente became boss and forged ties with a number of regional drug barons (Library of Congress, 2003). The CFO remains a powerful force in Mexican drug circles and is worthy of its designation as a "polydrug" organization because it deals in cocaine, heroin, marijuana, and methamphetamines.

The sophistication that Amando Carrillo Fuentes brought to the cartel remains. Its cell organization, multifaceted leadership, and extensive money-laundering network give this organization both stability and power. The north-central Mexico base of the CFO enables its leaders to micro-manage the shipment of tons of drugs into the United States. Recently the cartel's operations have expanded to include Cancun and Yucatan.

The death of Amado Carrillo Fuentes in 1997 weakened the powerful Juárez cartel. Guzman and the Sinaloa cartel began to move in on the territory of the weakened Juárez cartel, and the violence between these two groups continues. The Juárez cartel has in the past formed alliances with the Sinaloa-led Federation, but now has become an enemy allied with Los Zetas and the BLO. Ciudad Juárez has a reported murder rate of 165 deaths per 100,000. The Juárez cartel has used the Barrio Azteca gang to engage in battles against other cartels and at times against U.S. citizens. The Juárez cartel has created its own police known as La Linea in its battle against the powerful Federation (Stewart, 2010).

Subsidiary and Emerging Organizations

Each of the four major Mexican DTOs works with a variety of mid-sized drug smuggling groups. While regionally based, these groups often have connections to organizations in other Mexican states and frequently do business with international contacts. They have been linked to a number of incidents since 2000 involving murder and seizures of large quantities of drugs and money. Many of the leaders of these organizations are wanted by Mexican authorities but have remained at large for several years.

Beyond the more visible drug organizations are a number of small, corporate-style trafficking groups that may become the prototype of the future (Library of Congress, 2003). These groups emulate the cartelitos that have developed in Colombia in the post-cartel years. Mexican President Vincente Fox has attributed their emergence to the crackdown on the larger cartels in Mexico. Bruce Bagley describes the result as the "atomization of the industry," with new players joining in the game. The presence of these new faces promises to bring more complications to an already layered and overlapping multitude of drug organizations. Bagley and Jorge Chabat, a Mexican drug trade expert, suggest that these new players will resort to violence and brutality to eliminate their rivals (Harman, 2004).

A number of other, more specialized gangs operate on Mexico's northern border with the United States (Library of Congress, 2003). These groups are often linked to the larger DTOs and provide drug smuggling services for contraband going across the border. Rivalries between these gangs have resulted in numerous assassinations.

La Familia Michoacan

The southwestern Mexican state of Michoacan is famous for its marijuana production and as the epicenter of Mexican drug trafficking and violence. The Colima cartel, whose members are known as the kings of methamphetamine, has controlled the drug trade in this state in the past. The Millennium cartel is now reported to have taken control in 2007.

La Familia Michoacan (LFM), which now aspires to control the area, was formed in the 1980s by local marijuana farmers. LFM refers to itself as a vigilante group whose intention is to protect members from police corruption and the violent cartels (Grayson, 2009). Originally, this organization operated under the name La Empresa Organization and trained with Los Zetas to become the Gulf cartel's paramilitary presence in Michoacan, securing arms, carrying out kidnappings, and collecting payments for other cartels in exchange for access to their drug routes. In 2004, the group formed alliances with the Sinaloa and Tijuana cartels, which enabled it to quickly expand. In 2006, it began operation as LFM and became more violent. In particular, members were known for beheading their enemies. LFM members left behind a message at one such event: "The family doesn't kill for money. It doesn't kill women. It doesn't kill innocent people, only those who deserve to die. Know that this is divine Justice" (Cook, 2009). The cartel describes its existence as a necessary evil, to protect the interest of its people.

This cartel lives a seemingly paradoxical existence: Its members are ruthless and violent, yet demand religious discipline and preach family values. LFM may be described as being "cult-like." In 2009, this group was led by Nazario Moreno Gonzales, known as "The Craziest One." He is guided by the New Jerusalem religious movement and has written his own "bible"; all members of LFM are required to carry this bible. Another leader in this group is Alberto Espinoza Barron, know as "La Fresa" ("The Strawberry"), who was captured by the Mexican army in 2008 and has been charged with a grenade attack in the capital of Michoacan that killed 8 people and wounded more than 100 others (Grayson, 2009).

The business-like structure of the LFM is headed by an executive council that employs specialists in the areas of security, recruitment, and public relations, much like the Cali cartel of Colombia. The cartel often recruits new members from people who are released from drug rehabilitation centers, some of which the cartel owns. It forces the graduates of the program to work for the cartel/cult or be killed.

LFM is now the major producer of methamphetamine used in the United States. It is said by the cartel that selling to Mexicans is prohibited; drugs may be sold only to Americans. Group members deal in cocaine, heroin, and marijuana; sell pirated DVDs; and are involved in human trafficking. This cartel is extremely violent, torturing and assassinating its opposition and resorting to boiling, burning, and decapitating its enemies' bodies in the name of "divine right." LFM also uses political corruption to further its aims, much like the other organized crime groups. As discussed previously, LFM often forms alliances with other groups and cartels.

In 2009, Project Coronado, a massive law enforcement effort directed toward the Mexican drug cartels operating in the United States, concluded a 44-month investigation that led to arrests in 19 U.S. states and 49 cities. In the raids, low- and mid-level members of LFM were arrested for trafficking in drugs and purchasing firearms to ship back to Mexico (Cook, 2009; Grayson, 2009; Pilkington, 2009).

Los Zetas

As discussed earlier in this chapter, Los Zetas was originally a group of Mexican special forces agents who worked in counter-narcotics before leaving to become enforcers for the Gulf cartel. Los Zetas got its name from its radio code, the letter Z (Inskeep, 2009). Members have also operated under the name of "The Company."

Los Zetas is extremely dangerous and well organized and is now considered to be a separate cartel. Its members operate in small cells throughout Mexico from Cancun to Sonora. The group, which is thought to have as many as 4000 members, is led by Heriberto Lazcano and Miguel Trevino ("El Cuarenta"). The U.S. and Mexican governments have offered a total of $7 million in rewards for their capture. Like La Cosa Nostra, Los Zetas has expanded its activity in traditional organized crime activity. including kidnapping, extortion, and stealing oil and petroleum. The group has control of a number of areas that border Texas, including Ciudad Acuna, Reynosa, Matamoros Nuevo Laredo, and Piedras Negras. Members own businesses on both sides of the border that include car lots, liquor stores, and restaurants (Corchado, 2009).

Los Zetas has formed and dissolved alliances with a number of cartels, street gangs, and prison gangs—the Gulf cartel, BLO, LFM, Mexican Mafia/La Eme, Texas Syndicate, MS-13, and Hermanos Pistoleros Latinos, among others (Swecker, 2005). This trend will likely continue.

The structure of Los Zeta is complex, and its description varies from source to source. However, the two following examples give some idea of how this organization functions. According to Manwaring (2009), Los Zetas has a multilayered and networked structure that he describes as horizontal concentric circles. The command structure of senior individuals who provide guidance to the group is at the center of the circles (or at the top of the pyramid). The second circle is made up of management and oversight leadership, including intelligence, operational, planning, financial, and recruitment and training functions. The third circle consists of cell members involved in lower-level activities. The forth circle is made up of a variety of groups referred to as "clickas," whose members may be specialist or aspirants:

- Los Halcones (The Hawks)—keep watch over distribution zones

- Las Ventanas (The Windows)—signal others to warn of unexpected dangers in an operational area

- Los Manosos (The Cunning Ones)—acquire arms, ammunition, communications, and other military equipment

- Las Leopards (The Leopards)—attached to the intelligence section and extract information from their clients (may be prostitutes)

- Direccion (communications experts)—intercept phone calls, follow and identify automobiles and persons, and sometimes engage in kidnapping and executions

Los. Zetas was modeled after the U.S. Green Berets, with members being trained in rapid deployment, aerial assault, marksmanship, ambush, intelligence collection, counter-surveillance techniques, prisoner rescue, sophisticated communications, and the art of intimidation. Its arsenal includes AR-15 and AK-47 rifles, MP5 submachine guns, .50-caliber machine guns, grenade launchers, ground-to-air missiles, dynamite and other explosives, rocket launchers, and helicopters (Grayson, 2010). Los Zetas has recruited from the Guatemalan Special Forces known as Kaibiles, whose members adhere to the mantra: "If I advance, follow me. If I stop, urge me on. If I retreat, kill me" (Grayson, 2010, p. 185). In addition, the Mexican military lost more than 100,000 troops to desertion between 2008 and 2009, and these deserters are often recruited by groups such as Los Zetas. However, not all recruits are elite Mexican deserters; the group now recruits all who will join it.

Grayson (2010) offers a list of subgroups of Los Zetas who are decentralized into a number of cells:

- Los Halcones—the lowest tier, who gather information
- Los Cobras—provide security for drug shipments and Zeta leaders
- Zetas Nuevos—shock troop who carry out bloody assaults
- Cobras Viejos—more experienced individuals who are in charge of coordinating trafficking and security efforts
- Zetas Viejas—individuals who have been with the organization since the beginning, control a plaza, and serve in a command position

Many of the Mexican cartels, including Los Zetas, engage in extortion of Mexican police and offer them "plata o plomo" (silver or lead). Members of Los Zetas subject their captives to prolonged torture and often use decapitation, immolation, and strangulation as methods of death; the letter "Z" is sometimes carved into the backs of their victims. Collectively, these groups spend more than $200,000 each week on bribes. They provide their recruits and people in their area with food, entertainment, and other benefits to obtain the support and cooperation of the public (Grayson, 2009; Logan, 2009). Like many in organized crime, from the pirates of yesteryear to today's transnational criminal groups, corruption and support of the public remains a necessity for success of the Mexican DTOs.

Current Activity

Events during the last two to three years indicate that the Mexican drug scene is still changing and that Mexican traffickers are now in control of areas and activities in which they formerly either shared with others or played a subsidiary role. A case in point is the Mexicans' success in taking over aspects of cocaine and heroin trafficking from the Colombian cartels. The latter, which often now operate in smaller units (cartelitos), still control production, but Mexican DTOs are vying with one another for control over the process of conveying the drugs into the United States and subsequent distribution here. This new Mexican dominance has fostered the violence described elsewhere in this chapter.

One recent report by the Bureau for International Narcotics and Law Enforcement Affairs outlined the extent of current Mexican control over the U.S. drug market:

• Mexican traffickers supplied 90% of the cocaine sold in the United States in 2004.

• Mexico is the number two supplier of heroin and the largest foreign source of marijuana.

• Mexico is now the leading supplier of methamphetamines (Harman, 2005). According to one DEA agent, the Mexican version of "ice" in crystalline form has become increasingly popular in the United States (Harman, 2005).

Methamphetamine ("meth") labs have been emerging in Mexico in response to the crackdown on "backyard" meth labs in the United States. A significant portion of the drug sold in the United States (65%) is now manufactured in Mexico or in Mexican-run labs in California (Harman, 2005). The past three years have seen significant increases in the seizure of Mexican-made methamphetamines. In addition, the restrictions placed on pseudo-ephedrine sales in the United States have led to the increased importation of that key meth ingredient into Mexico from factories worldwide.

A recent newspaper article about a seizure of Mexican meth in Greenwood, Indiana (an Indianapolis suburb), highlighted the major role played by Mexican drug traffickers in supplying the U.S. market (Bird, 2006). The shipment, which was worth $300,000, was smuggled from Mexico to Arizona by a predominately Hispanic organization and then transported to Indiana. Greenwood police noted that "ice" was only one of several drugs dealt by Mexican DTOs. The large volume of truck traffic into the United States makes border seizures difficult and ensures that sizable amounts of drugs will reach their destinations in various areas of the United States.

Another important development in the Mexican drug scene has been the Russian mafia's collaboration or penetration of various DTOs (Hayward, 2003). Opportunities for this activity were provided by the weakening of some of these drug gangs as a result of arrests and deaths. Russian mobsters have given advice and laundered money for the Mexican groups. Bruce Bagley points out that Russian drug "thugs" maintain a low profile but, at the same time, are "the bloodiest human beings you can imagine" (Hayward).

The war on the major Mexican cartels by both the Fox and Calderón administrations and the constant evolution of other groups and cartels have provided other organized crime groups such as the Russian mafia a chance to become more involved in the supply of drugs and other illegal activity along the southwest border of the United States. These new players have provided smaller groups with assistance in protection, transportation, and money laundering.

The drive for innovation has not been lost by the Mexican crime groups. In 2009, drug smugglers parked a car transport trailer on the Mexican side of a security fence and drove two trucks loaded with marijuana into Arizona. When U.S. Border patrol agents engaged the group, the Mexican drug smugglers begin firing machine guns at the agents. More than $1 million of marijuana was seized in one of the trucks, and the other drove back over the fence into Mexico. Mexican drug cartels continue to transport large shipments of drugs using such tactics as well as by excavating new tunnels across the U.S.–Mexican border (Moore, 2009), such activity was reported in 2010, for example.

Drug Policies: Impact and Consequences

The increase in drug trafficking by Mexican cartels has prompted U.S. policies designed to aid Mexico's counter-drug efforts. Some of these policies are similar to those employed in Colombia and have had the same effects in Mexico. The Mexican military, with support from the United States, has assumed an increasing role in drug control efforts. This trend has had the effect of strengthening the military's position in the Mexican government and making it a more autonomous force. Fox's appointment of a former brigadier general and military prosecutor to lead this effort has led to closer ties between the military and Mexico's equivalent of the U.S. Department of Justice. It is no coincidence that the military's share of drug-related arrests and cocaine seizures has increased dramatically since the mid-1990s (Freeman & Sierra, 2005).

The increased responsibility of the Mexican military for government counter-drug activities, notwithstanding any effect on drug traffic, has had some notable consequences. One is the continuation of human rights violations that have characterized Mexican politics for decades (Freeman & Sierra, 2005). Mexican soldiers have committed a variety of heinous acts—including torture, rape, and murder—in their capacity as drug control agents. A second consequence is the greater opportunity for corruption provided by the increased exposure of the Mexican military to drug trafficking. Drug-related crimes have become common among military personnel during the last decade.

President Fox's counter-drug campaign has been hailed as a success by various U.S. and Mexican officials, including the former president himself. Fox has contended that the increased violence in recent years is a sign of the program's success and has suggested that drug gangs are challenging one another as well as the authorities as a result of the initiative (Freeman, 2006). Arrests of cartel kingpins have certainly been impressive. In 2006, Fox said that Mexico was willing to extradite "all of those who have pending matters with U.S. Justice" (*Orlando Sentinel*, 2006). This is an essential and important part of Mexican history. Fox's policies have been continued and supplemented under President Calderón.

Yet, despite these positive signs, a closer examination suggests a different outlook for the Mexican DTOs. Although the bulk of the attention was given to the arrest of cartel kingpins, most of those convicted on drug charges by the Fox administration were actually indigenous people who transported drugs simply to survive. Incarceration of these individuals presumably has had a minimal effect on drug smuggling volume. Furthermore, the deaths and arrests of major traffickers have had little effect on the overall flow of drugs across the U.S.–Mexican border because rival traffickers or "newbies" quickly replace the departed criminals.

As discussed earlier, the crackdown on drug trafficking by the Calderón and Fox administrations may have made a complicated situation even more complicated. Weakening the larger organizations produced more instability, which was then exploited by newly formed groups eager to grab a share of the drug trade profits. The increase in the number of players has ratcheted up the level of drug-related violence, a consequence of the never-ending allure of the illegal drug market.

The current president of Mexico, Calderón, has used the military as a security force owing to the massive amount of corruption among the police of Mexico. Calderón has also continued Fox's policy of extraditing drug traffickers to the United States. Because of such efforts, the Merida Initiative was established as a multinational campaign designed to strengthen the ability of authorities to combat criminal organizations by equipping and training police, supporting judicial reform, building prosecutorial capacity, and increasing cooperation among border security, corrections, customs, and the military. The United States has pledged $1.6 billion to the project to support countries that cooperate with this initiative, which includes Mexico and other Central American countries. The Merida Initiative includes $74 million in funding for the purpose of stopping the flow of illegal weapons from the Unites States to Mexico (Merida Initiative, 2009). This plan's structure was based on Plan Colombia, and the effort is directed against transnational organized crime and money laundering.

Organized crime groups based in Mexico now operate in more than 200 cities in the United States. Their criminal activities include money laundering, human trafficking, arms trafficking, and now acts of terrorism against their country, in addition to their major source of income, drug trafficking. Numerous reports of both clandestine laboratories and marijuana fields within the United States operated by Mexican cartels have added to their criminal enterprises. The ongoing war between the Mexican criminal groups has turned both Mexico and the United States into battlegrounds, as authorities continue to wage a war on "narco-terrorism" that has led to loss of control of states within Mexico and significant loss of life and property in both Mexico and the United States.

The most recent development has been the involvement of Hezbollah in Mexican drug operations. Personal communication with DEA agents assigned to the Mexican cartel investigation and a news release by DEA have confirmed that the terrorist group is involved in drug trafficking for profit (see Chapter 14, *The Nexus of Transnational Organized Crime and Terrorism*).

Conclusions

There are several reasons for pessimism regarding Mexico's role in drug trafficking, including the ceaseless demand for illegal drugs that drives these activities, the multitude of elusive groups vying for a share of the smuggling profits, the corruption that pervades every level of Mexico's political and legal institutions, and the fear generated by drug-related violence. As Freeman and Sierra (2005) point out, these conditions are compounded by the extreme poverty of millions of Mexicans. Cultivation of drugs and involvement in their production and transportation is a means of survival for some and a means of mobility for others (Freeman & Sierra). The presence of these factors suggests that there will continue to be a thriving business in illicit drugs and continued futility in battling drug entrepreneurs and their allies.

The escalation of violence and loss of control over significant areas of the country by the Mexican government has resulted in the perception that Mexico may qualify as a failed state (Friedman, 2010; Manwaring, 2009). However, the country has benefited from the massive influx of cash from the criminal enterprises. The banking industry and real estate industry in Mexico have grown considerably due to these activities. If the cartels make peace and continue business without the violence, a shadow government may develop that allows the cartels to operate as long as there is no violence against the government or its population. There is no way to accurately predict who will control the criminal activity in Mexico and which way the government will go—that is, whether it will become a shadow government or regain control. However, due to the enormous profits from the criminal activity in Mexico, enterprises such as drug trafficking will almost certainly continue.

Discussion Questions

1. Discuss the development of the Mexican DTOs. What are the current major DTOs and why are they so successful?

2. How are the Mexican DTOs structured? Is this structure susceptible to law enforcement efforts? How and why?

3. Which characteristics of Mexican DTOs match the characteristics of organized crime discussed in Chapter 1?

4. Discuss the Mexican DTOs' activities and methods of operation. What are the most successful law enforcement strategies against the Mexican DTOs?

5. How are the Mexican DTOs different from other organized crime groups?

References

Army Soldier Charged with Capital Murder in Mexican Drug Cartel Killing. (2009, August 11). *FoxNews.com*. Retrieved March 11, 2010, from http://www.foxnews.com/printer_friendly_story/0,3566,538951,00.html

Bird, P. (2006, October 24). Imported Meth: State's New Scourge? *The Indianapolis Star,* pp. A1 & A6.

Carl, T. (2006, September 17). Drug Lord Suspect Extradited. *The Miami Herald.* Retrieved September 22, 2006, from http://infoweb.newsbank.com

Chepesiuk, R. (2003). *Drug Lords: The Rise and Fall of the Cali Cartel.* Wrea Green, UK: Milo Books.

Cook, C. W. (Ed.). (2007, October 16). Mexico's Drug Cartels. CRS Report for Congress, Congressional Research Service. Retrieved March 11, 2010, from Congressional Research Service Digital Database.

Cook, C. W. (Ed.). (2009, October 16). Mexico Drug Cartels. CRS Report for Congress, Congressional Research Service, p. 11. Retrieved March 11, 2010, from http://www.fas.org/sgp/crs/row/RL34215.pdf

Corchado, A. (2009). Mexico's Zetas Gang Buys Businesses Along Border in Move to Increase Legitimacy. Retrieved March 11, 2010, from http://www.cleveland.com/world/index.ssf/2009/12/mexicos_zetas_gang

Freeman, L. (2006). *State of Siege: Drug-Related Violence and Corruption in Mexico: Unintended Consequences of the War on Drugs.* Washington, DC: Washington Office on Latin America.

Freeman, L., & Sierra, J. L. (2005). Mexico: The Militarization Trap. In: C. Youngers & E. Rosen (Eds.), *Drugs and Democracy in Latin America: Its Impact on Latin America and the Caribbean* (pp. 263–302). Boulder, CO: Lynne Rienner.

Friedman, G. (2010). Mexico and the Failed State Revisited. Retrieved April 10, 2010, from http://www.stratfor.com/weekly/20100405_mexico_and_failed_state_revisit

Grayson, G. W. (2009). La Familia: Another Deadly Mexican Syndicate. *RSD Reports.* Retrieved March 12, 2010, from http://www.robertstevenduncan.com/2009/02/la-familia-another-deadly-mexican.html

Grayson, G. W. (2010). *Mexico: Narco-violence and a Failed State?* New Brunswick, NJ: Transaction.

Hall, K. G. (2006, March 12). Mexican Drug Traffickers' Violence Spreads Inward. *The Philadelphia Inquirer.* Retrieved October 17, 2006, from http://infoweb.newsbank.com

Harman, D. (2004, December 13). Drug "Cartelitos" Hit Mexico Resorts—17 Mexican Drug Agents Were Picked Up Last Week for Alleged Involvement in Drug Trafficking in Cancun. *The Christian Science Monitor.* Retrieved October 17, 2006, from http://infoweb.newsbank.com

Harman, D. (2005, August 16). Mexicans Take Over Drug Trade to US: Ciudad Juárez, Mexico. *The Christian Science Monitor.* Retrieved October 9, 2006, from http://www.csmonitor.com

Hayward, S. (2003, August 11). Russian Mafia Worms Way into Mexican Drug Cartels. *The Miami Herald.* Retrieved October 17, 2006, from http://infoweb.newsbank.com

Inskeep, S. (2009). Mexico's Ferocious Zetas Cartel Reigns Through Fear. Retrieved April 15, 2010, from Points of View Research Center.

Jones, N. (2008, June 15). *Using Counterinsurgency Strategy to Reassert the Westphalian State Against Criminal Networks: The Case of the Gulf Cartel in Mexico.* International Studies Association, 2009 Annual Meeting, pp. 1–47. Retrieved March 10, 2010, from http://0-search.ebscohost.com.umiss.lib.olemiss.edu/login.aspx?direct=true&db=aph&AN=45099422&site=ekhost-live&scope=site

Kellner, T. (2010). The Forever Drug War: Inside the Mexican Drug Wars Quickly Consuming a Nation. Retrieved March 10, 2010, from http://www.huffingtonpost.com/tomas-kellner/the-forever-drug-war-insi_b_531005.html?v

Library of Congress, Federal Research Division. (2003, February). *Organized Crime and Terrorist Activity in Mexico, 1999–2002.* Washington, DC: Author.

Logan, S. (2009). The Evolution of "Los Zetas," a Mexican Crime Organization. Retrieved April 15, 2010, from http://www.mexidata.info/id2194.html

Manwaring, M. G. (2009, September). A "New" Dynamic in the Western Hemisphere Security Environment: The Mexican Zetas and Other Private Armies. Retrieved March 10, 2010, from http://permanent.access.gpo.gov/fdlp924/PUB940.pdf

Merida Initiative: Myth vs. Fact. (2009). Retrieved April 30, 2010, from http://www.state.gov/p/inl/rls/fs/122395.htm

Moore, S. (2009, February 2). Tougher Border Can't Stop Mexican Marijuana Cartels. *The New York Times.* Retrieved March 10, 2010, from http://www.nytimes.com/2009/02/02/us/02pot.html?_r=1&wanted=print

National Drug Intelligence Center. (2009, April). North Texas High Intensity Drug Trafficking Area Drug Market Analysis 2009. Retrieved March 10, 2010, from http://www.justice.gov/ndic/pubs32/32781/dtos.htm

Nortimex News Agency. (2006, July 9). Mexican Drug Gangs Funding Colombian Mafias. Retrieved October 17, 2006, from http://infoweb.newsbank.com

The Orlando Sentinel. (2006, September 20). Mexican Leader Vows to Send Drug Lords to U.S. Retrieved September 22, 2006, from http://infoweb.newsbank.com

Pilkington, E. (2009, October 23). Crackdown on La Familia Cartel Leads to More Than 300 Arrests Across US. *Guardian.co.uk.* Retrieved March 10, 2010, from http://www.guardian.co.uk/world/2009/oct/23/la-familia-drugs-us-mexico

Rodriguez, O. R. (2010, April 12). Mexico: Cartels Team Up to Destroy Hit Men Gang. Associated Press. Retrieved March 30, 2011, from http://www.signonsandiego.com/news/2010/apr/12/mexico-cartels-team-up-to-destroy-hit-men-gang/

Stewart, S. (2010). Mexico: The Struggle for Balance. Retrieved March 10, 2010, from http://www.stratfor.com/weekly/2010040_mexico_struggle_balance?utm

Swecker, C. (2005, November 17). Congressional Testimony: Statement of Chris Swecker, Assistant Director Criminal Investigative Division, Federal Bureau of Investigation, Before the U.S. House of Representatives Committee on Judiciary Subcommittee on Crime, Terrorism, and Homeland Security and the Subcommittee on Immigration, Border Security and Claims. Retrieved March 10, 2010, from http://www.fbi.gov/congress05/swecker111705.htm

U.S. Department of Justice, National Drug Intelligence Center. (2010, February). National Drug Threat Assessment 2010.

Chapter 6

The Russian Mafia

Act locally, but think globally.

—René Dubos, French-born American microbiologist (1901–1982)

Objectives

After completing this chapter, readers should be able to:

- Discuss the origins of Russian organized crime and how they differ from the origins of other organized crime groups.
- Describe the structure of the "Russian Mafia."
- Understand the unique challenges to U.S. law enforcement that Russian organized crime groups present.
- Discuss the various criminal activities of Russian organized crime.
- Explain why Russian organized crime groups are considered a serious threat to the United States.

Historical Perspective

The former Soviet Union is the birthplace of the sophisticated and violent criminal group called the *organizatsiya*. Now operating in the United States, this group is considered a national threat by the FBI and other law enforcement agencies.

Understanding criminality in the former Soviet Union is key to understanding Russian organized crime. Until the 1980s, the Communist Party held absolute power in the Soviet Union. Members of the Party had close associations with the black market. At the time of the breakup of the Soviet Union in 1991, an estimated 700 criminal gangs operated in Soviet bloc countries. Organized along both ethnic and family lines, these groups often were controlled by a leader known as the *Vory V. Zakone* ("thief-in-law"; Handelman, 1993). Viewed as protectors of the poor and peasants, they robbed government entities or officials and then divided the profits among the group (Handelman, 1995). These thieves outlasted both the czars and the Communist Party and were publicly perceived as rebels. They became folk heroes and their outlaw culture continued even as both Lenin and Stalin tried to wipe them out, sending many to the *gulags* (Soviet slave labor camps). While in prison, they tattooed themselves, and these tattoos became symbols of status much like a business card. Tattoos offered a picture of the

Russian Mafia tattoos.

inmate's criminal history: The more tattoos, the more convictions.

During World War II, many members of these gangs betrayed the thieves' code and fought in the Soviet army against Hitler. When the war ended, the government sent most of them back to the gulags, where they were either killed or became "bitches" for the prison administration. Like their counterparts in U.S. prisons, Russian prison officials had to deal with these gangs if they wanted to maintain peace and order. Once gang leaders and members emerged from prison, many began relationships with corrupt government officials and these alliances became part of organized crime in Russia.

A rapid growth in crime and corruption occurred in conjunction with the flourishing post-war black market for goods and services. In an attempt to build a utopia, the Soviet government engaged in a process of negative selection, and its mass human rights abuses resulted in an ethnic and social conflict that produced the growth of Mafia-type organized crime—and resulted in an extremely violent country (Abramkin, 1996).

Modern organized crime in the former Soviet Union has evolved from four centers of criminality: the Russian criminal elite (Vory V. Zacone), the *nomenklatura* (those holding powerful positions or jobs), ethnic groups, and regional criminal groups.

As mentioned earlier, the Vory V. Zakone developed in the gulag prison system in a similar fashion as the U.S. organized crime groups such as the Mexican Mafia, Black Guerilla family, La Nuestra Familia, and other prison gangs. Russian gangs developed to help inmates survive attacks by other groups and to enable them to gain power or privileges while in prison. The Vory are highly structured, with well-established rules. A series of 18 rules called the *Voroskoy Zakon* have been reported by law enforcement to control behavior of the gangs and make them follow the orders of the boss. Known as "the thieves' code," these rules include the following:

- Members cannot have a family (no wife or children) but can have a lover.
- They forsake all relatives.
- Members cannot have a legitimate job.
- They must assist other thieves.
- Members can never reveal information about thieves' activities, identities, or locations.
- Members must make good on promises to other thieves.
- Members do not gamble if they cannot afford to pay.
- They must teach young thieves the trade.
- They cannot help the authorities or testify in court.
- Members cannot serve in the military.
- They cannot cooperate with law enforcement.
- Members carry out punishment against any rule-offending thief.
- Members must participate in an inquiry to settle disputes between thieves.
- They should not lose the ability to reason by using drugs or alcohol.

The second group of criminals was formed from corrupt Communist officials and business leaders who were the power elite of the country, or *nomenklatura*. A "gray" or illegal economy developed where corruption ruled.

A third source of criminal activity consists of ethnic groups, such as the Chechens, Armenians, and Georgians. Formed along ethnic lines, these criminal groups are extremely violent, and their members are very loyal to other gang members. Such a group is typically intergenerational, where succession and ethnic traditions pass from one generation to the next.

The largest criminal groups are formed within geographic regions of the former Soviet Union, and are based on a specific criminal activity, shared experiences, or bonding to a particular leader. These groups control much of the power within their regions, and are similar to gangs in the United States with membership in certain clubs or in control of a specific geographic region.

Due to the enormous size of the black market, organized crime in the former Soviet Union has become very powerful over the years. At one point, as much as two-thirds of the economy may have been controlled by organized crime. In 1997, the Center for Strategic and International Studies on Russian Organized Crime estimated that 40% of private business, 60% of state-owned enterprises, and more than half of the country's banks were under the control of organized crime. Organized crime corrupted officials at all levels of the bureaucracy, developed crime bosses, and took over large legal enterprises through violence and intimidation. A Russian prosecutor reported more than 6000 cases of military corruption in one year. What the Russian Mafia has done in the former Soviet Union has become a goal for these criminal enterprises in the United States.

The economic "crisis" that has prevailed in the wake of the breakup of the Soviet Union has resulted in a large number of Russians earning as little as $11 per day. Thus many go into crime not to have a lush lifestyle, but simply to survive.

After the breakup of the Soviet Union, even more gangs emerged. In 1991, a thieves' world meeting occurred just outside Moscow where the most powerful organized crime leaders planned specific actions and structured their operations to take the most lucrative advantage of the fall of the USSR. The U.S. market potential was discussed, and it was decided that someone needed to go to the United States to develop and organize operations there.

The Russian Mafia (also known as the Red Mafia) exploited the new unstable governments in the former Soviet Union in a similar fashion as the Sicilian Mafia did in Sicily. As much as 30% of earnings were extorted from nearly every business operating in Russia. Unlike other organized crime groups, however, these Russian criminal groups did not invest their earnings in the local economy. Instead, they placed billions of dollars in personal Swiss bank accounts. Today, the Red Mafia is the most diverse organized crime group in the world, having operations in as many as 60 foreign countries and offshore islands, and continuing to exploit unstable governments.

In 1993, the Russian Ministry of Internal Affairs estimated that more than 500 organized crime groups were operating in Russia. These groups had a membership of more than 100,000, with 18,000 people in leadership positions. The structure, membership, and activities may well be evolving, and the reach of such groups is definitely expanding into the global community, including the countries of Mexico and the United States.

Following the breakup of the Soviet Union, Russia became a free enterprise battleground where there were no rules. More than 1400 murders were reported in Moscow in 1993; those killed included journalists, businesspeople, and their families. Eighty percent of Russian businesses paid protection to criminal groups. By the 1990s, there was massive institutional corruption, with more than 6000 organized crime groups in operation in the former Soviet Union (Center for Strategic and International Studies, 1997).

Educated and creative, the Russian Mafia is very well suited for international operations. Although the former Soviet Union remains the center for its operations, the United States began to experience an incursion of Russian organized crime in the 1970s and 1980s. Due to the U.S. policy of expanding immigration, 200,000 Russian immigrants came to the United States during this period, many of whom had criminal records. The Jackson-Vanik Amendment allowed Soviet Jews visas to trade in the United States, and it is estimated that 2000 criminals came into the country during this period. With many having advanced degrees, they presented a new challenge for U.S. law enforcement, which had to cope with their unique mixture of sophistication and extreme violence. The Russians are considered by most law enforcement agencies to be the most violent of all organized crime groups.

The majority of the Russian immigrants settled in southern Brooklyn, New York, in an area called Brighton Beach. It is believed that the Soviet government deliberately released criminals who were sent to the United States, while others from Odessa smuggled themselves out of the country via Israel or various cities, and then later immigrated to the United States. However they got to the United States, the Red Mafia posed a new challenge for U.S. law enforcement (Kelly, Chin, and Schatzberg, 1994). Brighton Beach became known as "Little Odessa" (Odessa was a center of the Soviet black market).

In 1996, the FBI estimated that more than 30% of Russia's 6000 gangs operated in at least 30 of the U.S. states. For instance, there was at least one incident in Mississippi where Russians became involved in a casino scam operation. This criminal enterprise has expanded from Russia to Brighton Beach, and on to a large number of cities, with the Odessa Mafia being the prominent group operating in the United States (Macho, 1997).

Structure and Organization

More than 200 of Russia's gangs are considered global entities or conglomerates. Because these groups are so diverse, it is difficult to characterize their organizational structure. Finckenauer and Waring (1998), for example, suggest that the structure is not like that of other groups such as La Cosa Nostra (LCN). **Figure 6-1** illustrates the parallel structure of the Russian Mafia and traditional organized crime (Lindberg & Markovic, 2001).

The Russian-run networks do not appear to be highly centralized, nor are they dominated by a small number of leaders, unlike the Yakuza, LCN, or drug cartels. A typical boss controls four specialized cells through a brigadier and two underbosses or spies. The structure of a boss, called a *Pakhan*, controls four cells through a brigadier, with enforcers operating at the bottom of the structure (Financial Crimes Enforcement Network, 1996).

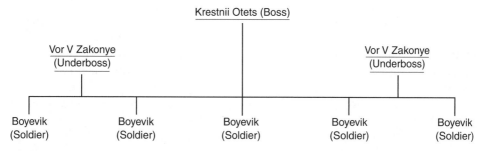

Figure 6-1 The parallel structure of the Russian Mafia and traditional organized crime.

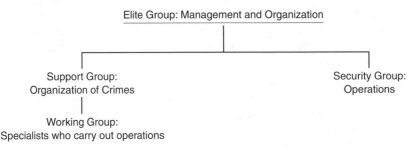

Figure 6-2   The four separate levels of Russian crime groups.

Criminal groups are divided into four levels (**Figure 6-2**). The elite group consists of management, organization, and ideologists who develop plans and strategies for operation. The second tier is called the support group; its members plan a specific crime for a specialized group or choose who carries out the operation. The third group is charged with security and intelligence. The last group, the working group, consists of the individuals who actually carry out the crime (Kelly, Chin, & Schatzberg, 1994).

The *nomenklatura* were once considered the most worthy Communist Party members. Today, their members are very sophisticated and highly educated, and they employ modern technology in their criminal operations. Many have degrees in economics, physics, or engineering. Often they are former KGB (Soviet Security Agency, incorporating both intelligence and secret police) officials or agents and are involved in exploiting financial institutions in Russia and abroad. They also are involved in the illegal export of Russia's natural resources. Extortion is a specialty of this group.

The most potent threat to the United States may come from this group of former state officials and KGB agents. The investigator who identifies members of the Russian Mafia belonging to this group should be prepared to face the same tactics that were used in Russia. Enforcers known as *Kryshas* are extremely violent as well as cunning, and are often employed to protect a company from other criminal organizations. In 1995, more than 400 Ministry of Internal Affairs (MVD) officers were killed while many others were bribed by criminal organizations in Russia.

Russian groups in the United States are ad hoc teams that came together for a specific criminal opportunity. These teams are flexible and project oriented. Their structure is described as being similar to that of many modern legitimate organizations that are more horizontal than vertical. Members typically have been acquaintances in their home country of the former Soviet Union and now are professional entrepreneurial criminal groups. These groups have powerful leaders, although one individual does not monopolize the leadership. While similar to criminal groups that operate in the former Soviet Union, they are evolving criminal organizations whose structures can change as needed to adapt to new situations (Finckenauer & Waring, 2001).

Abadinsky (2003) concluded that most Russian groups operating in the United States are fluid, with most including from 5 to 20 members. He compares them to the ICE

Sicilians (Zips) groups (discussed further in Chapter 7) because of the similarity of their loose structure. Groups are formed around regional backgrounds or a specific enterprise; members may be of Armenian, Chechen, Georgian, Latvian, or Ukrainian origin. Structure does vary among groups. For example, the Chechen groups tend to be highly structured, with a hierarchy based on relationships formed from families or clans, similar to that of the Sicilians. They honor a code of silence like the LCN's *omerta,* and most often recruit from within their families. A clear line of authority exists from the leader to the lowest member (Abadinsky, 2003; *Columbia Daily News,* 2002).

Other groups form around unique criminal opportunities, with their structures being tweaked as necessary to carry out the operation. After completion of the operation, the structure may dissolve and another form to take on another criminal operation. Groups may also form around a dominant individual.

Whatever their structure, Russian organized groups include an amalgamation of thieves-in-law, corrupt officials, and businesspeople working as criminal syndicates to reap huge profits from a wide variety of criminal enterprises. The investigator must identify the structure and leadership of groups operating within his or her jurisdiction to be able to develop strategies for attacking this particular leadership as well as the group's assets and methods of operation. The structure of Russian organized crime groups is likely to be fluid and dynamic.

Because of changing markets, geographic locations of activity, and enforcement strategies, this educated and experienced criminal group changes its approach when necessary to continue earning enormous profits while avoiding arrest and prosecution. It is difficult for law enforcement to identify leaders and structures because membership and leadership shift rapidly from gang to gang. Apprehension of even identified leaders and members is difficult.

Activities and Methods of Operation

It is essential for the investigator targeting the Russian Mafia to examine the past and present activities of organized groups in cities such as Moscow, where as many as eight major criminal groups operate. Other crime groups are active in other major cities such as St. Petersburg and Odessa.

Theft, Kidnapping, and Murder

Russian groups operate in any market or enterprise that offers profits, power, or both. Extortion, drug trafficking, prostitution, forgery, art theft, and auto theft are among the many criminal activities of Russian organized crime groups. A group located in northern California, for example, consists of Ukraine and Western Russians who specialize in auto thefts and "chop shops," selling both automobiles and auto parts. This group has also expanded into narcotics, extortion, and prostitution, employing violence to succeed in its operations. In 2002, prosecutors in California indicted leaders of Russian criminal groups for kidnapping and murdering Soviet immigrants involved in an extortion scheme. Victims included the chief of Matador Communications, Georgy Safiev; a film producer, Nikolai Kharabadze; the president of Advanced Mobile Technologies, Alexander Umansky; a financial clerk, Margarita Peckler; and Meyer Muskalel, director of a home building company. These victims, all of whom were wealthy, were kidnapped for ransom, and were forced to call relatives or business partners to provide the money needed to win their release.

The Odessa Mafia headquarters in Brighton Beach is highly structured, with satellite operations located in several major cities in the United States. Money laundering, fraud, loan sharking, murder, and narcotics are this group's areas of specialization.

An Armenian group that operates in the Hollywood area of Los Angeles has an estimated 450 members. They are involved in fuel fraud, extortion, credit card fraud, and narcotics. Members also have been convicted of kidnapping and attempted murder. Many groups make huge profits from rackets in Russia dealing with anything from narcotics to illegal exports of resources, such as tin, aluminum, bronze, and other natural resources, including weapons-grade uranium (Frankel, 1995). These profits are now being sent to countries such as the United States at a rate of more than $1 billion a month, and once laundered, are returned to Russia.

Complex fuel frauds perpetrated by these organized crime groups cost the U.S. government more than $2 billion in lost tax revenues between 1990 and 1995. This type of fraud involves the creation of a fictitious company or companies that exist in name only (a so-called *burn company* existing for the purpose of hiding the true identity of the owners); such companies then alter the fuel chemistry or fraudulently sell low-grade fuel labeled as premium, rig fuel pumps to cheat customers, and do not pay taxes on the fuel. Called a *daisy chain*, these strategies are used to transfer fuel a number of times and create a massive paper trail until it is sold to the burn company, which disappears without a trace soon afterward, with the organized crime group pocketing as much as 50 cents per gallon in federal and state taxes. The fuel is sold below market prices, which forces legitimate fuel companies out of business. These groups commit crimes such as bombing, kidnapping, assault, and murder to ensure that the competition is eliminated or the company is turned over to the organized crime group.

In 1995, 13 members and the leader of a Russian–Armenian group known as the *Mikaelian organization* were convicted of multiple acts of mail and wire fraud, money laundering, extortion, and narcotics trafficking charges. This group had gained control of independent diesel fuel wholesale and retail gas stations throughout southern California, and were pocketing 42 cents per gallon by not paying federal and state taxes.

Cybercrime

Russian organized crime groups also have been involved in telecommunication fraud, including cloning cellular phones, which cost billions in lost revenues to legitimate service providers. The FBI, Interpol, and British and Australian authorities have also investigated

Russian cybercriminals who are targeting bookmakers and online betting. When the bookmakers refuse their demands for ransom, the Russian Mafia shuts down these networks. In 2004, Russian Mafia attacks in Alice Springs, Australia, crashed Telstra's online gambling network for five hours in an attempt to extort protection money. The Russian organized crime group can often bring these booking operations to a standstill by hacking into their systems (O'Brien, 2004).

Extending Their Reach

Medical and insurance fraud may be committed by means of staged auto accidents, resulting in billions in false medical billing. Auto theft rings, money laundering, and murder are common with this type of Russian organized crime activity. Intelligence indicates that alliances with LCN and the Colombians have also allowed the Russians to become heavily involved in narcotics distribution in areas of New York, California, and other states. A 1993 seizure of 800 kilos (kilograms) of cocaine and the arrest of Russian organized crime members indicated that distribution was being conducted in Detroit, Los Angeles, and New York.

The 1991 RICO indictment of Boris Goldberg as head of a criminal enterprise is further evidence of Russian organized crime activity in the United States. Goldberg was indicted for an enterprise involving cocaine trafficking, armed robbery, extortion, attempted murder, weapons charges, and fraud. Members of the Russian Mafia have associated themselves with the Mexican drug trafficking organizations (DTOs; see Chapter 5). In particular, Mexican authorities have reported Russian penetration of DTOs in the cities of Tijuana, Mexico, and Baja and San Diego, California.

In 2001, Steven Casteel, Director of Intelligence for the DEA, reported Russian organizations laundering Mexican DTO drug money for a fee of 30% or more in addition to approval to operate in the DTOs' area. Casteel suggested that the Russian infiltration of Mexican DTOs is consistent with the globalization of organized crime. Much of the Russian money laundering occurs in offshore sites and countries such as Haiti, Russia, Puerto Rico, Cuba, and the Dominican Republic. An April 2001 seizure of 13 tons of cocaine near Acapulco and the arrest of 10 Russian and Ukrainian crew members confirmed the involvement of the Russian Mafia in the Mexican DTOs' operations (Hayward, 2003).

Pirated music and computer crime are also targets for Russian organized crime. As many as 40 companies in 20 U.S. states have been the victims of Russian hackers, who target trade secrets, customer databases, and credit card information (Lorek, 2001). An estimated 95% of the music assets sold in Russia are illegal, and $310 million in annual U.S. losses from this source has been reported (Manjoo, 2000).

Undercover operations by U.S. Customs have confirmed that Russian organized crime groups working with corrupt government officials and businesses are involved in illegal weapons trafficking. In one incident, two Lithuanians were arrested after a two-year (1995–1997) undercover operation. The sting agents used the cover story of working for Colombian drug traffickers when attempting to purchase shoulder surface-to-air missiles. They were negotiating with the Lithuanians to buy 40 missiles for $1.3 million and nuclear weapons in a deal to follow the missiles' purchase. A Bulgarian state-owned company was alleged to have agreed to sell the missiles to the undercover agents. The Minister of Defense of Lithuania signed false documents to allow the shipment to appear legal when it was loaded aboard a cargo ship to Puerto Rico, where the agents expected to receive delivery (Lungren, 1996).

The following incidents from reports prepared by the California Attorney General highlight evidence that Russian organized crime groups have been expanding their narcotics operations:

- On March 4, 1993, a Russian émigré was arrested for petty theft. The Burbank Police Department recovered two kilos of cocaine and $2200 in cash from the émigré's vehicle. It was later learned that this individual was also involved in shipping stolen vehicles to Russia.

- On May 1, 1993, a Russian émigré was arrested for immigration violations. Information from the Immigration and Naturalization Service indicates that this person was involved in smuggling cocaine from the United States to Russia through his import/export business in southern California. This émigré had spent 13 years in a Russian prison.

- In February 1995, Tracey Hill, believed to be a courier for a Russian organized crime group, was arrested in Redding, California, for possession of 18 kilos of cocaine. Hill was en route to Vancouver, British Columbia, from the Los Angeles area.

- On May 4, 1995, seven kilos of heroin was seized from a member of an Armenian organized crime group based in the Glendale area. The heroin came from the Middle East and was intended for distribution in the United States (Lungren, 1996).

- In 2005, U.S. officials charged 18 Russians with arms trafficking and smuggling. The 62-page complaint detailed a plot to traffic in machine guns and other weapons and sell automatic weapons. According to FBI Special Agent Andy Arena, this group was willing to do business with anyone as long as it generated money for the organization. The defendants, who had Armenian, Russian, and Georgian backgrounds, were offering to sell shoulder-fired "Stinger" missiles, AK-47 automatic weapons, rocket-propelled grenades, and Claymore mines. The weapons allegedly were offered by KGB officials and came from Russian military surpluses in Chechnya (Hirschkorn, 2005).

- A European law enforcement operation resulted in the arrest of 69 Russian organized crime members for robbery, drug smuggling, and money laundering. Operation Java began as a probe into the Russian mob in Spain, and ended with arrests in Austria, France, Germany, Italy, and Switzerland. Those arrested included Armenians, Russians, and Georgians who operated a highly structured international criminal organization that resulted in seizure of large mansions and enormous amounts of money. Mobsters from the former Soviet Union who operate outside Russia may number as many as 300,000 and dominate the criminal underworld in several countries, including the United States (Adams, 2010).

- A report in the *Sun-Sentinel* concluded that the biggest change in the long history of organized crime in South Florida was the movement of the Russians into the area after the fall of communism. The Russian groups have also opened banks in Antigua and Aruba (Franceschina & Burstein, 2010).

Semion Mogilevich

In May 1995, Czech police raided a meeting of Russian Mafia bosses in Prague. "The owner of the restaurant, Semion Mogilevich, also owns a chain of companies called ARIGON with headquarters at St. Helier on the island of Jersey with branches in Prague, Moscow, Kiev, Budapest, Los Angeles, Philadelphia, New York, and Johannesburg" (Miroslev, 2001).

Money laundering operations by this college-educated, Ukrainian-born Jew were discovered when more than $6 billion (and possibly even as much as $10 billion) was laundered through the Bank of New York in 1999. The transactions were said to have begun in October 1998. "U.S. investigators suspect that government officials and politically connected businessmen who had access to billions in International Monetary Fund loans to Russia may have cooperated with the Mafia to spirit huge transfers out of the country" (Mendellhall, 2001). The Bank of New York failure is the largest in U.S. history to date.

Mogilevich, who was reported to be the leader of a Russian organized crime group with more than 250 members, was declared an undesirable and cannot enter the United States. Despite that impediment, he continues to run a company in Philadelphia. Known as the "Brainy Don" because of his economics degree and viewed by the FBI as the most powerful mobster in the world, Mogilevich is considered a grave threat to the stability of Israel and Eastern Europe. "According to the FBI and Israeli Intelligence, he rules over arms-trafficking, money laundering, drug running, and art smuggling Red Mafia. . . . He is expected to have more than $100 million to spend with a guaranteed backup source of revenue according to British officials. Part of the cash is being laundered through a very willing London Bank" ("Russia," 2001). Mogilevich and his partner Vladimir Nekrasov, a millionaire Russian businessman, were arrested on charges involving decades of major international crime. The charges included racketeering, securities. and mail fraud.

The FBI has described Mogilevich as a major player in international organized crime who holds passports from Ukraine, Russia, and Israel. Mogilevich began his career as a petty thief and was jailed twice for petty theft and fraud. He has lived and worked in the United Kingdom, the United States, and Canada, where he was allegedly involved in prostitution and smuggling. In the past, he owned a factory that produced anti-aircraft guns and was involved in trading art and antiques among other enterprises, both legal and illegal (Harding, 2008).

The illegal activities of Russian Mafia groups are known to be highly lucrative: "It is estimated that foreign companies pay up to 20% of their profits to the Mafia as the ongoing price of doing business in Russia" (Lindberg & Markovic, 2001). This practice definitely affects the willingness of foreign investors to consider Russia as a potential location for their businesses. Gwen McClure, the FBI agent who led Interpol's organized crime division, has said of the Red Mafia, "They have enough money to corrupt and destabilize entire countries" (Krane, 1999). Experts estimate that $100 billion had been laundered by these groups by 1994, $200 billion by 1996, and $300 billion by 1999 (Idea House, 2001). It is clear that Russian organized crime groups are rapidly becoming the most threatening in organized crime today.

Other Bank Fraud Schemes

Some Caribbean banks are also eager to get involved in fraud, especially when Russian Mafia are involved. "Billions of dollars are believed to be flowing through such offshore bank havens as Antigua, Aruba, the Cayman Islands, and St. Marten" (Farah, 1996). Caribbean governments have made it very easy to own and operate banks on their shores, and the Russian Mafia taking advantage of their hospitality. "In some Caribbean nations, money laundering is not even a crime" (Farah). Typically, these governments require secrecy restrictions be placed on all depositor and transaction information. It seems the Russian Mafia has indeed found a haven in the Caribbean. Other organized crime groups—the Colombian and Mexican cartels—have also used Caribbean banks for laundering their ill-gotten gains.

For example, the European Union Bank located in Antigua was chartered as an offshore subsidiary of Menatep, a large Russian bank. Its sole shareholder was Alexander Konanykhine (Farah, 1996). It is alleged that Konanykhine siphoned millions out of Russia through this Caribbean Internet bank. For the last decade, he has been in a U.S. prison on charges of violating conditions of his visa; his 2003 deportation to Moscow was blocked by U.S. courts. Konanykhine is wanted in Russia for allegedly embezzling $8.1 million from the Exchange Bank in Moscow in 1992.

The Russian Mafia has infiltrated Canada as well, where its operations have played out primarily in Ontario, British Columbia, and Quebec. These Russian Mafia groups have become involved in the manufacture and use of counterfeit currency and false identification documents, and have organized shoplifting and large-scale theft of consumer goods that are then shipped to Russia and elsewhere. A Canadian car can be stolen and shipped to Russia and sold for twice its Canadian value, for example.

Vyacheslav K. Ivankov

One case that may be a valuable case study for the investigator is the story of Vyacheslav K. Ivankov. This notorious Vladivostok Russian crime boss was born in the 1940s in Georgia (Soviet Union), grew up in Moscow, and was known for his political stand against communism. His family had suffered under both the Lenin and Stalin regimes. Ivankov was not a member of a street gang, but rather excelled in amateur wrestling and became a popular champion. First put in prison after a bar fight for allegedly defending a woman's honor, Ivankov began a long association with the criminal element in the Soviet Union.

By the 1970s, the black market in Russia was thriving. Ivankov formed a criminal gang and frequently impersonated a police officer to rob other criminal groups. Arrested and sentenced to 14 years, Ivankov, by then known as Yaponchik ("Little Jap"), became a high-ranking Vory V. Zakonye ("thief-in-law"). Like other crime bosses, such as Luciano, Gotti, and Escobar, Ivankov continued to conduct his criminal business from prison. After his early release from the gulag in 1991, he again began to prey on other criminal groups, such as the Chechens. Known for his violence, including murder and torture, he became a target for both gang rivals and Russian law enforcement. During the summit meeting in Moscow of crime bosses, leaders of the Vory allegedly decided to send Ivankov to the United States to take control of Russian organized crime in North America. Despite having a prison record and countless files bearing witness to his criminal past, he was able to obtain a visa and enter the United States.

Ivankov established his organization in Brighton Beach, allegedly to direct movies. A very intelligent individual, he had extensive experience in many rackets along with a propensity for violence and torture. Many in U.S. law enforcement describe Ivankov as a typical Russian organized crime boss, an intelligent thug, unlike an LCN boss. Ivankov was probably not a "Godfather," but certainly was a high-ranking Russian mobster. He became a feared gangster in the United States and established a number of front companies for his criminal operations. Allegedly, his organization was involved in prostitution, narcotics, money laundering, and a variety of other violent criminal activities. He paid a U.S. citizen $15,000 to marry him so that he could gain U.S. citizenship. Eventually, his operations extended to New York, Miami, Los Angeles, Denver, Boston, and San Francisco, and he traveled extensively outside the U.S. border to Russia and other countries.

The reign of Ivankov ended in 1995 when two Russian immigrant businessmen reported an extortion scam. Alexander Volkov and Vladimir Voloshin, whose investment advisory firm (Summit International Corporation) served Russian émigrés, had been kidnapped and forced to agree to pay $3.5 million in extortion money. Voloshin's father was beaten to death in a Moscow train station during the extortion attempt. Ivankov was personally involved in plotting the extortion and threatening the two businessmen. Unbeknownst to him, the two businessmen had gone to the FBI, whose agents used electronic surveillance to record much of the extortion attempt; the case was terminated early due to life-threatening situations. Ivankov was arrested, along with 8 members of his reputed 100-member gang in the United States, for the extortion scam. He served 10 years in a maximum-security prison for his crime. In 2004, Ivankov was released to Russian authorities to face murder charges in Moscow stemming from the 1992 shooting deaths of two Turkish citizens in a Moscow restaurant. (Ivankov had been on probation in Russia when he fled to the United States in 1992.)

While Ivankov's legacy remains a role model for young Russians in both Moscow and the United States, many in law enforcement believe that these criminals are not the real power. The most serious threats, they suggest, come from the former KGB and other state officials of Russia.

Links with Other Organized Crime Groups

In 2000, the television network MSNBC reported an alliance of Russian organized crime with FARC (Revolutionary Armed Forces of Colombia). Using Russian IL-76 cargo aircraft, the smugglers were loading planes with arms and ammunition and flying out of airstrips in Russia and the Ukraine, with stops in Amman, Jordan, to refuel. With the assistance of corrupt officials in Jordan, the planes passed through customs and traveled to airstrips in Colombia to air drop their cargo, where members of FARC were waiting. The aircraft then returned to Amman with huge shipments (up to 40,000 kilos of cocaine) of drugs, where part of the load was used to pay the middlemen in Amman. The remaining cocaine was flown back to Russia for distribution there and in Europe or the Persian Gulf area.

This alliance poses a national threat to the Colombian government because it brings an unlimited supply of sophisticated weapons to FARC's 16th Front under the leadership of Tomas Medina Caracas, also known as Negro Acacio. The impact on the United States is obvious. As FARC becomes more powerful, it will be able to import more drugs into the United States through its alliances with LCN, Russian organized crime groups, and others. The resources of these combined organized crime groups pose an unprecedented challenge to U.S. law enforcement.

Such diversity and innovation are hallmarks of Russian organized crime groups. In 1998, a warehouse in New Jersey was raided and 55-gallon drums containing alcohol were seized. Six companies, including McCormick Distilling in the United States, were the subjects of the investigation. The drums were labeled as "industrial solvent" and the liquor inside was dyed blue to resemble solvent. The drums were being shipped to Russia as solvent to avoid paying the customs duty. Once in Russia, the dye was removed and the alcohol bottled and sold as vodka. Because Russian consumption of alcohol amounts to 6 to 12 gallons per capita per year, this is a lucrative market. This huge operation resulted in enormous profits for the Russian organized crime groups that were in alliance with these elements of American business.

DEA and Canadian law enforcement have reported that the Russian groups are also involved with Mexican organized crime groups in the production of methamphetamine. Russian groups have smuggled large amounts of R-11 Freon, which is used for extracting meth from chemical solutions. Russians have also supplied weapons to the areas of Ensenada and Baja, California, and Norte, Mexico.

In yet another undercover operation, DEA agents arrested Ludwig Fainberg (also known as "Tarzan") for arms trafficking. In 1984, Fainberg was living in "Little Odessa" (Brighton Beach) and became known as a "torch" man (arsonist) for the LCN around New York. By 1990, he had moved to Miami, Florida and opened Porkey's, a strip club known to be a frequent meeting place of Russian and Colombian organized crime members. Here, Fainberg established himself as an international dealer in the sex trade industry, buying women in Russia and Eastern Europe and then importing them to the United States. In 1993, he purchased six helicopters, and negotiations to purchase a nuclear submarine for $60 million were under way when a DEA sting operation halted the transaction. Fainberg was arrested by DEA and later cooperated, giving evidence against major Colombian drug traffickers; he served only 30 months in jail before being deported to Israel. A year later, he was doing business in Canada; in 2003, the Canadian government deported him to Israel.

Prosecution in the case was successful because the agencies involved took advantage of extensive undercover operations, informants, and electronic surveillance. This outcome demonstrates that global arms trafficking is a major operation for Russian organized crime groups and that law enforcement can be successful.

Russian organized crime groups involve themselves in professional sports (fixing of the 2002 Olympic figure skating competitions) and have been implicated in fixing amateur sports as well. They intervene in sports in other ways, too. There have been reported cases of embezzlement of funds from the Central Red Army Sports Club. The president of the Russian Ice Hockey Federation was murdered in April 1997. Another major sports club, Moscow Sporteak, lost its director general in June 1997 in a contract murder. Three professional hockey players may have been targeted for extortion by the Russian Mafia. U.S. sports groups are not innocent in this type of activity. "Over $10 million in 'transfer fees' were paid to Russian hockey clubs by the National Hockey League in an effort to sign Russian talent" (Center for Strategic and International Studies, 1997). Their criminal activity has extended into many more competitive sports as well, including bodybuilding and weight lifting (Center for Strategic and International Studies).

Members of these Russian organized crime groups often come to the United States with years of experience in manipulating government systems as well as financial institutions, and they have a history of extreme violence and torture. The diversity of activities demands that investigators become knowledgeable in many areas of criminal activity to effectively deal with Russian organized crime.

A summary of findings by numerous task forces, media, and government reports on Russian or Eurasian organized crime offers additional understanding of these criminal groups:

- Eurasian organized crime is a threat to the national security of the United States owing to its ability to provoke instability in a nuclear-armed major power.

- Russian organized crime has alliances with its criminal counterparts in more than 50 countries, with more than 200 Russian organized crime groups operating globally.

- Corruption is a major obstacle in addressing organized crime in Russia as well as in other countries.

- Russian organized crime groups have the opportunity to procure and traffic in nuclear, biological, and chemical weapons of mass destruction and extraordinary weapons or arms that are desired by terrorist groups as well as powerful criminal groups.

- Russian organized crime members in Russia do not operate like the "Robber Barons" in the United States. Such groups do not invest their earnings to grow the domestic economy in ways that can result in a modern infrastructure.

- Assassinations, bribery, fear and intimidation, and weak governments have derailed efforts to deal with Russian organized crime.

- Russian organized crime has become a shadow government in the former Soviet Union, in particular in the banking industry.

- Russia, like other countries, may become a criminal state due to corruption of business, government, and law enforcement. The state may be controlled by corrupt officials, businessmen, and criminals.

- The absence of an effective judicial system in Russia and countries where Russian organized crime operates has allowed the criminal syndicates to become de facto adjudicators.

Investigative Strategies

Russian organized crime groups present a new challenge for U.S. law enforcement. A comprehensive knowledge of their activities and prison terms in the former Soviet Union, uncovering of their methods of operation, and identification of the members and their associates are necessary to build an effective U.S. law enforcement effort against the Russian Mafia. The close relationship with banking and business and the use of *Kryshas* (enforcers who use violence) are strategies that are likely to be repeated frequently in the United States by Russian organized crime groups.

Cooperation with the source country is paramount to successfully dealing with these sophisticated groups. Countries where these groups operate must share accurate, timely, and complete intelligence. Members frequently operate in seven or eight countries simultaneously. Corruption must be addressed before information is shared; otherwise, any efforts or strategies will fail. The problems of intelligence sharing and collection, communication between law enforcement in several countries, and the legal definitions of organized crime and other criminal activities combined with jurisdiction questions are significant obstacles to overcome. The case studies presented in this chapter illustrate the present diversity and complexity of these groups in their U.S. operations.

Crime prevention officials and organizations in the United States must act quickly to prevent expansion of the criminal operations of Russian organized crime groups before they become more entrenched. Task forces dedicated to Russian organized crime are necessary to focus on this national threat. Their alliances coupled with their ability to engage in diverse criminal activities—from drugs to weapons of mass destruction to complex financial crimes—require every kind of resource, technology, and expertise law enforcement has in its arsenal. The 1996 case where four Russians were charged in New York for conspiring to defraud 24 Russian companies, including a charity to establish aid to victims of the Chernobyl nuclear disaster, of more than $10 million is further evidence that the task force concept can be effective in addressing these groups (Freeh, 1996).

Implementation of appropriate training for both U.S. and foreign law enforcement is a strategy that will result not only in greater expertise in addressing organized crime, but also in closer relationships and networks between the many countries affected by these groups. Creation of the International Enforcement Academy in Budapest (in 1995), as well as the development of courses and training, can supplement more established entities such as the National FBI Academy in the United States in providing state-of-the-art training for law enforcement personnel worldwide.

The International Crime Control strategy, initiated in 1998, establishes eight goals, including countering international financial crime and high-tech or computer-related crime. This strategy also includes the establishment of new legislative provisions. The Organized Crime Strike Force Unit under the Criminal Division of the U.S. Attorney's Office has already placed state, local, and federal offices under one roof, thereby combining resources, expertise, and intelligence. As a consequence, there were more than 250 pending investigations targeting Russian organized crime enterprises (Finckenauer, 2001).

Because of their activities in the last decade, stopping Russian organized crime groups requires that law enforcement efforts focus on financial institutions. This includes being knowledgeable about statutes, regulations, methods of investigation, and international banking to effectively address the level of sophistication of Russian criminal activity. The Money Laundering Acts of 1986 and 1994, the Currency and Foreign Transactions Reporting Acts, and other legislation that can result in arrest and prosecution of criminal organizations should be required training for any investigator who is responsible for Russian crime investigation.

The diverse nature of Russian organized crime criminal activity lends itself to violation of conspiracy and RICO laws. The predicate acts under RICO are commonly used for Russian group members operating in the United States and abroad. Addressing these complex organizations will require development of complex statutes and long-term investigations that utilize the entire arsenal of law enforcement tools and strategies. Both U.S. and international task forces must be created to address this level of criminal sophistication.

Investigators must be prepared to deal with a Russian community that is not eager to cooperate with law enforcement because of the intimidation and fear produced by the numerous murders, assaults, and threats carried out by the Russian Mafia. Murders of government officials, businessmen, police, and even journalists should be expected. An example is the Moscow murder of Paul Klebnikov, a 41-year-old *Forbes* editor who wrote about millions being stolen by corrupt officials and Russian organized crime. His alleged murderers were arrested, but were subsequently acquitted.

Investigators must always be cognizant of the corruption potential when dealing with organized crime groups from Russia. As many as 1500 officials have been under investigation for corruption in Russia. The element of addressing and identifying corruption will likely be a key part of the strategy for dealing with Russian organized crime groups operating in the United States.

Undercover operations and informants can be effective but also present an enormous risk of injury or death. Carefully planned operations with maximum security must be part of every operation where undercover agents or informants are employed. Investigators must develop a high level of expertise in handling and protecting informants. Witness protection must be available to those in the Russian communities who do cooperate. In New York, the majority of Russian refugees are Jewish, just as most Russian organized crime members are Jewish. The New York Police Department has few Russian-speaking police and even fewer reliable Russian émigré informants. These citizens fear not only for themselves but also for their families who live in both the United States and the former Soviet Union. Protection is required for the cooperating Russian witnesses and family members here and abroad.

Conclusions

As with dealing with other organized crime organizations, alliances with law enforcement around the world are necessary to effectively target Russian organized crime. International databases, training, innovative strategies and laws, global communication systems between law enforcement agencies, and cutting-edge technologies, such as electronic surveillance and tracking, are needed to combat their sophisticated criminal operations. Investigative grand juries are essential for these types of long-term, sophisticated investigations. Immunity and protection for those who cooperate with authorities will likely result in additional cooperation from the U.S. Russian community. U.S. law enforcement must meet the challenge presented by Russian organized crime with not only federal efforts, but state and local operations as well.

Much of what is written about Russian organized crime groups is often debated. The need for more accurate and complete intelligence regarding their structure, methods of operation, activities, and membership is crucial to the development of effective enforcement strategies. What is certain is that these groups are expanding their operations both in the United States and throughout the world, as they are forming alliances with many other organized crime groups. U.S. law enforcement must meet this challenge with its own alliances of law enforcement organizations, including government agencies, the business community, and community members where Russian organized crime members live and work.

As pointed out in the work edited by Finckenauer and Schrock (2004), the face of Russian organized crime is changing. Today, such groups represent a blend of the "Thieves' World" (an online gaming program based on a science-fiction novel) and the highly educated entrepreneurs of the Russian states. Although internal conflicts exist among the various groups, the quality of management of the Russian clans ensures their success and expansion into other countries. Russian transnational organized crime groups and Eurasian organized crime groups with extraordinary skills in executing financial crimes are certainly some of the newest faces in organized crime and will likely remain a major threat to society and governments worldwide.

Discussion Questions

1. What are the origins of Russian organized crime, and how are they different from the origins of other organized crime groups?

2. What is the structure of the "Russian Mafia"?

3. Which additional unique challenges to U.S. law enforcement do Russian organized crime groups present?

4. Why should investigators study the history of men like Ivankov?

5. Discuss the different criminal activities of Russian organized crime. Include the reported criminal alliances between Russian organized crime groups and other organized crime groups.

6. Why are Russian organized crime groups considered a serious threat to the United States, and how can American law enforcement respond to them?

References

Abadinsky, H. (2003). *Organized Crime* (7th ed.). Belmont, CA: Wadsworth/Thompson.

Abramkin, V. (1996). *In Search of a Solution: Crime, Criminal Policy, and Prison Facilities in the Former Soviet Union.* Moscow: Human Rights Publishers.

Adams, J. (2010, March 16). At least 69 Alleged Russian Mafia Arrested in European Crackdown. Retrieved June 24, 2010, from http://www.csmonitor/World/terrorism-security/2010/0316/at-least-69-alleged-Russian-mafia-arrested-in-Europe-crackdown

Center for Strategic and International Studies. (1997). Task Force Report. *Global Org.* Retrieved April 20, 2004, from http://www.CSIS.org

Columbia Daily News. (2002). Organized Crime Task Force. Retrieved July 20, 2003, from http://www.CSIS.org

Farah, D. (1996, October 7). Russian Crime Finds Haven in Caribbean. *Washington Post Foreign Service,* p. A15.

Financial Crimes Enforcement Network. (1996). Annual report.

Finckenauer, J. (2001). Russian Organized Crime in the United States. United Nations Activities. Retrieved November 24, 2006, from the National Institute of Justice, International: http://www.ojp.usdoj.gov/nij/international/russian.html

Finckenauer, J., & Schrock, J. R. (Eds.). (2004). *The Prediction and Control of Organized Crime: The Experience of Post-Soviet Ukraine.* New Brunswick, NJ: Transaction.

Finckenauer, J., & Waring, E. (1998). *Russian Mafia in America.* Boston: Northeastern University Press.

Finckenauer, J. O., & Waring, E. (2001, April). Challenging the Russian Mafia Mystique. *National Institute of Justice Journal,* 2–7.

Franceschina, P.. & Burstein, J. (2010, March 20). Mafia Has Long History in South Florida But New Ways and New Rivals. Retrieved June 24, 2010, from sun-sentinel.com/news/broward/Rothstein/fl-rothstein-south-florida-mob-history-20100317,0,529206.story

Frankel, B. (1995, September 14). Extortion Now the Least of Its Activities. *USA Today,* p. 1A.

Freeh, L. (1996, April 30). Hearing on Russian Organized Crime: Testimony before the House Committee on International Relations. Retrieved November 24, 2006, from http://www.fas.org/irp/congress/1996_hr/h960430f.htm

Handelman, S. (1993, January 24). Why Capitalism and the Mafia Mean Business. *New York Times Magazine,* pp. 12–15.

Handelman, S. (1995). *Comrade Criminal.* New Haven, CT: Yale University Press.

Harding, L. (January 25, 2008). Russia's Most Notorious Mafia Boss Arrested in Moscow. Retrieved June 24, 2010, from http://www.guardian.co.uk/world/2008/jan/25/russia.lukeharding

Hayward, S. (2003, August 11). Russian Mafia Worms Way into Mexican Drug Cartels. Knight Ridder News Service. Retrieved June 15, 2006, from http://www.cdi.org/russia/johnson/7285-14.cfm

Hirschkorn, P. (March 15, 2005). U.S. Charges 18 in Russian Weapons-Smuggling Plot. Retrieved June 25, 2010, from http://www.cnn.com/2005/LAW/03/15/weapons.trafficking/index.html=newssearch

Idea House. (2001). *Russian Organized Crime Is Big Business.* Dallas, TX: National Center for Policy Analysis.

Kelly, R. J., Chin, K. L., & Schatzberg, R. (1994). *Handbook of Organized Crime in the United States.* Westport, CT: Greenwood Press.

Krane, J. (1999, March 17). Russian Mobsters Kick Down the World's Doors. *APB News.*

Lindberg, R., & Markovic, V. (2001). *Organized Crime Outlook in the New Russia.* Schaumburg, IL: Search International. Retrieved June 14, 2006, from http://www.search-international.com/Articles/crime/russiacrime.htm

Lorek, L. (2001, July 16). Russian Mafia Threatens Net. *Interactive Week.*

Lungren, D. (1996, March). Russian Organized Crime. State of California, Office of the Attorney General. Retrieved June 15, 2006, from http://www.fas.org/irp/world/para/docs/rusorg1.htm

Macho, S. (1997). FBI Director Warns Russian Organized Crime Threatens U.S. National Security. *ERRI Daily Intelligence Report.* Chicago: Emergency Response and Research Institute. Retrieved June 14, 2006, from http://www.emergency.com/rusn-mob.htm

Manjoo, F. (2000). Russians Pirate, Rule the CD's. *Wired News.com.* Waltham, MA: Lycos. Retrieved July 15, 2002, from http://www.wired.com/news/culture/0,1284,39234,00.html

Mendellhall, P. (2001, August 31). Russian Crime Creeps into Kremlin. *MSNBC News.* New York: NBC News.

Miroslev, A. (2001). *The Network of International Organized Crime in the Czech Republic.* Institute of International Relations.

O'Brien, N. (2004, September 7). Russian Mafia Crashed Telstra. *The Weekend Australian.* Retrieved June 13, 2006, from http://www.theaustralian.news.com.au/printpage/0,5942,10687986,00.html

Russia. (2001). Retrieved from http://11members.tripod.com/orgcrime/rusorder.htm

Chapter 7

The Italian American Mafia

There are no problems we cannot solve together, and very few we can solve by ourselves.

—Lyndon B. Johnson, 36th U.S. President

Objectives

After completing this chapter, readers should be able to:

- Understand why the Mafia has been able to survive so long under intense pressure from law enforcement.
- Explain how the American Mafia differs from other organized crime groups.
- Discuss the history of the Mafia in the United States.
- Describe the structure of the Mafia and explain how it is susceptible to law enforcement efforts.
- Explain how law enforcement has been successful against Mafia operations.

Introduction

Although the "new organized crime"—composed of the Russian/Eastern European crime groups, Mexican and Colombian drug trafficking organizations, Japanese Yakuza, Chinese Triads, and a variety of gangs—has supplanted much of the traditional organized criminal activity, this realm was once dominated by Italian organized crime groups known as the Mafia. Currently, the American Mafia is somewhat dormant, though it has not disappeared altogether. In fact, many of the newer organized crime groups are allied with or pay tribute to Mafia members.

Known by many other names, including La Cosa Nostra (LCN), the Mob, the Outfit, the Office, and the family, Italian criminal organizations have existed in America since the 1850s. Italian organized crime groups became very active during the Prohibition years of the 1920s, consolidated their power in the 1930s, and evolved into established criminal organizations known as the Mafia and LCN in the 1950s and 1960s.

The first official mention of an Italian American crime organization known as "the Mafia" occurred in the 1950 Kefauver Hearings, and the term "La Cosa Nostra" was first used by gangster Joe Valachi in 1963 while testifying before the U.S. Senate Subcommittee on Investigations (Albanese, 2004, pp. 115–133). However, the first admission by Italian American crime figures that the Mafia actually existed came in the 1987 "Commission" trial when leaders of the five New York City Mafia families—Gambino, Genovese, Lucchese, Columbo, and Bonnano—admitted that the Mafia existed and that they were members.

The Mafia is one of the few criminal organizations in the United States that has bridged the gap between the legitimate upperworld and the criminal underworld. It repeatedly has demonstrated its power and innovation by corrupting both law enforcement and the U.S. political system. It has controlled many labor unions and major businesses through monopoly, violence, intimidation, and corruption. The Mafia remains the only organized crime group to exercise such extensive power and control in America.

The saga of the Mob and politicians remains one of the most debated crime topics in America. Due to extreme pressure from law enforcement, the Mafia has evolved into even a more secret organization, making the identification of Mob bosses more difficult. Their trend toward becoming legitimate has advanced over the decades as well. Federal prosecutions in the 1980s, 1990s, and early 2000s have resulted in the Mafia becoming more of an underground operation and even dormant in many areas of America. The current state of the Mafia is "down but not out."

Historical Perspective

Overview

The origins of the American Mafia as well as other Italian organized crime groups (Sicilian Mafia, the Camorra, the Ndragheta, and Nuova Sacra Corona Unita) are all connected to the culture of southern Italy and the island of Sicily. For centuries, Sicily was invaded and ruled by a series of "outsiders." These foreign rulers were viewed as unfair because they established laws that rigidly controlled the peasants. The "mafia" was organized to protect the elite landowners and their property when the weak "outsider" governments failed to maintain order. Landowners hired small armies of Sicilians called *com pagnediarm* to oversee and protect their property. Because many of these protectors were recruited from the local criminal elements, there was a natural progression toward unifying tactics for profit and forming alliances with other criminals. This led to the development of a lifestyle known as "mafioso." Even the Catholic Church sanctioned these brutal protectors, and thus they were known as *Ndragheta* (Society of Men of Honor) for their services to the church and community. The more powerful leaders of these gangs began to collect a "tribute" for "protection" from both landowners and peasants.

By the time Italy became unified, these protection organizations had evolved into a very powerful political force in Sicily. Considerable debate remains about the development of organized crime in Sicily. The *gabelloti* (peasant entrepreneurs who were the estate managers for large landowners) were the bridge between peasants, the weak governments, and the landlords. Over time they become very powerful and violent because there was no police force or military on the island. Each Sicilian village had its own *cosa* (a group of gabelloti), but there was no centrally organized leadership; collectively, the many groups of village gabelloti became referred to as the *Mafia*. This system became one of patron-client, with the gabelloti providing land and jobs to peasants in return for their support and tribute (Blok, 1974).

It appears that no single organization controlled Italian crime. Criminal groups also emerged in other regions of Italy, such as the Camorra, Ndragheta, and Nuova Sacra Corona Unita. Some groups were more structured than others, and the various organizations developed for different reasons. As Italians immigrated to the New World and elsewhere, the loose system of these criminal groups gradually became established in the United States and other countries worldwide.

The current American Mafia continues to rely on many of these old traditions while maintaining an ability to adapt to changing markets and social conditions. Visible but not omnipresent, the Mafia has cannily survived over a century and remains a serious challenge to U.S. law enforcement. The essence of their success is the group's ability to form alliances between businesspeople, politicians, and other criminal groups to take advantage of criminal opportunities for profit.

Immigration Years: The Black Hand

Italian crime groups known as *Mafia*, after the Sicilian protective groups, were spawned in the major U.S. cities during the 1850s, when a massive wave of Italian immigration occurred. New Orleans is believed to be the first city where the Mafia from the Old World settled among Italian immigrants. Italian government anti-Mafia campaigns had pressured many Sicilian Mafia members to migrate alongside approximately 80% of the population of Italy's rural south and approximately 20% of the population from Sicily. First known as the *Black Hand* because of the inked handprint signatures that they left at a few crime scenes, Sicilian gangs formed to continue the same types of criminal activities that had existed in Italy for decades. Each gang was engaged in the traditional crimes of extortion, gambling, and kidnapping, and each operated independently under a leader or boss. Groups known as the Black Hand in the New York criminal gangs soon spread to other major cities such as Chicago.

One of the most extraordinary events connected to the Black Hand group based in New Orleans was the murder of the Chief of Police, David Hennessey, in 1890. Control of the Italian vote in New Orleans was hotly contested between the Provenzano crime family and the gang led by Anthony and Charles Matranga. Hennessey went on record regarding his disdain for Italians. A later series of murders allegedly committed by Italians prompted Hennessey to investigate the activities of these groups. At the time, Hennessey was reported to align with the Provenzano faction and began a campaign to remove the Matranga faction.

Hennessey publicly announced that he would expose the Italian criminal organizations in a special hearing. He was assassinated on October 15, 1890, a short time before he was supposed to testify. After the arrest and trial of several Italians for his murder, all of whom were found not guilty, a crowd gathered in downtown New Orleans and broke into the jail where other Italians were being held for Hennessey's murder. The mob lynched 11 people, some of whom were not connected to the Hennessey case (Gambino, 2000). Despite the fact that no evidence existed of a large secret Italian Mafia, the press created a moral panic, establishing the impression of a dangerous Mafia organization already embedded in the United States. This myth quickly became accepted in the minds of the American public despite the fact that most Italian émigrés and Italian Americans were law-abiding citizens. There remains no evidence that the Black Hand was the first stage of the Mafia's invasion of America.

A significant early development of the Mafia was the formation of criminal gangs in New York and Chicago, who began to establish ties with Italian gangsters in other cities. The climate for the evolution of crime was ripe in most major cities, which were characterized by severe overcrowding, rampant crime, disproportionate wealth, gang activity, corruption of public officials, and widespread gambling and prostitution. Alliances among politicians, gamblers, gangsters, and businesses were also commonplace.

Like many other immigrant groups arriving in the United States, Italian immigrants spoke little English and tended to settle in pocket communities alongside other Italians. When these Italians became victims of a crime, they were often ignored by U.S. police and politicians. Authorities were suspicious of the people who did not speak their language or understand American culture. As a result, those in the Italian community often turned to local gangsters for protection and their form of rough justice.

By 1829, well-organized gangs began to emerge such as the Five Points, Plug Uglies, Forty Thieves, and many others (Asbury, 1928). By the late 1800s, gangs had strongly infiltrated politics and businesses, and new leaders such as William "Boss" Tweed in New York and Michael McDonald in Chicago emerged as powerful crime bosses. Long before Prohibition, drug trafficking networks in cities such as Philadelphia, led by men such as "Dopey" Benny Fein, were doing business with the Italian American crime groups.

The Prohibition era, which extended from the early 1920s into the early 1930s, was an important period of growth in income and power for the Mafia. Although the 18th Amendment did result in reduction of alcohol consumption (an annual consumption of less than one gallon per capita), substantial demand by the public prevailed and alcoholic drink prices increased, allowing the Mob to reap huge profits from bootlegging. To protect their healthy profits from this business, members of the Mafia expanded their corruption efforts to infiltrate and control government officials and police. Over time, the Mafia became a more efficient and effective criminal organization, growing in both size (number of members) and power. During the Prohibition years, the subverted politicians and businesspeople helped this group to become firmly entrenched in the economic and political systems of America.

Each city and family has its unique story. Organized crime groups in each city also evolved differently. Many of the established operations in smaller cities were simply an expansion of the powerful Mafia families from the larger cities such as New York, Chicago, New Orleans, and Philadelphia. However, once established in smaller cities, these groups had a great deal of independence from their sponsoring family. Boston, Buffalo, Detroit, Las Vegas, Los Angeles, and New Orleans all have their own horror stories of assassinations, murders, corruption, and takeovers by Mafia organizations.

Violation of Omerta

One reason for the secrecy among Mafia members was their strict vow of *omerta* (discussed in detail in the "Structure and Organization" section). Members swore that names and activities would never be revealed, and violators of this oath were tortured and/or murdered.

From 1950 to 1951, Senator Carey Estes Kefauver chaired the meetings of the Special Committee on Organized Crime in Interstate Commerce known as the *Kefauver Hearings*. The Committee investigated corruption and organized crime in the United States by interviewing hundreds of witnesses in 14 states. Its proceedings were also the first televised hearings of a congressional committee. Americans were fascinated by the secret dealings of the underworld and the criminal organization known as the Mafia. But despite the testimony and publicity surrounding the Mafia criminal organization, many Americans concluded that there was no valid evidence that this secret organization existed in the United States and that the findings of the special Senate committee were dramatized.

It was the Apalachin incident in 1957, where Italian American crime bosses had convened a meeting in upstate New York, that provided further corroboration of the existence of an Italian American crime organization known as the Mafia. Among those arrested at this meeting were Vito Genovese, Carlo Gambino, Paul Castellano, and Joseph Profaci, all of whom were bosses or high-ranking Mafia members (see "The FBI and the Mafia" section).

The next confirmation of an American Mafia came in 1963. The first Mafia turncoat, Joseph Valachi, testified before a U.S. Senate subcommittee and confirmed that there was a structured crime organization known as La Cosa Nostra. However, no supporting evidence was found by the Senate subcommittee to support such a nationwide crime organization. In 1980, another Mafia turncoat, Jimmy Fratianno, testified that there was an Italian American crime organization known as the Mafia or Cosa Nostra (Albanese, 2004).

The highest-ranking Mafia turncoat, Salvatore "The Bull" Gravano, provided similar testimony in the 1992 trial of John Gotti, Jr.

More than 100 Mafia members have testified in court about this group's members and operations, many of whom are currently in the federal witness protection program. The trials of the 1980s and 1990s finally put an end to the debate concerning the existence of both the Mafia and its Commission (a group that settles disputes between crime families). Indeed, the defense in the 1986 "Commission trial" conceded the existence of both the Mafia (also known as La Cosa Nostra) and the Commission. This trial resulted in the sentence of 100 years for the leaders of the five families of New York City (except for Paul Castellano, who was murdered by John Gotti, Jr., during the trial).

The FBI and the Mafia

The FBI did not formally recognize the existence of the Mafia until 1957, when an enormous underworld conference was busted in Apalachin, New York (Lyman & Potter, 2006, pp. 32–33). In this incident, a local police officer noticed the extra traffic and out-of-state license plates, and upon discovering the meeting called in the FBI. More than 60 mobsters were arrested in the largest roundup of Mafia in U.S. history to date.

Some believe that J. Edgar Hoover (FBI director for 50 years) purposely diverted law enforcement attention away from these criminal groups to preserve his passion for race-horse betting, as his tips came indirectly from Mafia bookies who fixed the races. Others point to the unusual relationship between Hoover and his second-in-command, Clyde Tolson. Alleged Mafia photos circulated in the 1970s showed Hoover and Tolson together in drag. Still others subscribe to the theory that if the extent of Italian organized crime had been exposed to the U.S. public, it would have tarnished the shining image of the FBI and its famous director. Hoover also may have believed that the organizations were too rich and powerful to take out. For whatever reason, what is true is that FBI agents were directed away from investigating organized crime and toward easier targets (except for brief periods of time) until Hoover's death.

The New York Mafia

Arnold Rothstein

Perhaps somewhat oddly, an orthodox Jew, Arnold Rothstein ("The Brain"), is considered the first chief ("Don") of an American organized crime group. In the mid-1920s, Rothstein was the first to form a criminal organization that supplied illegal goods and services (Lyman and Potter, 2006). His main contribution was applying organization to the gang's formal structure and hierarchy. These elements included specialization, a clear chain of command, and defined operating procedures—ideas similar to those espoused by the organizational theorists Max Weber (theory of bureaucracy) and Fredrick W. Taylor (theory of efficient operations). Rothstein was the model for the next generation of organized crime, and many of his lieutenants grew in power to rank among the most famous gangsters of the 1930s to the 1960s.

One Rothstein protégé was Frank Costello, a Calabrian émigré who much later became boss of the Luciano family after Luciano went to prison in 1935. Costello expanded Mafia operations into other cities such as New Orleans, where the primary Italian American gangs consisted of Neapolitan and Calabrian immigrants and smaller groups of Sicilians. Despite being similar in many respects, differences between these crime groups and perceived territory violations led to the Castellammarse Wars (discussed later in this chapter). This conflict ultimately ended with the formation of the Commission, which was developed to prevent such disputes in the future.

Over the years, Rothstein's organization grew in power. In addition to gambling and prostitution rackets, he expanded into narcotics, which became an enormous source of illegal income. Another of Rothstein's men was Jack "Legs" Diamond. Diamond and his brother Eddie were in the business of hijacking and later became associated with mobsters such as Dutch Schultz, Charles Luciano, and "Little Augie" Orgen. Other Rothstein protégés included Lepke Buchalter and Jacob "Gurrah" Shapiro. These two criminals, along with Orgen, were in the pavement business. As has happened frequently in criminal organizations, the Orgen and Diamond factions became enemies owing to conflicts over turf and illegal enterprises. Orgen was killed and Buchalter was executed for his crimes in 1944. Schultz was murdered by Luciano, who went on to become the next major player in the history of the American Mafia. Rothstein was shot and killed in 1928 for reasons yet unknown, although it was speculated that he was killed for supporting the Diamond brothers in their attack on Schultz and his partner, Joey Noel.

Charles "Lucky" Luciano

Although Rothstein often is described as the founder of American organized crime, another of his protégés, Charles "Lucky" Luciano (born Salvatore Lucania) is credited with the creation of today's American Mafia. Known for his leadership ability, Luciano appeared to be a dapper and charismatic lady's man, but he was also a ruthless, cold-blooded killer.

Luciano's story is a valuable lesson for those seeking to understand modern organized crime. His family emigrated from western Sicily in 1907 when Luciano was 14, and settled in a Jewish community in New York City. By age 14, Luciano had dropped out of high school, and by age 18 he had been charged with possession of heroin and was a suspect in a number of murders.

Charles "Lucky" Luciano.

After serving six months of a one-year sentence, Luciano was released from prison and joined the Five Points gang. His criminal career can best be described as being in the right place (New York) at the right time (Prohibition). Luciano was known for his ability to work with anyone, regardless of their ethnicity. While a teenager, he had formed close friendships with fellow minor hoodlums, Benjamin "Bugsy" Segal and Meyer Lansky, both of whom were Jewish. Learning about the structure of organization and the inside nature of criminal activities from Rothstein helped make Luciano an important figure in U.S. Mafia history.

In 1927, Giueppe "Joe the Boss" Masseria asked Luciano to become a major player in Masseria's faction against the Sicilian group led by Salvatore Maranzano. Each group had invaded the other's territory and tensions had escalated. Around 1930, a vicious battle known as the *Castellammarse Wars* erupted between the two groups. More than 60 men were killed during this intensely brutal rivalry for control of criminal activities and profits. The Masseria group was losing the war despite having major players such as Luciano, Schultz, Frank Costello, Vito Genovese, Al Capone, Meyer Lansky, and others. Maranzano approached Luciano about coming over to his side and betraying Masseria. When Luciano refused, he was beaten and left for dead.

In April 1931, after deciding to betray Masseria, Luciano switched factions. He and Genovese arranged for Masseria to meet them at a restaurant on Coney Island, New York. "Joe the Boss" Masseria was shot and killed, and Maranzano declared himself "Boss of Bosses." However, after making Luciano his powerful ally, Maranzano decided that he could not trust Luciano or Luciano's allies. Using information obtained from Meyer Lansky, Luciano turned the tables on Maranzano, however: He sent a hit squad posing as police to kill the last "Boss of Bosses" of the Mafia. After the hit, Luciano became the most powerful Italian organized crime boss in New York and probably the United States.

The Commission

Luciano knew that gang war was bad for business, so he negotiated with other Italian crime leaders and formed what became known as *the Commission* in 1931. This body would handle disputes and act as a semi-governing body for the U.S. branch of the Mafia. Charter members included Joseph Bonanno, Joseph Profaci, Thomas Gagliano, Vincent Margano, and Luciano from New York City; Stefano Maggaddino from Buffalo; and Frank Nitti from Chicago. (This body continues to exist, but its representation has evolved to include more cities and bosses.) With peace between the Mob families, the American Mafia became the most powerful organized crime group in the world. Luciano led a very public and glamorous lifestyle, including ownership of an apartment in the Waldorf Towers.

Although the new American Mafia had abandoned many of the traditional Sicilian customs, it kept the strategies of violence, corruption, omerta, and monopolizing the rackets. Luciano was chairman of the board of *Murder Inc.*, the enforcement arm of the Commission. Members of the Commission assigned territories, adjudicated disputes, and carried out internal discipline. The now-consolidated American Mafia had surpassed the accomplishments of both the Irish and Jewish crime groups under Luciano's and the Commission's leadership.

Luciano's extravagant lifestyle made him a target of New York prosecutor Thomas Dewey and his staff, and multiple investigations into his criminal activities began in the early 1930s. Finally, Dewey was able to convict Luciano of running a prostitution racket; Luciano was sentenced to 30 to 50 years for his crimes. While an inmate in the dreary Dannemora prison, Luciano was treated as a special case. The warden allowed secret visits as well as phone calls from friends and family, which enabled Luciano to continue running his organized crime empire from his prison cell. His two partners left New York, with Lansky moving to Florida and Segal to Hollywood.

In 1942, Mob and government interests narrowed to confluence when members of U.S. Naval Intelligence, anticipating interference with the U.S. shipping industry by Nazi saboteurs, arrived for a secret meeting with Luciano at Dannemora prison. Through Lansky, they approached Luciano with a request for the Mob to provide protection and intelligence for the United States on the international shipping docks. After agreeing to help, Luciano was transferred to the "country club" Great Meadow Prison, where he continued to confer with his Mob connections and gained access to alcohol and the comforts of women.

Luciano again was visited secretly by Navy Intelligence while he was in Great Meadows Prison, when officials asked him to help negotiate with his Sicilian Mafia contacts to aid the Allied Forces with the 1943 invasion of Italy. In return for his cooperation, Luciano was pardoned in 1946 by then New York Governor Dewey, who, after prosecuting Luciano years earlier, had launched a successful political career. Subsequently, Luciano was extradited to Italy and not allowed to return to the United States. Simultaneously, however, he was issued a Cuban passport. In that same year, Luciano left Italy for Havana, where he called a summit of Mob bosses in December 1947. Among the attendees were Gambino, Albert Anastasia, Costello, and Lansky. At the meeting, these Mafia leaders discussed establishing an international narcotics operation, the hit (assassination) on Segal for his failure in Las Vegas, and other Mob enterprises such as gambling and prostitution.

When the DEA discovered Luciano's activities in Cuba, officials arranged for his expulsion back to Palermo, Italy. In 1957, Luciano again arranged for a summit in Palermo in an attempt to establish an international drug trafficking operation. At the time, most of the narcotics already were processed in Italy before being smuggled into the United States for distribution. That meeting resulted in the cooperation between the Sicilian and American Mafias for narcotics distribution in the United States, a contract that continues today. In return for Luciano's negotiation of this deal, in addition to profits, he received a $25,000 per month tribute from the American Mafia as a demonstration of respect.

Similar to other organized crime bosses, Luciano developed a reputation for charity and became extremely popular with the public, often being asked for his autograph by both Americans and Europeans. Eventually, however, Luciano became alienated from other Mafia bosses and groups because they began to resent his larger share of the profits. Additionally, he wanted to make a movie about his life—a project not approved by the other organized crime bosses. Some believe that the same Commission he had established took out a contract on him. Luciano died of a heart attack in 1962 at the age of 64 and is buried in Queens, New York.

Charles "Lucky" Luciano was a gangster genius whose contributions of structure and diplomatic ability to negotiate with other crime bosses led to the formation of an international criminal organization, the legacy of which continues today. Identification and prosecution of leaders such as Luciano negatively impacted the American Mafia, however, and such efforts remain a priority of organized crime investigations.

The Five Families of New York

In addition to the Luciano-Genovese family, four other powerful crime families emerged in New York: the Lucchese, Columbo, Gambino, and Bonanno families. These Mafia families were among the most powerful in America, and all have had representatives on the Commission from its beginning to the present day.

Joseph Bonanno was a major figure in the evolution of the Mafia in America. Born in 1905 in Sicily to a reputable and wealthy family, his story differs from those of Luciano, Capone, Costello, and others. His family immigrated to America but returned home in 1911. After the death of his mother, Bonanno went back to New York in 1924, in the midst of the Prohibition years. Because his family was connected to the Mob in Sicily, the young man arrived in America with good references. Maranzano, impressed with his ability for administration and seeing profit opportunities, became his mentor and put him in charge of the bootlegging operation.

Bonanno and Luciano made peace after the Castellammarse Wars, and Bonanno became boss at the age of 26. He assisted in the formation and was a charter member of the 1931 Mafia Commission. In addition, Bonanno approved Carmine Galante's arrangement with the French and Sicilian crime groups, which established a lucrative international narcotics operation between America, Sicily, and France.

Bonanno's cousin, Stefano Maggaddino, established a crime family in Buffalo, New York. Eventually, bad blood between Bonanno and his cousin led to the removal of Bonanno as boss of his New York family. Bonanno's son became a "made man" (see the "Membership" section later in this chapter) in 1941 and married a Profaci, which united two powerful New York families.

At the age of 52, Bonanno met with the Sicilian Mob in 1957 to form a strong alliance that remains in existence today. As early as the 1930s, Bonanno had become extremely wealthy and owned a number of legitimate businesses, including the Brunswick Laundry, Morgan Coke Company, and a hotel in New Jersey. Bonanno successfully ran the powerful family for four decades, an unusually long tenure for a Mafia boss.

In 1963, Joseph Valachi's chilling testimony during a Senate hearing exposed Joe Bonanno as the family head. In 1968, after two years of family wars (the *Banana Wars*), Bonanno retreated to Arizona after a failed attempt to murder the top bosses of rival families in New York. Joseph Massina inherited the position of boss in 1989 and still ran the family from prison following his racketeering conviction. Bonanno also flouted omerta when he cooperated with the publication of a biography (*Honor Thy Father* by Gay Talese, 1971) and produced a movie about his life in the Mob (*Bonnano: Godfather's Story,* 1999). At the time of his death at age 93, he was the last of the charter members of the Commission.

Bonanno's contributions to the American Mafia's success included narcotics connections and the movement of the Mob into legitimate business investments. It is interesting to note that prosecutor Rudolph Giuliani successfully used Bonanno's book as evidence in the trial of Mafia members. Much of Bonanno's later problems arose from his efforts to make his son Bill succeed him as boss while ignoring other prominent and productive members. Bonanno served only 18 months in prison during his entire career as a Mafia member and boss.

Due to extensive prosecution and convictions of many bosses and members of the American Mafia, identification of current members, bosses, and active families is difficult. Major families that are active today include the five families of New York, although their power has been weakened considerably. The Carlo Gambino family remains the largest criminal group, with an estimated 300 made members and 2000 to 3000 associates. John Gotti, Jr.'s son, John III, and his uncle Peter Gotti became bosses after John Jr. was sent to prison in 1992. The Vito Genovese family, headed by Vincent "The Chin" Gigante of Greenwich Village may be the second largest Mafia group, with 150 to 200 made men and 1200 associates. Dominick "Quiet Don" Cirillo took over control of this group after Gigante went to prison in 1997. The Gretano Lucchese family has been under intense government scrutiny, with bosses Anthony "Ducks" Corallo and Salvatore Santoro eventually being convicted. Corallo has since died and was succeeded by Vittorio Amuso, who is now in prison as well. At last report, Joe DeFede was the acting boss. The Joseph Colombo family boss is Andrew Russo, but has been weakened by turf wars and government prosecution. The Joseph Bonanno family fell apart following the 1968 plan by Bonanno to murder the top bosses of other families; Joseph Massina was the last reported boss.

Mafia boss John Gotti.

Other Mafia Groups

Chicago

Unlike New York, which has traditionally had five bosses and five families, most major cities have only one Mafia boss. In Chicago, Johnny Torrio was considered the Arnold Rothstein of organized crime. Exceptionally intelligent, Torrio began as a member and then became leader of New York's James Street Boys, who were associates with Paul Kelly's Five Points gang. Chicago gangs evolved somewhat like those in New York, going from leadership under "king of the gamblers" Michael McDonald, to Al Capone, to Sam Giancana, to today's Outfit, for which it is difficult to identify the boss.

Like New York, Chicago was the site of Mafia wars and Mob violence. From 1923 to 1926, nearly 400 murders were connected to the Mob. The battles between the Torrio-Capone and Dion-O'Banion organizations (later the Hymie Weiss organization) left a history of murder and violence that Chicago has yet to repeat. The Capone faction eventually killed Weiss and O'Banion. Today's Outfit is much smaller and far less visible than that of the Capone years, yet remnants of the old Mob can still be found in satellite cities such as Cicero. For the most part, the Outfit has moved into competitive business strategies and away from violence and intimidation. The Chicago Mafia is characterized as more of a cooperative operation with other ethnic groups; in contrast, the New York families keep much of their business within the blood family.

Gangs in cities such as Chicago, where organized crime had evolved from gangsters such as "Big Jim" Colosimo to John Torrio, Hymie Weiss, and Al Capone, were not considered a federal problem in the early years. During the 1940s, bosses such as Tony Accardo brought rock-solid discipline to the Chicago conflict between the warring Italian American crime groups. Before Accardo, Al Capone, Frank Nitti, and Paul Ricca had been the bosses of the Outfit. Although Accardo was tough like Capone, he learned from what he considered operational mistakes. In his opinion, too much publicity brought too much attention to the Mob. Accardo's philosophy was to be a parasite without disturbing the host. He allowed Sam Giancana, a gangster who had started as a driver for the bosses and rose quickly to power because of his willingness to commit murder, to take over the policy and numbers operations from the Jones brothers (Edward, George, and McKissack), who were kings of the policy rackets in the so-called *Black Belt* located in south Chicago. The transition (turf battle) resulted in a number of murders and much violence, but it turned out to be very profitable for the Chicago Outfit.

After the repeal of Prohibition, the American Mafia looked for other means of illegal and legal income. Gambling, narcotics, and Las Vegas enterprises replaced bootlegging. By the mid-1950s, the Chicago crime group had moved part of its operation to Las Vegas.

Las Vegas and Sam Giancana

The Flamingo was the first casino operated for the American Mafia. Skimming money from casino profits before reporting it to the IRS provided yet another substantial source of income for the Mob. In 1957, Accardo remained in control of Chicago, while Giancana became the operational boss and assumed the flashy public lifestyle associated with Capone. At the same time, the Apalachin meeting had been an embarrassment to the FBI, and the agency had begun to put its considerable resources to work toward interrupting Mob business, including engaging in illegal wiretaps and bugs.

The 1960 Presidential election is a major source of debate about the power of the American Mafia. Mafia members believed that they and the Richard Daly (then mayor of Chicago) political machine delivered the election to John F. Kennedy at the request of his father, Joseph Kennedy. In return, Mafia leaders expected favors from the Kennedy family. After Robert Kennedy was named U.S. Attorney General, however, the government went after the Mob with a vengeance.

Giancana was under intense surveillance and made history when he successfully sued the FBI, which then was forced to curtail its surveillance of his movements. Whether Mafia members were actually involved in the assassination of President John F. Kennedy is still debated. Giancana's actions attracted much unwelcome heat and allegations to the Chicago Mob. He eventually served a year in jail for contempt of court, when he refused to testify after being guaranteed transactional immunity.

Giancana also was known for his romance with Phyllis McGuire (of the McGuire Sisters singing group), his association with singer/movie star Frank Sinatra, and the girlfriend he shared with President John F. Kennedy, Judith Exner. The secret arrangement between the Giancana Outfit and the Central Intelligence Agency (CIA) to assassinate Fidel Castro again focused a lot of attention on Chicago organized crime. Relationships between members of the Mob and the U.S. government during the Kennedy years are obscure, and few people who are still living know if any agreements actually existed between these crime groups and the Kennedys.

Forced into exile in Mexico by Accardo, Giancana returned to Chicago in 1975 and was killed on orders from Accardo. Later, Mob trials in the 1980s ended Accardo's nearly 40-year rule of the Chicago Outfit. Although he was not convicted, many of his associates were convicted and sentenced to long prison terms (Roemer, 1995). At the age of 86, Accardo was one of the few bosses who died of natural causes.

Today, the Chicago Outfit is now smaller, with 50 to 200 made members and multiethnic crews, unlike other Mafia families. The last reported boss was Joseph "The Clown" Lombardo; after being a fugitive from justice for nearly a year, he was captured and sentenced to prison in January 2006.

Philadelphia and Atlantic City

It is believed that the Philadelphia/Atlantic City family was organized by a Sicilian, Salvatore Sabella, who was boss from 1911 until 1927. The Philadelphia organized crime scene was not dominated by the Mafia Commission, but it did have ties to Meyer Lansky, Bugsy Siegel, and others during the early years. Angelo Bruno (1927–1946) was integral to the American Mafia's development in Philadelphia. In the early years of its existence, the

"Boo-Boo" Hoff and Nig Rosen syndicate was a loose confederation of bootleggers and gamblers that had a strong connection to Lansky. This confederation operated in several states, including New York, New Jersey, Delaware, Maryland, and Pennsylvania. Bruno was the successor to Rosen's syndicate and was a Commission member until his murder in 1980. Bruno's successor, Philip Testa, was killed in a bomb blast; afterward, Nicodemo "Little Nicky" Scarfo took control of the Philadelphia group. Other bosses included Frank "Flowers" D'Alfonso and John Stanfa.

New Orleans

The Marcello family of New Orleans has played a significant part in the American Mafia's history. Three bosses or families preceded Carlos Marcello, including Antonio and Carlo Matranga, who controlled the docks, freight lines, and fruit and vegetable markets in this city in the early years. The Matranga brothers were from Palermo, Sicily and established probably the first Mafia family crime group in America in New Orleans.

By 1953, Marcello had become a seasoned criminal who had amassed substantial business enterprises, both legitimate and criminal. His early career included a 1930s bank robbery for which he served four years of a 12-year sentence in Angola. By age 25, he was a made man in the Mafia (see the "Structure" section). He was convicted in 1938 for selling marijuana but served only nine months. Marcello's club, The Brown Bomber, was known for drugs, gambling, and prostitutes. Governor Huey Long was believed to have introduced Marcello to Frank Costello. In 1947, during a meeting in New Orleans that included Tom Rizzuto, Nick Grifazzi, Frank Lombardino, Anthony Carolla, and Joe Capro, Carlos Marcello became the undisputed boss of the New Orleans family. His organization was known for its intimate involvement in bribery and corruption of government, including judges, police, sheriffs, and even a congressman.

Marcello's alleged involvement in the assassinations of Martin Luther King, Jr., and both John and Robert Kennedy is still debated today. After his death in 1993, Anthony Carolla became boss of the New Orleans family and Frank Gagliano became underboss.

Prosecutors and law enforcement describe the New Orleans Mafia since the death of Carlos Marcello as dormant but not extinct. Marcello's organization rarely had disputes, unlike the families in Chicago and New York. There was more autonomy of activities among family and associates, and the organization was even less structured than other Mafia families. Marcello had the power to approve a made man without Commission approval. His underboss was his brother, Joe Jr., and his caporegimes (lieutenants) were Norfio Pecora and Joe Poretto. Other brothers who helped run the family businesses were Peter, Vincent, and Pascal. Like other Mafia families, Carlos "The Little Big Man" Marcello owned motels, restaurants, and other businesses that served as fronts as well as a string of legitimate enterprises. His organization spanned the states of Louisiana, Mississippi, Texas, and parts of California, as well as Mexico and the Caribbean. He had ties to presidents, judges, the Dixie Mafia, and sheriffs (including Leroy Hobbs in Mississippi), as well as to other Mafia families. His structure and power allowed him to manipulate politics, crime, and business throughout his empire.

The Philadelphia and Atlantic City Mafia may have interests in New Orleans and has leadership that is somewhat active under Ralph Natale. The 1989 conviction of Nicodemo Scarfo and others has led to the alleged decline of this family's activities, however.

The American Mafia Today

Some American Mafia organizations have established alliances with other ethnic groups, while other groups have kept their organizations primarily ethnic Italian operations. In cities such as New York and Chicago, these groups experienced tremendous violence during their evolution; in contrast, in other cities such as New Orleans, Mafia groups have had relatively little violence attributed to their struggle for power and control among factions. One characteristic cuts across all modern-day Mob groups in major cities, however: It is more difficult to identify today's Mafia bosses.

The modern American Mafia has evolved beyond the traditional crimes of extortion, narcotic trafficking, gambling, and vice. It now has acquired a number of legitimate businesses and become deeply infiltrated both government and political environments. The American Mafia had to become a far more complex and sophisticated organization to continue to be as successful as it has been in the past. Although it is impossible to explore the history of the Mafia in all of the cities in which this group exists, it would be prudent for any investigator to study the history of the Mafia organization in his or her respective jurisdiction to better understand the development of such a successful criminal enterprise.

What the American Mafia is today continues to be influenced by its past. These considerations include how these groups recruit, operate, and survive, by continually adapting to changing law enforcement methods. Will the Mafia acquire shares of multinational corporations, become major players in the elections and appointments of government leaders, develop information systems capable of obtaining critical intelligence and technology, manipulate databases to their advantage, form global alliances that are more powerful than any ever encountered by law enforcement, and develop global money laundering operations that are almost impossible to detect? If Mafia organizations have not achieved these goals already, these are the likely Mafia objectives in the near future.

The following events point to the ongoing existence of LCN and the activities in which its members continue to be involved:

- Genovese boss Daniel ("The Lion") Leo was given an additional 18 months after pleading guilty to RICO, loan sharking, and illegal gambling charges. He became the boss of the Genovese family in 2005. He was ordered to forfeit $1.3 million from the family's illegal gambling operation (McCain, 2010).

- Fourteen members of the Gambino crime family were arrested and charged with murder, RICO offenses, prostitution of minors, and trying to locate and intimidate a sequestered jury according to the U.S. Attorney for the Southern District of Manhattan, New York. Daniel Marino, named as the current boss of the family, was one of those arrested following the indictment. The operation include a prostitution business that operated from 2008 to 2009, where women as young as age 15 were recruited as prostitutes (Guzzardo, 2008).

- Italian Mafia boss Gaetano Lo Presti and 89 other members of the Sicilian Mob were arrested in Sicily. Reportedly, the Sicilian group was making efforts to rebuild itself after the arrest of several top fugitives had left the organization in disarray. Although Sicily's La Cosa Nostra has experienced numerous blows from law enforcement, Italy's mainland groups such as the Calabrian Ndrangheta have grown increasingly more powerful and more violent. In addition, an investigation has been undertaken regarding alleged Mob-sourced corruption linked to oil drilling contracts in the oil-rich southern region of Italy off Basilicata—an especially noteworthy investigation in the aftermath of the BP oil spill and disaster off Louisiana's Gulf coast in 2010 (D'Emilio, 2008).

- There are more than 3000 Mafia members and associates in the United States, according to the FBI. The Mob is far from dead, even after two decades of vigorous prosecutions. LCN and Italian mobsters continue to engage in labor racketeering, infiltration of unions and the construction industries, gambling, and loan sharking. As the economy evolves, these groups evolve in tandem. LCN still has a powerful presence in New York, southern New Jersey, and Philadelphia. Although Asian, Russian, and Albanian organized crime groups have established their own operations, they remain smaller and more disorganized than their Italian counterparts. Forensic accounting, wiretaps, and development of informants continue to be effective tools against organized crime in general, however (Bohn & Arena, 2008).

- In recent years, 62 members of the Gambino, Genovese, and Bonanno families have been arrested on charges including money laundering, illegal gambling, and murder. The operations identified in the charges included sports gambling and toll-free telephones. Police in Italy made an additional 77 arrests in connection with this investigation, including the arrest of Salvatore Lo Piccolo, who was believed to be the new "boss of bosses." One report has stated that the Italians have been attempting to mend relations with the New York Mafia after the bloody internecine wars of the 1980s. The Mafia in Palermo, for example, has been attempting to reestablish a relationship with the Inzerillo family in the United States involving drug trafficking, illegal commercial ventures, and money laundering (Feyerick & Vinci, 2008).

- An acting caporegime of the Lucchese family was arrested for operating a sports betting ring in the Bronx and Manhattan, according to federal prosecutors. Other member of the family were charged with distributing cocaine. The group reportedly has access codes to an offshore gambling operation (Zambito, 2008).

Structure and Organization

The American Mafia is a subculture with its own rules and values for the purpose of profit sharing from legal and illegal activities. The organization's hierarchy insulates the bosses from arrest and prosecution. The so-called *Honored Society* of the Mafia has a hierarchical chain of command much like a legitimate business corporation. Most Mafia families are headed by a boss, an underboss, and a consigliore (counselor). **Figure 7-1** shows the typical organization chart of a Mafia family.

Associates (*Giovane D'Honore*) are not "made" members (see the "Membership" section), but rather made members direct their activities. Each *caporegime* oversees a "crew" of soldiers, who are made men and associates. The *consigliere* is an older member who has extensive expertise (and sometimes is an attorney). He advises the boss and also serves as a liaison between soldiers and administration. He may be a constable who serves as a financial advisor. A *piciotto* is a low-ranking soldier who serves as an enforcer (*hit man*). The

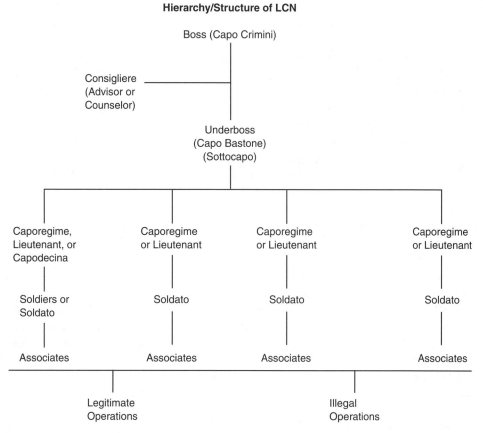

Figure 7-1   Hierarchy of a Mafia family.

made man is also called a foot soldier (*sgarrista*) and carries out the orders of the caporegime or lieutenant.

The Commission is the national organization believed to comprise the bosses of the five families of New York and Chicago, Buffalo, Detroit, and Philadelphia. This composition has changed over the years and continues to evolve with ongoing power shifts within the American Mafia crime organization. The Commission plays a coordinating and mediating role between families, settling disputes and approving hits, and assigning areas of activity for each family. The Commission also approves new membership and manages joint operations between American Mafia families and other organized crime entities such as the Sicilian Mafia. This structure allows for rapid replacement of any person, as someone in the next lower level is always ready to take over the vacant position.

Each family has its own territory or type of activity that it operates exclusively. The organization may have specialty crews who operate such activities as gambling, narcotics, or loan sharking for the family, while other crews may be responsible for all activity within a specific area of a city or state. Most crews act independently of other crews. The Chicago outfit may not use the same titles as other Mafia families.

Although all Mafia families have bosses, each city is organized in a different way. As noted earlier, New York has five separate families; in contrast, Chicago has the Outfit, which consists of separate street crews, each with a specific geographic area. Families are the basic unit of the organization, but the name changes from area to area. In Chicago, it is the "Outfit"; in New York, it is the family (*borgata*); in New England, it is the "Office." Respect and loyalty are expected, and betrayal of omerta results in death. Members are referred to as "friends of ours" and associates are "friends of mine."

The family's crime operations are put into action by crews of made members and associates under the direction of a *caporegime*. The daily routine of a crew member consists of violence, treachery, and boredom. The member works in one crew and checks in with his caporegime, letting him know what they are doing to score. Each score or operation must be approved. Crews usually work alone and only occasionally know about other crew members and their activities. Members rarely use their real names. Most conversations are face to face, and rarely does a crew member know of any family activity beyond that carried out by his crew.

The structure of the Mafia has allowed it to form what some term a *shadow government*. Members and associates at the bottom may be independent entrepreneurs, yet pass part of their earnings up the chain of command to be shared with bosses. Through bosses and the Commission, the administration acts as a government regulating and controlling the overall operation, including dividing up areas of operation by families or crews, settling disputes, approving new members, and enforcing rules. With characteristics of both a corporation and government, the structure of the American Mafia, along with its extensive exploitation of corruption, has allowed the organization to survive in America for more than a century. For the most part, the structure of the American Mafia has allowed this organization to avoid the turf wars that have erupted in the old country between the Sicilians and other Italians. By the 1930s, for example, the American Mafia had determined that the traditional *vendetta* (blood feud) was bad for business. When Luciano and others established the Commission in 1931, the ruling body prevented many all-out wars between families by having "sit-downs" to settle disputes and solve problems. Although members are not normally paid a salary by a family organization, the family connections allow members to establish lucrative operations.

Membership

As is true for most crime organizations, membership in the Mafia is exclusive, often based on ethnicity, familial relationships, and past criminal activities. Exclusive membership adds to the sense of trust among group members, which is a basic element necessary for criminal networks to come together and persist over time (Von Lampe, 2003). A man does not petition for membership in the Mafia; rather, a prospective member is "selected" by the other members and must undergo a series of "tests" to prove his worthiness. Clear boundaries exist between members and outsiders, and the group's specific rules (codes of behavior) are supported by oaths or affirmations at initiation that must be followed by members. The rules are enforced by a strict discipline system, with death being meted out as the punishment for violations.

As noted earlier, each Mafia family includes a number of *made men*. who are often referred to as *wiseguys* or *goodfellows*. To become a made man, a person must be a male of Italian descent on his father's side. In the old tradition, a member had to have committed a murder (*hit*) directed by a boss. This requirement prevented infiltration by law enforcement; also, because murder has no statute of limitations, the Mob had a lifetime guarantee that a member would not talk for fear of being prosecuted. To become a member today, a man may just have to be a good source of income for the organization—that is, be an earner. The prospective member also must have a sponsor who is a made man and obtain a unanimous vote admitting him to the group by all family members.

Although there has never been a time in U.S. history when more Mafia leaders and members were in jail, there remains a large pool of potential members and leaders waiting to replace them and fill vacant positions. Even though new membership in most families is not always available, the opportunity for membership in the past has opened up often enough to induct the most "worthy" gangsters. This situation may have changed today, however. According to Joe Pistone, an undercover FBI agent in the 1970s, the old values of the Mafia are fading as younger mobsters who are more about "my thing" than "our thing" replace the elder elite. The 25- to 35-year-old wiseguys do not have the same values as the older members and are more likely to engage in drug use and take greater risks.

Henry Hill: Wiseguy and Goodfellas

Many Mafia members grow up in neighborhoods committing crimes as youngsters—a practice that leads to associations with made men. Often their relatives are members of the Mafia, exposing these young men to the culture of crime. The attraction of the Mafia lifestyle and crew operations is perhaps best illustrated by the Henry Hill story.

Hill's mother was Italian and his father Irish (the reason he could not become a made man). Born in Brooklyn, New York, in 1943, the young Hill became fascinated with the power and lifestyle of the wise guys of the Lucchese family. His involvement in crime began at a young age with gambling and stealing. Caporegime Paul Vario took notice of Hill and began using him to run errands and do odd jobs. At age 16, after Hill was arrested for possession of stolen credit cards, Vario arranged for Hill to get a union card and receive a paycheck without going to work except on payday. Hill was a good con man with charming ways.

After enlisting in the Army in 1960, Hill was arrested for bookmaking and loan sharking, and in 1963 was discharged. He then returned to the Vario crew and worked with Jimmy Burke, an Irishman and Mafia associate. As is often the case with crews, they specialized in hijacking at the John F. Kennedy Airport. Arrested in 1965 for possession of untaxed cigarettes and later sentenced to 10 years for collecting money by force for the Mob, Hill was a favorite associate. He found life in prison not much different from that on the streets and, much like other mobsters who go to jail, continued to operate his criminal activities from prison. However, he broke a Lucchese rule by selling drugs. After he was paroled, Hill became an addict.

Hill was responsible for providing the Mob with information that resulted in the 1978 robbery of Lufthansa Airlines cargo. Crewmembers began spending the money openly and were eventually murdered on orders from the Mob boss, who feared drawing attention to the Lucchese crime family. In 1980, Hill was arrested for dealing dope. Certain that he would be killed for violating the rule against narcotics trafficking, Hill entered the witness protection program and testified against his role model Vario and fellow crewmember Burke. His testimony landed 30 mobsters in jail. After violating the rules of the witness protection program numerous times, he was kicked out of the program. In 1999, Hill finally seemed to beat his addiction and has since faded from the headlines.

Although recruitment into the Mafia has become more difficult today because of law enforcement pressure, there are still young men like Hill who are drawn to the seemingly glamorous lifestyle of mobsters. The 1990 book *Wiseguy: Life Inside a Mafia Family* (by Nicholas Pileggi) and the film entitled *Goodfellas* (by Martin Scorsese, Nicholas Pileggi, and Timothy Bricknell) are based on Hill's life.

Initiation

As stated earlier, some type of initiation ceremony is important for all crime organizations. This rite has both real and symbolic consequences. In such a ceremony, the former prospect signifies that he is ready for membership, and the members signify that he is now one of them forever with real consequences for betrayal of the group. Every crime organization, including biker gangs, has an initiation ritual that is a symbolic representation of this acceptance into the group, complete with oaths and affirmations.

The importance of the Mafia initiation ritual has faded somewhat, but some form of it persists in all groups. The initiation ceremony, which varies from family to family, may include drawing of blood and repeating oaths of secrecy and obedience, or it may be as simple as a meeting where the new member is introduced and welcomed to the family and boss. The FBI recorded the initiation ceremony for the first time in 1989. This recording gave credibility to information provided by Mafia members who had cooperated with the FBI and established the existence of the American Mafia.

The court testimony of Sammy "The Bull" Gravano, Joe Valachi, and Anthony Casso described the following initiation ceremony of a made man into the Mafia. First, the initiate's trigger finger is pricked and made to bleed on a card with a picture of a Catholic Saint on it. This card is burned in his hand, and the initiate swears that he will never betray the Mafia or he will burn like the card. The boss and other members lock hands with the new member in the middle of the circle, and they welcome the new member, proclaiming his membership into the brotherhood.

Usually, a list of proposed members must be produced for approval by the Commission and other Mafia families. At least one list of proposed members seized by the FBI contained the man's full name and street address.

Activities and Methods of Operation

Provision of Illicit Services and Goods

The American Mafia is very open to any enterprises that make money; however, ever since the Prohibition era, the provision of illicit services and goods has been the mainstay of its illegal activities. Lyman and Potter (2006) define illicit services as "those that legitimate businesses do not provide and are proscribed by law." Illicit services include gambling, protection rackets (basically a form of extortion in which businesses pay for protection from unforeseen misfortune, such as fire or vandalism), loan sharking (loaning money at exorbitant rates, with violence used if necessary as a means of collecting on the debt), and prostitution.

The provision of illicit goods involves supplying items that are not available from legitimate sources. Organized crime groups in America, including the Mafia, became wealthy and powerful supplying alcohol during the Prohibition era, but today the largest moneymaker is illegal drugs. The market for illicit goods is always expanding, and organized crime groups are quick to seize on new opportunities. One major market is for unregistered guns and stolen property that crime groups can supply at a lower price than legitimate businesses. Organized crime groups, including the Mafia, are major suppliers of pornography, cultural objects, counterfeit or pirated goods, untaxed cigarettes, wild animals, intellectual property, human organs, and people for the sex trade and general labor.

Gambling

Illegal gambling is not merely a minor part of traditional organized crime such as LCN, but rather the foundation upon which other illicit activities are supported. Online betting, including sports betting, is a major source of revenues, which are then invested in legitimate enterprises and other illegal operations (e.g., loan sharking, money laundering), and used to corrupt business, governments, and law enforcement. Sports betting is a major enterprise for LCN and has resulted in the corruption of sports and those involved. It is estimated that $380 billion annually is bet illegally on sports events around the United States. In Nevada, where sports betting is legal, the annual amount of betting is approximately $2.9 billion. The problems with this activity include the lack of uniform international law and oversight or regulation, the ability of funds to cross international borders, the high degree of anonymity, and the lack of the law enforcement attention due to the public accepting sports betting. This activity is a rapidly growing phenomenon that is becoming a law enforcement challenge ("Gambling and Organized Crime," 2009).

The Gaming Devices Act of 1951 (Johnson Act 18 U.S.C. &1804) is the federal criminal law used to monitor organized crime and gambling. Other statutes used for this purpose are RICO, 18 U.S.C. 1961, and the Bank Secrecy Act (31 U.S.C. & 103). The Treasury Department's Financial Crimes Enforcement Network and the Money Laundering Control Act of 1986 are used to oversee and implement policies to prevent and detect money laundering through such activities (U.S. Treasury Order No. 105-108).

In 2000, legalized gambling could be found in more than 28 states, mostly in the form of casino gambling in cities such as Biloxi, Mississippi, or on riverboats. Other casinos are found on Indian lands.

There appears to be a nexus to gambling and organized crime whether the gambling is legal or illegal ("Gambling and Organized Crime," 2010). The history of the infiltration of organized crime in Nevada's casino industry should serve as a warning of the existing and future interest of organized crime in such legal enterprises.

Labor Racketeering

Labor racketeering is defined as the infiltration and/or control of a union or employee benefit plan through illegal, violent, or fraudulent means (U.S. Department of Labor, 2006). Traditionally, it has been one of the American Mafia's fundamental sources of profit, power, and influence. According to the FBI, one-third of those arrested at the 1957 Apalachin crime conference listed their employment as "labor" or "labor–management relations." In the past, U.S. Senate investigations (the 1963 McClellan Committee and the 1986 President's Council on Organized Crime) have found extensive Mafia involvement in the International Brotherhood of Teamsters (the Teamsters), the Hotel Employees and Restaurant Employees International Union (HEREIU), the Independent Laborers Association (ILA; now the International Longshoremen's Union), and the Laborers International Union of North America (LIUNA). In 1978, Congress passed the Inspector General Act and placed the labor racketeering enforcement program in the Office of the Inspector General in the U.S. Department of Labor (Labor OIG). The Labor OIG reports that the unions mentioned previously still account for a significant portion of its racketeering investigations (Office of the Inspector General, 2004).

The industries most susceptible to labor racketeering include maritime, construction, surface transportation, garment manufacturing, motion picture production, legal gambling, and hotel services. Although nearly 50% of the Labor OIG's racketeering investigations involve pensions and employee welfare benefit plans, the American Mafia also has been involved in loan sharking to employees and companies, gambling in the work setting, embezzlement, and extortion. Labor racketeering also includes the use of force or threats to obtain money for ensuring jobs or labor peace (Albanese, 2004, p. 8). If the Mob is not paid by workers, there will be no jobs available for laborers; conversely, if the company does not pay the Mafia, the gangsters there may initiate violence, strikes, or vandalism.

The New York Lucchese crime family made millions soliciting labor-peace payoffs from freight-forwarding and trucking companies at John F. Kennedy International Airport in New York (Jacobs, 1999, pp. 58–59). This crime family controlled the unions' management, threatening to have workers go on strike if payoffs to the Mob were not made. A five-month strike against Emery Worldwide (a freight-forwarding company) cost the company $20 million in revenues and forced it into bankruptcy. Through the unions, the Lucchese crime family also controlled affiliated jobs such as truck drivers, warehouse workers, dispatchers, and clerical workers. Jobholders kicked back money to the crime family to continue in their employment.

Because of the Mob's labor racketeering activities, these organized crime groups have been able to control certain other businesses. In New York, the five families have controlled the Fulton Fish Market, the Javits Convention Center, and even air cargo services at John F. Kennedy International Airport. At times, "legitimate" businessmen have willingly cooperated with their demands to obtain benefits such as decreased labor costs, inflated prices, or increased business. However, the practice of "shaking hands with the devil" has consequences. The Mafia may loan money to stockholders of companies that are in debt or that want to expand their businesses, only to then buy the same stock at a low price before it becomes available to investors on the stock market. Of course, the value of the stock is inflated so that the Mafia "investors" can sell their shares at excessive profits before the price of the stock eventually falls. Corruption and political influence are employed in concert with violence to conduct business and control legal enterprises or protect illegal enterprises.

Other Mob businesses include pornography distribution, interest in Las Vegas and Atlantic City casinos, the garment industry, trucking firms, and other businesses. At one time, 20% of the meat sold in the United States went through the New York meat market that was controlled by the Genovese, Gambino, and Lucchese families of New York. John Gotti, Jr., was president of Sampson Trucking Company. The Gambino family controlled ARC Plumbing Company, which had contracts with New York City valued at $20 million. Its control over unions, trucking, businesses, and other industries, in addition to its illegal enterprises, allowed the Mafia to rise to unprecedented power.

New Partnerships

As the era of the political machine has faded, the political influence and corruption impact of organized crime has declined. Mayors in Kansas City, New York, Philadelphia,

Chicago, and Boston were once associated with the Mafia, but such linkages are now rare. Competition from other organized crime groups has added to the alleged decline of Mafia activities and power. However, evidence exists that other organized crime groups are partnering with the Mafia in a variety of ways. The American Mafia has employed outlaw biker, Puerto Rican, Mexican, and Colombian gangs as part of its operations, for example. Mob taxes have been collected from rackets and operations from African American numbers (gambling) operations in large cities as well as from Russians operating in Brighton Beach, New York. Many of the major organized crime groups pay *tribute* (taxes) to the Mafia because of their access to corrupt judges, politicians, and businessmen. While those other organized crime groups may be the peers of the Mafia and have much larger memberships, the Mafia maintains an uncanny ability to control many of the illegal markets.

Russian gangsters, for example, have been involved as partners in large fuel scams with the Mafia. Both Colombian and Mexican DTOs have major ties to the Mafia, so the United States is just one of the countries named in the global activity of these alliances. The political influence of the Mafia has been demonstrated by its attempts to pass legislation that would widen avenues for illegal enterprises in states such as Louisiana. Although the goal of their activities is profit, political objectives are part of the Mafia's overall plan to achieve power and control over both legal and criminal markets—an approach that is highly attractive to other organized crime groups desiring to operate in the United States.

Investigative Strategies

From the 1980s to the present, the law enforcement response has had a tremendous impact on the Mafia. By 1990, as many as 1400 Mafia members, representing all of the families throughout the United States, had been sentenced to prison terms. Ranking Mafia members in Las Vegas, New Orleans, Chicago, Philadelphia, Cleveland, Boston, New Jersey, Las Vegas, Buffalo, and other cities have been convicted because of the diligent work of task and strike forces, creative use of legislation, and strong prosecution efforts.

Exposure: Informants and Witnesses

The acknowledgment of the existence of the Mafia was likely the beginning of its decline. The 1951 Kefauver Committee hearings exposed Mafia bosses Carlos Marcello and his friends, Santo Trafficante of Florida and Joe Savela of Dallas, Texas. The success of this effort brought a greater pressure from law enforcement and public demand for more effective legislation to deal with organized crime groups, including the Mafia. The 1963 McClellan hearing was one of many that intensely investigated the Mafia. The 1972 House Select Committee hearings reported that Mafia boss Marcello was a menace to the U.S. government and its citizens. The 1979 House Assassination Committee concluded that Mafia members Carlos Marcello, Santo Trafficante, and their associate Jimmy Hoffa were probably responsible for the assassination of John F. Kennedy. This increased publicity and exposure led to increased efforts to "turn" members against one another and persuade them to violate the code of omerta.

As stated earlier, the first Mafia member to break omerta and testify in public was Joseph "The Rat" Valachi, a soldier in New York who testified on national television during the McClellan hearings in 1963. His story is laid out in the 1968 book by Peter Maas, *The Valachi Papers*. Based on Valachi's testimony, Congress passed new laws, including the RICO statutes and Title III, which included the federal authority to conduct electronic surveillance or wiretaps (see Chapter 12).

Since Valachi's conviction, a number of Mafia members have become government witnesses in a bid to avoid lengthy prison sentences after their conviction. One tool of law enforcement in this regard is the federal Witness Security and Protection Program (WITSEC). More than 6000 witnesses and 14,000 dependents have entered this program. More importantly, this valuable program has resulted in as many as 10,000 major criminals being convicted, in part on the testimony of protected witnesses ("rats") who were given new identities and then relocated.

Unlike Valachi, Jimmy "The Weasel" Fratianno was a ranking Mafia member. Fratianno's testimony resulted in the convictions of Mafia members and led to charges against Mafia boss Frank Tieri—the first boss to be convicted under the RICO statutes (receiving income from the Mafia). This was an important milestone in the law enforcement strategy. After Tieri's trial, a number of Mafia members and bosses were indicted under RICO laws, including John Gotti, Jr., Nicky Scarfo, Paul Castellano, and many Gambino family members.

The Sammy "The Bull" Gravano saga illustrates the use of informants and Mafia members who turned into government witnesses. At the age of 16, Gravano dropped out of school and became a gang member. By age 25, he had killed his friend Joey Colucci, whereby he "made his bones" (committed murder) and became a made member of the Colombo family. Later, he left the Colombo family and became a Gambino family member. Gravano became close to Paul Castellano and began taking over a number of the gang's companies. As the underboss to John Gotti, Gravano knew everyone and was privy to many activities of the Mafia. In 1992, after being arrested on a variety of major criminal charges, he became a government witness and testified against his boss. His testimony resulted in the convictions of 4 bosses, 9 caporegimes, and 30 Mafia soldiers. The book *Underboss* by Peter Maas (1997) describes Sammy Gravano's story. Gravano's testimony in 1997 was vital to the conviction of the Genovese boss, Vincent Gigante.

The strategy of developing informants and witnesses demonstrates the power of strong laws to force even powerful Mafia members to cooperate and provide testimony that convicts their criminal peers.

Sting Operations

Sting operations are commonly used police tactics designed to catch suspects committing a crime. They rely on deception—for example, when a police officer or an informant acting as a police agent purchases drugs while pretending to be a user or supplier. Stings are used in a variety of police operational strategies, including those directed against auto thefts (using a bait car to catch a thief), prostitution (pretending to be johns or prostitutes), pornography (pretending to be seeking pornography), child molestation (pretending to be a child in an Internet chat room), and other crimes. The nature of the sting depends on the crime and the actors involved. These operations have been used successfully by law enforcement authorities against organized crime, including the American Mafia.

One sting operation was used against the powerful New Orleans boss, Carlos Marcello. Joseph Hauser was a con man involved in scams and frauds; after his arrest, however, Hauser became a government informant and a witness against the Mafia. Operation BRILAB (an acronym for bribery and labor) used Hauser in a 1979 FBI sting to develop a case on Marcello. In this scheme, insurance contracts were awarded by Marcello's corrupt contacts. Hauser and FBI agents acted in undercover roles and used wiretaps and surveillance to collect evidence that could be used about these contacts and Mafia members alike. This case resulted in Marcello, Larry Montague, and others being indicted for engaging in interstate travel for the purpose of racketeering, RICO violations, and mail and wire fraud. Had the contracts been received, Marcello would have received revenues of approximately $1 million per month from this scam. Hours of audio tapes plus the sworn testimony of Hauser and two FBI agents during an 18-week trial in 1981 ended in a conviction and a 12-year sentence for 72-year-old Marcello; later Marcello was also found guilty of bribing a federal judge in Los Angles.

Government Oversight

Historically, the conviction of one or more Mafia-controlled union officials had little effect on the long-term operation of a corrupt union and business, because the officials were merely replaced and "business as usual" continued. More recently, however, civil actions under RICO have allowed courts to use restraining orders, injunctions, and trusteeships to prevent racketeering; these means are also used to purge Mafia members and their associates from these unions and businesses and prevent them from gaining a foothold in the defendant organization (Jacobs, 1999, pp. 223–233). The trustee, who is typically appointed for a lengthy or indefinite term, oversees the operation of the union or business to prevent the return of Mafia members, which signals to the membership that there will be no return to the status quo. Any interference with or ignoring of the monitor's or trustee's orders can result in the union being held in contempt of the court's orders. Monitors and trustees have been appointed to oversee the operation of the Fulton Fish Market, the garment industry, waste hauling, and the trucking industry in New York City, for example.

Grand Juries and Legislation

Grand juries are panels of citizens called together by state and federal courts to hear evidence and determine whether criminal charges should be initiated. They also can serve an investigative function, with the extraordinary power of handing down subpoenas and conferring immunity on witnesses. A witness who lies to a grand jury can be charged with perjury, although a person can invoke his or her 5th Amendment right against self-incrimination in this setting. Investigative grand juries are one of the most effective tools a prosecutor can use against organized crime members. An organized crime member can be called before the grand jury, granted immunity, and then questioned about criminal activities, including the involvement of those persons higher up in the organization. If the Mob member lies, the charge is perjury. If the person refuses to answer after being granted immunity, the charge is contempt of court.

Attacking the Mafia requires law enforcement to not only deal with individuals or perhaps the entire criminal organization, but also the subculture that produces continued Mafia membership. Eliminating the role models for potential new members is essential to eliminate the attraction of this lifestyle. RICO, conspiracy, and CCE statutes continue to be used successfully in prosecutions of the upper ranks of the Mafia and have affected its subculture in detrimental ways.

Regulatory initiatives are effective administrative tools that have helped reduce Mafia control over such entities as waste disposal, inspection services, the construction industries, and the transportation system. Licensing entities must also be monitored to fight against bribery.

To have success against groups like LCN, the investigator must know who the players are, develop accurate and complete intelligence on the group and its activities, identify the leadership, know how they launder money and finance their operations, understand how and who they recruit and handle their membership, and develop an understanding of their methods of operation. Only the Russian Mafia and possible the Yakuza have organizations as complex and effective as LCN, and this sophistication presents a major challenge for law enforcement. Electronic and physical surveillance along with financial accounting and development of informants or sources of information are effective means of going up against LCN.

Conclusions

Although many Mafia bosses are now in jail or dead, the threat of organized crime run by these families remains palpable. Promises to remove the Mafia were made in the past by powerful politicians and prosecutors such as Dewey and Kennedy, yet the Mafia persists. No other organized crime entity has so successfully bridged the gap between the everyday world and the underworld. While still a potent organized crime group in the United States, the Mafia is now less powerful, in part because of progressive investigation and prosecution strategies.

There will always be debate over the structure, history, and method of operations of the Mafia. The successful investigator will discover the truth about these characteristics and activities of the Mafia in his or her jurisdiction, and develop effective strategies to deal with this criminal enterprise. Like other crime groups, the Mafia forms alliances with other organized crime groups and operates transnationally. It is learning from the mistakes of those members who have been killed or placed in prison, and will undoubtedly evolve into a more complex and secretive organization that will become even more indistinguishable from legitimate enterprises. The phrase "down, but not out" best describes the current state of the Mafia. Its future will likely be a repeat of the past, with the American Mafia adjusting to the new environment and continuing to survive.

Discussion Questions

1. Why has the Mafia been able to survive so long under intense pressure from law enforcement?

2. Why is the American Mafia considered unique relative to other organized crime groups?

3. Discuss the history of the Mafia in the United States.

4. Discuss the structure of the Mafia, and explain how it is susceptible to law enforcement efforts.

5. What are the major activities of the Mafia? How has law enforcement been successful against Mafia operations?

References

Albanese, J. S. (2004). *Organized Crime in Our Times* (4th ed.). Cincinnati, OH: Anderson.

Asbury, H. (1928). *The Gangs of New York: An Informal History of the Underworld.* New York: Thunder's Mouth Press.

Blok, A. (1974). *The Mafia of a Sicilian Village, 1860–1960.* New York: Harper and Row.

Bohn, K., & Arena, K. (July 16, 2008). Mafia Feels Heat from Feds, Crime Rivals. Retrieved June 20, 2010, from http://www.cnn.com/2008/CRIME/07/16.fbi.mob/index.html?iref=newssearch

D'Emilio, F. (2008, December 17). Alleged Mafia Boss Hangs Himself in Sicily Jail. Retrieved June 20, 2010, from http://www.foxnews.com/printer_wires/2008Dec17/0,4675,EUItalyMafia.00html

Feyerick, D., &Vinci, A. (2008, February 8). Reputed Mobsters Rounded Up in U.S. and Italy. Retrieved June 20, 2010, from http://www.cnn.com?2008/CRIME/02/08/gambino.arrest/iondex.html?iref=newssearch

Gambino, R. (2000). *Vendetta* (2nd ed.). Toronto, Canada: Doubleday.

Gambling and Organized Crime. (2009, June 23). *Journal of Gambling Issues, 23.* Retrieved June 20, 2010, from http://www.camh.net/egambling/issue23/pdfs/07turner.pdf

Gambling and Organized Crime. (2010, January 15). Retrieved June 25, 2010, from http://law.jrank.org/pages/1243/Gambling-Gambling-organized-crime.html

Guzzardo, J. (2008) 14 Alleged Members of Gambino Crime Family Charged. Retrieved June 20, 2010, from http://cnn.site.printthis.clickability.com/pt/cpt?action=cpt&title=14+alleged+members+of+

Jacobs, J. (1999). *Gotham Unbound: How New York City Was Liberated from the Grip of Organized Crime.* New York: New York University Press.

Lyman, M., & Potter, G. W. (2006). *Organized Crime* (4th ed.). Upper Saddle River, NJ: Prentice Hall.

Maas, P. (1968). *The Valachi Papers.* New York: Putman.

Maas, P. (1997). *Underboss: Sammy the Bull Gravano's Story of Life in the Mafia.* New York: Harper Collins.

McCain, N. (2010, March 24). Ex-mobsters Get Jail Time for Pattern of Racketeering. Retrieved June 25, 2010, from http://www.courthousenews.com/2010/03/24/25858.htm

Office of the Inspector General, U.S. Department of Labor. (2004). The Evolution of Organized Crime and Labor Racketeering Corruption. Retrieved November 20, 2006, from http://www.oig.dol.gov/public/reports/laborracpaper.pdf

Roemer, W. F. (1995). *Accardo: The Genuine Godfather.* New York: Donald I. Fine.

Talese, G. (1971). *Honor Thy Father.* New York: World Publishing.

U.S. Department of Labor, Office of the Inspector General. (2006). The OIG's Labor Racketeering Program. Retrieved November 20, 2006, from http://www.oig.dol.gov/laborracprogram.htm

Von Lampe, K. (2003). Criminally Exploitable Ties: A Network Approach to Organized Crime. In: E. Viano et al. (Eds.), *Transnational Organized Crime: Myth, Power and Profit.* Durham, NC: Carolina Academic Press.

Zambito, T. (2008, November 24). Bronx Sports Gambling Ring Led By Lucchese Family Member Busted. Retrieved June 25, 2010, from http://www.nydailynews.com/news/ny_crime?2008/11/24/2008-11-24_bron

Chapter 8
The Yakuza

Just when you think you've graduated from the school of experience, someone thinks up a new course.

— Mary H. Waldrip, journalist

Objectives

After completing this chapter, readers should be able to:

- Discuss the origins of the Yakuza and explain why they are important to the investigation and prosecution of Yakuza members.
- Identify the major Yakuza clans and describe their structure.
- Discuss the activities of the Yakuza and describe how this group differs from other organized crime groups.
- Explain the six sacred oaths and how they contribute to the success of the Yakuza.

Introduction

The term *Yakuza* is derived from a Japanese card game, *Oicho-Kabu*, which is played similarly to the American card game of blackjack. The goal in Oicho-Kabu is to obtain a score of 19. Because the words *ya* (8), *ku* (9), and *za* (3) sum to 20—a worthless hand in the game—the word "Yakuza" literally means "useless hands in society" (Haberman, 1985).

Believed to have originated in the early 1600s, the Yakuza group of organized crime now owns approximately $85 billion in assets and has approximately 150,000 members. Known for corporate extortion, gambling, prostitution, and drug trafficking, the Yakuza ranks among the most powerful and successful organized groups in the world. Like other organized crime groups, the Yakuza is considered a "shadow government" of Japan, and its alliances with other large organized crime groups makes it a threat to the global community. Although most of the 3000 Yakuza organizations are based in Japan, it is well established in the United States as well as in most of Asia and other countries. Hawaii and California, in particular, have experienced the impact of the Yakuza. As with other organized crime groups, expansion of Yakuza activities in the United States is anticipated.

Historical Perspective

Early Criminal Groups

The origins of the Yakuza can be traced back to the early 15th century, when the *Kabuki-mono* (crazy ones), who wore odd clothing and carried swords, were terrorizing their communities. Once the servants of Shōgun (*hatamota-yakko*), these eccentric *samuri* became unemployed during the Tokugawa (peace) era of Japan. As *Ronin* (masterless *Samurai* fighters), many became criminals who robbed villages to survive. These bands of outlaws assumed various names and developed a slang language of their own. The Yakuza have been described as "gangs or networks of adult male criminals who have structures of hierarchies and bosses similar to legitimate corporations and are involved in illegal, semi-illegal, and legal enterprises with strong ties to politicians" (Kersten, 1993).

The Yakuza, who are referred to by the Japanese government as *boryokudan* ("violent group"), deny their roots as Ronin or Kabuki-Mono. They believe that their ancestors were the *Machi-Yakko* (city servants), who were considered the people's heroes and defended them against the oppression of the Kabuki-Mono. To this day, many bosses and members believe that they live the way of *Ninkyo-do*, the myth describing how the Yakuza opposed the strong to help the weak. These groups are not homogenous, nor are they made up of blood relatives.

Other suggested origins of these underworld groups are that they consisted of traditional gamblers (*Bakuto*), street peddlers (*Tekiya*), political right-wing extremists (*Uyoku*), and common thugs (*Gurentai*). The common thread among these groups was a background of landless, poor misfits who where characterized as delinquents or worthless and violent. Although much of the history of the Yakuza is debatable, they did form "families," clans, or gangs with close relationships, wherein each member was seen as the protector of all other members.

The Tekiya are believed to have come from the *Yashi* (peddlers), who were traditionally traveling merchants of patent medicines. These outlaw merchants distanced themselves from the feudal caste system of Japan, forming groups for protection as well as to control lucrative markets. Considered deceptive merchants who often misrepresented the quality and origins of their products and preyed on poor and middle class by cheating them out of their money or goods, these groups or families formed relationships known as the *Oyabun-Kobun* (father–child role). The Kobun (child) became the servant and was loyal to the Oyabun (supreme boss). The Oyabun supervised the Kobun, controlling the goods and services that the family provided. These groups became influential in Japan's feudal system.

The Bakuto originated during the Tokugawa era, also known as the Edo period (1603–1867). These gamblers were alleged to have been employed by the government to gamble with workers to get back much of the wages they were paid. The Bakuto sponsored gambling games (gambling is illegal in Japan) and, in addition to owning legitimate banks, owned gambling houses and were involved in loan sharking and extortion.

Both the Bakuto and Tekiya criminal groups survived because of economic and political events until 1945.

The Industrial Age Through the Post–World War II Era

Industrialization of Japan allowed these criminal groups to ally with the capitalists, providing cheap labor and controlling labor through violence and threat. Also employed as strike breakers, these groups provided similar services as the U.S. La Cosa Nostra (LCN). This affiliation with the ultraconservative party led to the formation of the political right wing.

The Uyoku are the nationalists or political right and are anticommunist. Although they target large corporations, the Uyoku also have strong ties to politicians. This group is believed to have a pro-monarchist and anti-Western imperialistic philosophy. During the industrialization of Japan, the Yakuza began to create different secret organizations "that trained its members in warfare, languages, assassination, blackmail, etc." (Skold, 2002). Known as ultranationalists, their violence became more public. "They murdered two prime ministers, two finance ministers, attacked several politicians and industrialists" (Skold).

The Yakuza exploited Japan during the industrial and social changes of the late 19th and early 20th centuries. "They began recruiting heavily within the shipping and construction industry and also began to cooperate with authorities in return for more favorable treatment from police" (Murphy, 2001). Membership rose steadily until World War II. During the American occupation of Japan after the war, food was rationed, creating an enormous black market for the scarce goods. A new kind of Yakuza known as the *Gurentai* (street hustlers or hoodlums) arose, whose members were mostly former Japanese militia. Patterning themselves after the American gangster Al Capone, these groups used intimidation and extortion to achieve their profits. Just like the Italian Mafia, the Gurentai began to dress in dark suits and wear sunglasses.

After the war, the Allied Command liberated the Chinese and Korean captives, who had been held in Japan and used as slave labor during the war. The gangsters among the former captives initially controlled the black markets, but after many turf battles, the Gurentai took over. Eventually, the Bakuto, Teriya, Uyoku, and the Gurentai merged and became more powerful and much more diverse in their criminal activities. Between 1958 and 1963, the Yakuza ranks rose to 184,000, which was larger than the Japanese army. More than 5000 gangs in Japan jostled for positioning against one another. Epidemic violence and turf wars over profits resulted in a situation similar to the LCN wars in the United States (Kaplan & Dubro, 1986).

The Yakuza crime group was formalized in the early 1960s through the negotiations of Yoshio Kodama, a thug who during the war had been recruited to establish a spy network in northern China and was given the title of rear admiral by a grateful Japanese government. During those years, he also dealt in supplies (nickel, copper, cobalt, and heroin) and parlayed his company (*Kodama-Kikan*) into a $175 million enterprise. Kodama was considered a war criminal and a threat to the stability of the Allied-occupied post-war Japan, however; thus he was imprisoned, only to be released later. Upset over the ever-increasing violence, the Allied Command later asked Kodama, known as the "Godfather" of the Japanese underworld, to negotiate peace between all of the rival gangs. It was this alliance between Kazuo-Taoka of the Yamaguchi-gumi, Tosei-Kai (Hisayuki Michii, Korean crime boss), the Kanto-Kai, and the Inagawa-Kai factions that formed the Yakuza — the coalition that created peace among Japan's organized crime groups.

Yamaguchi-Gumi Crime Group

The largest and most powerful Yakuza group is the Yamaguchi-gumi. In 1902, this subgroup had more than 23,000 members. The third Oyabun of this faction, Kazuo Taoka, was responsible for much of its growth and power. The Yamaguchi-gumi was formed in 1915 in the Kobe area. Taoka ruled as a violent dictator, developing strong ties to politicians, which increased the success of the organization. Kobe Harbor, a main port of Japan, was controlled by Taoka labor forces, which led to the control of other harbors.

As with many organized crime groups, a split occurred within the Yamaguchi-gumi, with Hiroshi Yamamoto creating the Ichiwa-Kai syndicate, which became the third largest organized crime group in Japan. The syndicate of the Inagawa-Kai boss, Kakuji Inagawa, absorbed many of the old Bakuto.

Yoshinori Watanabe

Bosses became heroes in the public's eyes and were subjects of songs, movies, and media glamorization. The saga of Yoshinori Watanabe illustrates the rise of powerful bosses of the Yakuza.

The leader of the largest Yakuza clan (the Yamaguchi-gumi clan) is Yoshinori Watanabe. Born in 1941, Watanabe came from a huge family of farmers and a prosperous life. After finishing middle school, he worked in a Tokyo restaurant. He later moved to Kobe and became involved with the Yamaken-gumi gang, a subgroup of the Yamaguchi-gumi clan. When Watanabe joined the Yamaguchi-gumi sometime around 1960, its members were embroiled in a series of deadly turf wars (Amoruso, 2002). During this time, he began to show leadership skills, and the bosses began to take notice of him. He rose quickly through the organization after the war.

When the Yamaguchi-gumi clan began having troubles during the early 1980s, law enforcement thought this discord could be the end of the group. "They had lost their third boss in 1981 due to a heart attack, his successor to liver failure, and his eventual successor to assassins" (Amoruso, 2002). Watanabe became the fifth boss of the Yamaguchi-gumi in 1988 when the Yamaguchi-gumi were the largest Yakuza clan in Japan. During the 1980s, however, they split into two rival factions and lost power during the war that followed. Twenty-six members were killed during this war (Amoruso).

During the 1990s, Watanabe began to drastically change the structure of the Yamaguchi-gumi. The original centralized power structure was split into seven semi-autonomous regional groups, a move that made it more difficult for the police to penetrate the group, and made it easier for the leaders of the clans to control internal and external friction (Amoruso, 2002). Watanabe focused on developing new alliances with rival clans while strengthening others. The clan's offices expanded from 39 to 43 of Japan's 47 prefectures. By 1999, the Yamaguchi-gumi had 165,000 full-time members, which is five times the size of the entire U.S. Mafia at its peak in the 1950s (Amoruso).

Under Watanabe's leadership, the Yamaguchi-gumi survived the Japanese depression and the government's crackdown on organized crime. Other Yakuza clan bosses and members were jailed, and the police scrutiny and economic recession that followed caused many members to shift alliances. "The Yamaguchi-gumi grabbed what was left and managed to muscle in on the new economy" (Amoruso, 2002).

Because Watanabe was the most powerful Yakuza boss, police attempts to attack him met with little success. Distancing himself from the crimes of his group, he helped raise money and get out the vote for scores of politicians. Because of Watanabe's political power, it was believed that the police could do little to stop him unless they took on his political allies, too.

According to some sources, Watanabe is a simple man who lifts weights, avoids rich foods, and jogs. He likes to hike and ski and was an "avid student of Chinese history and Japanese's law" (Amoruso, 2002). He enjoys karaoke, and is especially fond of the music from the movie *The Godfather*. Some sources suggest that he sees himself as a public servant who helped losers who could not hold down a regular job. "Since the Yakuza provides work for such people, and helps keep their frustration in check, or at least directed mainly at one another, he thinks of it as a pragmatic solution to an intractable problem" (Amoruso). Watanabe considered that the alternative to the Yakuza solution of keeping these people in check was disorganized crime.

Yakuza Mergers

In the wake of ever more successful struggles by police to control the Yakuza's activities, by the mid-1960s smaller groups were absorbed by larger groups such as the Yamaguchi-gumi, Sumiyoshi-Kai, and the Ingawa-Kai as they sought to survive; more than 60% of Yakuza members belonged to one of these three groups at one time. *Koiki* ("wide area")

TABLE 8-1 Criminal Groups Operating as Yakuza in 1992

Clan or Group	Approximate Membership
Yamaguchi-gumi	23,100
Sumiyoshi-Kai	8,000
Inagawa-Kai	7,400
Aizu Kotetsu	1,600
Kudo-rengo Kusano-ikka	600
Okinawa Kyokurya-kai	570
Dojin-kai	510
Kyokyryu-kai	430
Aida-ikka	370
Kyosei-kai	330
Kozakura-ikka	190
Asano-gumi	150
Yamano-kai	100
Ishikawa-ikka	100
Soai-kai	80
Shinwa-kai	80

Source: Data are from Keiza, N. (1993). "Anti-gang law wracks mob ranks." *The Nikkei Weekly*

is the term police used to characterize their large criminal operations. These groups became extremely powerful because they operated both legal and illegal enterprises. By 1992, 16 groups were named by the police under a new law against Japanese organized crime to help target Yakuza members for arrest and prosecution (Act for the Prevention of Unlawful Activities by Boryukudan Members). Totaling 43,960 members, these groups are defined in **Table 8-1**.

In recent years, organized crime crackdowns have resulted in a 70% increase in serious crime in Japan, with the arrest rate falling from 90% to 70%. Corruption is rampant, however, as scandals and cover-ups have plagued law enforcement agencies (Amoruso, 2002).

Yakuza Today

Modern Yakuza members are more economically motivated and materialistic than the early Yakuza. Research on members indicates that most Yakuza are high school dropouts. The majority join this group because of the perceived glamour and monetary success of Yakuza organizations. Many members were delinquents and involved in drug use (Uchiyama, 1989).

The Yakuza have been active in the United States since the mid-1950s. It is likely that the Yakuza factions will operate in the United States in a similar fashion as they have in Japan. However, these groups are fluid and dynamic, and continue to evolve both in their legal and illegal enterprises. Notably, Yakuza activity in the United States has increased since the 1990s as members of this group have sought to take advantage of the arms trade potential and lucrative investments in areas such as real estate. One Yakuza entity, Rondlan Doyuki, is alleged to own stock in a number of U.S. corporations, including Chase Manhattan, Citicorp, IBM, Dow Chemical, Bank of America, General Motors, Atlantic Richfield, and Sperry. Many believe that the major activity in the United States by the Yakuza is money laundering. These groups are extremely active in California, Hawaii, New York, and Nevada.

There is good reason to believe that these enterprising groups will continue to expand their operations in the United States and other countries as they overcome the culture and language barriers. Intelligence reports indicate that meetings between major organized crime groups from many countries have occurred to discuss how to divide areas where more profits and less turmoil are possible. The Yakuza's history has resulted in diversity in their criminal operations, which include prostitution, child pornography, gambling, entertainment, liquor distribution, drugs, arms, money laundering, and extortion (Tuohy, 2000). The Koiki-Boryokudan faction, for example, has made alliances with other global organized crime groups such as the Chinese Snake Head, South American drug cartels, and Russian organized crime groups, and has expanded its operations into most of Asia, the United States, and Australia.

The Yakuza remain active in Japan as well as other countries and are considered a major threat to governments. Violence linked to this group continues to plague Japan. CNN reported the death of Takashi Ishizuka of the Sumiyoshi-kai clan by a gunman dressed in a dark suit, face mask, and sunglasses. At the time of his murder, Ishizuka was being treated in Nippon Medical School Hospital after being shot in the stomach on the streets of Tokyo. The assailant shot him through a window as Ishizuka lay in his hospital bed, where he was guarded by the police. He was shot several times in the head in what is believed to be a gang-related crime. According to the CNN report, Japan's Yakuza clans earn billions from extortion, protection rackets, gambling, drugs and other kickback schemes ("Yakuza Boss Shot Dead in Hospital Bed," 2002).

Another clan leader was convicted in the shooting death of Mayor Iccho Ito of Tokyo, who was campaigning for reelection to his fourth term. Tetsuya Shiroo, a reported clan boss of the Yamaguchi-gumi clan, was allegedly angry over the city's refusal to compensate him after his car was damaged at a public construction site (Kageyama, 2008).

In other activity related to the Yakuza, the University of California–Los Angeles (UCLA) received a donation of $100,000 from a suspected Japanese mob boss. Some believe that other donations for transplants have occurred and involved other clan bosses (Spak, 2008). These reports are a good indication that the Yakuza is alive and well and will continue to exist as it has for hundreds of years.

Structure and Organization

Membership

Each Yakuza group consists of a highly structured leadership that is pyramidal and stratified. This "boss and his henchmen" structure is based on the Oyabun-Kobun (father–child) relationship, in which the Kumicho or Oyabun is head of the clan (parent) and his followers are the Kobun (children). These clans consist of members with quasi-blood relationships, similar to the structure of the old Japanese feudal system. Subgroups are formed under each boss. The *Saiko-Komon* is a senior advisor who has advocates, accountants, bookkeepers, and his own gang of "children." The *Waka-Gashira* is the number two man of the clan in authority and carries out orders from the Oyabun. The *Kyodai* (older brother) has a boss referred to as the *Shatei-Gashira,* who has a higher rank than the Waka-Gashira but less authority. Younger brothers are called *Shatei* and junior leaders are known as *Wakashu.* The children can be leaders over their own gangs. Thus the clan becomes a large group with many subfamilies. All members must obey their leader, under threat of punishment for disobedience ("Yakuza," 2000). **Figure 8-1** shows the Yakuza ranking system.

The structure of the Sumiyoshi-Kai differs from the other Koiki-Boryokudan in that it has a conglomerate structure, in which several bosses of the top Yakuza groups form a federation with an elected president.

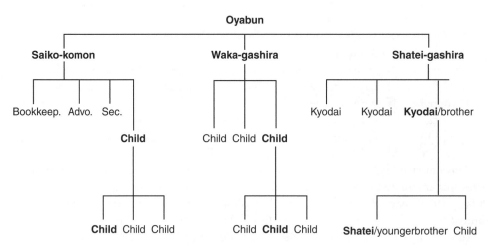

Figure 8-1   Organizational chart for some clans of the Yakuza.

Code of Conduct and Oaths

All groups are very traditional and must abide by a code of conduct, which demands loyalty to bosses and honored nondisclosure of the secrets of the Yakuza. Four types of sanctions may be applied for breaking these rules. The most severe punishment is lynching for serious offenses as viewed by the boss. *Yubitsume* is the amputation of the fingers at the joints — this bakuto custom signifies a weakening of the hand, which at one time meant that the member's ability to handle a sword was diminished. Yubitsume is performed as an act of apology to the boss, and the amputated finger is presented to the boss as a constant reminder of the error of the offending member. Currently, yubitsume is rarely practiced. The third form of sanction is *zetsuem*, which is the severing of the relationship between the boss and the offender. The offender may return to his former Yakuza gang after a period of time. The last sanction, *hamon*, is where the offender is removed from all Yakuza membership forever.

The Yakuza include both members (*Kumin*) and associates (*jun-Kumin*). The Kumin are initiated into the clan by a ritual involving the exchange of sake (rice wine) cups to symbolize entry into the family and the father–child relationship. This ritual takes on a religious appearance and often is performed at a Shinto shrine or altar (Kaplan, 1986). In the Yakuza initiation ceremony, the sake symbolizes blood. The Oyabun and the initiate sit face-to-face as their sake is prepared by *azukarinin* (guarantors). Mixed with salt and fish scales, the sake is then carefully poured into cups and the Oyabun's cup is filled to the brim, befitting his status, while the initiate gets much less. They drink a bit and then exchange cups, and each drinks from the other's cup, sealing the Kobun's commitment to the family. From that moment on, even the Kobun's wife and children must take a backseat to his obligations to his Yakuza family.

New members are required to abide by six sacred oaths:

- Never reveal the secrets of the organization.
- Never violate the wife or children of another member.
- Do not withhold money from the clan.
- Do not fail to obey supervisors.
- Do not become involved with narcotics.
- Do not appeal to the law or the police.

The similarity between the Yakuza culture and the LCN culture of omerta/oaths and rules for members and associates is obvious. Like other organized crime groups, the Yakuza began as a group to provide protection from government or landowners and communities, but later became corrupted by greed and power. Nevertheless, the image of the Yakuza as outlaw hero persists among many members and the public, who see little wrong in who they are and what they do.

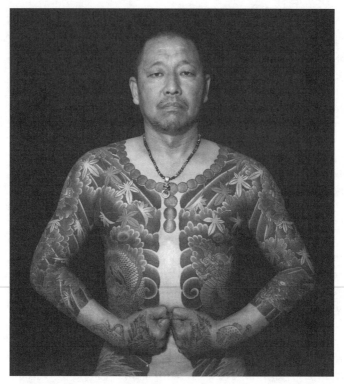

Example of Yakuza-style tattoos.

The older Yakuza system was an apprenticeship in which the Kobun (child) would be trained by a member in the techniques of the occupation and criminal subculture of service to the clan. The clan is bound together by the traditions, rituals, and the concepts of *Ikka* (whole family; Kaplan & Dubro, 1986). The Yakuza display both *Otoki* (masculinity) and *Kao* (face, meaning "respect"). The Bakuto also use the body suit style of tattooing the body. In the past, criminals in Japan were marked by a tattoo around an arm for each offense. Illegal until 1948 and still considered shameful by most Japanese, the tattoo became a symbol of strength and masculinity among organized criminals, and identified the Yakuza as a misfit. (This practice is similar to the tattoos of U.S. outlaw motorcycle gang members.) The tattooing of the entire body and missing finger joints can easily identify some Yakuza members.

The Yakuza have numerous ceremonies that are required under the concept or ethics of *Giri*, which requires them to honor and proclaim their clan name. These ceremonies are held to celebrate or mourn an event. All Yakuza are required to attend and contribute money. The ethics of Ninkyo-do were practiced more by the older Yakuza than by the now materialistic Yakuza or Keizal Yakuza, who have done away with many of the old rituals and traditions (French, 2001). Japanese youth have become much like their Western counterparts, who are individualistic and materialistic as well as opposed to the degree of service demanded of apprenticeship.

All members are required to pay a membership fee and contribute money during ceremonies. The huge amount of money going to the boss may allow him to prosper without having to be involved in criminal activity, which insulates him from arrest and prosecution while assuring him control over his group. Much of the recruiting of members is done in martial arts clubs, in boxing clubs, and among misguided youth seeking avenues for success. Today's young Yakuza are more street thugs than their warrior ancestors. Group members are promoted based on the amount of money they contribute to the bosses and organization. Once a younger member reaches a certain rank (usually Shatei), he can establish his own "children" (gang). By this method, the clan can grow into the thousands in membership. All members obey their gang leaders, and everyone obeys the Oyabun.

The group that most mirrors the origin of criminal groups such as LCN is the Gurentai, who took economic advantage of the chaos and confusion in Japan after World War II. These thugs excelled by using threats, violence, and corruption to control the black markets, labor, and gambling.

Unlike other organized crime groups, the Yakuza do have ultranationalistic, conservative, and anticommunist political ideologies. Their long-term, rather peaceful relationship with the police is beginning to crumble, however, because of the changing laws of Japan and public opinion. Unlike other organized crime groups, the Yakuza maintain a very public image and presence. The headquarters of the clans are well marked with the symbol of the clan. Each clan has a distinct symbol that is worn as a label on the black suits that have become their uniform. Displayed as power symbols, the pins and tattoos are signals for rivals and victims to give them respect and fear. Investigators of Yakuza clans should become familiar with the symbols of Yakuza members to identify and trace their movements and activities.

Most clan headquarters are very elaborate and are technologically advanced, as both their means of physical and electronic security are prominently displayed. Well-armed guards are obvious to the public and police.

Concerned with their own image and that of their cities and country, the Yakuza often contribute to good causes and offer or provide assistance in times of disaster. By ingratiating themselves with the public, the Yakuza hope to hamper enforcement of the new laws of Japan. At the same time, they have used violence to maintain their image when portrayed in an unfavorable manner in a movie. Yakuza still portray themselves as protectors of society's weaker members by maintaining a code of honor and exhibiting chivalry. Many in law enforcement believe that Yakuza associates—who may outnumber Yakuza members by 10 to 1—are the most serious threat posed by the clans because they maintain a low profile and are more difficult to identify. Given their diversity, long history of survival, extensive blending into legitimate businesses, and ability to adjust to change, the structure of the Yakuza will likely survive and continue to expand globally.

Activities and Methods of Operation

The Yakuza traditionally operated wherever a Japanese population was found. They followed Japanese immigrants to establish operations in places such as Hawaii, California, and Australia's Gold Coast. An estimated 80% of their revenue comes from illegal activities. However, they are rapidly becoming developers as they amass vast real estate holdings. Their objective appears to be becoming more legitimate by investing their illegal profits into legal businesses—a plan that will even further diminish the ability of law enforcement to identify members and their operations. In addition to their traditional partnerships with Chinese Triads, the Yakuza have formed alliances with both Korean and Vietnamese gangs in California and possibly other U.S. states.

Business Acquisition

A typical approach to taking over a business is to visit the owner of a Japanese business involved in tourism and offer to steer large numbers of people to the business in return for a percentage of the profits. If the owner refuses, group members resort to threats or violence, which eventually concludes with the Yakuza owning the business.

Protection and Extortion

Another tradition of Yakuza is the protection and extortion racket. Members provide "protection" in exchange for money, working as bouncers or security in bars, restaurants, gaming houses, and other sites. Most owners pay the money and do not report the extortion for fear of reprisal.

Gambling

Like LCN and other organized crime groups, the Yakuza have filled the public's demand for illegal services and products. Gambling is a long tradition of the Bakuto faction and continues to be a source of its revenue. Horse racing, bicycle racing, and a variety of other sports betting, along with loan sharking and book-making, offer the Yakuza a steady source of revenue.

An Oyabun who testified at the President's Commission on Organized Crime in 1984 described the structure and activities of the Yamaguchi-gumi and the Sumiyoshi-rengo. He told the Commission that the clans try to identify any company having financial difficulty and then develop elaborate plans to take it over. By employing threats and entering fraudulent contracts with the company, the Yakuza ensure that the company eventually fails because of profits directed into the clan's coffers. Other methods of business takeover include actions by the Sokaiya (thugs), who specialize in disrupting stock markets and stockholders' meetings.

One of the more powerful groups of Sokaiya is the Rondan Doyukai. They have been very successful in Japan, where most stockholders decide it is less expensive to pay them off rather than risk the negative impact these groups can have on a company's stability. These groups have operated in the United States by targeting large corporations such as Chase Manhattan, Bank of New York, Bank of America, IBM, General Motors, and a number of Japanese-owned banks, investment firms, and other companies. They normally begin by attending a stockholder meeting and introducing themselves as "your Japanese stockholders" and offer their praise of the company, wish them luck, and then leave.

The United States is a viable target for the Yakuza, given the more than $80 billion in trade that occurs each year between the United States and Japan. The Yakuza may resort to using force to take over major stock positions in corporate entities within the United States and Japan. They make millions of dollars annually through corporate extortion, with the Sokaiya (shareholders' meeting men) being the masters of this enterprise. Sokaiya will buy a small number of shares in a company so that they can attend shareholders' meetings. In preparation for the meeting, they gather damaging information about the company and its officers. Secret mistresses, tax evasion, unsatisfactory working conditions, and pollution—all of these sordid details represent opportunities for the Sokaiya. The Sokaiya then contact the company's corporate management and threaten to disclose whatever embarrassing information they have at the shareholders' meeting unless they are "compensated." If management does not give into their demands, the Sokaiya go to the shareholders' meeting and raise a ruckus, shouting down anyone who is to speak, making a boisterous display of their presence, and shouting out their damaging revelations. In Japan, where people fear embarrassment and shame far more than physical threat, executives usually give the Sokaiya whatever they want. While this practice has been outlawed by the Japanese government, verified reports demonstrate that this strategy is still prevalent; indeed, such activities of the Yakuza are well documented in American *Fortune* 500 corporations. This mastered craft is providing a lucrative entrance into the legitimate businesses of the United States to an extent that is unfathomable by U.S. law enforcement authorities.

Narcotics Trafficking

By far, the largest revenue source of the Yakuza is drug trafficking. Stimulants such as amphetamines and methamphetamines are in high demand in Japan, and the Yakuza are the primary suppliers of these illegal substances. Intelligence indicates that the Yakuza are involved in cocaine distribution as well. If this allegation is true, an alliance with the Colombian cartels as well as other groups such as Chinese organized crime may be a reality.

As early as the 1930s, Harry Anslinger, then Director of the Federal Bureau of Narcotics (now DEA), warned that Japanese gangs were major world suppliers of illicit "white drugs," referring to morphine and heroin. Japanese morphine was seized from Japanese immigrants in the 1930s in Hawaii, Washington, and Oregon. Although World War II interrupted the Japanese drug supply, it is not surprising that their drug trafficking operations in the United States have resumed.

Pornography

Hard-core pornography is prohibited in Japan, where it is illegal to sell photographs or films showing human genitalia. Of course, whenever any kind of prohibitions are put in place, a public demand creates huge profits for the enterprising criminal. Women from the United States and other countries are often imported into Japanese crime circles for prostitution or pornography purposes, either willingly or by subterfuge. U.S. fronts have been created using English-speaking Yakuza agents, who place enticing advertisements for actors, singers, and dancers, offering auditions in Japan. Once the woman is in Japan, the job requirements change to prostitution or servitude. Those who are trapped cannot earn enough money to return to their home country and so become permanent employees of the Yakuza. Often these women act as hostesses (prostitutes) in the Yakuza clubs, where Japanese men will pay large fees for sex with a Western woman. The Los Angeles Police Department (LAPD) has reported that hundreds of women fall victim to this type of exploitation.

Sex tours for Japanese men with nude dancing and prostitution are also offered by Yakuza-owned facilities. These facilities are located in many countries, including the United States.

Weapons and Smuggling

Another enterprise of the Yakuza is the arms business. American-made firearms and ammunition are 10 times more valuable in Japan than in the United States. Although firearms are not part of the Japanese tradition of swords and knives, many gangs and clans in Japan have become quite heavily armed. Clans often corrupt military personnel and entice them to supply weapons, in addition to seeking out the purchase and smuggling of weapons by American civilians.

As with the narcotics trade, the methods of smuggling are inventive and have a high success rate in ensuring that the illicit goods reach Japan, where the weapons are then sold to gangs. The United States is not the sole supplier of firearms, however; other countries are becoming involved in this trade. With the fall of the Soviet Union and the globalization of Russian organized crime groups, it may be that alliances between the Russians and Yakuza have formed based on the drug and weapons markets. Intelligence indicates that the Yakuza are becoming more involved in the global transportation industry, which certainly will affect their ability to move illicit goods from country to country.

Money Laundering

Money laundering goes hand-in-hand with profits from the Yakuza's diverse legal and illegal operations. Some methods involve washing the money through high-volume cash businesses such as bars, construction companies, trucking or transportation companies, restaurants, and tourist gift shops. Japanese bankers are often reluctant to cooperate with law enforcement in stemming this practice because of threats and intimidation. Many bank executives are either employed by the Yakuza or recruited to become members of the organization. When the Yakuza own their own financial institutions, concealing the source and existence of their illegal funds is not difficult. Money can be transferred anywhere, anytime.

The Yakuza continue to explore new avenues of revenue as well as ways to improve their image, while simultaneously expanding operations. Insider stock trading and attempts to purchase or develop casinos in the United States have been documented. Japanese businessman, Ryoichi Sasakawa, who was alleged to have ties to the Yakuza, and his son, Takashi, had been involved in investments in the United States. The father had contributed money to U.S. universities, institutes, and even the presidential library of Jimmy Carter, who publicly praised the work of Sasakawa. Internationally, Sasakawa financed the United States–Japan Foundation with a $48 million endowment; made donations to the Nippon Foundation and World Health Organization, among others; and was generous to disaster relief agencies and environmental causes. Some believe these moves are intended to enhance his image, which is a typical ploy of those who live the lifestyle of the upper-echelon Yakuza.

In still another effort to expand Yakuza operations, a Tokyo real estate firm, West Tsusho, led by Ishii Susumu, boss of the Inagawa-Kai clan, purchased two U.S. companies. In 1991, *Time* magazine reported that West Tsusho purchased Quantum Access and Asset Management International Financing and Settlement with the help of Prescott Bush, Jr., brother of then President George H. W. Bush. Prescott Bush received a $250,000 fee, but reportedly was unaware of the connection of West Tsusho to the Yakuza.

Investigative Strategies

Many members of the Yakuza have been arrested during their criminal careers in Japan, and some members and associates have been arrested in the United States and other countries. Payments to Sokaiya are now an illegal practice in Japan; however, there is evidence that the Yakuza are still employing this method of extortion. In the late 1990s, the banking industry of Japan suffered a major financial disaster when it made bad loans to Yakuza members and bosses, who then refused to repay the loans. Efforts to collect these loans resulted in the death of at least one banker and an executive of another financial institution (Kaplan, 1998). These bad investments hurt the Yakuza in their wallets as well as their image. Companies are now reluctant to deal with the Yakuza because of their financial history and the violence associated with the groups. It appears that the financial difficulties due to their loss of face and the new anti-Boryokudan law have resulted in a more desperate and violent Yakuza.

Laws and Statutes

The Boryokudan Countermeasures Law of 1992 defined the Yakuza as an organization that uses violence to commit illegal acts (National Criminal Justice Reference Center, 2000). This legislation, which places strict restrictions on Yakuza activity, actually designated clans as targeted for law enforcement arrest for their style of extortion. The following acts of the clans are prohibited under the law:

- Demanding gifts
- Demanding subcontract jobs
- Demanding *mikajime* (muscle fee)
- Demanding protection money
- Collecting on high-interest loans
- Demanding exemption from loans or financial obligations
- Demanding loans
- Demanding that security brokers conduct credit transactions
- Demanding that companies and others purchase certain stock
- Demanding payment for return of evacuated land and buildings that are subject to public auction
- Illegally assembling on property
- Engaging in extortion by taking advantage of a person's weak points
- Demanding money on fraudulent facts
- Intervening in court cases or out-of-court case settlements

These restrictions provide insight into the activities of the Yakuza and should be part of the investigative strategy. The Japanese law also restricts gangs from recruiting juveniles to join them by coercing, threatening, or enticing the youths.

The United States can expect the Yakuza to employ similar tactics and must be prepared for expanded operations within its borders. Specialized law enforcement groups such as the LAPD Asian Task Force must be trained and established throughout the country, especially in areas with large populations of Japanese Americans. Although Yakuza activities in the United States may be difficult to distinguish from legitimate enterprise, the law enforcement community must be trained, educated, staffed, and equipped to investigate corporate America. The current successful investigations of Enron, WorldCom, and others are indicative of the government's ability to take on this type of criminal activity. Changes in the statutes and laws in many countries are also needed to ensure U.S. cooperation with other countries. Money laundering violations, RICO, drug laws, and conspiracy statutes must be created to address the nature of criminal organizations such as the Yakuza.

Special Task Forces

On numerous occasions, Peter Lamb of the National Crime Authority of Australia has stated that law enforcement is playing catch-up and must form teams capable of dealing with the economic and complex crimes of the Yakuza. Task forces need forensic accountants, attorneys, experts, analysis, and innovative techniques to address this crime organization. As with many other organized crime groups, the Yakuza's new tool for moving money is the Internet. Law enforcement must develop expertise in dealing with transnational crime to curtail such activities.

Because the Yakuza quickly adapt to pressure from law enforcement and can develop new modes of operation, simply taking out the leaders is not enough. There is always a replacement who lusts for the power and money offered by being boss of a clan, and who is willing to do anything to get to that position. Centuries of Yakuza history attest to the group's uncanny ability to survive. Global cooperation is needed to deal successfully with this confederation of gangsters. Law enforcement must be able to cross national boundaries and attack the groups where they live. The new criminal alliances between Colombian, Chinese, Russian, Yakuza, and other organized crime groups must be broken.

Follow the Money

Yakuza are now investing in real estate and corporate America. The economic benefits of U.S. investments were close to what the Yakuza had enjoyed in Japan, until bad loans and the economic slump seriously damaged their profit margins. The United States cannot afford to allow these investments to continue. Members and leaders of the Yakuza, along with their assets, must be identified, targeted for investigation, and prosecuted to the fullest extent of the law. Following the money from illegal enterprises such as arms trafficking, sex-related enterprises, and drug trafficking to the legal enterprises must be a priority of U.S. police and their foreign law enforcement counterparts. Sting operations or reverse undercover operations that have been successful against other organized crime groups, such as the Medellín and Cali cartels of Colombia and the Mafia in Italy and the United States, also may be effective against the Yakuza.

More international agreements such as the Council of Europe's *Convention on Laundering, Search, Seizure, and Confiscation of the Proceeds of Crime* (also known as the Strasburg Convention), which was signed in 1990 and went into effect in 2001, are necessary (reported by the *Brama News* and *Community Press*, December 1, 2002; National Criminal Justice Reference Center, 2000). These agreements require that each nation adopt legislation creating the criminal offense of money laundering of funds from serious crime. Attacking the assets of the Yakuza is a proven strategy that must be developed further. Financial institutions and banks that assist organized crime groups such as the Yakuza are known to law enforcement (e.g., in Hong Kong, Switzerland, and the Cayman Islands) and must become targets of investigations. These semi-legal enterprises collect fees as high as 20% in exchange for laundering millions with very little risk of prosecution. The Yakuza process their profits through layers of complex financial transactions to conceal the sources of that illicit income. The use of net worth, source, and application financial analysis can identify unexplained income of members of the Yakuza. Reconstruction of expenditures versus income will allow investigators to form plans to legally pursue charges for money laundering, income tax violations, and reporting violations.

Conclusions

The Yakuza may be the most effective organized crime group that invests its illicit profits into legitimate business. Corrupting legitimate business is probably the most serious threat posed by groups such as the Yakuza. U.S. law enforcement authorities must overcome the language and cultural barriers to develop intelligence related to this group that is credible, accurate, and timely.

Past performance is a predictor of future activity of the Yakuza. Although the players change, the activities, structure, and patterns of these gangsters remain fairly constant. The dual goals of intelligence are both tactical and strategic. Intelligence leads to effective plans, actions, and decisions. Investigators must identify the Yakuza goals, methods of operation, and structure as group members operate in the United States. This intelligence can provide an assessment of the level of threat and the nature of expansions, violence, and aggressiveness of the Yakuza. A proactive approach needs to be developed using solid tactical and strategic intelligence. Investigators must increase their understanding of the relationships between the many global organized crime groups to determine how they communicate, where they meet, how they operate, and how and where the money flows.

Physical surveillance, undercover operations, electronic surveillance, and informants are the major tools of investigations of organized crime. The properly managed and developed informant is perhaps the ultimate source of information regarding organized crime. Charts produced by analysis of this information are invaluable to both plan and develop courtroom presentations. Financial analysis is particularly effective in money laundering investigations. Both commodity and event flow analysis give an instant understanding of how the organization operates. Communication analysis offers strategies for capturing and providing evidence to obtain court orders for electronic surveillance. Electronic surveillance provides evidence of violations that can be prosecuted under RICO and CCE statutes, conspiracy, money laundering, and many other criminal acts. Note that experts are often needed to break codes or ciphers and explain conversations captured or recorded during electronic surveillance.

Major laws and statutes such as the Organized Crime Act of 1970, Money Laundering Act of 1986, various controlled substance acts, and conspiracy statutes such as RICO must be understood by the criminal investigator who takes on the Yakuza. Standardized and innovative training and education must be utilized by law enforcement to catch up to the complex operations of the Yakuza. Language fluency and a deep knowledge of the Japanese culture and history are crucial.

The Yakuza will continue to evolve into a more complex and sophisticated organization as the group seeks to maintain its level of profit and success. This Japanese criminal organization will continue to form and strengthen alliances with other organized crime groups, and employ corruption and violence to protect its operations. International drug trafficking, gambling, and the sex trade will always be part of the illicit operations of the Yakuza, but the infiltration of legitimate business may pose an even more serious threat to the United States. Determining how the Yakuza launder their money may be more difficult than developing other types of criminal cases. The money trail is complex, and it requires team efforts by well-trained and equipped law enforcement to unravel its intricacies. Complex infrastructures of large numbers of people make up the overall structure of the Yakuza, so the successful investigation of this organization will require a dynamic law enforcement response by well-trained, globally cooperative, and highly technical investigators.

The Yakuza may well prove to be more threatening to the United States than the American Mafia and drug cartels. Their ability to infiltrate legitimate business and governments is well documented, and their money laundering operations and real estate investments may expand to pose a serious threat to the economic stability of United States and other nations. The Yakuza also will continue to form alliances with other organized crime groups, which will make them even more of a challenge. As early as 1988, the Yakuza had a gross income of more than $10 billion per year (Skold, 2002). In the near future, members probably will operate more like underground or "shadow figures" while expanding their operations to move more deeply into economic crime and appear less like the traditional Yakuza.

Because of the lack of verifiable intelligence and penetration by law enforcement, much remains unknown about the current state of Yakuza organized crime. The challenge for law enforcement is to develop current and accurate information about the structure and activities of today's Yakuza. Although the Yakuza are not currently as much as an ingrained part of the government of Japan as in the past, the group remains a major transnational organized criminal organization with a large membership that has moved more underground. It represents yet another major threat to a number of governments worldwide, including the United States.

Discussion Questions

1. Discuss the origins of the Yakuza. Why are they important to the investigation and prosecution of Yakuza members?

2. Who are the major Yakuza clans? What is their structure?

3. Why do you think the Yakuza has been so resilient to efforts to arrest and prosecute its members? What does the future hold for the Yakuza?

4. Discuss the activities of the Yakuza. How does this organized crime group differ from other organized crime groups such as the DTOs or the LCN?

5. What are the six sacred oaths and how do they contribute to the success of the Yakuza? How are these oaths similar to rules of other organized crime groups?

6. What do you believe are the most effective enforcement tools against the Yakuza?

References

Amoruso, D. A. (2002). Yoshinori Watanabe. *Gangsters, Incorporated*. Retrieved June 20, 2006, from http://gangstersinc.tripod.com/Watanabe.html

French, J. W. (2001, October 4). Even in Ginza, Honor Among Thieves Crumbles. *New York Times*. Retrieved April 20, 2011, from http://www.nytimes.com/2001/10/10/world/tokyo-journal-even-in-ginza-honor-among-thieves-crumbles.html?src=pm

Haberman, C. (1985, February 6). TV Funeral for Japan's Slain Godfather. *New York Times*. Retrieved April 20, 2011, from http://www.nytimes.com/1985/02/01/world/tv-funeral-for-japan-s-slain-godfather.html

Kageyama, Y. (May 26, 2008). Alleged Gangster Convicted in Mayor Shooting. Retrieved June 24, 2010, from http://www.foxnews.com/wires/2008May26/0,4670,JapanMayorShoo

Kaplan, D. (1986). *Yakuza: The Explosive Account of Japan's Criminal Underworld*. Reading, MA: Addison-Wesley.

Kaplan, D. (1998, April 13). Yakuza Inc. *U.S. News and World Report*. Retrieved November 14, 2006, from http://www.usnews.com/usnews/biztech/articles/980413/archive_003691.htm

Kaplan, D. E., & Dubro, A. (1986). *Yakuza*. Reading, MA: Addison-Wesley.

Kersten, J. (1993). Street Youth, Bosozokoy and Yakuza: Subculture Formation and Societal Reactions in Japan. *Crime and Delinquency, 39*, 277–295.

Murphy, D. (2001). *Things Japanese: Yakuza*. Yamasa, Japan: Achi Center for Japanese Culture. Retrieved June 20, 2006, from http://www.Yamasa.org/acjs/network/english/newsletter/ThingsJapanese12.html

National Criminal Justice Reference Center. (2000). *Present Situation of Organized Crime in Japan and Countermeasures Against It* [abstract]. Washington, DC: Department of Justice. Retrieved November 14, 2006, from http://www.ncjrs.gov/app/publications/Abstract.aspx?id=197906

Skold, D. (2002). Yakuza. *Oldman's homepage*. Retrieved November 24, 2006, from http://w1.313.telia.com/~U31302275/yakuza.html

Spak, K. (2008, May 31). Japanese Mob Boss Gave $100K to UCLA. Retrieved June 24, 2010, from http://www.newser.com/story/28895/japanese-mob-boss-gave-100k-

Tuohy, J. W. (2000). *Sayonara, Don Corleone*. Retrieved May 2, 2011, from http://www.americanmafia.com/Feature_Articles_34.html

Uchiyama, A. (1989). Economic Life of Member of Organized Crime Gangs. *Reports of NRIPS, 30*(1).

Yakuza. (2000). Gangland.net. Retrieved June 20, 2006, from http://www.gangland.net/yakuza.htm

Yakuza Boss Shot Dead In Hospital Bed. (2002, February 15). *CNN.com*. Retrieved June 24, 2010, from http://archives.cnn.com/2002/WORLD/asiapcf/east/02/25/japan.shooting/index.html

Chapter 9
Triads and Tongs

Opportunity is a moving target: The bigger the target, the faster it moves.

— Richard Gaylord Briley

Objectives

After completing this chapter, readers should be able to:

- Explain the difference between a Tong and a Triad.
- Discuss the structure of the Triads and its importance to investigators.
- Discuss the Triad culture and its importance to tactical and strategic planning and operations.

Introduction

Hong Kong Triads began in the same way as many organized crime groups—that is, they formed naturally as benevolent societies or guilds for protection of the community or to represent the interest of their community. In 1994, the Serious Crimes Ordinance of Hong Kong defined a Triad as "any society which uses rituals that are common to triad societies, or uses any ritual similar to that used by triad societies and adopts triad title or nomenclature." This ordinance also defines organized crime as "a schedule offense connected to activities of a triad with extensive planning and organization by two or more persons to commit two or more schedule acts."

Historical Perspective

In the United States, the presence of Chinese organized crime is complex and consists of Triads, Tongs, secret societies, and gangs.

Triads are secret societies that, like the Yakuza, date back to the 17th century. Today, an estimated 57 Triad societies operate in Hong Kong, which is the base for all Triad societies worldwide. Only some 20 of these Triads are involved in criminal activity. Membership ranges from 20 to 50 for small groups to more than 30,000 members in each Triad group. The recognized expert on Chinese organized crime, Ko-lin Chin, believes that these groups are not structured or coordinated like the U.S. La Cosa Nostra (LCN), and that there is no single Chinese Mafia (Chin, 1996). Nevertheless, substantial evidence exists of alliances between many Chinese street gangs and adult organizations such as the Triads and Tongs.

While most Triads are based in Hong Kong, Macau, or Taiwan, *Tongs* are an American phenomenon like the outlaw motorcycle gangs (OMGs; discussed in Chapter 10). Developed around the 1850s in San Francisco during the Gold Rush era, these family associations were created among people having common surnames, such as "Long." Tongs were organized by persons (some were Triad members in their home countries) with less common surnames to ensure representation in negotiations within their communities. The Chinese Consolidated Benevolent Association, comprising six companies, was formed as a political entity of the Chinese community.

Most Tongs are respectable fraternal organizations. Some Tong members became active in criminal activities, however; thus their groups can be characterized as organized crime organizations. Known as *fighting Tongs*, these groups soon controlled gambling, prostitution, and narcotics distribution by forming monopolies. They were linked to gangs and Triads in Hong King, Taiwan, and Macau that exist today. For example, the Wah Ching Tong originated from a 1960s street gang that, through extortion, violence, and other typical criminal activities, established a monopoly on Chinese entertainment in the United States.

Chinese organized crime activity exists in most major U.S. cities. According to law enforcement intelligence reports, the Triads, Tongs, and their street gang associates prey mainly on the Chinese community. Although alliances are sometimes formed between the three groups, they are separate entities that control their own activities. Some Chinese organized crime groups, such as the United Bamboo Crime Syndicate, began as street gangs in Taipei, Taiwan, in the 1950s. Today, the United Bamboo Crime Syndicate is an international organization with more than 40,000 members. This group is no longer active solely in predominantly Chinese communities known as *Chinatowns*, but rather operates networks that supply narcotics and human smuggling worldwide. Chinese organized crime groups are major suppliers of heroin to the United States.

The reported alliances between the Yakuza, Triads, LCN, and others present a major threat to law enforcement efforts, which is compounded by cultural and language barriers.

The loyalty, secrecy, brotherhood, righteousness, and nationalism that characterize these groups result in enterprises that are difficult for outsiders to penetrate. These organizations may form networks rapidly when opportunities arise, and then dissolve just as fast upon completion of the criminal activity. The dynamic nature of the Triads, Tongs, and street gangs allow them to be fluid and mobile so as to take advantage of emerging market opportunities.

Chinese culture emphasizes intergenerational family loyalty. *Guanxi*, a phenomenon where individuals are bound to others with mutual obligations (much like the American Mafia's omerta), is the basis for the strong loyalty displayed by Triad or Tong members. Family and mutual reciprocity (*qinqing*) allow all resources to be shared with each member, who in turn is obligated to contribute to the family, which lies at the heart of Chinese culture. Another impediment to law enforcement efforts to penetrate these groups is the fact that most Chinese people in the United States are reluctant to provide information to law enforcement because of the known corruption and harsh treatment of citizens in their homeland by police and government.

In addition to the activities of the Triads, Tongs and street gangs, some evidence suggests that mainland Chinese syndicates have established operations in the United States. These new groups tend to be more aggressive and loosely organized than the traditional Triads. All of these organizations are becoming more diverse in their criminal activity than the old Triads, and have moved into committing Internet crimes, product counterfeiting, and fraud (Robinson, 1999).

With a world membership of more than 100,000, these Chinese organized crime groups pose an obvious threat to the United States. Alliances among Chinese factions and others may be a turning point in how their organized crime groups function. Chinese criminals are becoming increasingly more competitive with other organized crime groups, and are penetrating legitimate businesses in ways much like the American LCN. The United States has become a major market for Chinese organized crime's goods and services. It is important to realize that not all Triads, Tongs, and their members are involved in criminal activity, however.

Although Triads, Tongs, Chinese gangs, and the new mainland societies/groups are separate entities, they occasionally form alliances to achieve specific criminal goals. Steve Macko (1997), a crime analyst, reported that the Chinese Triads are more dangerous than the Italian and the Russian groups for two reasons. First, the Chinese Triads are not a tightly unified crime organization. A Triad may exist anywhere there is a Chinese community and operate a number of legal enterprises. Second, while Russian gangsters are considered to be very violent organized crime groups, Macko believes that the Chinese are less violent and much more subtle in their organizations' workings. Most Chinese Triads will try to avoid committing violent acts that might draw attention to themselves, whereas other organized crime groups may commit frequent violent acts in the struggle to establish dominance over the marketplace. Triads commonly employ well-placed corrupt political contacts to control their enemies.

Because the Triads in mainland China are the forerunners to the U.S. Tongs and street gangs, knowing some of their history is helpful in understanding Chinese organized crime.

The Fighting Shaolin Monks

Many experts trace the origins of Triad societies to the 17th century. Legend has it that the foundation for these societies was laid when the second Manchu emperor, Kiang Hsi, asked for help from the Siu Lam monastery, which trained monks in the martial arts. Facing a rebellion in Fukien, the emperor believed that, with their assistance, he would be able to quell any disturbance that should ever arise.

The fighting Shaolin monks agreed to aid the emperor and began their mission. After they helped to successfully end the revolt, emperor Kiang Hsi rewarded them with vast imperial power for their efforts. The monks returned to their Shaolin Temple and continued their monastic lifestyle as they had known it before. However, the emperor began to fear that the monks—who had easily defeated the rebellion in Fukien—could one day turn against him. With this fear in mind, he searched for a way to end the potential threat the monks presented. To prevent them from ever having the chance to overthrow his power, the emperor decided to destroy the monks and their temple, and soon afterward sent his army to murder the monks. Knowing that the monks maintained stringent security over their temple, the emperor bribed one of them to assist his army to break in. Because this bribed monk was considered the number seven monk in the temple's hierarchy, he had the ability to sneak the army past security (Black, 1991).

Once inside the temple, the emperor's army caught the monks off guard and quickly murdered most of them. Only 18 monks managed to escape from the carnage. After fierce battles during the army's hot pursuit and despite their attempts to hide by splitting up, all but five monks were eventually murdered. These five escapees later formed their own monasteries in the areas in which they settled (Raamsdonk, 2001). Deeply angered by the emperor's betrayal, they also founded secret societies within their monasteries. The secret societies had one purpose: to destroy the Manchu (also known as the Ching dynasty) and restore the previous rulers, who were the Ming. The Ming family had ruled over China during what would become known as the country's finest era of peace and culture. The monks believed that by restoring the Ming to power, they would not only have fitting revenge upon the emperor for his treachery, but their country would also benefit from their actions (Black, 1991).

The Ming family name was "Hung," and the family's color was red; Hung and red are both closely associated with the Triad societies of today. Nearly all societies pay homage to the original five monks by displaying the triangular symbol from which the term *Triad* (heaven, earth, and man) was derived, and the color red is prominent. These secret societies began to use the motto, "Crush the Ching, establish the Ming." To avoid detection by the emperor and his spies, each society developed secret handshakes and gestures to identify themselves to other members (Black, 1991).

Around the world today is a martial art practiced by several thousand individuals known as Hung Gar Kung Fu. While few realize it, the foundation for this martial art may be one of the secret societies of the original monks. The martial arts association's red flag shows a hand with outstretched palm and all fingers bent except for the pointer finger. One of the original slogans during the attempts to overthrow the emperor was "If every Chinese will lift but one finger, we can bring down the Ching and restore the Ming." The training forms of this martial art begin with this hand signal. Individuals who practice this school of martial art may be using one of the original secret hand signs of the ancient rebellion.

Chinese Rebellions Through the Revolution

Because of the secrecy these societies maintained, the constant martial arts training that occurred in these monasteries, and economic pressures, the Chinese societies eventually evolved from being political organizations to criminal organizations. Despite their reputation for criminal acts, these societies are still viewed by many members of the public as protectors of the people from an oppressive ruler, much in the same way that the Italian Mafia and Japanese Yakuza were perceived as protectors of their respective communities in their early years. Likewise, members see themselves and their organizations as being protectors of society, rather than filling the role of common criminals.

The Chinese organizations did play important roles in several rebellions throughout their native country — most notably, the Boxer Rebellion (1896–1900), which involved the White Lotus Society, one of the original five societies. From 1910 to 1918, Chinese warlords, foreign commercial concerns maintaining their own governments along the coast, and Chinese intellectuals who were bitter over the burden imposed by foreign imperialism fought for power and control. China was not unified at this time. Oddly enough, the China dynasty tottered into its grave after being overthrown in 1911 by the Nationalist government, but by that time there were no longer any Mings to restore to the throne (Black, 1991).

Sadly, while the societies were fighting to overthrow their emperor, other countries — most notably Japan — took advantage of the Chinese. These countries imported Chinese citizens as menial labor, forced the sale of opium through war, and stole countless gold artifacts from the Chinese.

By 1927, the Nationalist government was established in China. Its leader, Chiang Kai Shek, was a known killer and member of a Triad named Shang Hai Green Gang. The new Chinese government and other Western countries used this gang to control the communists and to quell any unrest among laborers.

Global Dispersal of the Triads

With the 1947 attack by the Japanese army during World War II, the Chinese Triads began to work for the Japanese Yakuza running their criminal enterprises out of Hong Kong. During this time, the only complete unification of the Triads took place. The

Japanese organized the Triads into one organization known as the *Hing Ah Kee Kwan* (Asia Flowering Association). The Triads were entrusted with policing responsibilities as well as handling any anti-Japanese sentiment. After the war, these groups' focus shifted once again to attempting to control the rising power of the communists. Membership in the Triads had grown to an estimated 300,000 members by 1947. During this time, the 14K Triad was organized by the Nationalist army lieutenant general, Kot Siu Wong, whose headquarters was located in Canton. When the communists finally took over the Chinese government, Triad members fled to safe havens around the world, with groups appearing in Hong Kong; Macao, Thailand; San Francisco, United States; Vancouver, Canada; and Perth, Australia (Black, 1991).

Since the communist era began, the United States has experienced a significant influx of Chinese immigrants. During the 1990s, Triads increased their presence in this country by investing in legitimate U.S. businesses. The Big Circle gang and the Fukching gang became very active in the United States during the 1980s and the 1990s, and currently are engaged in drug trafficking, high-tech crimes, and fraud. The Big Circle has been made part of the Tranquil Happiness Triad, and the Fukching gang is associated with the Fukien American Association Tongs.

The criminal culture, relationships, and structure of the Triads, Tongs, gangs, and their associates are complex. This complexity requires investigators to invest time and effort in understanding these criminal organizations so as to develop effective strategies to attack the structure and operation of these groups. Drug trafficking does appear to involve more groups among the various components of Chinese organized crime.

Structure

The structure of the Triads, Tongs, and gangs varies somewhat between groups. The most commonly reported structure is for the Triads. The British coined the term *Triad* to describe these gangs based on the triangle symbol that these societies maintained in their Hong Kong headquarters.

Triad Membership

Ancient numerology (a system based on the I-Ching that describes mystical associations between words and numbers) determines the positions in the Triads. Each element is assigned a number in Chinese criminal societies. These numbers are always multiples of 3, where the number 36 means heaven, 108 is the number for man, and the number 72 is assigned to earth. Numerology plays an important role in determining the amount of money a new member must pay to join the Triad. Also of importance is the number 7. Because the Manchus (who destroyed the original Shaolin Temple) were aided by the number 7 monk in the Shoalin hierarchy, the number 7 is never used in the initiation ceremony. Failure to abide by this rule could result in various punishments, including death (Raamsdonk, 2001).

As with initiates of the LCN, individuals who want to join the organization need a Triad sponsor of sufficient rank to vouch for them. During the initiation, the candidates swear oaths to the leaders of the Triad they are attempting to join. To show respect for the original five founders of the five original Triads, everyone drinks from a cup of blood drawn from each of the new recruits. Ceremonies in the past lasted from hours to three days; today, however, the length of the initiation ceremonies varies between Triads, Tongs, and gangs.

The control structure of the Triads is not the same as in other organized crime groups. While the headquarters of every Triad is based in Hong Kong, those in the headquarters do not always supervise or control their subgroups' activities. The headquarters is responsible for maintaining the image of the rituals and the Triad as a whole. Each of the major leadership roles in the Triads is assigned both an alphabetical name or rank and a numeral designation for that position.

Within each Triad is a head figure who is the leader. This individual, named the *Shan Chu* (Dragon Head or Hill Chief), is denoted by the number 489. This title is extended to all heads, so the main leader at the headquarters will bear this title, as will the heads throughout the world. Directly under the Shan Chu is his assistant, the *Fu Shan Chu*, who is denoted by the number 438. Also known as the *Lungtau*, this individual is an advisor or counselor. Interestingly, the leader and his assistant may also be called by the title *Tai-Lo* (elder brother) and *I-Lo* (second elder brother), respectively. Regardless of which title is applied, these two men are responsible for major decisions affecting the Triad. Notably, one of the decisions reserved for these two individuals is the issuing of death sentences for either members or outsiders.

Equal in rank but not decision-making power are the *Heung Chu* (incense master) and the *Sing Fung* (vanguard), both of whom are denoted by the number 438. Carrying the spiritual responsibility of the Triad, the Heung Chu is responsible for overseeing the rituals and oaths of new members. The Sing Fung may assist the Heung Chu in his duties, but the Sing Fung is charged with establishing subgroups of the Triad. In essence, he serves as a "franchise officer." The Grass Slipper, number 432, is the liaison for communications and interactions between units.

Next in the administrative hierarchy is the *Hung Kwan* (military commander), who is denoted by the number 426. Also called the Red Pole, this individual takes responsibility for ensuring the protection of all gang territory as well as overtaking properties of rival gangs, and supervision of the soldiers.

The next level is the *Pak Tsz Sin*, denoted by the number 415. This individual, who is also known as the White Paper Fan, is responsible for providing all financial and business advice to the Triad.

The lowest level of Triad membership is the *Sze Kau*, denoted by the number 49. These individuals are the common gang members or soldiers.

Figures 9-1, **9-2**, and **9-3** depict the structure and associations of Chinese organized crime in the United States.

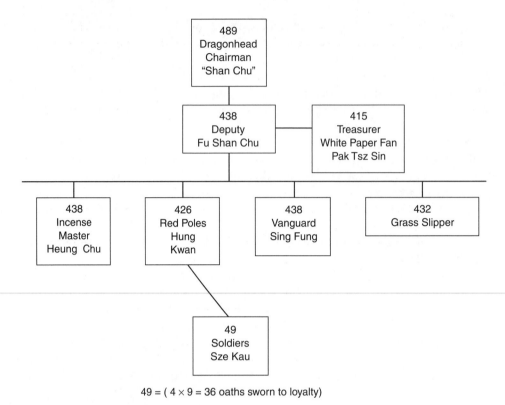

49 = (4 × 9 = 36 oaths sworn to loyalty)

Figure 9-1   Structure of a Triad.

Triad members also work in a variety of departments that are not denoted by a number:

- *Accounting* — responsible for the various financial activities of the Triad; money laundering is also this section's responsibility.

- *Recruiting* — Responsible for arranging social activities, developing spies for the Triad, and finding new members (some of whom are forced to join the organization).

- *Operations* — Responsible for the drug trafficking and prostitution businesses.

- *Communications* — Responsible for maintaining ties to the other Triads and the main lodge in Hong Kong.

- *Training and Welfare* — Responsible for ensuring quality martial arts and weapons training. This department also makes sure that families of jailed Triad members are provided with adequate income for survival, and provides the medical coverage these families may need (Black, 1991). (LCN also sometimes practiced this policy for its members who were jailed.)

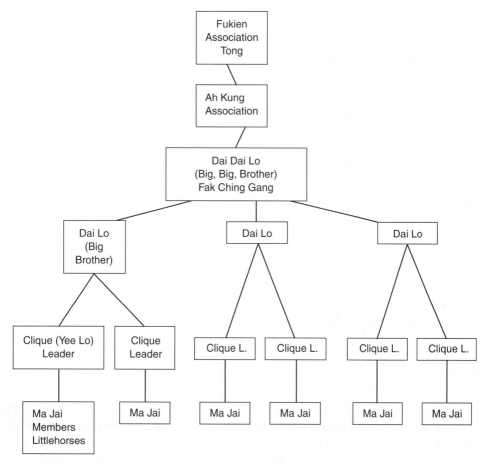

Figure 9-2 Structure and association of a Tong-affiliated gang.

The Shan Chu (supreme leader) is usually elected at an annual or biannual meeting; at the same time, the treasurer is elected. The leader controls promotions in conjunction with a committee, supervises internal discipline, and settles disputes. The leader does not control or dictate to members in which criminal activities they will or will not engage.

All members of the Triad communicate through secret hand symbols. A newer method of secret communication may involve the tea ceremony and organization of the teacups and the teapot. To date, there has been nothing published that indicates what the various positions mean to Triad members.

Tongs

Tongs are structured much like political action groups, as they represent their constituents. The Tongs that are involved in criminal activity often use street gangs to provide security for their gambling operations or other criminal activity.

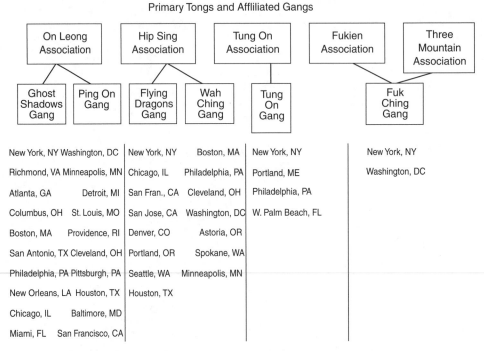

Figure 9-3 Chinese organized crime groups operating in the United States.

The top position in the Tong-related gang is the *Dai Dai Lo*. Below the Dai Dai Lo are the *Dai Lo*, the *Yee Lo*. and the *Ma Jai*. An *Ah Kung* (grandpa) or *Skuk Foo* (uncle) may direct operations through the Dai Dai Lo; the Tongs communicate through this grandfather or uncle figure. However, Tongs do not have direct control of the gangs, despite the fact that the gangs act out many of the traditions of the Triads. In particular, these gangs have the connections needed to import large quantities of Southeast Asian heroin (also known as China white).

The larger Tong organizations provide the gangs with meeting places and places to hang out, and they allow the gangs to operate in their territories, providing opportunities for making money from their criminal enterprises.

Investigating Triads and Tongs Based on Structural Considerations

The major Triads are known to have multiple subgroups. A Hong Kong–based expert on Chinese organized crime, Peter Chong, has identified the major Triads with their subgroups as shown in **Figure 9-4**. This structure is similar to the OMGs and their puppet clubs, as described in Chapter 10.

Triad	14K	Chiu Chau	Wo Group	Luan group	Tung group	Chuen Group
	Hau	Shing Ye On	Shing Wo	Kung Lok	Kwan Ying	Yat Chee
	Yan	Fukye Hing	On Lok	Lok Tong	Luen She	Chui Ying
Sub	Chun	King Yee	Sing Yee	Ying She	San Wo	Hing Yee
Group	Tak	Tai Ho Choi	Lee Kwan			
	Mui	Yee Kwan	Lee Wo			
	Tung		Kwan Lok			

Figure 9-4 Major Triads and their subgroup.

Linking these Chinese subgroups to their Triad or Tong groups allows the investigator to better understand the operations of Triads as well as to employ the strategy of vicarious liability in conspiracy cases. Using appropriate methods to gather intelligence, the investigator must determine which Triads, Tongs, and gangs are operating in his or her jurisdiction. The identity and structure of the organization can serve as a starting point for tactical and strategic planning, but sharing this information with the (presumably secure) officials in the country of origin is also important. Many leaders of these organizations who profit by the criminal activity reside outside the United States. These leaders can be indicted in the United States and in the country where they reside through international cooperation and by employing conspiracy statutes. All Triads must have the approval of their headquarters in Hong Kong, Taiwan, or other source countries to establish territory in the United States. These Triads operate independently until disputes or major problems occur, which is when the boss at the headquarters will become involved. Thus these subgroups and cell leaders are involved in a variety of complex criminal activities.

Activities and Methods of Operations

In many parts of the world, more money is spent on drugs than is spent on food. Although the heroin market is a major source of revenue for Chinese organized crime, other activities of Triads, Tongs, and gangs include debt collection, prostitution, human smuggling ($30,000 to $50,000 per person), loan sharking, gambling, and other narcotics trafficking. Like other organized crime groups, Triads and Tongs are moving into legitimate businesses such as banks, the music and entertainment industries, tourist markets, and software, among many others.

Triad Activities

With an estimated 1.5 million members in China, the Triads are dynamic and are expanding rapidly—despite the fact that it is a crime in China to be a member of a Triad. Many members of these groups have alliances with both the new government of Hong Kong and illicit organizations such as the Yakuza. It is said that the Triads kill their enemies and only maim or injure their victims. They abide by their code of silence and are bonded to their organizations. Often referred to as *dragon syndicates*, their organizations pose a serious threat to the United States.

Triads have become transnational in terms of the scope of their operation. For many reasons, it is difficult to determine which is the strongest of the Triads. The three reported largest and most powerful are the 14K, Wo Sing Wo, and Sun Yee On groups (Macko, 1997). Major Triads in Taiwan include the Sung Lian, Tian Dao, Four Seas, and United Bamboo. Although each of these organizations is considered dangerous to the future of society, the Sun Yee On is the one that Macko identifies as being the most fearsome. Citing the Triad's adoption of business tactics, he believes that the Sun Yee On are following in the tradition of the Japanese Yakuza, and are currently becoming more and more involved in corrupting the activities of legitimate businesses.

The Triad societies still follow a rather unique code of ethics. As an example, Graham (1997) cites the *United Bamboo's Code of Ethics*, which became available when the Los Angeles County Sheriff's Department seized it as a member was attempting to enter the United States. The United Bamboo, which is considered the strongest Triad in Taiwan with more than 10,000 members, has expanded internationally and is already established in California and other U.S. states. Its code of ethics serves as one example of Triad culture and activity:

1. Harmony with the people is the first priority. We have to establish good social and personal connections so as not to create enemies.

2. We have to seek special favors and help from uncommitted gang members by emphasizing our relationship with outside people. Let them publicize us.

3. Gambling is our main financial source. We must be careful how we handle it.

4. Do not take it upon yourself to start things and make decisions you are not authorized to make. You are to discuss and plan all matters with the group and the elder brother first.

5. Everyone has their assigned responsibility. Do not create confusion!

6. We must not divulge our plans and affairs to outsiders—for example, to our wives and girlfriends. This is for our own safety.

7. We have to be united with all our brothers and obey our elder brother's orders.

8. All money earned outside the group must be turned over to the group. You must not keep any of it for yourself. Let the elder brother decide.

9. When targeting wealthy prospects, do not act hastily. Furthermore, do not harass or threaten them. Act to prevent suspicion and fear upon their part.

10. If anything unexpected happens, do not abandon your brothers. If arrested, shoulder all responsibility and blame. Do not involve your brothers.

Clearly, this code of ethics indicates that, despite the lack of a single leader as found in other organized criminal groups, these Triads do have a strict hierarchy. As mentioned earlier, this hierarchical structure gives the investigator the potential to apply vicarious liability for conspiracy cases. Several times in these codes, the individual is instructed to seek the guidance or the permission of the elder brother. Investigators must be aware of this vulnerability.

Secrecy is also paramount to the Triads. At the same time, the Triads do not appear to be concerned with keeping themselves out of the spotlight, as the rules mention that they must let others publicize them. The code does require a vow of secrecy. Failure to abide by this rule most likely would end in death for the offender, because the code states that this rule is important for the safety of all members.

Currently, the Triads are experiencing growth due to a relaxation of state control over many activities of the Chinese people. It would be wrong to believe that the Chinese Triads are seeking to expand only in China, however. These criminal groups focus on opportunities wherever there is a chance for financial growth, regardless of the geographic location. Stephen Vickers, head of the Hong Kong police criminal intelligence bureau, writes that Western law enforcement would be wasting its time preparing for an onslaught of Chinese Triads in places such as the United States. Vickers is certain that the Chinese criminals who are going to come are already in America (Macko, 1997).

There is documented growth of Triad activity in several other countries as well, including South Africa. In South Africa, the Triads are involved in the illegal growth and export of abalone. Abalone is considered a delicacy and an aphrodisiac in China. Although its export is not necessarily illegal, this industry is highly regulated in China. Thus the Triads are secretly exporting the abalone to China, reaping extraordinary prices for their product on the streets. It is likely that this activity in South Africa will result in alliances with organized crime groups in that country. Again, the trend for global alliances is a major challenge for U.S. and other nations' law enforcement. In addition to the abalone trade, Triads are focusing worldwide on smuggling, drug trafficking, control of the fish and produce markets, and, in an interesting development, control of karaoke bars.

Tong Activities

Tongs exist along with Triads and other societies or gangs, and contribute to the organized criminal activity in all major cities that have a significant Asian or Chinese population. In Chicago, for example, the On Leong and Hip Sing Tongs are major players in heroin trafficking to the United States from the Golden Triangle (Laos, Burma, and Thailand).

The U.S. Tongs trafficked in opium and other drugs and operated gambling and prostitution rings in New York, San Francisco, and Chicago in the 19th century, and they continue these activities today. The Tongs are also involved in cocaine distribution. The strict limitations imposed on membership in these secret ethnic societies have limited infiltration and research into their functioning; thus verifiable intelligence is lacking, and their precise operations and extent of activity are difficult to determine. Some evidence suggests that they engage in extortion, protection rackets, alien smuggling, murder, assault, money laundering, bribery, and corruption, in addition to their traditional criminal activities of controlling prostitution, drug trafficking, and gambling.

Tongs, like the Triads, engage in initiation rituals and have established codes, symbols, and rules with punishment for their organization and members. They are well integrated into the culture of the Chinese community and have survived more than 100 years in the United States because of their method of operations, secrecy, loyalty, and provision of needed services to the community. For a number of reasons, including physical and cultural barriers such as racism that separated Chinese immigrants from other settlers, Chinatowns began to become integrated into the larger American community only after antidiscrimination laws were passed in the 1960s.

Of course, while Tongs provided services to the Chinese community, their criminal aspects victimized them as well. Tongs became the unofficial government that provided arbitrary services including a credit and banking structure, schools, and ways to provide for the needy. Tongs are very powerful and influential because of both their legal and illegal services to the community (Booth, 2000).

Chinese Gang Activities

Tongs are connected to the Chinese gangs (Figure 9-3) that formed in the mid-1960s during the wave of immigration in which large numbers of youths moved from Hong Kong to the United States. These Chinese gangs became predatory businesses. Tongs employed the gangs to do their dirty work and to serve as security forces for their operations. Often classified as a young form of organized crime (Danner, 1992), these gang affiliates produce profits for the Tongs through protection fees collected from nearly all of the businesses in U.S. Chinatowns. Tongs do not control the gangs and most alliances are temporary or job specific.

Chin (1996) and Finckenauer (2003) found that most Chinese gangs lack the professionalism and sophistication of the Triads and Tongs. However, Chin and others believe that the gangs are capable of corrupting government officials and police. California's dominant Chinese gangs or groups include the Wah Ching and the Wo Hop To. The Triad-affiliated Chinese gangs appear to be expanding their criminal activities

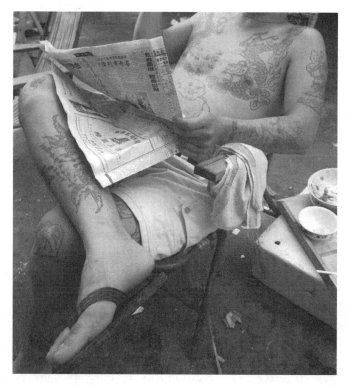

Example of Triad-style tattoos.

into such areas as human smuggling and are becoming more structured in similar ways as that of the Triads and Tongs.

Like other American street gangs (i.e., Bloods, Crips, Vicelords), Asian gang members have initiations and rituals and wear tattoos that represent their membership in a particular gang. In addition to gang wars, gang alliances often evolve around drug distribution or other criminal activity. Asian, Black, Latino, and other youth gangs often engage in collusion to make profits from criminal activity. Chinese organized crime groups are involved in illegal arms trading, and they deal weapons to many gangs; Tongs may employ gang members to do contract murders. Armed robberies and auto theft are common activities of Chinese gangs.

Violence and Intimidation

Violence is part of the power that Triads, Tongs, and other gangs employ to gain compliance from their victims. So-called *hatchet men* use a meat cleaver to chop up and injure their victims, and are widely feared by the Chinese community. Wounds produced by chopping are a symbol of both the Tongs' and Triads' retribution for noncompliance.

Conflicts between Tongs, between Triads, and between gangs have led to ongoing bloodshed in Chinese communities in the United States. As early as 1909, On Leong and Hip Sing (New York Tongs) were at war over turf and the drug trade. Similar wars occurred in both Chicago and California (Abadinsky, 2003). In addition, Chinese gangs have fought against other Asian gangs such as Vietnamese, Viet Ching, and Cambodian groups. The Chinese Green Dragons' gang and the Vietnamese gang Born to Kill (BTK) are bitter enemies whose members often murder one another, bringing violence to the community.

The Big Circle Gang members, who sometimes wear a red arm band symbolizing their history as communist Red Guard militia, have cells in the United States and are involved in a variety of high-tech crimes such as credit card fraud, financial crime, and complex theft operations. This gang is also involved in drug trafficking, gambling operations, prostitution, and extortion of the Chinese business community. New York gangs such as the Fuk Ching Tung On, Ghost Shadows, and Flying Dragons have a capacity for violence that is their defining characteristic. At the same time, these gangs are involved in legitimate businesses, often owning retail stores, restaurants, video stores, fish markets, and even banks.

Human Smuggling

Because of U.S. restrictions on female immigration in the 1800s, early Chinatowns were predominately male. The Tongs and Triads (snakeheads) smuggled young women from China who were deceived into thinking they would have good jobs in America. Known as *sing-song girls*, they were forced into prostitution and produced profits for the Tongs.

Zhang and Chin (2002) found in their research that nontraditional criminals are currently responsible for the majority of human smuggling of Chinese nationals. These groups are not associated with Tongs, Triads, or street gangs. Chin (1999) identified two categories of snakeheads through his research: Big snakeheads simply invest money and oversee smuggling operations; little snakeheads act as the recruiters and middlemen for the operation. These studies indicate that human smuggling today is somewhat different from the traditional operations of the traditional Tongs and Triads.

Business Investments

Perhaps the Tongs' greatest criminal asset is their ability to invest the profits from their criminal activities into legitimate businesses. Their ability to corrupt both business and government officials makes Chinese organized crime a national threat comparable to other organized crime groups such as the Yakuza and LCN.

Investigative Strategies

Similar to other organized crime groups, Chinese organized crime is a result of myriad social, economic, and legal conditions. As an ethnic organized group, the "Chinese Mafia" is not a single organization, but rather a number of groups operating independently but effectively. Although sometimes allied, they are often at war.

The centuries-long history of Chinese crime offers the investigator an opportunity to examine the methods of operation and activities so as to develop a better understanding of these criminals and to create strategies for dealing with yet another formidable adversary. Like other organized crime groups, the Triads and Tongs are driven by profit and power. Alliances between Triads to divide tasks between groups are common and efficient. Activities and methods of operation are dynamic. These groups need to be monitored and their activities and membership updated through effective and continuous intelligence-gathering efforts to ensure intervention by law enforcement.

Chinese groups are known to have formed alliances with Dominican, Mexican, Colombian, and Italian crime groups, and they also maintain connections with their origin groups in Mainland China. The ever-expanding nature of Chinese organized crime is a factor that must be considered when examining the trend of transnational organized crime.

Cultural and Language Barriers

One of the biggest problems U.S. law enforcement encounters when addressing Chinese organized crime is the lack of understanding of the Chinese culture. U.S. history has trained the Chinese community to be distrustful of law enforcement and this factor, combined with intimidation from the crime groups, often deters individuals from providing the information needed for successful investigations. Ambivalence toward the organized criminal activities of the Triads, Tongs, and gangs exists as well. The investigator must become familiar with each Chinatown's informal economy, and note which criminal groups serve as providers and protectors while victimizing this economy and culture. Learning one or more Chinese languages will prove greatly beneficial in this endeavor.

Factors that must be addressed by U.S. law enforcement include the cultural and language barriers, the Chinese community's lack of understanding of the U.S. justice system, and the fear of retaliation by members of the Chinese criminal groups. Gangs have often been successful in intimidating the community not to report, testify, or cooperate in criminal cases. The challenge for U.S. law enforcement is to build respect and trust among members of the Chinese community by addressing their problems and providing adequate protection for those who do provide assistance. Separation of the criminal element from the culture will require innovative strategies and constant positive contact with the Chinese community.

Criminal Tongs, Triads, and gang members must be removed from the community and replaced with officers who can provide the security and stability greater than what is now provided by the criminal element. This has proven to be a difficult task. Understanding the complex nature and structure of the Tongs and Triads, the dynamics of Chinese communities, and the complex nature and history of Chinatown is essential for successful intervention and investigation.

Surveillance and Sting Operations

The law enforcement response to Chinese organized crime includes electronic and physical surveillance, undercover operations, and undercover sting operations. Although the development and recruiting of informants is a difficult task, many members have cooperated and became witnesses for the government. Similar to LCN members who have violated omerta, Chinese organized crime members face severe penalties (including execution) under statutes such as RICO, CCE, and conspiracy, plus traditional statutes governing murder, extortion, and assault, among other crimes. The FBI has developed cases on the On Leong gang in Chicago, and the New York, San Francisco, and Los Angeles police departments have developed cases on many individuals in their areas. Although most members failed to cooperate, some did become informants for law enforcement.

Nevertheless, insufficient intelligence remains a major problem when investigating Triads and Tongs. Chinese organized crime methods of operation and activities are complex and differ from those used by LCN—the organized crime group with which U.S. law enforcement agencies are most familiar. The Tongs and Triads have not suffered the prosecutions and setbacks like LCN and the OMGs.

Often a member who is under investigation or indictment will flee to China. International cooperation is crucial for not only intelligence sharing, but also extradition and joint investigations between countries. Each agency and individual investigator, in addition to the U.S. government, must develop contacts (including personal contacts) and networks to ensure cooperation with foreign law enforcement.

Conclusions

The international law enforcement academy in Bangkok, Thailand, and the International Asian Organized Crime conferences are excellent avenues to develop contacts and networks for cooperation. FBI Academy and other federal training programs must continue to be offered to foreign law enforcement agencies as a means to develop the understanding and cooperation necessary for successful transnational investigations. China, Macau, and other countries have made progress in addressing organized crime, but much room for improvement remains. Unfortunately, a lack of resources, training, intelligence, and adequate statutes and laws continue to hamper the efforts of many countries.

International or transnational task forces are an idea whose time has come in the face of the global organized crime alliances, networks, and cooperation. Interpol was created for the purposes of data gathering, sharing information, and tracking criminal activity around the globe. The next step to creating an international investigative agency seems possible and is certainly needed, although the potential for corruption would be the major obstacle to the efficacy of such an agency. The U.S. effort itself is fragmented owing to turf wars and lack of interagency cooperation. An international-scale agency would certainly face the same problems.

Some Chinese organized crime groups, such as the Big Circle gang, have become so sophisticated that both physical and electronic surveillance are unlikely to be effective and are often compromised. Perhaps financial investigative strategies will remain effective if the underground financial system used by the Chinese groups can be identified. Investigators must become more familiar with computer technologies and emerging telecommunications systems to determine where money is being moved. The monitoring and interception of communications and money transfers are essential to investigation of organized crime. Information systems must continue to improve so that law enforcement can track and monitor the organized crime activities of groups such as the Triads and Tongs. Traditional practices of asset forfeiture, witness protection programs, intelligence collection, and informant development all must be improved in the Chinese community to demonstrate that law enforcement can be effective, and can serve and protect the Chinese community. Much of what occurs in the local Chinese community is shaped by events occurring in other countries, states, or jurisdictions within the United States. In the Chinese community, there is an inseparable merging of organized crime, business, and culture.

Understanding the phenomenon of *guanxi* and the concept of *quinqing* is essential to understanding Chinese culture. Because Chinese secret societies have existed for hundreds of years, they have replicated themselves in many parts of the world (including the United States) with great efficiency and efficacy. Like other organized crime groups, they employ violence, long-range planning, and corruption to ensure their continuity and effective recruitment. The investigator must understand that each group is formed in the local community, is protected by corruption, and engages in providing illegal services and goods to the local market. The networks of Chinese organized crime groups are extensive and global. Identifying these networks and their membership is instrumental to effective intervention and enforcement efforts. Improvements in global communication, transportation, and technology have provided groups such as Chinese organized crime the means to become more effective. Law enforcement, in turn, must take advantage of global networks and improved technology to address the Triads, Tongs, and others involved in complex criminal activity.

Discussion Questions

1. Discuss the history of Chinese organized crime. Why is it important?
2. What is the difference between a Tong and a Triad?
3. Discuss the structure of the Triads and its importance to investigators.
4. Which action would you, as an investigator, take to address Chinese crime?

5. Discuss the Triad culture and its importance to tactical and strategic planning and operations.

6. What are the profitable activities of Chinese organized crime in the United States?

References

Abadinsky, H. (2003). *Organized Crime*. Belmont, CA: Wadsworth/Thompson Learning.

Black, D. (1991). *Triad Takeover*. London: Sidgwick & Jackson.

Booth, M. (2000). *The Dragon Syndicates: The Global Phenomenon of the Triads*. New York: Carroll & Graft.

Chin, K. (1996). *Chinatown Gangs*. Oxford, UK: Oxford University Press.

Chin, K. (1999). *Smuggled Chinese: Clandestine Immigration to the United States*. Philadelphia: Temple University Press.

Danner, F. (1992, November). Revenge of the Green Dragons. *New Yorker*. Retrieved April 20, 2011, from http://www.newyorker.com/archive/1992/11/16/1992_11_16_076_TNY_CARDS_000365255

Finckenauer, J. O. (2003). Chinese Transnational Organized Crime: The Fuk Ching. Retrieved December 1, 2006, from http://www.ojp.gov/nij/international/chinese.html

Graham, J. (1997, April). Taiwan's Triads. *Asia, Inc*. Retrieved December 1, 2006, from http://orgcrime.tripod.com/taiwanstriads.htm

Macko, S. (1997, December 23). *Chinese Triads: An Update*. Chicago: ERRI EmergencyNet News Service. Retrieved December 1, 2006, from http://www.emergency.com/chi-tria.htm

Raamsdonk, R. V. (2001). The Triads. *Wing Chun Viewpoint*. Retrieved from http://www.wingchun.org/~danlucas.wcw.html

Robinson, J. (1999). *The Merger: How Organized Crime Is Taking Over Canada and the World*. Toronto, Canada: McClelland & Stewart.

Zhang, S., & Chin, K. (2002). Enter the Dragon: Inside Chinese Human Smuggling Organizations. *Criminology, 40*, 737–809.

Chapter 10

American Outlaw Motorcycle Gangs

What we see depends mainly on what we look for.

—John Lubbock

Objectives

After completing this chapter, readers should be able to:

- Name the major outlaw motorcycle gangs (OMGs) in the United States and describe how they evolved.

- Identify the typical structure of an OMG and explain how this structure is important to law enforcement.

- Discuss the investigative strategies that are most effective against OMGs.

- Describe the current trends of activity and method of operation of OMGs.

Introduction

Unlike the American Mafia and other organized crime groups, outlaw biker gangs are an American phenomenon. They were not formed for power and profit or greed, but were World War II veterans who rejected society's norms as boring and restrictive. Outlaw biker gangs were glamorized in such films as *The Wild Ones, Easy Rider*, and *Angels on Wheels* as rebellious groups whose members wanted to create their own rules and lifestyle. This image has changed to one of gangs oriented toward the profit motive through crime, including regional, national, and international organized crime (Barker, 2004).

Historical Perspective

There is no accurate count of the number of outlaw biker clubs in the United States today; however, the great majority of clubs are not believed to be criminal or organized crime groups (Barker, 2005). Nevertheless, a few have evolved into complex groups that are classified as organized crime. According to the National Alliance of Gang Investigators' Associations (2005), an estimated 300 active outlaw motorcycle gangs (OMGs) use their clubs as conduits for criminal enterprises. They vary in membership from fewer than a dozen members in a single chapter to a large number of chapters with thousands of members (Barker, 2005). OMGs are major distributors of illegal drugs and are considered extremely violent in their efforts to control and expand their criminal activities. They are allied with international drug trafficking organizations (DTOs) and may operate through chapters in foreign countries (Barker, 2004).

The National Drug Intelligence Center (NDIC) reports that 11.5% of state and local law enforcement agencies indicate OMG involvement in drug distribution is moderate to high in their areas of jurisdiction (*High Intensity Drug Trafficking Areas*, 2006). Foreign-produced drugs and precursor chemicals are smuggled from Mexico and Canada by OMGs. The OMGs purchase multiple-pound quantities of these substances from Mexican DTOs and smuggle the drugs into the United States. OMGs, particularly the *Bandidos*, maintain close relations with prison gangs such as the *Texas Syndicate* to distribute methamphetamine (meth). *Hells Angels Motorcycle Club* (HAMC) members allied with Asian criminal groups were indicted in March 2004 for operating a drug distribution network involving $20 million in high-grade marijuana, known as BC Bud or Quebec Gold, to customers in southern Indiana (*Intelligence Bulletin*, May 2004). Another OMG, the *Pagans,* is known to obtain large quantities of illicit drugs from both Colombian and Dominican criminal groups.

Many OMGs are considered organized crime because of their complex structures, ability to penetrate legitimate businesses, and practice of laundering money through businesses and casinos. These groups conduct much of their criminal activity through puppet clubs—groups that are allied with the larger clubs but are not members of the larger club (Barker, 2005). Most criminally oriented OMGs now include smaller OMGs in their organizations ("patching over") and then use puppet clubs to carry out much of the diverse criminal activity of OMGs. Perhaps not surprisingly, OMGs present a considerable challenge for U.S. law enforcement. (*Intelligence Bulletin*, May 2004).

The Post–World War II Era

The Hells Angels are considered to be the first and most powerful of the groups that were classified as organized crime (Barker, 2005). The Hells Angels began as a group of

California-based World War II veterans, who named themselves the *Pissed Off Bastards of Bloomington* (POBOB). Early criminal activities of the POBOB included vandalism, public drunkenness, fighting, and traffic violations. Members of the group considered themselves to be tough guys who had their own rules of behavior. The term "outlaw" was first used by law enforcement officers in California to distinguish lawbreakers such as the POBOB from other law-abiding members of the American Motorcycle Association (AMA).

Rallies and Runs

The outlaw biker image was created at the 1947 Hollister, California, motorcycle rally. According to Yates (1999), it was at Hollister that OMGs made their national debut. Approximately 1000 motorcyclists attended the event, including the clubs formed by World War II veterans such as the Market Street Commandos, the Pissed Off Bastards of Bloomington, the Galloping Gooses, and the Boozefighters. The rally resulted in the drunken veterans driving the town's six police officers crazy and filling the jails. For some unknown reason, a photographer for the *San Francisco Chronicle* staged a photograph of a drunken motorcyclist that subsequently was printed in *Life* magazine along with a distorted account of the incident, and the putative "Hollister Riot" made national headlines (Reynolds, 2000).

In 1948, a Labor Day motorcycle rally was held in Riverside, California. More than 1000 motorcyclists attended, and the events of Hollister were repeated with tragic results. The rally turned into a riot that left one person dead. The violence was blamed on "outlaw" bikers visiting the city, cementing the OMG's dangerous image in the public's eyes.

During the 1950s and 1960s, the OMGs became a symbol of rebellion, freedom, and outrageous deviant behavior. Unlike the American Mafia, their goal was uninhibited behavior and good times rather than profit and power. The earlier events gave rise to a tradition of runs by these OMG groups. A run occurs when a group of bikers from one or more clubs travel together on a club-sanctioned road trip by motorcycle to a specific location for some special reason. Some club members will travel as far as 20,000 miles per year on different runs. One traditional run, until 2006, occurred on Labor Day weekend to Hollister, California, the site for the Independence Day Rally. The run was canceled in 2006 for security reasons and its future status is in doubt.

In August each year, the Sturgis Rally draws thousands of bikers from many different groups to South Dakota. This event lasts as long as 10 days and is the largest run or rally in the United States for OMGs and other motorcyclists. The runs are highly organized into a formation of two motorcycles traveling abreast. Those members belonging to a particular OMG ride in a specific order that includes club officers, members, prospective members, and the club's associates (**Figure 10-1**). Bikers generally are not allowed to carry firearms, drugs, or alcohol on their motorcycles during a run, and they usually travel within speed limits. Crash trucks, vans, or cars associated with the club travel a distance in front of or behind the bikes, and those riding in the vehicles may be carrying firearms and drugs as well as sleeping bags, motorcycle parts, alcohol, and police scanners. Women or probates (members who are on probation before becoming a full member) usually drive the vans.

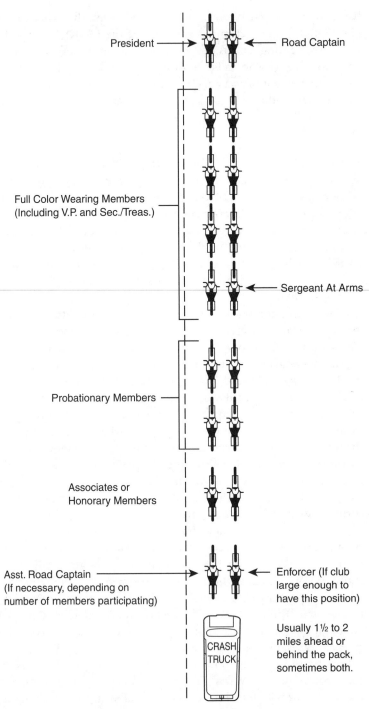

Figure 10-1 Formation and line up of a typical OMG during a run.

Most gangs own their own buildings (clubhouses) as part of the OMG culture; these locations are used for business meetings, motorcycle repair, and partying. Most OMGs disallow drugs, weapons, or stolen goods in the clubhouses, which are guarded by members against attacks by rival gangs. There are strict rules for behavior in the clubhouses.

Outlaw motorcycle gangs are also known as *one percenters*. AMA president William Berry coined this phrase when he declared that only 1% of motorcyclists in the United States were involved in lawlessness such as the outlaw clubs. This term has since become a rallying cry that appears on the stitched appliqué patches (colors) worn by OMG members.

From 1947 to 1970, OMGs experienced enormous growth. During this period, the early outlaw motorcycle clubs patched over other clubs, expanded their territory in the United States and overseas, and moved into drug trafficking, becoming gangs oriented toward profit from crime (Barker, 2004, 2005).

1970 to Today

Nomads, or roaming members of various chapters, formed alliances with smaller groups and recruited new OMG members throughout California and other areas of the United States in the 1950s and 1960s. By the 1970s, the OMGs had developed a stable structure and had an established leadership. During the 1970s and 1980s, as the American drug culture expanded, the OMGs evolved into major players in drug trafficking. Over time, these groups became more complex and diversified in their criminal activities.

Most biker gangs remain strong white supremacy groups, allowing only white males to become members. Although some black and other ethnic OMG members have been admitted, the majority of the gangs remain white males only.

The twin goals of OMGs today are profit and power. Members remain opposed to society and its laws and wear patches with the FTW ("F**k the World") logo. The motorcycle is seen as a symbol of pride, freedom, and power. Most groups require members to have a U.S.-made motorcycle with at least a 900-cc engine, usually a Harley-Davidson.

OMGs have also developed their own rules and dress codes. Each member's identity is displayed on his sleeveless denim shirt, leather jacket, or vest. This patch is referred to as *colors*. Each club has a patch design that identifies the club, and each club has very strict rules about wearing, respecting, and placing patches on the clothing. The colors have three sections, known as *rockers*. The top rocker is usually the club name, the center rocker is the club emblem, and the bottom rocker is the geographic location of the club. Only authorized patches are allowed on the jackets, and loss of colors is a serious offense for members. Some members have the emblem tattooed (mandatory for Hells Angels and some others) on their bodies. Each club demands uniformity with regard to dress, colors, and type of motorcycles.

The Big Four

Although many OMGs continue to grow and expand by forging alliances with other OMGs, law enforcement in the early 1970s recognized the "Big Four" as the OMGs that most typically exhibit the characteristics of organized crime: Hells Angels, Outlaws, Pagans, and the Bandidos. These groups evolved as paramilitary organizations with a bureaucratic structure (**Figure 10-2**).

Hells Angels

Members of the POBOB formed a new gang on March 17, 1948 in San Bernardino, California. The name *Hells Angels* was taken from a World War II bomber plane; this image can be seen in their crest, which shows a skull with wings. The original chapter was named the "Berdoo" chapter and the Mother Chapter (headquarters and home of the national president) was located in San Bernardino, California. In the 1960s, Ralph Hubert (Sonny) Barger, who was then president of the Oakland chapter, became the national president and the Mother Chapter moved to Oakland, California.

Hells Angels expanded during the 1960s and 1970s as the result of attention given to them through national coverage, movies, and even the Vietnam War. Some bored veterans returning home from Vietnam, for example, became members of biker groups like the HAMC. The actual number of HAMC chapters is unknown and probably unknowable by outsiders (Barker, 2005). The club has an estimated 4000 colors-wearing members,

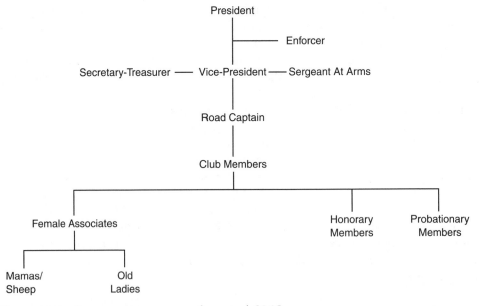

Figure 10-2 Bureaucratic structure of a typical OMG.

who belong to more than 100 HAMC chapters—65 in North America and 35 in countries outside the United States, including Denmark, Brazil, New Zealand, Canada, Great Britain, Australia, Europe, Japan, and others (Veno, 2002). HAMC is estimated to have more than 700 members in the United States (Barker, 2005). Although the number of chapters and members fluctuate, the Hells Angels are considered to be the largest, wealthiest, and most powerful of the Big Four. They serve as a model for other OMGs and have puppet clubs such as the Red Devils Motorcycle Club, whose members assist them in their criminal activities such as drug trafficking.

Canadian law enforcement believes that the HAMC is the most powerful and well-structured criminal organization in Canada (Criminal Intelligence Service, Canada, 2004). A two-year sting operation ended in January 2006 with the arrest of 27 people associated with the HAMC near Thunder Bay. Five of those arrested were patched members.

Outlaws

The *Outlaws* motorcycle club was formed in Chicago in 1935 by John Davis. At that time, the group was known as the McCook Outlaws Motorcycle Club "out of Matilda's Bar on Route 66 in McCook, Illinois, outside Chicago" (Barker, 2005). According to the group's official website, the club's name was changed to the Chicago Outlaws in 1950; in 1965, the club became the Outlaws Motorcycle Club Nation. The Mother Club was originally located in Chicago but later moved to Detroit.

Since their beginning in 1935, the Outlaws have grown into one of the largest motorcycle clubs worldwide (Barker, 2005). The Outlaws website lists 80 chapters in 20 states; it also lists 116 chapters in 14 countries outside the United States. Barker (2005) estimates this OMG's membership at 3900 worldwide.

The Outlaws and Hells Angels have been at war since the late 1960s. Battles over territory and drug markets have escalated to blowing up each other's clubhouses, murders and assaults on members, and the theft of each other's stolen property. The Outlaws frequently have allied with the Bandidos, who are also enemies of the Hells Angels.

Outlaws chapters continue to cluster in the Great Lakes, Midwest, Northeast, and Southeast regions, including Florida, Wisconsin, Illinois, Kentucky, and Indiana. The club motto is "God forgives; Outlaws don't." The Outlaws' colors consist of a skull over crossed pistols, a graphic known as "Charlie." (This emblem design was taken from *The Wild Ones* film, which starred Marlon Brando.)

In April 2003, the U.S. District Court of the Northern District of Ohio indicted 38 members of the Outlaws motorcycle gang on charges ranging from murder, drug distribution, and firearms violations, to possession of stolen property. The case involved large quantities of illicit drugs confiscated: 800 pounds of cocaine, 500 pounds of marijuana, 100 pounds of meth, 900,000 units of Valium, and more than 100,000 doses of LSD.

Bandidos

Donald Eugene Chambers founded the Bandidos OMG in Houston, Texas, in March 1966. Chambers expanded the club in Texas until he was arrested for murder in 1972. In 1974, Ronald Jerome Hodge was elected national president to replace Chambers. However, as with many organized crime leaders, Chambers continued to exert considerable influence over the group's operations from his jail cell.

Power in the Bandidos is pluralistic, in that it is divided among the group's elected officers. Like other OMGs, members consider themselves to be a law unto themselves. The club is referred to as the *Bandit Nation,* and members consider it to be separate and independent of the U.S. government. The club motto is "Bandido by profession, biker by trade, lover by choice," and members describe themselves as "the people our parents warned us about." The colors of the club are yellow, gold, and red. In the center of the colors is the *Mexican Bandido* logo, a pot-bellied cartoon figure wearing a sombrero and brandishing pistols. If a member has been in the group for five years, he is considered a charter member and is allowed to wear this patch.

Incorporated in Texas in 1978 as a nonprofit organization, the club's stated purpose is to provide social activity for its members who have a common interest in large motorcycles. This club has incorporated in other states such as Washington and Alabama as well. Bandido members must abide by specific rules and bylaws.

The history of the Bandidos is one of escalating violence and criminal activity, and its members have been convicted of many serious offenses. Clubs are located in the South, in the state of Washington, and in other regions of the western United States, as well as in France, Scandinavia, and Australia. Membership is estimated to total 3000 worldwide, with a large number of associates; there are more than 80 chapters in 12 countries. Within the United States, the Bandidos have more than 700 members and approximately 70 chapters in 14 states. There is evidence of the expansion of chapters, with the Utah chapter being established in 2003; the president of this chapter has been arrested for suspicion of murder.

In 2006, five members of the Canadian Bandidos were arrested on charges stemming from an in-group massacre. Eight murdered Bandito members were found in their vehicles on a remote farm near London, Ontario. At first, the Hells Angels were suspected, but later the Royal Canadian Mounted Police (RCMP) implicated fellow Bandidos in an apparent power struggle. In-group killings are not uncommon among OMG groups. As with all organized crime groups, the sense of brotherhood often breaks down when power or profit gets in the way.

Pagans

Established in 1959 in Prince George County, Maryland, by then president Lou Dobkin, Pagan chapters are now located along the eastern U.S. seaboard as well as in Louisiana (New Orleans), Florida, Texas, California, and West Virginia, although group activities

Examples of a Hells Angels patch.

are primarily centered in Pennsylvania, New Jersey, and New York. This OMG was a fairly benign group until 1965, when the Pagans evolved into a fierce biker gang with ties to organized crime groups such as the American Mafia (Barker, 2005). Their violence grew under the leadership of John "Satan" Marron in the early 1970s (Lavigne, 1987). There is no evidence of international clubs and the Mother Club is not in a fixed location, although it has been generally located in the Northeast.

Pagan leaders consist of 13 to 18 members who are chapter presidents, with the largest chapter located in Philadelphia. The Pagan membership has been dropping in recent years owing to law enforcement pressure, competition from other biker gangs (particularly the Hells Angels), and internal dissension (Barker, 2005). The estimated membership is between 600 and 900 patch-wearing members. Their colors show a Norse fire god.

The Pagans have grown by merging with other smaller OMGs. Considered by law enforcement to be almost as complex and diversified as the Hells Angels, the discipline and structure of the Pagans are the most rigid of the Big Four OMGs. The Pagan Outlaw Motorcycle Clubs' constitution, shown in **Box 10-1**, explains much of the culture of OMGs.

Box 10-1 Pagan Club Organization and Rules

The Pagan motorcycle club is run by the Mother Club. The Mother Club has last and final authority over all club matters. Any violation of the constitution will be dealt with by the Mother Club.

Six (6) members are needed to start a chapter. No new chapter may be started without approval of the Mother Club.

President—Runs chapter under the direction of the Mother Club. Keeps the chapter organized, makes sure chapter business is carried out, inspects all bikes before runs, and makes President meetings.

Sergeant-at-Arms—Makes sure the President's orders are carried out.

Vice-President—Takes over all the President's duties when the President is not there.

Secretary-Treasurer—In charge of minutes of meetings and treasury.

No member may change chapters without the permission of the Mother Club members in his area. All present chapter debts are paid and are approved by the president of the new chapter he wishes to change to. If a member has a "snival," he must use the chain of command—in other words,

1. His Chapter President,
2. A Mother Club member in the area,
3. The President of the club.

Meetings

1. Chapters must have one organized meeting per week.
2. Chapter meetings are attended by members only.
3. Members must be of sound mind (straight) when attending meetings.
4. If a Mother Club member attends a meeting and a member is fouled up, he will be fined by the Mother Club member.
5. Miss three (3) meetings in a row, and you're out of the club.
6. A member must attend a meeting to leave the club and turn in his colors and everything that has the name PAGANS on it (T-shirts, wrist bands, mugs, and so on).
7. If a member is thrown out of the club or quits without attending a meeting, he loses his colors, motorcycle, and anything that says PAGANS on it, and probably gets an ass kicking.

8. When a member is traveling, he must attend the meeting of the area he is traveling in.

9. If a vote is taken at a meeting and member is not there, his vote is void.

10. The member must have colors with him when attending meeting.

Bikes

1. All members must have a Harley Davidson 750–1200 cc.

2. If a member is not of sound mind or is too fouled up to ride his motorcycle in the opinion of another member, his riding privilege may be pulled by said member until he has his head together.

3. All bikes must be on the road April 30, or otherwise directed by the Mother Club.

4. All members must have a motorcycle license.

Mandatories

Two (2) mandatories, July 4, and Labor Day; Mother Club may call additional mandatories if need be.

Funerals

1. If a member dies in a chapter, it is necessary for all members in his chapter to attend his funeral.

2. The chapter is in charge of taking care of all funeral arrangements, parties, police, procession, and so on.

Parties

Pagan parties are Pagan parties only. Each chapter must throw (1) party or run a year.

Respect

1. Respect is to be shown to all Mother Club members, officer members, member's personal property, bike, old lady, house, job, and so on. In other words, if it's not yours, "Don't Mess with It."

2. No fighting among chapter members is allowed; any punches to be thrown will be done by the Sergeant-at-Arms or a Mother Club member.

3. No stealing from members.

4. Respect your colors.

(continues)

Box 10-1 Pagan Club Organization and Rules—Continued

Colors

1. The President gets colors from a Mother Club member in the area when a new member is voted in.

2. When a member leaves club, the President of his chapter turns over his colors to the Mother Club member in his area.

3. Respect your colors; don't let anyone take them from you except the President of your chapter or a Mother Club member.

4. No colors are worn in a cage, except during funerals and loading or unloading a bike from a truck.

5. Nothing will be worn on the back of your jacket except your colors, Diamond, 13 Patch.

6. No Hippie s**t on the front.

7. Colors are to be put on cut off denim jackets only.

8. The only member who may keep his colors if he leaves the club is a Mother Club member.

Old Ladies

1. Members are responsible for their Old Ladies.

2. Members may have more than one (1) Old Lady.

3. Members may not discuss club business with their Old Lady.

4. No Old Ladies are allowed at meetings.

5. No property patch is worn on an Old Lady—so if you see a chick, you better ask before you leap.

Prospects

1. Prospects must be at least 18 years old.

2. A prospect must be sponsored by one member who has known him at least one year.

3. The sponsor is responsible for the prospect.

4. The prospect must have a motorcycle.

5. The prospect must ride his bike to the meeting at time of being voted into the club.

6. The prospect cannot do any drugs.

7. Prospects cannot carry weapons at meetings and Pagan functions, unless otherwise directed by the president.

8. No stealing from Prospects is allowed.

9. Prospects must attend all meetings and club functions.

10. The prospect must do anything another member tells him to, that a member has done or would be willing to do himself.

11. The prospect must be voted in by all members of the chapter and three (3) Mother Club members.

12. The prospect must pay for his colors before receiving them.

13. The probation period for the prospect is determined by the Mother Club member.

14. Pagans M.C. is a motorcycle club and a nonprofit organization.

Other OMGs

Although the Big Four are considered the most formable threats, many smaller OMGs are involved in what can be classified as organized crime activity. The structure, method of operation, activities, and culture of these smaller OMGs are very similar to those of the Big Four. Many of these smaller OMGs act as puppet clubs for the Big Four or as their co-conspirators in illegal activities. A partial list of other independent clubs/gangs includes the Pistorellos, Warlocks, Vagos, Sons of Silence, Iron Horseman, Mongols, Grim Reapers, Kingsman, Red Devils, Ghost Riders, Diablos, Devils Disciples, Galloping Goose, and El Forastero.

These smaller OMGs are often involved in significant criminal activity. For example, the former national president of Diablos OMG was given a life sentence in U.S. court in 2002 for his role in the distribution of 40 pounds of meth in Indiana. In December 2005, several members of the Diablos were arrested on drug and weapon trafficking violations in Connecticut.

Grim Reapers

The Grim Reapers Motorcycle Club (GRMC) is a typical example of an independent OMG, with a 44-year history and chapters in Tennessee, Iowa, Illinois, Kentucky, and Indiana. Considered an ally of the Outlaws OMG, the Grim Reapers has ties to the Ku Klux Klan (KKK) and state militia groups. This OMG is an advocate of white supremacist beliefs and is considered extremely violent. Grim Reapers OMGs in Canada are independent of the U.S. club and are allied with Hells Angels, with some chapters becoming Hells Angels' chapters.

The origin of the Grim Reapers is believed to date back to 1959 in Louisville, Kentucky. Like other OMGs, the Grim Reapers are involved in distribution of large quantities of illicit drugs, stolen motorcycles and other vehicles, money laundering, mail fraud, and firearms violations. Much like the Big Four, the GRMC has national rules that govern conduct, membership, and operations.

Officials in the club have national authority and are located in the northern and southern regions; the national president is elected to a two-year term. Clubhouses, which are normally residences, serve as meeting locations and are most often found in remote and well-fortified areas. There are two mandatory national runs and two regional runs each year. High-level meetings are called presidentials, where each chapter and regional president has one vote.

The structure of the GRMC is depicted in **Figure 10-3**. Membership has varied from 70 to 200, and the Mother Chapter is located in Louisville. Similar to the Pagans' rules, to join the Grim Reapers individuals must be 18 years old, cannot be African American, and must own a 1000-cc American-made motorcycle. During the clubs' probationary period, prospects are subjected to intense physical and mental abuse. As part of the proof that they are not members of law enforcement, prospects often must commit crimes and provide an address for the next of kin.

GRMC colors are highly regarded (as with all OMGs); the logo shows a red-shrouded Grim Reaper holding a red scythe. Club tattoos are required for members and are located on an arm after three years and on their back after eight years of membership. Members cannot be drug addicts, and must pay 10% of their profits from drug sales and any profits from criminal activities to the treasurer of the club as a road tax; this money is split between the national, regional, and chapter treasuries.

In the future, the GRMC appears likely to be absorbed into one of the larger OMGs, such as the Hells Angels, and continue to be involved in criminal activities, primarily drug distribution, smuggling, and theft. Law enforcement lacks information on this group, such as expansion of its chapters. Although not the same threat as the Big Four, clubs such as the GRMC pose a serious concern for law enforcement and should be a focus for intelligence and law enforcement efforts (*Intelligence Bulletin,* April 2004).

Mongols

The Mongols Motorcycle Club is another example of an outlaw biker group that is extremely violent and poses a problem for law enforcement. The group is described in former ATF agent William Queen's (2006) book *Under and Alone.* Queen infiltrated this group as an undercover agent for ATF and tells his story. His book is recommended reading for anyone interested the workings of an outlaw biker group.

The Mongols continue to make headlines, with more than 60 of this OMG's members being arrested in six states. A law enforcement operation named "Operation Black Rain" resulted in the arrest of the gang's former national president, Ruben Cavozos. The group was infiltrated by four ATF agents who became patched full members. The former

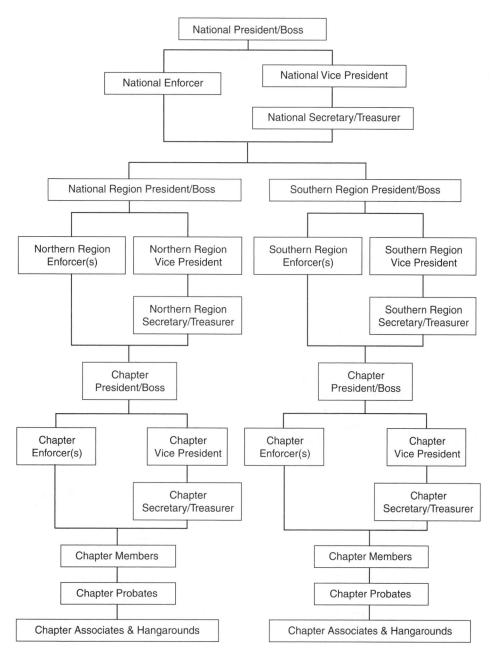

Figure 10-3 Organizational structure of the Grim Reapers OMG.

president, Cavazos, has written a memoir titled *Honor Few, Fear None: The Life and Times of a Mongol,* published by Harper Collins (Watkins, 2008).

The Mongols are a Latino ethnic gang and are rivals of the Hells Angels. AFT agent Mike Hoffman reported that the gang was recruiting members of Los Angeles street gangs to assist in its operations. The Southern California–based biker clan is believed to have approximately 600 members. The U.S. Attorney has stated that members are involved in drug trafficking, murder, assault, and arms trafficking. He plans to ask a federal judge to seize the Mongol's trademarked name, which would result in members not being able to wear their colors.

A recent indictment describes the Mongols as tightly organized and engaging in violence against black people, committing robberies, stealing motorcycles, and stealing credit card account information. The group is structured much like the Hells Angels and has strict rules and a rigid hierarchy.

Structure

Membership

OMGs are paramilitary organizations with a bureaucratic structure. **Figure 10-4** shows the chain of command within a typical OMG. **Figure 10-5** provides an ecological map of the social structure among members. The leader (national president) rules from the Mother Club (national headquarters). Chapters and regional representatives are selected in each geographic territory of the club. OMGs insulate their leaders from criminal activity through layers of members, puppet club members, probates, associates, and biker women. All major problems are submitted to the Mother Club or national leaders for resolution. Each club has its own elite enforcement unit: the "SS" for the Outlaws, the "Filthy Few" or "Death Squad" for the Hells Angles, the "Black T-Shirt Squad" for the Pagans, and the "Nomad Chapter" for the Bandidos. These elite enforcement groups move from chapter to chapter, serving as the "hit men" and "fixers" for the club.

Biker women are treated as property and wear colors with the inscription "Property of [club name]." There seems to be no shortage of women willing to become *old ladies, mamas,* or *sheep.* Often forced to work as prostitutes, dancers, or masseuses to support biker or OMG members, biker women are abused frequently and are considered property of the club. Most are initiated into the OMG by undergoing a "gang bang" (rape by most members). Mamas or sheep belong to the entire club and are expected to submit to sexual activity at any time with any member. Although they do not attend club meetings, they do work at the clubhouse as needed. Women referred to as old ladies belong to only one club member and cannot be touched by another member without reprisal; they do not attend club meetings. Biker women frequently provide housing for club members and work regular jobs to provide income for the member(s). These women often drive the crash truck during runs. Because they often carry guns or drugs for the members, biker women present a danger to anyone, including law enforcement.

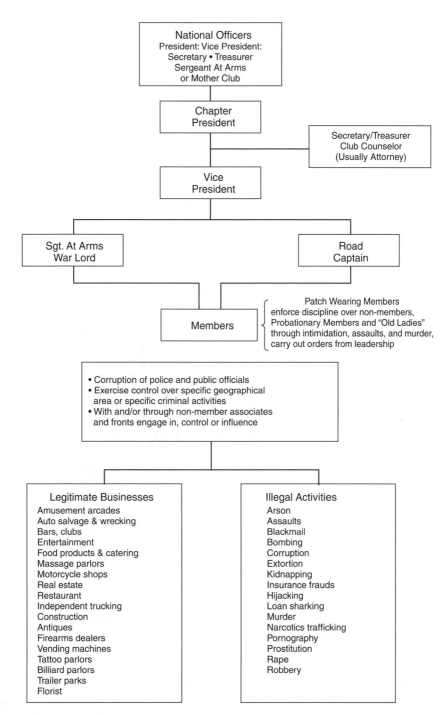

Figure 10-4 Typical structure of a major OMG chapter.

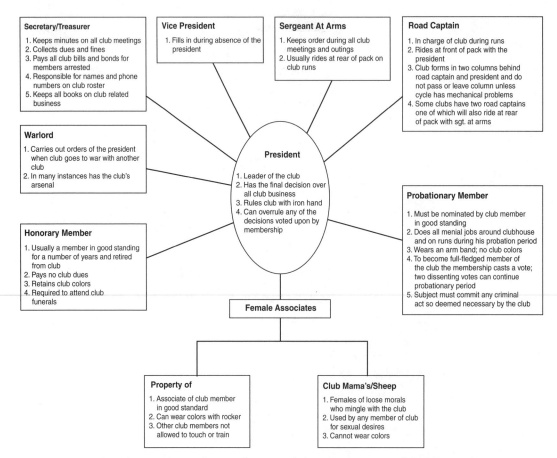

Secretary/Treasurer
1. Keeps minutes on all club meetings
2. Collects dues and fines
3. Pays all club bills and bonds for members arrested
4. Responsible for names and phone numbers on club roster
5. Keeps all books on club related business

Vice President
1. Fills in during absence of the president

Sergeant At Arms
1. Keeps order during all club meetings and outings
2. Usually rides at rear of pack on club runs

Road Captain
1. In charge of club during runs
2. Rides at front of pack with the president
3. Club forms in two columns behind road captain and president and do not pass or leave column unless cycle has mechanical problems
4. Some clubs have two road captains one of which will also ride at rear of pack with sgt. at arms

Warlord
1. Carries out orders of the president when club goes to war with another club
2. In many instances has the club's arsenal

President
1. Leader of the club
2. Has the final decision over all club business
3. Rules club with iron hand
4. Can overrule any of the decisions voted upon by membership

Honorary Member
1. Usually a member in good standing for a number of years and retired from club
2. Pays no club dues
3. Retains club colors
4. Required to attend club funerals

Probationary Member
1. Must be nominated by club member in good standing
2. Does all menial jobs around clubhouse and on runs during his probation period
3. Wears an arm band; no club colors
4. To become full-fledged member of the club the membership casts a vote; two dissenting votes can continue probationary period
5. Subject must commit any criminal act so deemed necessary by the club

Female Associates

Property of
1. Associate of club member in good standard
2. Can wear colors with rocker
3. Other club members not allowed to touch or train

Club Mama's/Sheep
1. Females of loose morals who mingle with the club
2. Used by any member of club for sexual desires
3. Cannot wear colors

Figure 10-5 Social interrelationships and responsibilities among typical OMG members.

Biker women often are used to gather intelligence. One way to provide this service is through their employment in strategic locations such as utility companies, telephone companies, and police departments. Operating in places such as court houses, law offices, and licensing agencies provides these women with opportunities to falsify documents and create new identities as well as monitor law enforcement and task force efforts.

During the 1970s, the attempt to attain legitimacy by the four major OMGs in their home communities resulted in formal charters with rules and bylaws. Each club now has a constitution and bylaws (the Hells Angels' bylaws are listed in **Box 10-2**).

As seen in Figure 10-5, each chapter president makes decisions about all club business and can overrule any decision voted on by chapter members. The vice president fills in when the president is absent. The Bandidos, Pagans, and Outlaws OMGs have a national president and four regional vice presidents. The Pagans' Mother Club consists of 13 to 18 former chapter presidents, who wear the number 13 on black T-shirts with their colors to signify their leadership position. Currently, the Hells Angels are divided into the East and West Coast divisions. Presidents of the chapters meet to discuss runs, club business, and admission of new chapters. Criminal activity is not discussed at these sanctioned club meetings.

Each club has a secretary/treasurer who keeps minutes of club meetings, collects dues and fines, and keeps all business records for the club. The national secretary answers to the national president, handles national violations, and keeps business records. He also may serve as a bodyguard to the president. Order is kept by the sergeant-at-arms, who often doubles as the enforcer and "hit man" for the chapter. The warlord keeps the weapons for the chapter and works directly for the chapter president. The road captain plans the runs, which includes dealing with issues of security, logistics, and supplies.

Each chapter may have a clubhouse where club business is discussed and parties are held. Some have referred to the meetings in clubhouses as "church" (Tretheway & Katz, 1998). The Hells Angels have a "Church of Angels" with ministers, which allows them to visit incarcerated members as well as provides the club with tax exemptions. Clubhouses are frequently protected by both interior and exterior security, steel doors, special locks, safes, barbed wire, chain-link fences, guard dogs, armored plating, burglar alarms, surveillance cameras, police scanners, booby traps, and a variety of high-tech

---

Box 10-2 Hells Angels' California Bylaws

1. All patches will be the same on the back; nothing will show on the back except the HELL ANGELS PATCH. A city patch is optional for each chapter. One patch and one membership card is allotted per member. The member may keep the original patch if it is made into a banner. Prospects will wear the California rocker on the back and a prospect patch left from where top of pocket is on a Levi jacket.

   FINE: $100 for breaking above bylaw.

2. No hypes. No use of heroin in any form. Anyone using a needle for any reason other than having a doctor use it on you will be considered a hype.

   FINE: Automatic kick-out from club.

3. No explosives of any kind will be thrown into the fire where there is one or more HELLS ANGELS in this area.

   FINE: Ass-whipping and/or subject to California President's decision.

4. Guns on California runs will not be displayed after 6 P.M. They will be fired from dawn until 6 p.m. in a predetermined area only. This rule does not apply to anyone with a gun in a shoulder holster or belt that is seen by another member if it is not being shot or displayed.

   FINE: $100 for breaking above bylaw.

   (continues)

Box 10-2 Hells Angels' California Bylaws—Continued

5. Brothers shall not fight with each other with weapons; when any HELLS ANGELS fights another HELLS ANGELS, it is one on one; the rule for prospects is the same as that for members. If members are from different chapters, the fine goes to the California Treasurer.

   FINE: $100 for breaking above bylaw or possible loss of patch.

6. No narcotics burns. When making deals, persons get what they are promised or the deal is called off.

   FINE: Automatic kick-out from club.

7. All HELLS ANGELS fines will be paid within 30 days. Fines will be paid to that chapter's treasurer to be held for the next California run.

8. There is one vote per chapter at California officers' meetings. For California, two no votes instead of a majority is required to kill a new charter; if a charter goes below six, they must freeze or dissolve on the decision of the California officers' meeting.

9. If kicked out, a member must stay out one year and then go back to his original chapter. The HELLS ANGEL tattoo will have an in-date and out-date when the member quits. If a member is kicked out, the HELLS ANGELS tattoo will be completely covered with a half X through the tattoo.

10. Runs are on the holidays; the three mandatory runs are Memorial Day, July 4, and Labor Day.

11. There is no leave period except for hospital, medical, or jail reasons.

anti-intrusion devices. Both turf wars against rival gangs and the potential for infiltration by law enforcement keeps members constantly alert for intrusion.

OMGs have restricted membership, with members paying dues to continue belonging to the club. A probationary member or prospect must be nominated by a club member in good standing who has known the prospect for at least a year. Prospective members perform menial jobs at the clubhouse and on runs. The prospect must commit whatever criminal act is deemed necessary by the club. Once a period of time has passed, and he has completed all requirements and demands by the club, the prospect is voted in by the members. Rituals for initiation are disgusting and often involve humiliating acts. These rituals or initiation rites vary from club to club. The prospect may be allowed to wear an armband with the club's colors during the probationary period.

Honorary members are those who have retired and are usually in good standing (see the next section).

All members, prospects, and honorary members are required to attend runs, funerals, and sanctioned meetings. The larger clubs or OMGs invest a portion of their profits into legitimate businesses, which then become club assets. Many members are employed, some as lawyers, some as famous entertainers, and some in a variety of white-collar professions. Membership has evolved from mostly war veterans to individuals from diverse backgrounds, although most come from the criminal element of society. For every colors-wearing member, there are approximately 10 associates who serve the club's interests.

Retirement Bylaws

Very little is known about aging OMG members, but it is clear that most of the Vietnam veteran–era members are facing retirement. Those who have survived the gang's brutality and escaped prosecution must follow a set of rules, just as regular members.
The following list of regulations applies to Hells Angels retirees:

1. You cannot change a bylaw at anytime (no ands, ifs, or buts—no exceptions).
2. After five years of active duty, you automatically keep your rag. Plus, you still must serve two and a half years on mandatory runs and other mandatory get-togethers.
3. You have to make four runs a year. (This is mandatory.)
    a. Steve Jamail is one run that you must be there or you will be fined $50.00.
    b. You can pick any other three mandatory runs of your choice.
    c. If any mandatory runs are missed, you will automatically be fined $50.00 for every run that you do miss.
4. If any mandatory runs are missed, you are fined for it. Also, if you are unable to pay the money you owe, the club can take your color and keep it until you can pay up.
5. After seven and a half years, you are automatically retired, or you have an option of staying in the club.
6. After retirement, you do not have to be at any meetings but you still must pay your dues.
7. After five years, you still have to pay whatever dues the club may have in effect at that time.

Activities and Methods of Operation

As stated earlier, OMGs are very sophisticated in their counter-surveillance techniques and security employed to protect their criminal activity against rival gangs and law enforcement. Although drug trafficking is their most common and profitable criminal activity, their other criminal activities include robbery, extortion, murder, arson, receiving stolen goods, white slavery, prostitution, rape, weapons trafficking, and assaults.

Networks

OMGs have a history of criminal relationships with LCN. For example, the Hells Angels have done work for the Gambino crime family of New York and Cleveland. The Pagans have been associated with LCN families on the East Coast, and have been used as enforcers for groups such as the Bruno crime family and the Philadelphia Mafia crime boss, Joey Merlino.

Cocaine, methamphetamine, and marijuana were the original drugs trafficked by OMGs; however, today the OMGs will venture into any market that has the potential for profit. In 1986, the President's Commission on Organized Crime estimated that OMGs earned more than $1 billion per year from drug trafficking and other criminal activities. OMGs have supported Mafia strip clubs by supplying women as dancers. These groups also have taken on legitimate businesses that act as fronts for criminal activity and avenues for money laundering, much like the methods used by the traditional Mafia groups.

OMGs control their networks through violence and intimidation of members, rivals, and potential witnesses. A current trend among OMGs is the employment of puppet clubs to conduct the criminal activity for the sponsor club. In Mississippi, the Pistorellos have seven chapters that are associated with the Bandidos' criminal activities. These puppet clubs take most of the risk and return most of the profits to the more powerful OMG members. This trend, along with the trend toward increasing Mafia associations, has allowed OMGs to expand their influence and become more diverse in both their legal and illegal enterprises.

Many of the associates act as a layer of security from prosecution and provide such services as clandestine laboratory operators, chemists for illicit drug labs, contract murderers, money launderers, and suppliers of weapons, chemicals, and high tech equipment. Attorneys who represent OMG members often help secure information regarding witnesses, who are then threatened with violence, injured, or killed. Like the Mafia, OMGs have used methods of bribery and corruption by means of money, surveillance, drugs, or sex to obtain information or favors for the enterprise. Today, OMG members are much more sophisticated than those who belonged to the original clubs. More educated and manipulative, they are adept at using the criminal justice system and technology to their advantage.

Angie Wagner (2002) reported on the April 2002 fight between the Hells Angels and the Mongols at Harrah's Casino in Laughlin, Nevada, where three men were killed. The investigation revealed that the Hells Angels were using high-tech equipment (such as night vision and quality weapons) to aid in their retaliation for the killing of another Hells Angels member, Christian Tate. A large amount of ammunition and a number of weapons were confiscated in a raid connected to this investigation. Although OMGs have become more educated and sophisticated, events such as this one are indicators that violence, revenge, and the outlaw behavior remain an integral part of OMG culture.

Similar to the Colombian DTOs, street gangs, and the American Mafia, OMGs sometimes change their public image from one of outlaw groups to that of service-type organizations that assist the community in good causes and charities. Like Al Capone feeding the hungry in Chicago, the OMGs have taken on behavior that makes them popular with the public. This practice garners favorable public support and decreases law enforcement attention.

Although OMGs have diversified their criminal activities, drug trafficking remains their primary source of income. The use of counterintelligence and infiltration of government and business has allowed some OMGs to rival such groups as the American Mafia in power and wealth in a particular region.

Investigative Strategies

Intelligence

The most important aspect of investigating OMGs is gathering intelligence to prove that these groups are actually a criminal enterprise engaged in a pattern of racketeering. The collection, analysis, and dissemination of accurate and timely information are keys to developing strategies to address OMG criminal activity. It takes a team effort to gather the right information and then implement a strategy for effective enforcement.

The first step is to identify the structure of the OMG and the members who occupy positions in the structure. Intelligence must identify this structure as a criminal enterprise. Because OMGs are considered groups involved in conspiracy to commit criminal activity, RICO, conspiracy, and money laundering statutes can be applied to bring the entire membership to trial as well as capture their assets.

The investigator must identify the associates, women, and puppet clubs who are an integral part of the club's criminal activities. During the intelligence gathering activity, investigators also must identify all connections with white supremacy groups, prison gangs, Mafia associates, street gangs, and any groups or individuals who are receiving services or goods or providing them to OMGs. This amount of information can be gathered only with interagency cooperation and by task force or strike force operations.

The creation of joint task forces and the Organized Crime Drug Enforcement Task Forces (OCDETF) in 1982 has proved to be the most effective approach to successful investigations of OMGs. Such organizations as the National Alliance of Gang Investigators' Associations are tremendous assets to investigators for networking, developing contacts for assistance, and remaining current on OMG trends and activities. Information on and identities of OMG members are much less difficult to obtain than details on the Mafia because of their public persona. OMGs openly flaunt their membership during their mandatory runs, established clubhouses, and frequent parties or meetings.

Numerous investigator organizations hold frequent conferences where training, education, and networking occurs. These working conferences should be part of any investigator's schedule.

Intelligence gathering is not without enormous risks to the agents as well as the informants. A few club members have agreed to divulge club activities after being faced with jail terms or committing particularly heinous crimes. Deep undercover agents often must participate in crimes to preserve their subterfuge, and some obfuscate or outright lie to their handlers, which can result in an operation going out of control. One Arizona sting ("Black Biscuit") in 2003 found that the informer, Solo Angeles biker president Rudy Kramer, continued to operate a meth lab and deal in weapons; he also brought a woman to a club party where she was subsequently murdered (Sher & Marsden, 2006). Although the Hells Angels organization was shaken by this sting operation in many western states, the tangle of court cases for Black Biscuit is still unraveling.

Laws and Statutes

Two of the more common criminal violations cited for OMGs are firearms violations and illicit drug trafficking. Federal statutes provide mandatory sentences for carrying or using a firearm during the commission of a felony (Title 18 U.S.C. Section 924). The Continuing Criminal Enterprise (CCE) statute (Title 21 U.S.C. 848) is a very potent weapon against supervisors, financiers, organizers, or managers of drug trafficking organizations such as OMGs. When these statutes are combined with RICO (18 U.S.C. 1961-68), investigators have an effective arsenal to wield against OMGs. Both criminal and civil RICO complaints can be used against members and assets of the OMGs. Add in the federal money laundering laws (e.g., Currency Transaction Report [CTR] and Currency and Monetary Instrument Report [CMIR] violations, the Money Laundering Act of 1986, the Money Laundering Prosecution Improvement Act of 1988), and the investigators have no excuse not to prosecute OMGs members, both individually and as part of an enterprise. These statutes are discussed in Chapter 12.

The Financial Crimes Enforcement Network (FinCEN), which was created in 1990 under the Department of Treasury, is an excellent resource to use during money laundering investigations. The El Paso Intelligence Center is another excellent resource for following the money when conducting investigations of OMGs. The U.S. Treasury Department's TECSII System is helpful for tracking the criminal activities of OMGs. Currently, the Patriot Act is the broadest money laundering statute and has expanded the scope of such investigations; the definition of an illegal money-transmitting business was expanded with this legislation, as was the concept of specified unlawful activity.

In addition to becoming members of task forces and networking with other entities, the development and proper management of informants can provide the evidence of structure and criminal activity necessary for an OMG to be classified as a criminal enterprise. Informants are very difficult to develop in OMGs because of the expectation of violent reprisals (including murder of themselves and their families) as punishment for anyone who provides information to law enforcement. Although confidential informants (CIs) have been very effective on occasions, they are difficult to control, protect, and develop. In addition, the CI may be able to provide only limited information about the enterprise.

Both electronic and physical surveillance can be extremely valuable to the investigation. However, placing a listening device in the right location at the right time can be problematic because the target area is often secured by both physical and electronic security and counter-surveillance measures. Identifying the proper location where valuable information can be intercepted (which phone, vehicle, business, clubhouse, or home) can be time consuming and dangerous. Undercover operations have been successful (Hells Angels, Bandidos, Outlaw, and other U/C operations) but are long-term ventures, are expensive, and require a great deal of risk by highly trained officers (Sher & Marsden, 2006).

Developing intelligence for prosecution requires enormous resources and time. In the case of OMGs, external and international cooperation is a frequent requirement. Other programs not previously mentioned, such as the Regional Information Sharing System (RISS) and the High Intensity Drug Trafficking Areas (HIDTA), can be additional valuable resources in moving against OMGs.

Grand Juries

As the investigation of an OMG is certain to be long term, the use of the investigative grand juries can be extremely beneficial. The subpoena power and grant of immunity available with this format are highly useful during the investigation. Educating a jury gradually empowers them to synthesize the complex information and allows for a higher probability of an indictment. The intelligence analyst's role is critical in this regard so that the enormous amount of data can be organized and summarized in a fashion that clearly defines the enterprise, provides a logical chronology of events, and details the illegal scheme/scam and money laundering activities. The adage "Follow the money" remains one of the best investigative strategies for proving the existence of a criminal enterprise. A flow chart of conversations and dates/times of phone calls is very enlightening to juries, because it can demonstrate correlations of criminal activity when combined with electronic surveillance videotapes.

Dozens of statutes concerning drug trafficking at the state and federal levels can be used to investigate OMGs (see Chapter 12). Any criminal violation discovered must be noted as a possible avenue for prosecution. However, taking all the assets, members, and associates to court is the only possible means to completely destroy the enterprise. RICO, money laundering, and conspiracy charges are the best opportunities to ensure near total destruction of OMGs.

The traditional Uniform Crime Reporting (UCR) Index Crimes of arson, assault, murder, theft, and robbery are additional avenues for developing prosecutable cases or proving a pattern of racketeering activity of a criminal enterprise. Crime scene investigations must be complete, with investigators using all available means to collect and analyze evidence to prove these traditional crimes stem from OMG activities, by connecting violators, crime scene, and victims.

Because drug distribution and production remain a major source of income for OMGs, there is a trend toward these groups forming alliances with smaller OMGs and major criminal enterprises such as the Mexican DTO; the profits from these liaisons can then strengthen these organizations both domestically and internationally. Larger and more powerful OMGs are likely to be observed in the near future. Lack of intelligence about these groups remains a concern, including the extent of alliances among OMGs, their U.S. and foreign chapters, and other organized crime groups, as well as the sources of weapons that OMGs are stockpiling.

Conclusions

In the end, it is the ability, perseverance, and fortitude of the investigators and their teams that brings about a successful prosecution of the OMG. They will find a way to address such a national threat as the OMG. The goal for the team is to collect, develop, and present evidence to juries, who will make their decisions based on the evidence and competency of the investigators.

Outlaw biker gangs are likely to continue to expand with the consolidation of many smaller gangs into the major groups. The trend toward establishing puppet clubs will continue, with some of these clubs eventually becoming major players and breaking away from their sponsoring clubs. Outlaw biker clubs will undoubtedly expand more into legitimate businesses and, like the Yakuza, abandon many of the traditions of the past. These trends will make the outlaw bikers more of an enterprise that, while criminally oriented, will be more difficult for law enforcement to address effectively.

Rivalries will continue between the major clubs, but alliances will also occur between clubs and other organized crime groups. OMGs will expand their use of technology in an effort to increase their efficacy. Their growth is likely to lead to development of larger groups—more than the current Big Four—for law enforcement to target. The future of OMGs will depend on their ability to evolve into more complex structures, by adding more layers between members and their criminal activities, and using their Hollywood-type glamour to recruit new members as well as infiltrate legitimate business, as the Yakuza and Mafia have done, especially in the last two decades. If the OMGs become more diverse and form alliances with other organized crime groups, they will continue to grow both in membership and power.

Discussion Questions

1. List and discuss the major OMGs in the United States. How did they evolve?

2. What is the typical structure of an OMG? Why and how is this structure important to law enforcement?

3. Which criminal activities do the OMGs commit? What are the most profitable for these groups?

4. Which investigative strategies are most effective against OMGs?

5. Which parts of the Patriot Act are most effective against organized crime such as OMGs? How can they be applied?

6. What are the current trends of activity and method of operation of OMGs?

References

Barker, T. (2004). Exporting American Organized Crime: Outlaw Motorcycle Gangs. *Journal of Gang Research, 11*(2), 37–50.

Barker, T. (2005). One-Percent Bikers Clubs: A Description. *Trends in Organized Crime, 9*(1), 101–112.

Criminal Intelligence Service Canada. (2004). *Organized Crime in Canada: Annual Report.*

High Intensity Drug Trafficking Areas (HIDTA). Rockville, MD: Office of National Drug Policy. Retrieved December 3, 2006, from http://www.whitehousedrugpolicy.gov/hidta/index.html

Intelligence Bulletin. (2004, April). Grim Reapers Motorcycle Club.

Intelligence Bulletin. (2004, May). Outlaw Motorcycle Gangs and Drugs in the United States.

Lavigne, Y. (1987). *Hells Angels: Taking Care of Business.* Toronto: Ballantine.

National Alliance of Gang Investigators' Associations. (2005). *National Gang Threat Assessment.* Washington, DC: Bureau of Justice Assistance.

Queen, W. (2006). *Under and Alone.* New York: Random House.

Reynolds, T. (2000). *Wild Ride: How the Outlaw Motorcycle Myth Conquered America.* New York: TV Books.

Sher, J., & Marsden, W. (2006). *Angels of Death: Inside the Biker Gangs' Crime Empire.* New York: Carroll & Graf.

Tretheway, S., & Katz, T. (1998). Motorcycle Gangs or Motorcycle Mafia? *Police Chief, 66*(4), 53–60.

Veno, A. (2002). *The Brotherhoods: Inside the Outlaw Motorcycle Clubs.* Crows Nest, Australia: Allen & Urwin.

Wagner, A. (2002, April 27). Three Dead in Nevada's Worst Casino Shooting as Bikers Clash. *Reno Gazette Journal.* Retrieved October 9, 2006, from http://rgj.com/news/printstory.php?id=13147

Watkins, T. (2008, October 21). Mongols Motorcycle Gang Arrested in Federal Sweep. Retrieved June 20, 2010, from http://www.foxnews.com/printer_friendly_wires/2008Oct21?0,4675,Biker GangBusts,00.html

Yates, B. (1999). *Outlaw Machine: Harley-Davidson and the Search for the American Soul.* New York: Broadway Books.

Chapter 11

Hispanic and African American Gangs

The critical responsibility for the generation you are in is to help provide the shoulders, the direction, and the support for those generations who come behind.

— Gloria Dean Randle Scott, educator and president, Beaumont College (1938–)

Objectives

After completing this chapter, readers should be able to:

- Discuss the history of black organized crime in the United States.
- Describe gang culture and explain why it evolved.
- Explain how and why some gangs evolve into organized crime.
- Discuss the different structures of gangs in the United States.

Introduction

The definition of a gang varies according to perspective. Gang definitions are found in state statutes (such as those for California) as well as in academia and among a variety of law enforcement agencies. Curry and Spengel (1988) define gang activity as "law violating behavior by juveniles or adults in a group that can be complexly organized or unorganized and that is often cohesive with leadership and rules. They have a tradition of symbols, colors, turf, signs, and language, and engage in a wide variety of crimes frequently involving violence" (pp. 381–382).

Gangs, particularly street gangs, have been of interest to academics, community groups, and law enforcement officials since Frederick Thrasher's (1968) classic study of 1313 Chicago juvenile gangs in the early 1920s. These early gangs were juvenile play groups that evolved into identifiable entities that engaged in conflict with one another and committed petty crime. By the 1950s and 1960s, social and economic conditions had changed in Chicago and other urban areas, and these early street gangs had become crime groups. Dominated by African American and Hispanic gangs, they became involved in serious criminal behavior, including drug trafficking. They later expanded outside their original communities and emerged as regional and national crime threats, requiring new approaches by law enforcement.

Developing crime analysis and intelligence units is an essential investigative strategy when dealing with gangs, because the gang culture and language barriers are often difficult to overcome. By understanding the group's history, culture, and methods of operations, investigators become more effective in their efforts to deal with gangs that have the potential to rise to the level of organized crime.

Historical Perspective

Gang crime and violence are not recent phenomena, but rather have been around for millennia. In the United States, such groups as the "Forty Thieves" of New York in the 1930s, the Jones Brothers gang of 1930s Chicago, and the Italian "Black Hand" and the Irish "White Hand" gangs operated in most major cities of early 20th-century America (Ianni, 1974). During the era that saw tremendous growth in the Sun Belt cities, many people from depressed urban centers in the north and west began to move to the south. Gangs and gang violence moved with them, becoming commonplace throughout Mississippi, Georgia, Tennessee, Arkansas, Louisiana, and Alabama. Social dissatisfaction, lack of education or opportunities to succeed, and rebellion were motivating factors for those urbanites who migrated south. Many of these newcomers brought their culture of crime with them, and new gangs began forming.

The 1980s were years of considerable expansion of gangs in the United States, primarily because of Americans' insatiable appetite for illegal drugs. Most discussions of organized crime in the United States tend to focus on activities in the major cities. However, rural states, such as Mississippi, have also experienced a tremendous increase in violence and drug distribution associated with gang activity. The Crips, Bloods, Folk Nation, and People Nation all had criminal groups in Mississippi by the 1980s and were involved in drug distribution in the region. Other states experienced the same kind of growth in gang activity.

Today, groups such as the Gangster Disciples have members in more than 70 cities in more than 35 states. With the Gangster Disciples' membership at an estimated 20,000 in Chicago alone (Knox & Fuller, 2004), the FBI has designated them as a major organized crime group. Whether gangs can be considered organized crime remains a topic of debate, as some—but not all—groups appear to have many of the characteristics of organized crime.

Hispanic/Latino Gangs

The origins of Hispanic gangs are rooted in 19th-century U.S. history (i.e., the 1852 annexation of the Southeastern territories) and continue to play a major role in current gang criminal activities. (African and other ethnic minority groups share this same kind of disturbed American history.) Many Latinos were left without a country and were removed from their homes and ranches after annexation; these families tended to gather in small towns known as *barrios*. The word *varrio* is used to reference a gang, and "barrio" and "varrio" are often used interchangeably. After economic and political events (similar to those experienced in the source countries of the Italian, Jewish, and Irish Americans), there was a significant migration of immigrants from Mexico into the United States. The ensuing rivalries that developed among immigrants led to the formation of what most believe to be the first U.S. gang.

Today, one in five immigrants to the United States is from Mexico. Correspondingly, Hispanic gangs are predicted to continue to increase in number.

Gang Communication: Language, Graffiti, Hand Signals, and Dress

Dress, language, graffiti, hand signs, and tattoos all must be understood by law enforcement to help identify members and predict activities of the gang.

The street slang known as *Caló* (which incorporates ancient Spanish Gypsy, Mexican, and English words; it is similar to "Tex-Mex" and "Spanglish" except that Caló is used in rhymes) is the dialect created by the gang that often appears in their graffiti. This language of Latino gangs is a combination of English and Spanish made to form new words or phrases. Much of this dialect/regional slang has been incorporated into the American lexicon, too.

Graffiti is an important part of gang tradition. Hispanic gangs call their inscriptions *plaquesos* or *placas*. This artwork and writing proclaims to the world the status of the gang, marks its turf, and offers a challenge to rivals. "Cross cuts" (mark-outs or destruction) of these writings are territorial insults that may escalate to violence, including "shoot-outs." *Monikers*, which are the street names of gang members, appear in the graffiti and can be valuable in identifying an individual gang member and his level of activity. Investigators must receive training and education in Spanish, Mexican/Latino culture, and local street language to be able to communicate with members, informants, the community, and to interpret graffiti correctly.

The dress of gangs has changed over the years. Because of the popularity of gang-type dress among non-gang members, however, it is now more difficult to determine membership in a gang. Some Latinos still wear the Pendleton-type wool shirt, khaki pants, watch or knit cap or a bandana (*moko rag*), and the popular highly polished leather shoes, but sports clothing and athletic shoes have become more common.

Hand signs and tattoos are the other two means of nonverbal communication of gangs (discussed in the next subsection).

Clicas

Divisions within the gang, known as cliques (*clicas*), are organized by age range. Seven- or eight-year-old gang members are referred to as *Inano* or *Tiny Locos*. *Veteranos* (veterans) are older and likely have spent time in prison. Role models (the veteranos) train the younger members in the ways and culture of the gang. Hand signs and tattoos are part of the intergenerational culture; one sign represents the initials of the gang and others are messages known to the members. Tattoos are cryptic symbols that express gang culture and are often crudely inked while the gang member is in jail. One common tattoo is three dots, which represents *mi vida loca* ("my crazy life").

Gang Culture

Most law enforcement officials believe that unrealistic and violent television and the brutal prison mentality have had powerful emotional impacts that have led to more violent gang activity. Other reasons why gang culture arises have been given by sociologists:

1. *Identity*: Most gang members identify themselves as warriors or soldiers.
2. *Recognition*: Belonging to a gang allows individuals to achieve a level or status that they feel is impossible to achieve outside the gang.
3. *Belonging*: The gang is a substitute for a family, and the gang becomes the member's family.
4. *Discipline*: Discipline is needed to achieve success; gang leaders provide this aspect to members.
5. *Love:* The gang is the family and the only place where members receive "love."
6. *Money:* Members assume that the gang will meet all of their needs and desires.

Just why certain young people are attracted to gang culture and remain involved with gangs are difficult questions. Lack of positive role models, jobs, lack of adult supervision, peer pressure, the need to belong, and the proliferation of working parents or single-parent households are a few of the factors contributing to gang culture. Many gang members are unsuccessful students who are high school dropouts or were expelled.

The rules set by these groups vary from gang to gang, and violation can result in assault and even death. Chief among gang values is loyalty. The gang becomes members' "god," and members will do anything to defend the gang.

A common paradigm of gang behaviors is the three R's:

- *Reputation*: Being "jumped in" or "beaten down" by members of the gang gives status to the new member. After the beating, members often hug one another and say they love one another, thereby psychologically linking violence and love. The status (rank) of the member and the gang's street reputation are very important to the culture of gangs.

- *Respect*: Respect is sought by both the individual and the gang. Disrespect (dis) demands retaliation.

- *Retaliation/revenge*: No challenge (dis) goes unanswered.

Gangs have their own rituals, languages, and so-called prayers that are part of the culture. The author of this book heard the following prayer from a gang member:

When I die and go to rest,
Lay two shotguns across my chest,
Tell all my vice lord brothers that I did my best.

Gang Structure

Gang structure may range from a loose coalition of individuals to a formal organization with an established leadership and ruling council of powerful members. The gang may have codified written rules or unwritten rules and procedures. When the gang develops leadership and rules, it becomes more powerful and displays more characteristics of organized crime. The gang will be unified in "peace times" (when the group is not in conflict with a rival gang) and will often display some type of unity in dress.

Members

Members are generally divided by types according to their level of involvement (Grennan & Britz, 2006):

- *Hard core*: need and thrive on gang activity. They determine the level of violence of the gang and are often the leaders or have the respect of all members. They are knowledgeable in legal matters, are streetwise, and are the most violent.

- *Affiliate*: associate with the gang for status and recognition. They are active in gang activity and wear tattoos, gang colors, or jackets,

- *Peripheral*: drift in and out of the gang based on interest in the current gang activity.

Recruiting into a gang can begin as early as age 9 or 10, although the majority of members are between 12 and 25 years of age. More often than not, they are underachievers with poor self-esteem, although there are some notable exceptions. Members join the gang by being "jumped in" and committing a crime.

Fagan (1988) classified gangs into four types:

1. *Social gang*: low level of delinquency and drug use or sales.

2. *Party gang*: acts of vandalism, extensive drug use, and cohesive operations based on patterns of drug use.

3. *Serious delinquents*: involved in drug sales and serious violent crime. They have organization and may be classified as organized crime.

4. *Young organizations*: extensive drug sales, highly cohesive, and organized. They have the most potential to become a formal organized group.

Another early work by Huff (1989) divided gangs into three types according to their activities:

1. *Hedonistic gangs*: minor crimes, getting high, and having fun.

2. *Instrumental gangs:* high volume of property crimes and not organized.

3. *Predatory gangs:* crimes of opportunity including robbery and theft. Serious drug abuse and drug sales are often used to purchase weapons. They are a target of exploitation by organized crime groups but are not considered organized crime.

Gang members may refer to themselves as warriors and have rules regarding their behavior. This is particularly true with white gangs, such as the Stoners, Cowboys, and Arkies (gangs identified in California).

Southeast Asian gangs are considered an especially serious problem by law enforcement. Laotian, Cambodian, Vietnamese, and Chinese gangs are common in major U.S. cities and along the coastal states, such as Louisiana, Texas, and Mississippi. Most of the previous information applies to these gangs because they are both organized in some groups and unorganized in others.

Major Gangs

Some of the major black gangs whose span of operations extend into multiple states include the Bloods, Crips, Vice Lords, Folks, Black Gangster Disciples, and Latin Kings. Membership in some gangs is multi-ethnic, wherein whites, Latinos/Hispanics, blacks, and other U.S. minorities may run in a single gang. The Vice Lord Nation also may be known as the *People,* whereas the Disciple Nation is sometimes called the *Folks*. Both the Folks and Disciple Nation had appeared in Chicago by the 1970s.

The origin and histories of these gangs are confusing and debated not only among academia and law enforcement, but also among gang members themselves. Their histories vary from state to state and from city to city. It has been reported that the Vice Lord Nation (the conservative Vice Lords) originated in 1958 in the Illinois State Training School for Boys known as "Charlie Town"; they were very active in the Lawndale area of Chicago. Known as a very violent gang, they believe that if you are fearless, you attack before you are attacked. The culture and pressures of inner cities cause a social bond to form between the gangs and their community that is a major factor in the continued existence of gangs.

Bloods and Crips

The Crips were probably first formed around 1967 in Los Angeles, California. They now operate in many major cities, such as New York, Kansas City, and Chicago, as well as in rural areas along the Mississippi Gulf Coast and Jackson, Mississippi. The Bloods include African Americans as well as Afro-Latinos; this gang formed when smaller gangs banded together in the early 1970s to protect themselves from the Crips' violence. More than 30 states report the presence of these gangs. The 2005 National Gang Threat Assessment reports that Bloods are operating in all regions of the United States (National Alliance of Gang Investigators' Associations, 2005). Although their leadership is constantly changing due to incarceration, death, and takeovers, these gangs display many characteristics of organized crime.

Along with the anti-Crips, players, and mob gangs, the Bloods began as a series of social groups (Piru Boys) with their own dress style; they were very "turf" oriented. Over time, their minor crimes evolved into auto thefts, drive-by shootings, and drug distribution. The Piru Boys of Compton or Piru Street had their primary color as red, and the Crips (from the East Side of Los Angeles around Fremont High School) used blue as their primary color. The Crips used the word "Cuzz" to greet one another, while the Piru Boys used the term "Blood" to greet another member.

Confrontations between the Crips and the Bloods (Piru Boys) soon led to extreme violence. After entering the criminal justice system, many members were placed into institutions such as the California Youth Authority, which merely fostered the gang culture. Many factions of different gangs began to form alliances with either the Bloods or the Crips. Today, membership in the two gangs is estimated at more than 100,000, and networks or subgroups centered on them have formed across the United States.

When gang members of the Crips or Bloods are incarcerated, they present a major problem for correctional facilities, much like the Gangster Disciples or Vice Lords do. Crips members join or align with the prison gang known as the *Black Guerilla Family* (BGF), which itself is aligned with the *Black Liberation Army* (BLA). BGF has a rigid structure inside the prison that includes a chairman, central committee, field general, captains, lieutenants, and soldiers. Most members of the BGF are African American street gang members who were sent to prison. The BGF enforces its own code of discipline. Although the gang was originally formed in San Quentin in 1966 for protection of African American inmates, it quickly became involved in diverse criminal activities inside the prison, and its members are connected to drug trafficking and other crimes outside the prison.

Despite the attempt by some leaders to unite the various factions and subgroups of the Bloods and the Crips with Disciple Nation or Vice Lord Nation, there is not much evidence of a united national gang. In some areas, these gangs include Asians or Latino members. Members may dress in designer clothing, such as baggy trousers that are worn on or have the appearance of riding low on the hips. Referred to as *Homeboys* (fellow gang members), many are third-generation (Triple OG or "original gangster") gang members. Members often locate to other states to avoid arrest, where they are welcomed and protected by the local gang. Relocation to rural areas or other states also opens new drug markets for the gang, as they recruit boys and young men into their criminal culture.

Jeff Fort and the Black P. Stone Nation

Jeff Fort was born in Mississippi, but moved with his family while still young. In the 1960s and 1970s, Fort's Black Power rhetoric ignited an already burning rage over American social conditions among young black men. A high school dropout, after leading the Blackstone Rangers (a group that he formed in 1966 as one of hundreds of rough-and-tumble neighborhood gangs in Chicago), Fort negotiated a coalition of 21 warring gangs that became the *Black P. Stone Nation* in 1969 (Knox, 2004). He was incarcerated in 1972 for embezzlement of federal funds from a federal grant of $1 million that had been awarded to the Black P. Stone Nation to help establish a learning program. While in prison, he formed *El Rukins,* allegedly as a quasi-Muslim religious organization. Fort maintained his contacts in Mississippi and later was arrested and convicted of conspiracy to distribute marijuana, based on a case developed by Mississippi Bureau of Narcotics (MBN) agents. Later, Fort was given money by the Democratic Party to campaign for Democratic candidates in the Chicago area and was invited to the 1969 inauguration of President Richard Nixon.

The Black P. Stone Nation gang had considerable assets, including many businesses and real estate ventures. A few of the group's properties were huge commercial buildings in Chicago that were later proved to have been purchased with illicit funds from criminal activity, including cocaine distribution. Fort and other gang members were convicted of terrorist acts against the United States in addition to conspiracy to distribute cocaine. In addition, during the 1980s, more than 60 members and Fort were charged and convicted of numerous crimes, including murder of rival gang members. In 1996, other El Rukins gang members, including Fort's son (known as "Nateta" or "The Prince") were convicted of cocaine distribution.

This gang's range of criminal activity is an example of the level and complexity of operations that some gangs achieve. Exerting an influence over politics strong enough to have federal grants awarded and gain the attention of the President of the United States, El Rukins members engaged in extensive criminal activity in remarkable fashion. Despite prosecutorial misconduct by the U.S. Attorney's Office in Chicago that resulted in the dismissal of the U.S. prosecutor and led to new trials and reduced sentences for members of the gang (Knox, 2004), by 1996 persistent local, state, and federal government efforts had resulted in the gang's demise and forfeiture of most of its assets. Although El Rukins may have been referred to as a "community group" by President Nixon and many Chicago area politicians, law enforcement never stopped their exhaustive pursuit of the illegal activities of Fort and his gang.

Larry Hoover and the Gangster Disciples

Larry Hoover was born in Mississippi, As a youth, he joined the *Gangster Disciples* (G.D.s) gang, a branch of which was active in Jackson. Like many other gangs, the G.D.s were loosely linked with major gangs in Chicago. Hoover was one of two protégés of the Black Gangster Disciple Nation leader, "King" David Barksdale. After Barksdale's death in 1974, Gangster Disciple Nation split into two factions—the Black Disciples and the Gangster Disciples—but the G.D.s became well known for their violence under Hoover's leadership. Most of their income stemmed from drug distribution, but they also were involved in petty crimes that included theft and prostitution. To strengthen bonds with the community, the G.D.s operated a political arm (21st Century V.O.T.E.) and "Save the Children" campaigns that essentially put on free rock concerts for young people.

Operating in a number of states, the Gangster Disciples soon established a formal structure similar to that of many other organized crime groups (Knox & Fuller, 2004). Members collected money from anyone who wished to sell drugs on their turf. Their rivals were other gangs, including the Black P. Stone Nation. Like the Black P. Stone Nation, the G.D.s involved themselves with politics by supporting candidates for office and sponsoring voter registration drives; in addition, considerable intelligence in Mississippi and other states suggests that this gang was involved in attempting to corrupt a number of law enforcement personnel. The gang has members—including Hoover—who are continuing to conduct criminal activity while in prison. **Figure 11-1** shows the reputed structure of the G.D.s gang.

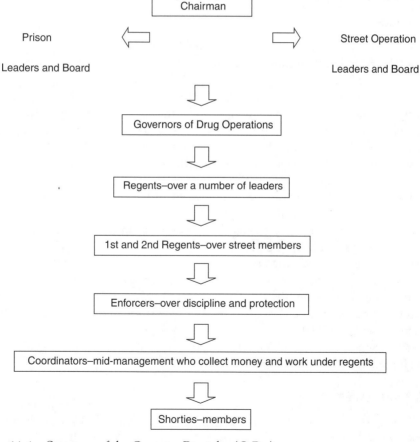

Figure 11-1   Structure of the Gangster Disciples (G.D.s) gang.

With more than 50,000 members (including very young *pee wees* and female counterparts), extensive leadership, and codified rules or laws, this gang is very bureaucratic and able to operate both outside and inside prisons (Knox & Fuller, 2004). The G.D.s present a challenge for wardens and correctional facilities because of their potential for security disruption. The leadership and management have kept detailed records of their structure and operations, including financial data, which helps to establish excellent cases against them. During the late 1990s, the gang and its leader (Hoover) suffered multiple indictments and convictions, which has made them much less of a current threat. A frequent subject of reporting in the *Chicago Tribune*, the G.D.s gang saga is also well documented in many city newspapers in Mississippi, Georgia, Missouri, and Illinois. The gang meets many of the criteria of organized crime, including corruption, violence, diverse criminal activities, hierarchy, money laundering, and profit sharing.

Historical Black Figures of Organized Crime

Frank Lucas

Until the 1970s, black criminals depended on the Italian connection for their drug supplies. This situation changed with the emergence of new-style criminals such as Frank Lucas, who created an international heroin ring. Through a relative in Bangkok, Thailand, Lucas established a direct source for supplying the illegal drug. His organization's scam was smuggling heroin in what appeared to be military and government coffins to Fort Gordon, Georgia, and then on to New York City, where it was distributed. Military personnel were bribed to ensure the operation's success.

Known as the *Country Boys*, Lucas's organization eventually expanded into Chicago, North Carolina, Los Angeles, and New Jersey. The profits of the drug smuggling operation allowed Lucas to become wealthy, and he owned numerous assets including several businesses in five states. Lucas was a high-profile drug trafficker who attracted the attention of law enforcement, becoming a major target of the DEA. He had connections to the LCN Genovese family, who provided him with a great deal of information about organized crime in New York and other areas. By using military personnel and restricting membership in the Country Boys to his relatives, the Lucas organization prospered. Once Lucas was convicted of drug trafficking, however, he parlayed information about the Country Boys' operations into a lenient sentence, through his cooperation with the government (Jacobson, 2000).

The three organizations described next resemble many of the larger organized crime groups, but operated on a much smaller scale.

Frank Matthews

After his early start as a numbers operator in North Carolina and later in Philadelphia, Frank Matthews became a major heroin trafficker in the 1960s. Matthews' claim to fame was his distribution network, which included the infamous French connection. His organization operated in as many as 20 states (Goddard, 1978).

Leroy Barnes

In the 1970s, Leroy "Nicky" Barnes (known as the "King of Harlem") made a fortune in heroin trafficking. Like Matthews, Barnes had connections to LCN in New York. He grew up in Harlem and was involved in drug trafficking early in life. Eventually, Barnes was convicted of drug trafficking and sentenced to life in prison.

Charles Lucas

Charles Lucas is another African American considered to be an organized crime figure. He developed an international heroin smuggling and distribution network. He established contacts in Southeast Asia, using African American veterans of the Vietnam War (who were mostly relatives, much like Matthews' gang). His network included the Bronx (a borough of New York City), New Jersey, Los Angeles, and North Carolina regions. Notably, his organization was arranged to provide a division of labor with leadership management positions; members employed extensive technology that produced a very effective and efficient business.

Other Black Criminal Organizations

Nigerian Organized Crime

An emerging threat is the Nigerian criminal organizations that are involved in financial crimes such as fraud and drug trafficking. Members of these groups are organized along their home tribal cities. They have established extensive smuggling operations that route Southeast Asia heroin and cocaine into Europe and the United States. To further their goals, these groups have developed connections to many street gangs. Although Nigeria is not a drug-producing country, it is a major transportation hub for heroin and cocaine. Nigerian organized crime is also involved in major money-laundering operations.

The elaborate fraud scams implemented by Nigerian organized crime typically promise high profits in exchange for a small investment. The scam usually requests a bank number and access to a place to transfer a large amount of money. For allowing them this access, the scammers promise the victim a large profit. They ask the victim to pay the transaction fees and taxes, and, once the victim supplies the bank account information, they clean out the victim's account.

Jamaican Organized Crime

Jamaican organized crime is another black organization that has been recognized as having an international scope of operations. The *Posses* first grew out of the political turmoil in Kingston, Jamaica. (Individual criminal gangs adopted the name "Posse" as a result of their fondness of American Western genre movies.) Later, they migrated to the United States to escape the extreme poverty and corrupt politics of their home country. In 2001, violence in Jamaica again resulted in a new wave of gang members migrating to the United States and elsewhere.

The Posses are most infamous for their level of violence, including more than 2000 drug-related murders between 1985 and 1990 (National Alliance of Gang Investigators' Associations, 2005). These groups are now involved with Mexican DTOs, and they are expanding into other countries. Because of their extreme violence (which attracted a great deal of attention) and effective law enforcement, their activities have declined in the United States, but they continue to act as importers, wholesalers, and distributors both in America and in other countries. While the large Posses have experienced a demise, these groups remain a part of drug trafficking.

Two groups—the Shower Posse and the Spangler Posse—were rivals in the cocaine and marijuana distribution business. During the 1980s, they were very active and employed violence using state-of-the-art weaponry. Both Posses have a structured leadership. Leaders control the Posse; lieutenants transport drugs and guns, and carry money to the leaders; and the members sell drugs to street gang members.

During the 1980s crack epidemic, approximately 40 Posses were active in the United States, with a membership estimated at more than 20,000. Members are non-ideological. Using their profits, they have infiltrated legitimate businesses. In addition to links to their Colombian suppliers, they have many connections with black street gangs, such as the Crips.

The arrest of Jamaican drug lord Christopher Coke of the Shower Posse reveals that an old group that has existed since the 1990s has not been defeated. According to the U.S. Attorney's Office, Coke directed and controlled cocaine and marijuana distribution in New York and other areas. His group was also involved in arms trafficking. The attempt to arrest Coke in Kingston ignited four days of gun battles that left 76 people dead. This case also demonstrates that public support of criminals and corruption remain necessary factors if organized crime is to continue to exist (Ripley, 2010).

Jamaica continues to be a transshipment area for Colombian cocaine. These gangs remain a problem in the United Kingdom because of their involvement in cocaine distribution in that country as well as their ongoing use of violence. Both the DEA and other U.S. law enforcement agencies still view the Jamaicans as a problem in the United States as well.

Prison Gangs

Gangs exist in all ethnic communities. Although African American and Latino/Hispanic gangs are the best known, Asian and white gangs—and more recently female gangs—have also drawn the attention of law enforcement officials.

Prison gangs are considered by some to be organized crime; however, these gangs do not meet the criteria established in Chapter 1. While these gangs normally have structure and a well-defined system of leadership, because of parole, transfers, and intervention by correctional officials, their leadership is inherently unstable. The objective of such a gang is to control the prison environment and acquire such items as drugs, money, and property inside the prison. Respect is obtained by any means necessary, including the use of violence.

One of the most discussed prison gangs is the *Mexican Mafia* (EME), which was organized in 1957 in Deuel Vocational Institute in Tracy, California. Members of this group control homosexual prostitution, drug distribution, and gambling within the prison walls; they also engage in extortion. Currently, they operate in a number of states and have networks outside of the prison. The EME has allied with the Aryan Brotherhood against the Nuestra Familia; both the Aryan Brotherhood and the Nuestra Familia are also major prison gangs.

The *Nuestra Familia* (NF) was organized in 1967 in Soledad Prison as a rival to the EME. Like other prison gangs, it has since established a presence outside the prison system by expanding into communities. This gang has a constitution, and its membership includes individuals from ethnic groups other than those of Latino or Hispanic origin. The NF's rigid structure includes established positions such as a general, captains, and lieutenants. Restricted membership and rules/creeds exist in the gang, with the death penalty applied for certain violations. NF has allied with the Black Guerilla Family (BGF) against the EME.

Other prison gangs include the *Texas Syndicates*, founded in Folsom Prison (Texas) in 1974; the *Aryan Brotherhood*, founded in the 1960s in San Quentin Prison (California); and the *Black Guerilla Family*, founded in 1966 in San Quentin Prison. Prison gangs are defined as close-knit disruptive groups of prison inmates, though their structure may

Mexican gang member.

range from a set of informal rules to rigorously structured leadership with written creeds and regulations (Walker, 2006). The purposes of these groups range from protection of their members while in prison to operation of large profit-producing enterprises.

One major problem in describing prison gangs' activities as organized crime is that these groups are ideological—that is, they have a political and often cultural agenda. For example, the Aryan Brotherhood is associated with the Ku Klux Klan and other right-wing hate groups. BGF goals include cultural unity and protection of black prison inmates. However, many prison gangs also have counterparts outside the prison walls that do engage in diverse criminal activities.

Investigative Strategies and Laws

One of the most significant skills an investigator can posses is the ability to obtain information that is accurate and truthful. These skills are taught by the Laboratory for Scientific Interrogation as developed by Avinoam Sapir of Phoenix, Arizona; John Reid and Associates, Inc., of Chicago, Illinois; Don Rabon of North Carolina Justice Academy; and Stan B. Walters (Kinesic Interview and Interrogation), among others. All of these entities have developed excellent publications and offer seminars that offer the investigator training in ways to gather more accurate information.

Investigation of black organized crime does not differ significantly from investigation of other organized crime groups. Notably, however, both adult and juvenile gangs are addressed in the Violent Crime Control and Law Enforcement Act of 1994, which brought more types of cases under the federal judicial system. This legislation includes enhanced penalties for using juveniles to distribute drugs and dealing drugs near schools, youth centers, playgrounds, and areas such as video arcades. The Anti-Gang Youth and Violence Act of 1997 provides for federal prosecution for serious and violent juveniles.

RICO, CCE, conspiracy, money laundering, electronic surveillance, undercover, and drug investigations are all strategies for dealing with black or other gang organized crime activities (see Chapter 12). Bans on military or automatic weapons and gun law violations may be used against these gangs as well. Unfortunately, the youths in gangs know they are not normally subject to the same penalties as adults and often use this leverage to their advantage.

Databases and intelligence that identify gang members, along with their activities, locations, street names, vehicles, and gang affiliations, are very important in developing investigative strategies against such groups. With gangs such as the G.D.s, whose membership may be as large as 25,000 people spread across 70 cities in the United States, developing a plan to deal with this type of organized crime is very difficult and requires extraordinary cooperation among law enforcement officials, plus support from federal agencies such as the ATF, DEA, FBI, IRS, and U.S. Customs. Many major cities have established gang units that are dedicated to the investigation of street gangs, such as the Crips, Bloods, G.D.s, and Vice Lords.

Conclusions

African American, Hispanic/Latino, and other gangs, which are currently expanding in terms of both number and level of violence in the United States, present a complex problem for law enforcement. While some gangs such as the Jamaican Posses have nearly disappeared, others like the brutally violent MS 13 remain strong. Associated with the Mexican DTOs, MS 13 is a loosely knit group of well-armed youths who are striving to become more powerful. Competition between gangs will continue to produce violence, and many gangs will likely become classified as organized crime in the future. The drug market will continue to be a major source of income for gangs. Gang alliances will undoubtedly form and dissipate, including alliances with other street gangs, prison gangs, and, in some cases, national and transnational organized crime groups.

How many gangs like MS 13 will develop into major organized crime groups is uncertain, but history tells us at least some will take this step. The complexity of the problem is such that law enforcement cannot resolve it alone. That is, a lack of positive role models, peer pressure, market demand, dysfunctional or unsupportive families, and the unsuccessful education and employment status of youth all contribute to the existence of gangs. These issues must be addressed in concert with sufficient and effective law enforcement to diminish the threat posed by these groups. Notably, some states have made it a crime to belong to a gang or be a gang member.

Although much less has been written about the histories and roles of groups such as African American organized crime, there is evidence that gangs with members from all ethnic groups have played a major role in organized crime activity throughout history. Unfortunately, that involvement is likely to contribute to organized crime activity in the future as well.

Discussion Questions

1. Discuss the history of black organized crime in the United States.
2. Compare black organized crime to La Costa Nostra's development and activities.
3. Discuss the gang culture and explain why it evolved.
4. Discuss the different structures of gangs in the United States.
5. How has law enforcement responded to gangs? Which statutes or acts apply specifically to gang enforcement and why?
6. How and why do some gangs evolve into organized crime?

References

Curry, G., & Spengel, I. (1988). Gang Homicide, Delinquency, and Community. *Criminology, 26,* 381–405.

Fagan, J. (1988). *The Social Organization of Drug Use and Drug Dealing Among Urban Gangs.* New York: John Jay College.

Goddard, D. (1978). *Easy Money.* New York: Farrar, Straus, and Giroux.

Grennan, S., & Britz, M. (2006). *Organized Crime: A Worldwide Perspective.* Upper Saddle River, NJ: Prentice Hall.

Huff, C. (1989). Youth Gangs and Public Policy. *Crime and Delinquency, 35,* 524–537.

Ianni, F. A. J. (1974). *Black Mafia: Ethnic Succession in Organized Crime.* New York: Simon & Schuster.

Jacobson, M. (2000, August 14). The Return of Superfly. *New York Magazine,* pp. 36–45.

Knox, G. W. (2004). Gang Profile: Black P. Stone Nation. In: G. W. Knox & C. Robertson (Eds.), *Gang Profiles: An Anthology.* Chicago: National Gang Crime Research Center.

Knox, G. W., & Fuller, L. L. (2004). The Gangster Disciples: A Gang Profile. In: G. W. Knox & C. Robertson (Eds.), *Gang Profiles: An Anthology.* Chicago: National Gang Crime Research Center.

National Alliance of Gang Investigators' Associations. (2005). *2005 National Gang Threat Assessment.* Retrieved December 4, 2006, from http://www.nagia.org

Ripley, K. (2010, June 24). Alleged Jamaican Drug Lord Christopher "Dudus" Arrives in U.S. Retrieved June 30, 2010, from http://www.politics.gather.com/viewArticle.action?articleId=281474978326344

Thrasher, F. M. (1968). *The Gang: A Study of 1,313 Gangs in Chicago* (abridged). Chicago: University of Chicago Press (originally published in 1927).

Walker, R. (2006). Gangs or Us. Retrieved December 4, 2006, from http://www.gangsorus.com

Chapter 12

Major Statutes, Legislation, and Methods of Organized Crime Investigations

Knowledge is the only instrument of production that is not subject to diminishing returns.

—John Bates Clark, neoclassical economist (1847–1938)

Objectives

After completing this chapter, readers should be able to:

- Compare the RICO statutes and investigation to conspiracy investigation.
- Recognize the elements of CCE.
- Discuss the issue of money laundering, including the definition, the 1958 and 1957 sections, methods of laundering, and ways to detect it.
- Discuss civil and criminal forfeiture and their impact on organized crime.
- Understand the controversies surrounding the statutes presented in this chapter.

Introduction

Numerous presidential commissions on crime and the U.S. Congress concluded in the late 1960s that existing laws were not adequate to address the complex criminal organizations that were operating similarly to legitimate businesses, but insulating their leaders and assets from traditional law enforcement methods. Major legislative actions increased the ability of law enforcement to address the complex and dynamic nature of organized crime.

The Omnibus Crime Control Act of 1968 allowed authorities to conduct electronic surveillance at state and federal levels. In 1970, the Organized Crime Control Act enhanced grand jury powers and allowed more authority to protect and secure witnesses. The Racketeer Influenced and Corrupt Organization Statute (RICO) of 1970 addressed the racketeering activity and funds gained through such activity. The 1986 Money Laundering Act (18 U.S.C. 1956 and 18 U.S.C. 1957) made it a federal crime to launder money. The Money Laundering Prosecution Improvement Act of 1988 allowed financial institutions to readily identify persons purchasing checks and money orders, and added special reporting requirements for these institutions. Both state and federal governments created conspiracy statutes that enhanced the ability to prosecute leaders of organized crime. The Continuing Criminal Enterprise (CCE) Statute of 1970 was directed toward major drug traffickers, as was the Foreign Narcotics Kingpin Designation Act of 1999, which applied to major foreign drug trafficking and provided extraordinary sanctions to the involved individuals and their organizations worldwide. These Acts followed federal and state statutes regulating controlled substances passed in the 1970s.

The USA Patriot Act, which was passed shortly after the terrorist attacks of September 11, 2001, expanded the scope of many of the previously enacted laws. It increased the ability of many governmental agencies to use surveillance in relation to terrorist and criminal activities, and it broadened regulations concerning the interception of communications. Particularly relevant are Sections 201 and 202 of the USA Patriot Act, which lay down rules on what communications can be intercepted and address sharing information about criminal investigations; Section 206, which covers roving surveillance authority; Section 209, which focuses on seizure of stored communications (such as voice mail); and Sections 210 to 213, which address subpoenas and search warrants.

Many other laws are constantly used by law enforcement to bring major cases against leaders of organized crime and their organizations and assets. This chapter examines the most important laws and the elements needed to establish a prosecutable case or seize the assets of major criminal organizations. Chapter 13 discusses the application of the intelligence function and its contribution in providing essential information to prosecute criminals under these statutes and laws. It is critical for the investigator to not only identify the "labeled" criminal element/enterprise and its activities, but also to establish the role of confederates in the upper world (i.e., corrupt business, government, and law enforcement); the twin goals are to seize these partners' assets and to prosecute them for their role in making organized crime such a successful enterprise.

The Hobbs Act and Extortion

One of the earliest statutes to deal with activity associated with organized crime was the Hobbs Act (18 U.S.C. 1951–1955), enacted in 1946. This Act made it a federal crime to obstruct or interfere with interstate commerce. Examples of obstruction include extortion (payment of money or other reward to avoid harm or harassment; involves fear and usually requires payment of a "street tax" to continue to operate a business) or robbery. The Act also makes it a crime to travel or use interstate facilities (e.g., telephones, computers, mail) to aid illegal activity. The Hobbs Act has been used to prosecute union officials who obtained kickbacks (a reward for using or buying a particular service or product), fees, loans, or any money or other reward for using their influence on the unions or people they represent.

Property is *extorted* under law by the Hobbs Act when a public official agrees that his or her official conduct will be controlled as promised or paid by another person. Extortion (also referred to as *blackmail*) is a practice often used by organized crime members to infiltrate legitimate businesses; it is a means to obtain property by way of threats or intimidation. Extortion can also be defined as obtaining property from another person, with his or her consent being obtained by use of force, fear, or under color of official right. Under the *color of official right* section, violation of the Hobbs Act is punishable by a fine of $10,000 and as long as three years in prison.

While the Hobbs Act remains a useful tool against organized crime, it is rarely used today because RICO or conspiracy laws have proven more effective. La Cosa Nostra (LCN; American Mafia) has been charged with more Hobbs Act violations than most other organized crime groups, but the Yakuza and Russian Mafia are also frequent violators of the Hobbs Act and its extortion statutes.

RICO

No other statutes used to address organized crime and white-collar crime have caused as much controversy and discussion as the 1970 Racketeer and Corrupt Organization Statute (RICO, 18 U.S.C. 1961–1965). In 1986, Robert Blakey (known as "the father of RICO") expressed concerns that there was no applicable definition of organized crime, racket, or racketeering. He believed that the then current legal attempts to define organized crime were constitutionally vague, in that they might violate the constitutional right to associate or assemble as well as the rights of due process or equal protection. His concerns remain controversial issues for some in today's society. RICO legislation has been attacked for being too vague, as constituting double jeopardy, as being an Eighth Amendment violation, and as interfering with the rights of due process, including the right to a speedy trial and to counsel of choice. Many applaud its use, whereas others call for restriction or elimination of RICO. The Patriot Act of 2001 is perhaps the only other crime-related legislation to be more controversial.

Before RICO, prosecution of major crime bosses was difficult at best because of the bosses' strategy of employing underlings to carry out the criminal acts, thereby insulating them from identification and prosecution. Rather than proving criminal agreement (conspiracy) or commission of a specific crime, RICO allows for prosecution of a pattern of crimes that are committed through an organization, referred to in the statute as an *enterprise*. RICO makes it a crime to acquire, receive income from, or operate an enterprise through a pattern of racketeering. Patterns of criminal acts committed by direct and indirect participants in criminal enterprises allow them to be prosecuted. Some believe that this statute leads to the prosecution of criminals who are not members of an organized crime group (crime by association), and that the statute is vague or too broad.

As part of the 1970 Organized Crime Control Act, RICO (or Title IX) defines 32 *predicate offenses* that can be classified as racketeering activities for profit by organized crime. Not only does the statute set out a mandatory punishment of 20 years in prison and a fine of $20,000, but it also has a civil section. Under both the civil and criminal sections, assets derived from racketeering activities can be seized and forfeited. The civil section allows anyone who has been injured in his or her property or business by racketeering activity to sue responsible parties for triple damages and attorney fees.

The RICO legislation specifically prohibits the following activities:

1. Using income received from a pattern of racketeering activity or through collection of an unlawful debt to acquire an interest in an enterprise affecting interstate commerce.

2. Acquiring or maintaining, through a pattern of racketeering activity or through collection of an unlawful debt, an interest in an enterprise affecting interstate commerce.

3. Conducting or participating, through a pattern of racketeering, racketeering activity, or collection of an unlawful debt, the affairs of an enterprise affecting interstate commerce.

4. Conspiring to participate in any of these activities.

Racketeering activity may include any of the predicate acts listed in the statute. A *pattern of racketeering* activity includes any two acts of racketeering by a person within 10 years of each other (this interval varies among state statutes, as some require a 5-year period). The acts do not have to be the same type of violation, but must be related by some criteria, such as motive or purpose, or design. The enterprise may be a corporation, association, or group whose members interact and are involved in the activities of the enterprise.

Predicate offenses include fraud, Hobbs Act violations, white slavery, drug trafficking, arson, extortion, obstruction of justice, kidnapping, loan sharking, and a number of other offenses. The offenses vary somewhat from state to state in the corresponding state legislation, but most are very similar in the offenses and elements of the crime.

For example, a growing problem with the Russian Mafia is the offense of white slavery. In 1910, the Mann Act (also known as the "White Slave Act") was passed to prohibit interstate transportation of women for the purpose of prostitution or any immoral purpose. Today, trafficking of humans—male and female, young and old—is common, with the Chinese Snake Heads, other Asian organized crime groups, and many Russian groups participating in this activity.

Several cases (e.g., *United States v. Teri,* 1980) brought against traditional organized crime groups have led to the expansion of federal RICO statutes to include publication of obscene materials, drug trafficking by street gangs, and police corruption. Its use in violent anti-abortion protest group cases was overturned by the Supreme Court in February 2006, however. The ongoing expansion of the RICO statute has caused concern among some in the legal community. Most states now have their own RICO statutes, which have also contributed to the increased number of RICO prosecutions.

Under RICO statutes, courts can enter restraining orders before conviction to prevent transfer of potentially forfeitable property or assets. A wide range of civil actions are possible under RICO, including divestiture, dissolution, and reorganization. These actions add to the complaints and controversy surrounding RICO. Prosecutors report that RICO statutes have been used to permanently dismantle large operations (such as prostitution rings); under local or traditional statutes, the offenders might have gone back into business after serving only short sentences while keeping their assets.

RICO cases do require excessive resources and time to develop and prosecute. The federal legislation allows the prosecutor to present a complete picture of the organization's activity, and it permits trials with multiple defendants where the activities of all are presented to the jury at the same time. For the investigator developing a RICO case, it is essential to prove a pattern of racketeering or long-term criminal activity, and to have the group classified as a criminal enterprise. According to Abadinsky (2003), RICO fails to specifically define organized crime and racketeering, which could be problematic for the case. Most prosecutors and law enforcement believe that RICO is not too complex, however. It has proved very successful in combating organized crime and white-collar crime, despite the fact that RICO has been applied inappropriately in cases brought by some prosecutors. The Colombian cartels, LCN families, and many other criminals have been prosecuted successfully under RICO, for example.

Another advantage of using the RICO statute to charge organized crime is that prosecution is allowed in any jurisdiction where overt acts were committed. More than 1200 major crime figures have been successfully prosecuted under RICO based on state and federal guidelines. While critics may view RICO as a threat to individual rights, it remains the law. It is used frequently as a tool in the arsenal of many law enforcement agencies to combat organized crime.

The forfeiture provisions specified in RICO allow the government to take away the profit incentive associated with criminal activities. Under civil forfeiture, the property can be frozen even though the owner is not charged with a crime.

Property Forfeiture

Civil forfeiture is a legal proceeding against property that either is purchased with profits from illegal activity or used to facilitate a crime. Vehicles, sea vessels, and aircraft can be seized when used to transport illegal contraband, such as drugs (e.g., cocaine or marijuana) and stolen goods. Criminal forfeiture requires that the defendant be found guilty of a crime and ordered to forfeit property or funds related to the crime.

The Federal Comprehensive Forfeiture Act of 1984 enhanced the government's ability to seize the assets of drug traffickers, including organizations such as the Mexican and Colombian DTOs, via civil forfeiture. The major advantage of civil forfeiture is that it imposes a lesser burden of proof (preponderance of the evidence) than does criminal forfeiture (beyond a reasonable doubt) to seize the assets. Probable cause is necessary before assets or property can be seized, which is the same rule as with any seized evidence. Once the property is seized, the burden shifts to the owner to prove the money or property was obtained legally (or did not facilitate a crime).

One advantage for law enforcement is that hearsay evidence can be used to establish probable cause. However, the U.S. Supreme Court (*U.S. v. Real Property*, 510 U.S. 43) has ruled that real property cannot be seized without notification of the owner and opportunity for the owner to contest the seizure. Another advantage of civil forfeiture, which is in *rem* (a lawsuit or legal action against a thing or property) rather than in *personam* (a lawsuit or legal action against a person), is that it allows the forfeiture of assets even when the owner is acquitted on charges of criminal activity.

Not just money and vehicles can be seized under this legislation, but also any assets that are proceeds of criminal activity or that have facilitated criminal activity. These items include aircraft, boats, houses, weapons, and real estate property as well as other tangible goods. Seized and forfeited assets are given to law enforcement agencies, which either auction them off or use them to supplement the cost of their operations (such as overtime, equipment, training, and property purchases). Defense attorney fees are also subject to forfeiture, which is a hotly debated issue. Criticism of forfeiture surrounds the issues of innocent owners (who are protected by law); excessive punishment, such as seizing a yacht for only marijuana traces; and taking vehicles, which may be necessary for a person to travel to work. The identification of hidden assets and tracing assets to criminal activity most often is a long-term and complex task. However, under civil forfeiture rules, it is necessary simply to link the owner to drug trafficking in some aspect; the owner then has the burden of proving how the assets were obtained.

Taking the profit out of crime by following the money is an excellent strategy for combating organized crime.

Violations of the Internal Revenue Code

During the 1960s, tax investigations by the Internal Revenue Service (IRS) produced most of the convictions of organized crime offenders. These investigations remain a useful strategy against organized crime because tax evasion (failure to pay taxes) is a crime commonly committed by these enterprises. Financial analysis is a major tool for developing cases against even the biggest violators. Many people involved with organized crime fail to keep required records and do not file a tax return, even as they spend large sums of money. LCN and Yakuza members often do not report gambling income, for example, and are guilty of evading income taxes. By examining the violators' spending habits and assets acquired, the investigator can establish a tax case.

A few of the methods employed by the criminal investigation division of the IRS include development of network and expenditure schedules, examination of the sources and applications of funds, and the bank deposit methods. The first two strategies are explained in Chapter 13. Both result in unexplained or unreported income. The bank deposit method examines bank deposits, cash expenditures, purchases, and any cash on hand. (Probably the most famous conviction for tax evasion was that of the notorious Chicago Mob boss, Al Capone.) Once the unexplained income is discovered by investigators, the burden of proof shifts to the suspect to verify that it was legally obtained.

Money Laundering Laws

A key strategy in fighting organized crime organizations is attacking their assets. Investigators need to be trained in banking and financial procedures to better understand how money is laundered.

Money laundering is always present in organized crime activity. Money laundering can be defined as all activities designed to conceal the existence, nature, and final disposition of funds gained through illicit activities. It has been a common theme in organized crime since the Prohibition era. Crooks need to "clean" the illegal funds before they can spend it. The massive amounts of money made by organized crime activity present a challenge for those who want to keep it, as they need to not only "clean" the money, but also protect it from seizure by law enforcement. The process used can be as simple as mailing or physically transporting the cash out of the country or as complex as engineering a bank takeover. The methods are often the same as those used in legal business transactions—except that the money was obtained illegally. The President's Commission on Organized Crime in 1984 observed that several new methods were being used to move organized crime funds—namely, wire transfers, avoidance of the Currency Transaction Report (CTR) and Currency and Monetary Instrument Report (CMIR) requirements, "fronts" and shell corporations, and bank transfers.

The Bank Secrecy Act of 1970 (31 U.S.C. 5311–5326) was the first attempt to combat money laundering by organized crime. The Act requires financial institutions to file a CTR on all cash transactions amounting to more than $10,000. This CTR must be filed with the IRS within 15 days of the transaction, and the bank or institution must keep copies for five years. Also, a CMIR exceeding $10,000 in value that leaves or enters the United States must be filed with the IRS. These records assist in tracking cash through the national banking system.

In response to these laws, organized crime members often make multiple smaller transactions (under $10,000) to avoid the reporting requirement. This practice, referred to as *smurfing*, is a violation of 31 U.S.C. 5324, known as the Anti-Drug Abuse Act of 1986. The penalty for smurfing (structuring for each transaction) is 5 years in prison unless the amount exceeds $100,000 during a 12-month period, which increases the penalty to a 10-year sentence. The Right to Privacy Act of 1978 was amended to allow the financial institution to give authorities the name of the suspect or organization, the account number, and the nature of the suspected illegal transaction.

Section 1956 of the Money Laundering Act of 1986 deals with violations in a domestic context and those that occur when monetary instruments or funds are transported between the United States and a foreign country. The violator must conduct or attempt to conduct a transaction *knowing* (or with "willful blindness") that the assets involved are proceeds of unlawful activity, even if the launderer does not know the precise activity. This action must promote *specified unlawful activity*, which means an attempt to conceal or disguise the source, origin, location, or ownership of the proceeds, or be designed to avoid federal or state reporting requirements.

Interestingly, before the passage of the 1986 Money Laundering Act, it was not a federal crime to launder money. The 18 U.S. 1957 law makes it a violation to engage in monetary transactions in excess of $10,000 with property derived from proceeds of specified unlawful activity. Both CTR and CMIR violations are predicate acts under RICO. Violators of the 1956 section may incur a penalty of up to a 20-year prison term and a fine of up to $500,000, or twice the value of the property involved. Violators of the Money Laundering Act may receive up to a 10-year prison term and a fine. Title 18 U.S.C. 981 and 982 provide for civil and criminal forfeiture, respectively.

Other key pieces of legislation that address money laundering include the following statutes:

- *The Drug Abuse Act 1988.* This law requires that offshore banks record any U.S. cash transfers in excess of $10,000. They must also allow government access to those records.

- *The Annunzio-Wylie Money Laundering Act of 1992 and the Money Laundering Suppression Act of 1994.* The Annunzio-Wylie Act makes it a crime to operate a money laundering business, but it also protects financial institutions from civil liability when reporting suspicious activity of their customers. This legislation requires that all financial institutions and gambling enterprises report suspicious activity.

- *The Money Laundering Prosecution Improvement Act of 1988.* This statute requires financial institutions to verify the identity of persons who purchase bank checks, traveler's checks, or money orders in amounts of $3000 or more. It also allows the government to target certain institutions or geographic areas for special reporting requirements (U.S.C. Sections 5325–5326).

More recently, the *USA Patriot Act* (United and Strengthening America by Providing Appropriate Tools Required to Intercept and Obstruct Terrorism Act of 2001) has been considered by American Bar Association (ABA) National Institute's Center for Continuing Legal Education to be the broadest money laundering statute on the books. Unlike Sections 1956 and 1957, it does not require a list of specific offenses or *specified unlawful activities* (SUAs) for prosecution of money laundering. This Act also expanded the foreign crimes list to include bribery of a public official, embezzlement and misappropriation, and theft. Although these transactions may not have any connection to terrorism, they are included in the legislation and may be used by prosecutors to bring charges. In this sense, the USA Patriot Act is a complement to the United Nations Convention against Transnational Organized Crime (held in Palermo, Italy, in 2000), which requires extradition of violators who are involved in transnational organized crime or "serious" crime, which may include corporate tax violations and fraud occurring in a foreign country, such as SUAs money laundering charges (which includes computer fraud). The Act expands the definition of the term "illegal money transmitting business" to include unlicensed businesses and those who transport or transmit illegal proceeds or money intended to promote or support unlawful activity. It allows IRS information (CTRs and CMIRs; Forms 4789 and 4790; and Form 8300, which covers reporting of cash payments greater than $10,000 received in a trade or business) to be available to law enforcement. Anyone who transports or transmits money by any method is considered subject to this Act.

All types of organized crime activities require money laundering to legitimize their income. Doing so allows the violator to spend money without suspicion of criminal involvement. To make transporting cash less demanding, large profits from illegal activities somehow need to be infused into the U.S. banking system and subsequently exchanged for smaller, less bulky transactions. Money from international or transnational organizations then can be delivered to the organizations' source countries in their own currency. Only then can the now-clean money be converted into tangible assets such as expensive homes, real estate, cars, marine vehicles, and operating/bribery expenses, among other cash outlays.

The Money Laundering Cycle

In 1990, the *Financial Crimes Enforcement Network* (FinCEN) was formed under the Department of Treasury to function as an intelligence center for all financial crimes. FinCEN divides money laundering into three stages:

1. *Placement*: The illegal proceeds are placed into the financial system unnoticed or transported outside the United States.

2. *Layering*: The funds go through a series of financial transactions in such frequency, volume, and complexity that they are difficult to trace and appear to be legitimate financial transactions.

3. *Integration*: The funds are integrated into the economy in such a way that they appear to be derived from legitimate income. At this stage, the investigation is faced with a major problem of distinguishing illicit from licit funds.

Cash transactions between the suppliers, transportation cells, and users can all be considered money laundering violations. Transportation of cash out of the United States leaves no paper trail to follow and is a common means used by organized crime; however, in today's nearly cashless society, other means are becoming more frequently used.

Financial institutions are often major players in the business of organized crime activity. The Western Union and U.S. banking system are two examples. These businesses can be used as black market exchanges to launder money, much like the *casa de cambio* or money exchange houses that convert U.S. dollars to pesos or buy U.S. dollars at a black market rate.

Remittance corporations operating as fronts under the guise of an investment company, broker, financial service provider, or check-cashing operation may receive and transmit illegal funds. The CTR or CMIR will often reflect only the name of the company and not the organized crime figure or organization. This money is transmitted through a number of "fronts" before being placed in the violator's account or company, so that it appears to be legal income. In fact, funds may go through 15 to 20 financial institutions or banks. Real estate transactions are an excellent way to launder illegal proceeds. Buying property for $2 million in visible cash and $1 million "under the table" allows the violator to launder $1 million of illegal proceeds.

Law enforcement must be properly staffed and equipped to find and fight money laundering. The El Paso Intelligence Center (EPIC) and FinCEN are staffed by experts from a variety of federal agencies who have access to the U.S. Treasury's computer system (TECS II). TECS II includes a database of all CTR, CMIR, and IRS Form 8300 transactions. The Multi-Agency Financial Investigative Center (MAFIC) was formed to identify, target, seize, and forfeit any significant assets of major organized crime figures. These agencies have been, and continue to be, essential partners for combating money laundering.

Controlled Substances Acts

Because drug trafficking is still the major profit producer of organized crime worldwide, acts that address illegal drug distribution are often used to convict major organized crime bosses and members. The Controlled Substance Act is a statute that has been codified in the laws of all U.S. states.

The Comprehensive Drug Abuse Prevention and Control Act of 1970, which has been amended nearly each year to add new substances, gives federal jurisdiction for investigating drug trafficking and provides substantial penalties for violation of the Act. This legislation divides substances into five schedules based on their potential for addiction and harm. Procedures for controlling a substance are provided in the Act. Requirements for legal distribution of pharmaceuticals are part of most statutes regarding controlled substances, which includes security, records, and reporting loss by pharmacists and the medical profession.

Other legislation that supplements this statute include the following statutes:

- The *1988 Chemical Diversion and Trafficking Act* controls substances known as precursor chemicals, which are needed to produce certain drugs. Records of purchases and transactions of these precursors are required by the Act; investigators can, in turn, use the records to trace these products to clandestine laboratories that produce or manufacture illegal drugs.

- The *Comprehensive Crime Control Act of 1984* and the *Anti-Drug Abuse Act of 1986* increased prison sentences for specific drug offenses.

Other drug abuse legislation and amendments have been directed at the demand side of the equation. They include penalties for using drugs and loss of license to drive, among other punishments.

Conspiracy Statutes

The term "conspiracy" gets at the essence of organized crime activity. A successful conspiracy is not necessary for conviction on this charge, as the conspiracy charge remains distinct and separate from the substantive crime that was the goal of the conspiracy. Conspiracy laws have a long history, having originated in England in 1305 A.D.

Most states and the federal government have passed conspiracy laws that identify substantial penalties for violators. Most prosecutors require proof of *overt acts* (any act that furthers the objective of the conspiracy, which may be a lawful or unlawful act). All participants do not need to know about the overt acts. The conspiracy or agreement may be established by any contrivance (either implied or tacit) for two or more persons to come to a common understanding to violate a law.

Conspiracy laws have many advantages for case development related to organized crime:

1. Conspirators do not have to know one another.
2. Each conspirator is responsible for the actions of the others (Pinkerton theory).
3. All conspirators are agents for one another.
4. Conspirators do not have to be aware of the actions of others.
5. Anything done to carry out the objective of the conspiracy is an overt act.
6. Overt acts need not be criminal in nature.
7. Overt acts need not be known by all participants.
8. Any act or statement by one conspirator can be used in court against all other conspirators.
9. All conspirators may be responsible for the substantive crimes of their co-conspirators, provided these criteria are met:
   - They were in the conspiracy at the time the offense was committed.
   - The offense was committed in furtherance of the conspiracy.
   - The offense was a foreseeable consequence of the conspiracy.
10. The venue lies in any jurisdiction in which an overt act occurred or where the agreement was made.

11. The conspirator must do something affirmative to withdraw from the conspiracy, such as inform the police about the conspiracy and inform known co-conspirators of his or her intention to withdraw.

12. The statute of limitations normally runs five years from the last overt act or when the conspiracy ends. (This period varies between states.)

13. The case can eliminate the entire criminal organization.

14. Evidence against one defendant is evidence against all.

15. Exception to the hearsay rule is allowed, so that a defendant can testify concerning statements, deeds, or actions of the co-conspirators.

16. Asset forfeiture laws apply to drug conspiracy cases.

The major disadvantage of prosecutions based on conspiracy is the need for a long-term commitment to gather evidence, which is likely to require the efforts of many personnel. In major investigations, extensive surveillance is conducted and the testimony of witnesses needs to be verified and corroborated, which often requires large expenditures in both overtime and human resources. Investigations spanning multiple venues often pose political and logistical problems as well.

Although conspiracy investigations are complex, they are much simpler to develop and understand than RICO offenses and money laundering cases. Conspiracy cases allow prosecution of the leaders of organized crime groups even when they attempt to insulate themselves by delegation of criminal activities to their subordinates or when they remain in a foreign country, never entering the United States where the objective of the conspiracy is reached. Statutes usually identify an offense of conspiracy as a violation of the RICO Act. It should be noted that mere association or knowledge of the existence of the conspiracy does not constitute joining the conspiracy.

Several types of conspiracies are possible in relation to organized crime activity:

1. *Historical:* The objective of the conspiracy has already been met. Investigators must locate witnesses; conduct warrants for physical evidence, including documents; and use informants to produce a case of this nature. Again, the goal is to prove that the agreement to violate the law existed.

2. *Ongoing:* The conspiracy still exists while it is being investigated.

3. *Chain:* All members are connected, yet only some members interact with the others:

$$A \leftrightarrow B \leftrightarrow C \leftrightarrow D \leftrightarrow E$$

In the chain type of conspiracy, not all of the members know one another, and no single member knows all of the members. In the diagram, persons A and B make the agreement to violate the laws, and persons C, D, and E carry out overt acts. Persons E and D do not interact with persons A and B, and C interacts only with B and D; person E interacts only with person D.

4. *Wheel*: As in the spokes of a wagon wheel, the area between the spokes interacts with certain members. Although all members are connected, only some of the links or members interact with others.

   Wheel conspiracies, which are also called cell structures or compartmentalization, are common structures found in terrorist and organized crime groups. A terrorist group may be referred to as a sleeper cell when the operatives are dormant, waiting for instructions to carry out their mission or objective.

5. *Combination Wheel and Chain Conspiracies:* In these conspiracies, members of the wheel and the chain frequently interact for operational purposes and are part of the same operations (cons) in the overall conspiracy. The structure contains a combination of smaller conspiracies that form a larger, more complex, interaction.

Opponents of conspiracy statutes argue that, too often, large numbers of people are forced to stand trial with people who were only distantly associated with a criminal operation. This practice may lead some defendants to be considered *guilty by association*.

Conspiracy Case Development

The development of a conspiracy case involves a wide variety of investigative techniques and methods. The investigator must be well trained in these methods, and must be given sufficient time and resources to conduct such complex and long-term cases. The following are some of the methods frequently used to develop conspiracy cases:

1. Management and development of informants
2. Title III investigations and electronic surveillance
3. Mail covers
4. Photo spreads and line-ups or show-ups
5. Use of grand jury testimony and immunity of witnesses
6. Physical surveillance
7. Asset or financial investigations
8. Undercover operations
9. Trash runs
10. Search warrants for documents
11. Grand jury subpoenas or investigative grand juries
12. Analytical and intelligence support
13. Testimony of co-conspirators

Federal and state prosecutors and investigators have praised conspiracy cases as a valuable tool against organized crime activity. The penalty for violations is normally the same whether the objective of the conspiracy was completed or failed.

Continuing Criminal Enterprise Statute

The Continuing Criminal Enterprise (CCE) statute (21 U.S.C. 848) was enacted as part of the Comprehensive Drug Abuse Prevention and Control Act of 1970. Nothing puts fear in a violator or defense counsel like the possibility of a CCE conviction. Most often, the violator is willing to cooperate and provide information in exchange for a lesser charge.

The CCE statute is directed at any person who occupies a position of organizer, supervisor, or manager in a narcotic production and distribution enterprise. The minimum sentence for a CCE conviction is 20 years in prison with no possibility of parole, but the court may impose additional years up to a life sentence and fines up to $2 million ($5 million if it is an organization; a second conviction is a mandatory 30-year sentence). Additionally, all profits and assets of the operation are subject to forfeiture as prescribed in 21 U.S.C. 853.

The CCE statute includes the following elements:

1. A person violates any federal drug offense law.

2. This violation is part of a continuing series of violations (three related transactions).

3. This person operates in concert with five or more persons and occupies a position of organizer or supervisor, or is in a management position.

4. This person receives substantial income or resources from the violations.

Proof of a CCE usually involves both direct and circumstantial evidence. It may include evidence of the defendant's position in the organization, the quantity of drugs involved, the amount of money that changed hands, or lavish personal expenditures without any legitimate source of income. The investigator must demonstrate specific illegal acts that were committed by a defendant to prove a CCE violation.

The Kingpin Act

The Foreign Narcotics Kingpin Designation Act was signed into law in December 1999 as an Amendment to Public Law 106-120, Intelligence Authorization Act of FY2000. Modeled after the Specially Designated Narcotics Trafficker (SDNT) program, it seeks to expose, isolate, and incapacitate the financial infrastructure of major drug trafficking organizations. Sanctions such as denying major traffickers and their businesses access to the U.S. financial system and prohibiting U.S. citizens and companies from conducting business with them are major parts of this Act.

Regulation and Monitoring of Business and Labor

Labor racketeering has been a major profit producer for such entities as LCN. According to numerous government investigative committees and subcommittees, four major international unions were long dominated by organized crime: the International

Brotherhood of Teamsters (IBT), the Hotel and Restaurant Employees Union (HRE), the Laborers International Union of North America, and the International Longshoremen's Association (ILA). Men such as Jimmy Hoffa, Jackie Presser, and Allan Dorfman are legends in the analysis of LCN history. By controlling the unions, LCN realized that it could control a number of associated businesses, such as labor, trucking, and shipping. Domination of a business or component of a business allows organized crime ventures to launder money while paying taxes to appear to be legitimate, and is another venue for profit through diversification and legitimate employment for associates, friends, family, and members of the organization. Organized crime's major activities include extortion (*strike insurance*) and so-called *sweetheart contracts* that garner profits at the expense of workers and misuse of union benefit funds.

Using union power for personal profit began with LCN bosses such as Arnold Rothstein in the 1930s (see Chapter 7). The business owners' benefits provided by organized crime range from harassment of competitors, controlling of union labor, and increased profits. Although money laundering statutes, RICO, and conspiracy statutes are intended to combat business and labor racketeering, it is the cooperation among law enforcement, financial institutions, businesses, and the judiciary that can prove extremely valuable in reducing organized crime's impact in the business world. Increased funding for regulatory agencies and partnering with these agencies will enhance the ability to monitor organized crime activity in an area that is not familiar to most law enforcement investigators.

The 1967 President's Commission on Crime reported a number of businesses that were considered especially vulnerable to organized crime:

- Construction
- Waste removal
- Real estate
- The garment industry
- Financial institutions
- Restaurants, bars, hotels, and legal gambling

This list continues to grow. Organized crime activities result in limited competition, higher prices, lower wages, a reduction of legitimate employment, and an enormous loss of tax revenues.

Electronic Surveillance

The federal government as well as state legislatures have authorized law enforcement to intercept telephone conversations and electronic communications, and record them for presentation as evidence during trials. Title III of the 1968 Omnibus Crime Control Act (18 U.S.C. 2510-2520) authorized federal law enforcement agencies to eavesdrop on suspects when authorized to do so by a warrant; most states have passed similar statutes.

The Electronic Communications Privacy Act of 1986 expanded electronic surveillance to include cellular and electronic mail.

To help establish probable cause that the communication device is being used to conduct criminal business, computerized pen registers (records of numbers of outgoing calls) and the *trap and trace records* (number of incoming calls) are placed on communication devices before a *wiretap* is started. The pen register and trap and trace capability are now integrated within a single computerized device that prints out the results of a link analysis of the calls, e-mails, or communication exchanges (location, time and length of call, and identification of callers).

The Patriot Act of 2001 has enhanced the ability of federal agencies to share criminal information obtained by electronic surveillance. This includes foreign intelligence and counterintelligence content obtained by the National Security Agency (NSA), Central Intelligence Agency (CIA), and any federal agency.

Prior to the passage of the Patriot Act, federal law enforcement had very limited authority to delay notification of "sneak and peak" searches. The Patriot Act expanded this capacity to "reasonable cause" showing of adverse impact on the investigation. Title III authorizes covert entry to install interception devices (such as *bugs*, or transmitters that pick up conversations in a room or area). Without court approval or an extension, the target of the interception operation must be notified of the wiretap within 90 days after the termination of the court-ordered intercept. Most orders for electronic surveillance are for 30 days unless they are extended.

The Patriot Act clarified that law enforcement can use Title III trap and trace and pen registers on computer networks. It also ensures that a warrant, once issued, is legal on any communication device a target uses and in any jurisdiction where the target travels (*roaming wiretap*). This type of warrant was used prior to the Patriot Act in major drug investigations.

Requirements to obtain an electronic intercept include the following criteria:

1. Probable cause exists to believe that a crime is being committed or about to be committed by the target, and that the crime is an offense under Title III.

2. All other investigative methods have failed or will not provide the evidence to meet the goals or objectives for a successful investigation.

3. Probable cause exists that the intercept will provide the communication evidence sought.

4. Probable cause exists that the area or device is being used or will be used by the target or targets to violate a particular law.

These types of investigations are extremely labor and time intensive. In addition, special equipment is often required to carry out these complex operations. Most departments cannot support the financial or technical aspects of an intercept operation. Specialized training is also required for investigators to use equipment and gain knowledge of the rules and limitations that apply to such use. Equipment must be monitored 24 hours a day, and monitoring must be discontinued when communication is privileged, not covered by the court order, or not related to an offense. There is also the possibility that no valuable evidence will be recorded despite the effort and expense. As communication becomes more "high tech," newer equipment and training inevitably become necessary to intercept communications (e.g., from digital and cellular phones, e-mail). For these reasons, electronic surveillance can be problematic, even though it may produce valuable evidence needed to develop a case and charge major organized crime members under RICO, money laundering, and conspiracy statutes.

Investigative Grand Juries

Federal and state prosecutors have experienced great success with the investigative grand jury concept. These juries have the authority to subpoena testimony and documents, grant immunity, and remain in session for six months or longer, which allows a complete investigation to be carried out while maintaining secrecy. Refusal to honor a subpoena results in punishment consisting of arrest and jail time. The testimony of reluctant persons can be compelled upon a grant of immunity from prosecution. Two types of immunity are possible:

- *Derivative use immunity*: A form of immunity that prohibits the information provided by the witness from being used against that person. However, if evidence of a crime is developed independently of the testimony, the witness can be prosecuted.

- *Transactional immunity*: A broad form of immunity that prohibits prosecution on the crime or criminal act the witness is testifying about.

The Witness Security Program (WITSEC), which was introduced in 1971, has facilitated organized crime investigations and encouraged witnesses to give testimony without fear of retaliation. The program gives a new identity to witnesses and places them in a secure location with lifetime protection. It has been successful in protecting essential organized crime witnesses.

Other Statutes Frequently Used During Organized Crime Investigations

The following statutes found in the United States Code (U.S.C.) should be incorporated in the investigator's arsenal when coping with criminals:

- 18 U.S.C. 4: Misprision of felony.
- 18 U.S.C. 111: Assaulting, resisting, or impeding federal officers.
- 18 U.S.C. 924 (c): Use or possession of a firearm during or in relation to drug trafficking offenses.
- 18 U.S.C. 1071: Concealing a person from arrest.

- 18 U.S.C. 1073: Flight to avoid prosecution or giving testimony.
- 18 U.S.C. 1341: Frauds and swindles (includes mail fraud).
- 18 U.S.C. 1503: Influencing or injuring an officer or juror generally.
- 18 U.S.C. 1503(a): Influencing a juror by writing.
- 18 U.S.C. 1510: Obstruction of criminal investigations.
- 18 U.S.C. 1511: Obstruction of state or local law enforcement.
- 18 U.S.C. 1512: Tampering with a witness, victim, or informant.
- 18 U.S.C. 1513: Retaliating against a witness, victim, or informant.
- 18 U.S.C. 1542: False statement in application of and use of a passport.
- 18 U.S.C. 1543: Forgery or false use of a passport.
- 18 U.S.C. 1621: Perjury generally.
- 18 U.S.C. 1952: Interstate and foreign travel or transportation in aid of racketeering enterprises/ITAR.
- 21 U.S.C. 843 (b): Use of a communication facility to facilitate a drug crime (also known as phone counts).

Most indictments include violations of a number of these statutes, and cases on these charges are fairly easy to develop. It is obvious that organized crime activity includes violations of all of these statutes.

Conclusions

Task forces, undercover operations, informant development, financial investigations, electronic surveillance, and technology are all useful tools that, when supported by powerful legislation and regulation, offer some hope of minimizing and even eliminating some organized crime groups. However, because of these criminals' political and economic relationships as well as ongoing public demand for their illegal products and services, organized crime refuses to go away. By creating policies that address market demand, the threat of organized crime can be controlled.

This law enforcement perspective is controversial, and some in academia and other organizations, such as the American Civil Liberties Union (ACLU), regularly produce position papers and lobby Congress to amend or repeal legal statutes that they believe infringe on Americans' constitutionally guaranteed rights. However, most of these statutes and methods have been applied to important cases against organized crime organizations and their membership for decades (with the exception of the Patriot Act), and they remain the most effective weapons for law enforcement.

Discussion Questions

1. Compare the RICO statutes and investigation to conspiracy investigation.

2. Name and discuss the requirements for obtaining a Title III wiretap.

3. What are the advantages and the disadvantages of electronic surveillance?

4. What are the elements of CCE?

5. Discuss the issue of money laundering, including its definition, the 1958 and 1957 sections, methods of laundering, and ways to detect it.

6. Discuss civil and criminal forfeiture, and explain their effects on organized crime.

7. Explore and discuss controversies surrounding the statutes presented in this chapter. Why do you think these controversies continue after so many years of the laws' application?

References

Abadinsky, H. (2003). *Organized Crime* (7th ed.). Belmont, CA: Wadsworth/Thomson.

Anti-Drug Abuse Act of 1986. (Pub. L. 99-570).

Bank Secrecy Act of 1970. (31 U.S.C. 5311-5326). *Regulatory: Overview.* Washington, DC: Financial Crimes Network, Department of the Treasury. Retrieved December 4, 2006, from http://www .fincen.gov/reg_main.html

Blakey, G. (1986). *Organized Crime in the United States: A Review of the Public Record.* Bellevue, WA: Northwest Policy Studies Center.

Chemical Diversion and Trafficking Act of 1988. (Pub. L. 100-690). *Diversion Control.* Alexandria, VA: U.S. Drug Enforcement Administration. Retrieved December 4, 2006, from http://www.dea.gov/ programs/diversion.htm

Comprehensive Drug Abuse Prevention and Control Act of 1970. (21 U.S.C. 881 (a) (7)). Controlled Substances Act. *Everything2.* Retrieved December 4, 2006, from http://everything2.com/index .pl?node=Controlled%20Substances%20Act

Continuing Criminal Enterprise (CCE). (1970). (21 U.S.C. 848). Retrieved December 4, 2006, from http://www.capdefnet.org/fdprc/contents/shared_files/titles/21_usc_848.htm

Electronic Communication Privacy Act of 1986. (Pub. L. 99-508). Retrieved December 4, 2006, from http://www.cpsr.org/prevsite/cpsr/privacy/communications/wiretap/electronic_commun_ privacy_act.txt

Federal Comprehensive Forfeiture Act of 1984. (21 U.S.C. 853).

The Foreign Narcotics Kingpin Designation Act. (1999). (21 U.S.C. 1901–1908, 8 U.S.C. 1182; Pub. L. 106–120). *What You Need to Know About U.S. Sanctions About Drug Traffickers.* Washington, DC: Office of Foreign Assets Control, U.S. Department of the Treasury. Retrieved December 4, 2006, from http:// www.ustreas.gov/offices/enforcement/ofac/programs/narco/drugs.pdf

Hobbs Act. (1970). (18 U.S.C. 1951–1955). U.S. Department of Justice. Retrieved December 4, 2006, from http://www.usdoj.gov/usao/eousa/foia_reading_room/usam/title9/131mcrm.htm

Internal Revenue Service Code. (1986). (26 U.S.C. 7201, 7206). Retrieved June 28, 2006 from http://www.geocities.com/CapitolHill/Senate/3616/TAXEVASION.html; http://www.geocities.com/CapitolHill/Senate/3616/FALSEINCOMETAXRETURN.html

Mann Act of 1910. (18 U.S.C.A. 2421 et seq.)

Money Laundering Control Act of 1986. *Bank Secrecy Act and Anti-Money Laundering*. Washington, DC: Federal Deposit Insurance Corporation. Retrieved December 4, 2006, from http://www.fdic.gov/regulations/examinations/bsa/bsa_3.html

Money Laundering Prosecution Improvement Act of 1988. (21 U.S.C. 801) (also known as the Chemical Diversion and Trafficking Act of 1988). Vienna, Austria: United Nations Office on Drugs and Crime. Retrieved December 4, 2006, from http://www.unodc.org/unodc/legal_library/us/legal_library_1990-06-21_1989-27.html

Omnibus Crime Control and Safe Streets Act of 1968. (18 U.S.C. 2510-2520). Washington, DC: U.S. Department of Justice. Retrieved December 4, 2006, from http://www.usdoj.gov/crt/split/42usc3789d.htm

Organized Crime Control Act of 1970. (18 U.S.C. 1956, 1957). Retrieved December 4, 2006, from http://trac.syr.edu/laws/18USC1956.html; http://trac.syr.edu/laws/18USC1957.html

President's Commission on Law Enforcement and Administration of Justice (1967). *The Challenge of Crime in a Free Society*. Washington, DC: U.S. Government Printing Office.

President's Commission on Organized Crime, 1988. (Executive Order 12435). Harry S. Truman Library: The American Presidency Project. Retrieved December 4, 2006, from http://www.presidency.ucsb.edu/ws/index.php?pid=41647&st=&st1=

Racketeer Influenced and Corrupt Organizations Act (RICO). (1970). (18 U.S.C. 1961-1965). Retrieved December 4, 2006, from http://usinfo.state.gov/usa/infousa/laws/majorlaw/rico/rico.htm

Title V of the Organized Crime Control Act of 1970. (18 U.S.C. 1546). Retrieved December 4, 2006, from http://trac.syr.edu/laws/18USC1546.html

United States Code (2006, November 6 update). *Database*. Washington, DC: GPO Access. Retrieved December 4, 2006, from http://www.gpoaccess.gov/uscode/index.html

Uniting and Strengthening America by Providing Appropriate Tools to Intercept and Obstruct Terrorism Act (USA Patriot Act) of 2001. Washington, DC: Electronic Privacy Information Center. Retrieved December 4, 2006, from http://www.epic.org/privacy/terrorism/hr3162.html

Chapter 13

The Intelligence Function in Organized Crime Investigations

People who see the big picture expand their experience because they expand their world.

—John Maxwell (1951–), author, pastor

Objectives

After completing this chapter, readers should be able to:

- Discuss the sources of intelligence involving organized crime.
- Recognize the problems encountered by intelligence units when gathering and disseminating information about organized crime.
- List and discuss the different products of the intelligence unit.
- Explain how the intelligence analyst evaluates information.

Introduction

This chapter examines the proactive process and application of strategic and tactical intelligence to the investigation of today's organized crime.

The development and application of criminal intelligence can pose a major threat to criminal organizations. Analytical models, association analysis, and event and commodity analyses are the most important processes used to identify the organization's structure, membership, activities, and methods of operation. This type of investigation results in the identification of patterns and trends, which are extremely valuable when developing

243

strategic, tactical, and administrative law enforcement responses to organized crime activity. Since 2001, the emphasis on terrorism by federal agencies has negatively affected the resources dedicated to organized crime intelligence, as state and local law enforcement are mandated to be more involved in antiterrorism efforts. Creating national and international databases and sharing intelligence are necessary to address today's organized crime in the most effective manner.

Current Assessment of Organized Crime in the United States

Organized Crime's Connection to Terrorist Groups

Globalization and the advent of the technology and information age have combined to enable crime organizations such as the Yakuza, Red Mafia, Triads, Colombian and Mexican drug cartels, and terrorists to operate as if there were no geographical boundaries. Formerly international threats have now become domestic threats for the U.S. public and American law enforcement.

As earlier chapters in this text explained, outlaw biker groups and La Cosa Nostra (LCN) are no longer the only organized crime groups operating within the United States. New organized crime groups and their partners are emerging, and alliances between these groups constitute an unprecedented threat to this country. Encryption, software, fiber-optic cables, digital cellular telephones, and satellite technologies allow these sophisticated enterprise criminals to realize a new immunity from law enforcement efforts (McDowell, 1991).

Organized crime's connection to terrorism has intensified during the past decade, especially when one considers that much funding of terrorist activity is derived from narcotics trafficking. In South America, the National Liberation Army (ELN), Revolutionary Armed Forces of Colombia (FARC), and United Self-Defense Groups of Colombia (AUC) are classified as both terrorist and organized crime groups, as all three derive much of their income from the drug trade. Hamas and Hezbollah (violent Palestinian Islamist revolutionary groups) are operating in Paraguay, Brazil, and Argentina; both of these organizations use drug trafficking to finance their activities in South America and the Middle East. The Taliban (a repressive quasi-Islamist ruling faction) has operated illicit opium production in Afghanistan and has connections to political extremists in Uzbekistan and Pakistan. Money from this operation partially funded the Al Qaeda terrorist organization. Drugs, geography, and money are common ground between terrorism and organized crime.

U.S. Drug Enforcement Agency (DEA) intelligence has also uncovered alliances between Russian organized crime, LCN, the Italian Mafia, Mexican and Colombian drug trafficking organizations, the Japanese Yakuza, Chinese Triads, and Nigerian crime groups. Terrorist networks are increasingly forging alliances with these organized crime groups and others to finance terrorist operations worldwide (Testimony of Steven W. Casteel, 2003).

Whether state sponsored or otherwise funded, these complex organizations have funneled illegal funds into the political and economic systems of many countries to influence these systems to support organized crime activity. They move their money and themselves from country to country with no regard for national boundaries, fleeing arrest and prosecution by means of corruption and influence. Neither rivalries, nor turf battles, nor geographic and ethnic differences have prevented these groups from working together.

Legislation

The National Security Act of 1947 prevented the Central Intelligence Agency from having law enforcement powers as well as from gathering and sharing intelligence with the FBI and other U.S. law enforcement agencies (Holt, 1995). Investigation of today's organized crime groups, however, requires economic intelligence not only from the U.S. banking system but also from abroad, because U.S.-based groups' alliances with foreign criminal organizations are often classified as international or transnational organized crime groups. If accurate, complete, and timely intelligence is not collected and analyzed from within and outside U.S. borders, these groups will become more secure, efficient, effective, and clandestine than ever before.

In 2001, the U.S. Congress passed the USA Patriot Act (discussed in Chapter 12). Although this legislation was intended to enhance law enforcement tools to deter and punish terrorists, it may well prove to be important in the battle against organized crime. Proof of links between terrorism and organized crime as well as less restrictive rules for U.S.-based intelligence gathering may open up new avenues of resources and support from other agencies to combat these criminal enterprises. Although it is opposed by the American Civil Liberties Union and other organizations, who cite it as a violation of many U.S. constitutionally granted freedoms, the Patriot Act allows major intelligence operations to be conducted with U.S. citizens as the target. Its expansion of financial investigations includes the use of information gathered under the Foreign Intelligence Surveillance Act (FISA, 1978; amended 1994–2006), and it creates new pathways by which the CIA and FBI can share information not only with each other, but also with state and local law enforcement agencies. The Patriot Act amends the FISA to widen surveillance regulations for criminal investigations, including the ability to intercept any communications (computer, satellite, or any passive or active signal).

Since 2003, additional legislation has been introduced by the House and Senate to temper the broad authority granted under the Patriot Act, and two sections (505 and 805) have been ruled unconstitutional by the courts. This Act is temporary in that some sunset provisions exist—that is, the law will not exist after a date set by Congress (this deadline had been extended twice at this book's publication).

Intelligence

Intelligence is not the same as information. Intelligence is a multistep process that involves collecting, collating, integrating, analyzing, correctly interpreting, and effectively disseminating the information. Crime incidents, criminal behaviors and characteristics, patterns, and trends are used in tactical, strategic, and administration functions and planning as part of the intelligence function.

For example, one study conducted by the Texas Law Enforcement Management and Administrative Statistics Program (TLEMASP, 1995) reported that 50% of information produced by crime analysis units in Texas was used for tactical purposes, 27% for strategic purposes, and 24% for administrative purposes. Tactical analysis functions were divided into four categories: crime series pattern detection; suspect–crime correlations; target/suspect profiles; and crime-potential forecasts. Analyses of administrative program evaluations were parlayed into cost-effectiveness reports and government support studies. Strategic analyses included the preparation of exception reports, crime trend forecasts, resource allocation, and situation analyses. As revealed by this study, crime analysis units were viewed by Texas agencies as being very useful and their reports were frequently utilized by officers. However, the survey also indicated that the officers may lack understanding of the precise function of a crime analysis unit. Although this study was not directed specifically at intelligence used against organized crime, the functions reported are very similar to those used for enterprise/organized crime (TLEMASP).

Historical Perspective

Intelligence and crime analysis have a rich history that began when the need for effective criminal investigation was first recognized. While criminal and intelligence investigations are distinct entities in many ways, these law enforcement units do operate in a similar manner. Criminal investigations are primarily reactive, however, whereas intelligence is proactive. Intelligence is an ongoing process of information collection, analysis, and dissemination. It provides information about people, places, organizations, and businesses that are specific targets.

Although criminal investigation case files are considered "open files" (i.e., the information could be known throughout law enforcement offices and agencies) with the goal of arrest and prosecution, intelligence files are "closed files" that often contain information about continuous activity that may not be corroborated or even factual. Information from intelligence files is never presented in courts and is protected from subpoena.

Criminal investigation and intelligence files are filed in separate locations. Most agencies also store their intelligence files in a different location than the site where the personnel of the intelligence unit work. A high-tech security system typically protects the files because they contain extremely sensitive reports, including allegations of corruption and alleged illegal conduct by high-profile people, locations, and businesses. This type of sensitive information is shared on a "need to know" basis, with very few people having access to it.

Frequently, intelligence information is used to create a report (product) that may provide guidance to investigators. These products may be transferred to a criminal investigation file after the information is validated. Once released, the information is presented in court cases in the form of flow charts, graphs, analytical models, financial analysis, and link diagrams.

Intelligence operations originally arose from military operations, as scouts would assemble information on topics such as the terrain and the opposition's troop movements that could be reviewed and analyzed by the military command. Crime analysis in America became more codified in the early 1900s, when the innovative Berkeley police chief and educator August Vollmer (and possibly others) developed *modus operandi* files. Vollmer's protégé, O. W. Wilson, is credited with coining the term "crime analysis" in his book *Police Administration*, which became the most influential text on administration for its era.

The Law Enforcement Assistance Administration created the Integrated Criminal Apprehension Program (ICAP), forerunner of the Violent Criminal Apprehension Program (VICAP) that is currently operated by the FBI. Over time, police departments in most major cities, many state agencies, and federal agencies have developed crime analysis/ intelligence units that are identified as a distinct unit on the structural chart of each department. Unfortunately, the resources dedicated to these intelligence units by state and local law enforcement in the United States are, all too often, inadequate and unable to address major organized crime operations. Federal units include the El Paso Intelligence Center (EPIC), Narcotics and Dangerous Drug Information System (NADDIS) of the DEA, Regional Drug Intelligence Squads (RDIS), and the Financial Crimes Enforcement Network (FinCEN). The CIA and the FBI have their own databases as well. Such entities as the National Drug Pointer Index and the Regional Information Sharing System (RISS) are also involved in supporting law enforcement in their efforts against organized crime.

Perhaps somewhat unexpectedly, there is a history of alliances between intelligence agencies and organized crime (Lyman & Potter, 2000). LCN provided intelligence during World War II and conducted counterintelligence operations for the U.S. government (see Chapter 7). The Air America operation of the CIA during the Vietnam War transported opium in return for support from the Hmong tribe for the U.S.–South Vietnamese forces. As late as the 1980s, the resistance of the Afghan Mujahideen (declared by Presidents Jimmy Carter and Ronald Reagan to be "freedom fighters" and trained by the U.S. military, these men evolved into the rigid Islamic Taliban extremist group) to the Soviet forces that were then occupying Afghanistan was financed by drug trafficking. The Iran–Contra political scandal during the 1980s, in which U.S. weapons and training were secretly given to Nicaraguan guerilla groups through America's avowed enemy (Iran) in a program funded by drug trafficking, is yet another example of alliances between organized crime and the intelligence community.

Sources who provide intelligence are often of questionable character and reputation. To what extremes the U.S. government should go to achieve its goals and gather intelligence remains debatable.

Other problems faced by intelligence units include the following issues:

- Little or no information sharing may occur (particularly on an international level) because of a lack of trust, communication, or corruption concerns.

- There is always a threat that strategic intelligence will be compromised for tactical operations or intelligence functions.

- Laws regulating intelligence confidentially differ among countries (for example, Canadian courts allow sources to be revealed).

- No qualified analyst is located in source countries, which compromises effective and accurate intelligence functions.

Europol has developed a system with strict rules regarding dissemination of sources that may reverse the tradition of not sharing intelligence across international borders. Both strategic and tactical intelligence information is critical to the success of long-term coordinated efforts against organized crime (Schneider, Beare, & Hill, 2001).

Evaluation of Information

Information evaluation is an important function of any intelligence unit. The Mississippi Bureau of Narcotics (MBN), for example, has developed a system for evaluating information that is currently used by many intelligence units across the United States. This system varies somewhat among agencies, but most evaluate the source and the information separately.

In the MBN system, letters are assigned to a particular source, who is rated numerically according to the degree of validity of his or her information (or vice versa). An example of such a system is the following:

Evaluation of Source

A = A reliable source who has a proven track record and is competent.

B = A source whose information is most often valid but has been wrong on occasion(s).

C = An unreliable source whose information is most often false.

D = A source whose accuracy of information cannot be determined.

Evaluation of Information

1 = Information is true and can be corroborated.

2 = Information is likely true and comes directly from a reliable source, but cannot be corroborated.

3 = Information is not of direct knowledge from the source, but can be partially corroborated.

4 = Information cannot be corroborated and is not from the source's direct knowledge (i.e., it is hearsay).

When information from such a system is distributed to those outside of a select group within the law enforcement agency or department, the coded report replaces each source name with the assigned letter and number.

Analysis of intelligence requires collation of data, where specific information is compared to information from other sources. However, information does not become intelligence until after it is analyzed and interpreted. A combination of technology, human review, and interpretation produce the final product. Experienced senior supervisors review the analyst's work before the report (product) is delivered to the user. The number and type of reviews performed vary from agency to agency, but often the end product will include suggested courses of action or alternatives in an effort to aid a criminal investigation (Price, 1991).

Sources of Intelligence

The enormous volume of information collected through intelligence operations requires a major effort geared toward filtering and sorting it. After sorting, the intelligence product is delivered to three levels: strategic (conduct and development of policy), operational (planning of effective deployment, tactics, and techniques), and tactical (execution of tasks).

Intelligence sources may be classified as human, open, or technical. *Human sources* are commonly used in organized crime investigations and include informants, businesspeople, undercover officers, physical surveillance, friends of targets, associates of targets, relatives of targets, and professional workers. *Open sources* include any type of publications, business records, vital statistics, court records, tax records, and financial records. *Technical intelligence* (i.e., active or passive electronic transmissions) involves imagery and/or signal intelligence. Imagery intelligence may be gathered from sensors of the light spectrum or from still or video cameras placed on satellites and aircraft. Signal sources include Title III electronic intercepts (bugs and wiretaps), computer fax transmissions, microwave transmissions, and satellite transmissions. Often, the most credible intelligence comes from technical sources (Graham & Kiras, 1995; O'Connell & Tomes, 2004). In contrast, informants and human sources are quite problematic in terms of control, protection, management, and determination of reliability; nevertheless, most successful organized crime investigations involve human intelligence. When combined, these three types of intelligence sources (human, open, and technical) allow the investigator to get inside the enemy's decision-making process.

Intelligence must take a holistic approach and be driven by innovative leadership (backed with adequate resources) to remain at least one step ahead of organized crime activity. Development of technology capabilities, data transmission, and protection of sources are essential to this approach (Graham & Kiras, 1995). Edmund J. Pankau (1992), a former special agent with the IRS Organized Crime division, offers excellent practical guidance in his book entitled *Check It Out,* which describes how to discover information about assets, people, and places. Data available without court orders include real estate records, bankruptcy records, voter registration, local permits, civil suits, and a large variety of other sources. Analyses of these data can provide valuable information and help to build profiles of organized crime groups and their members.

Application of Analytical Models to Organized Crime Investigations

With the current U.S. political emphasis on the terrorist threat, deep budget cuts, and the existence of fluid organized crime groups that are continuously becoming more complex and sophisticated, successful investigators require accurate, timely, and comprehensive information if they are to intervene effectively in organized crime operations. Law enforcement must become more efficient with the available resources to address enterprise crime. State and local enforcement must develop effective intelligence functions and methods for both sharing and gathering intelligence within the United States and abroad.

Good intelligence identifies the targets for effective police operations and provides direction for investigators. The focus expands from individuals to groups or organizations, with emphasis on establishing priorities for personnel, time, money, equipment, and other limited resources.

Although informants can be extremely valuable, their information should not be used when establishing priorities for police operations. Instead, as police supervisors or administrators develop their priorities, completion of intelligence and analytical products should be a vital step that enables them to grasp the broad scope of the problem (they can see the "big picture"). Unfortunately, failure to share sensitive information between law enforcement entities remains a major obstacle to effective decision making in this regard.

Computerized data banks are widely used as investigative tools. To fully realize their benefits, law enforcement personnel must be better trained at using them.

Global criminal intelligence and threat analyses are becoming effective tools in dealing with transnational and international organized crime. As these criminal organizations adapt to global markets, tracking the flow of money and identifying new markets of interest to these crime groups will require both strategic and tactical abilities. While tactical intelligence supports planning and execution of law enforcement operations, strategic intelligence supports policy formulation and broad plans at the administrative level to develop long-term solutions to combating organized crime. This might involve analyzing drug trafficking, money laundering, and drug abuse trends in a specific geographical area when developing a threat assessment based on both internal and external factors.

Coordination of enforcement activity between countries, to include money laundering operations, should be a focal point of intelligence unit (Price, 1991). Besides drug trafficking, other expanding markets for organized crime include small-arms trafficking, cybercrime, nuclear weapons and explosive devices, other weapons of mass destruction (biological and chemical), human body parts (for transplantation), slave trafficking of women and children, and environmental crime. As the world moves toward realization of a paperless, wireless, and cashless society, the intelligence unit must actively create methods for collecting, analyzing, and disseminating information by taking advantage of complex technology and data/information systems. Given that organized crime is now a lower priority among federal agencies, state and local divisions must fill this gap and become much more active in addressing its problems.

Data Analysis
Discovering the financial resources and funding strategies used by criminal organizations often results in the conviction of major players in organized crime groups. A number of sophisticated software programs are now being used in the intelligence development stages, which have resulted in an improved intelligence product that may even be able to predict future events. The increased speed at which relationships and patterns are discerned within huge amounts of data will enhance the ability to deliver timely information so necessary to deal with the dynamic and complex nature of organized crime.

Financial institutions are becoming an essential part of an organized criminal's method of operation. Identification of criminal patterns and trends is now possible by collecting and analyzing criminal information. Correlation of elements of criminal activity and identification of members of a criminal organization can establish links that give law enforcement administrators direction when planning strategies to address these activities. A good threat assessment provides a broad overview of the impact and vulnerability of organized crime in a specific area. Analyzing historical and current data can help to predict the future impact of these criminal activities. When an intelligence product elucidates the historical evolution of organized crime groups, including their structure, activities, goals and objectives, and method of operation, often the appropriate investigative strategies become obvious. The product also may suggest the best use of resources, including personnel, equipment, and funding (McDowell, 1991).

Structure and Responsibilities of Agency Personnel
Within every agency is a chain of command. The intelligence/crime analyst supervisor (normally a sworn, ranking officer who supervises both sworn and nonsworn personnel) reports directly to the agency head/director on a daily basis to keep the director informed on sensitive or critical issues and events. This report and the personnel who are permitted to receive it must be approved by the director of the intelligence unit. With very sensitive information (e.g., corruption or criminal activity involving a public official), it is easy to see why the scope of this dissemination must be approved by the agency head. Some intelligence/crime analyst units employ a few sworn officers whose primary responsibilities are to gather intelligence from human, open, and technical sources on targeted places, individuals, or organizations. Their goal is to gather valuable information rather than to develop a prosecutable case.

Agencies and departments may establish intelligence files under individual names, organizations or groups (such as the Bandidos outlaw motorcycle club, or the national and New Orleans family of LCN), and locations, businesses, corporations, and places. As noted earlier, access to these files is strictly controlled, and they are placed in a secure location separate from criminal investigation files. The index of these data contains thousands of names, locations, and organizations. Parts of these files may be transferred to criminal case files only if the content is corroborated and contributes to the prosecution.

Financial Analysis

One of the most productive products of a crime analysis/intelligence unit is the financial analysis. Adhering to the adage "Follow the money" has resulted in RICO, money laundering, and IRS cases against major violators and organizations. Two methods used for this purpose are the net worth expenditures schedule and an analysis of the sources and applications of funds. In case of organized crime, both will likely point to an amount of expenditures in excess of known legal sources of income or unexplained income. Most defendants are reluctant to take the stand and explain the source of this excess income because it probably derives from illegal enterprises. Many organized crime members invest this illegal income in a variety of legitimate businesses such as real estate, trucking, waste management, restaurants, and other assets.

Commodity Flow Analysis

Related to financial analysis is the commodity flow analysis, which is a graphic chart of the direction(s) of sophisticated intergroup activities. With organized crime, this pictorial definition of its operations illustrates the group's services, goods, materials, and products. Such charts often link illegal sources of income to legitimate businesses or corporations. The objective of a commodity flow analysis is to identify the network through which money flows between the leaders of major crime groups and the source of their crimes, which may include an apparently legal enterprise. A second chart may reveal the routes of transfer or shipments of illegal substances from source countries to street distribution. An intelligence product can then be produced that combines the commodity flow with operational structure (**Figure 13-1**).

Event Flow Analysis

Another product of the crime analysis/intelligence unit is the event flow analysis. It depicts the time and date of an event, such as tracking cocaine from the growing field to processing, to loading and transport, and from transport to distribution. Each step of the process can be detailed by location and people involved.

Crime by Association

A frequent product used in prosecutions of organized crime members is the association or link chart. These graphic displays show the relationships between members of complex organizations. They may include each person's position in the hierarchy, the connections of illegal activities to legitimate businesses, or the power, strength, and influence of the organization. A number of association matrices and link diagrams may be incorporated into this analysis. For example, Figure 10-4 depicts the organizational chart of the Grim Reapers Motorcycle Club, which is classified as an organized crime

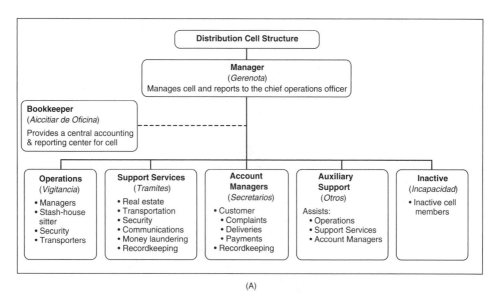

(A)

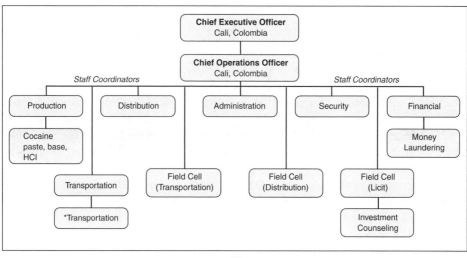

(B)

Figure 13-1 Sample of a commodity flow analysis. (A) Distribution cell structure. (B) Operational structure.

entity, albeit without the names of members who currently occupy these positions of authority. With the names added, the prosecutor may prove that this club is a criminal or continuing criminal enterprise. Conspiracy and RICO statutes then allow for the leaders of these types of organizations to be prosecuted for the criminal acts of their subordinate members (vicarious criminal liability).

Other link analyses include those involving telephone/cellular records and wire transfers of money by such means as Western Union. These products are part of the preliminary steps required for obtaining a court-ordered electronic intercept. Linking suspects by these records eliminates the possibility that a suspect might testify that he or she did not know other members of the conspiracy or never wired money to a known source of illegal goods or substances. Pen registers and the trap and trace technique may also be used to link suspects in the matrix by detailing all incoming and outgoing calls.

Units Within the Intelligence Division

The crime analyst in the intelligence unit can explore the overall scope of a criminal operation. An investigation may include the structure/hierarchy, gross income, quantities of illegal goods and services, processes employed to launder money, and roles of members of an illegal enterprise. This unit may perform cryptanalysis of recorded conversations and racketeering documents that may contain encrypted information — major violators often use codes or ciphers to disguise their criminal activities. Skilled analysts may be able to graphically lay out an entire criminal enterprise (such as LCN or the Colombian North Valley cartel) in a manner that jury members can easily understand. "A picture is worth a thousand words" is the prosecution's most satisfying adage when these materials are presented in court.

The importance of developing effective criminal intelligence is not limited to efforts conducted by the U.S. government and law enforcement agencies. Intelligence opportunities in Canada, for example, are described in a report created by the Alberta Solicitor General and the Alberta Criminal Intelligence Service. Goals of their strategic plan include providing effective collection, analysis, and dissemination of criminal intelligence; developing intelligence-based analytical products; and participating in the preparation of provincial threat assessments of organized crime for the benefit of senior police managers and various levels of government (Criminal Intelligence Service Alberta, 2002).

U.S. federal agencies such as the FBI, DEA, ATF, and Homeland Security, as well as state and local law enforcement, depend on accurate, comprehensive, and timely intelligence products to successfully deal with organized/enterprise crime. Organized crime poses a threat to U.S. political, economic, and social systems equal to that associated with terrorism. Our gaps in knowledge about these criminal organizations can be filled by increasing the resources dedicated to producing effective intelligence products. State and local law enforcement must become more involved and knowledgeable about their intelligence functions to ensure that adequate resources are dedicated to this vital function.

Conclusions

The success of complex investigations of organized crime groups depends on the ability to make sense out of the massive amounts of information that can be collected from a variety of sources. Skilled intelligence analysts are able to assemble a product from raw data that can assist administrators in developing the logistics for effective and efficient investigations as well as strategies to predict or deter future criminal activities. Accurate, comprehensive, and timely information is the goal of an intelligence unit. Agencies or departments that do not have this resource are unprepared to cope with organized crime and must depend on agencies with sufficient resources to take over this function.

Like many other professions, law enforcement is often overwhelmed by the demands of the information age and new technologies. Law enforcement personnel must become more innovative and technologically advanced, applying the proactive approach of criminal and intelligence analysis to keep pace with their organized crime foes' capabilities. Computer and wireless technologies will continue to play major roles in organized crime activities and investigations of these activities. Law enforcement efficacy will depend on creative and proactive strategies to address the ever more complex technologies that are sure to be introduced as well as the growing phenomena of transnational organized crime.

By using intelligence gathering strategies and qualified personnel, gaps in knowledge and interagency communication problems encountered throughout the world can be bridged. Networks and consolidation of efforts must be established between worldwide law enforcement agencies to ensure that valuable information is protected and shared with the goal of producing proactive strategic enforcement. The roles of intelligence analysts and criminal analysts must also continue to evolve into a variety of disciplines for these positions to remain effective. To staff crime analysis/intelligence units, universities must develop quality programs that produce creative professionals who are capable of staying ahead of the criminals they will face on the street and in the justice system.

Discussion Questions

1. Why are organized crime investigations vulnerable to the intelligence process?

2. Discuss the sources of intelligence involving organized crime.

3. Discuss the problems encountered by intelligence units when gathering and disseminating information about organized crime.

4. List and describe the different products of the intelligence unit.

5. How does the intelligence analyst evaluate information?

6. What does the future hold for the intelligence function?

References

Criminal Intelligence Service Alberta. (2002). *Alberta Solicitor General and Criminal Intelligence Service Initiatives.* Province of Alberta, Canada: Department of the Solicitor General.

Graham, C., & Kiras, J. D. (1995). Intelligence and Peacekeeping: Definitions and Limitations. *Peacekeeping and International Relations, 24,* 3–4.

Holt, P. M. (1995). Spying out new roles for Central Intelligence Agency. *Christian Science Monitor, 87,* 19.

Lyman, M. D., & Potter, G. W. (2000). *Organized Crime* (2nd ed). Upper Saddle River, NJ: Prentice-Hall.

McDowell, D. (1991). *Strategic Intelligence in Law Enforcement: The Development of a National Capacity for Production of Strategic Intelligence on the Criminal Environment of Australia.* Canberra, Australia: Attorney General's Department of Australia.

O'Connell, K., & Tomes, R. R. (2004). Keeping the Information Edge. *Policy Review, 122,* 19.

Pankau, E. J. (1992). *Check It Out.* Chicago: Contemporary Book.

Price, B. (1991). The Use of Intelligence in the Fight Against Drugs. In S. Flood (Ed.), *Illicit Drugs and Organized Crime: Issues for a Unified Europe* (pp. 131–141). Chicago: Office of International Criminal Justice.

Schneider, S., Beare, M., & Hill, J. (2001, April). *Alternative Approaches to Combating Transnational Crime.* Rockville, MD: National Criminal Justice Reference Service. Retrieved December 4, 2006, from http://www.ncjrs.org/nathanson/etranscrime.html

Testimony of Steven W. Casteel, Assistant Administrator for Intelligence, Drug Enforcement Administration, Hearing of the Senate Judiciary Committee. (2003, May 13). Narco-terrorism: International Drug Trafficking and Terrorism—A Dangerous Mix. Retrieved December 4, 2006, from http://www.ciponline.org/colombia/030513cast.htm

Texas Law Enforcement Management and Administrative Statistics Program (TLEMASP). (1995). *Crime Analysis: Administrative Aspects.* Huntsville, TX: Police Research Center.

Suggested Reading

Abadinsky, H. (2003). *Organized Crime.* Belmont, CA: Wadsworth/Thomson.

Baker, T. E. (2005). *Introductory Criminal Analysis: Crime Prevention and Intervention Strategies.* Upper Saddle River, NJ: Prentice-Hall.

Chapter 14

The Nexus of Transnational Organized Crime and Terrorism

Your eyes and your heart are intent only upon your own dishonest gain, and on shedding innocent blood and on practicing oppression and extortion.

—Jeremiah 22:17

Objectives

After completing this chapter, readers should be able to:

- Understand the motives for the nexus of organized crime and terrorism.
- Compare and contrast the structure of both a terrorist organization and transnational organized crime.

Introduction

Modern technology has created wireless, paperless, cashless, and global societies that have advanced the concepts of both terrorism and organized crime. These organizations now have the ability to conduct their operations anywhere in the world. The most recent development on this front is the increased cooperation and networking between organized crime groups and terrorist groups. Some criminal organizations are conducting both criminal acts and acts of terrorism, causing them to be labeled "hybrid" organizations. This phenomenon has created a major problem for law enforcement due to the tremendous impact of alliances between organized crime and terrorist groups.

The increased demand for illegal services and goods has both economic and political effects on governments; indeed, many people in academia and law enforcement consider this issue to be the most defining and compelling problem of the 21st century. This problem is fueled by the lack of consistency in law enforcement, regulation, and laws that address both terrorism and organized crime (Lyman & Potter, 2004; Shelley, 2002).

There is a question about the extent of these terrorist/organized crime alliances, and it remains unclear whether nuclear, chemical, or biological weapons of mass destruction have fallen into the hands of terrorists. A particular concern is whether drug trafficking and human trafficking networks are being used by terrorists or terrorist cells to enter the United States with weapons of mass destruction or other dangerous materials.

The connection between terrorism and organized crime includes a variety of criminal activities — for example, drug trafficking, arms trafficking, human trafficking, money laundering, armed robbery, counterfeiting, and fraud. Organizations such as Al Qaeda, Hezbollah, and Hamas have discovered that such criminal activity can support their operations when state sponsorship for these groups is lacking. In fact, some evidence indicates that state sponsorship of terrorism has declined in recent years and that terrorists have turned to enterprise crime and alliances with organized crime to fill this gap in financing (Curtis, 2002; Curtis & Karacan, 2002). Due to the nature of their criminal activity, there is a propensity for organized crime and terrorists to be linked and to depend on one another for their own respective reasons.

Defining transnational organized crime and terrorism can be controversial when it comes to delineating their structure, functions, activities, membership, and leadership. This chapter examines the history and nexus of transnational organized crime and terrorism by highlighting these aspects of both groups.

Comparing Terrorism and Transnational Organized Crime

When examining the 18 characteristics that define organized crime in Chapter 1, it quickly becomes apparent that many of these characteristics could be used to describe terrorist groups. The National Institute of Justice (2007) has defined organized crime as follows: "A structured group of three or more persons existing for a period of time and acting in concert with the aim of committing one or more serious crimes or offenses in order to obtain, directly or indirectly, a financial or other material benefit" (p.1). The definition of transnational organized crime developed by the National Institute of Justice adds the following conditions:

- Criminal offenses are carried out in more than one state.

- Crimes are prepared, planned, controlled, or directed in one state and conducted in another.

- Crimes are committed in one state by a group that operates in several countries.

- Crimes are committed in one state but have substantial effects in another state.

Shelley (2001) describes transnational crime as having the three following characteristics:

- Based in a single state
- Commit crimes in several countries as opportunities occur
- Conduct illicit activities with a low risk of discovery and arrest

As discussed in previous chapters, the goals of organized and transnational organized crime are twofold: money and power. These are characterized by a hierarchical structure, limited membership, violence and corruption, rules and regulations, specialization or division of labor, and a monopolistic approach in their activities of providing illegal goods and services.

The definition of terrorism has evolved somewhat over time. Burke (2000) and the Federal Bureau of Investigation (Terrorist Research and Analytical Center, 1993) define terrorism as the unlawful use of force against persons or property to intimidate or coerce governments, the civilian population, or any segment thereof, in achieving political or social goals. For Hoffman (2006), terrorism is fundamentally and inherently political and is about power — the pursuit of power, the acquisition of power, and the use of power to achieve political goals. Swanson, Territo, and Taylor (2008) list four categories of terrorism:

- Domestic terrorism (home-grown terrorism)
- International terrorism
- State terrorism
- Transnational terrorism

According to Dishman (2005), these groups may rely on different organizational structures — hierarchal, centralized cell structure, and leaderless resistance. Today, home-grown terrorists are becoming more of a concern in the United States, as shown by events such as the attempted bombing in Times Square in New York and the shootings at Fort Hood.

The activities, structure, and methods of operation of both phenomena and the characteristics that classify a group as terrorist or organized crime are critical to comparisons of such groups and reveal how the two achieve their goals. Both groups operate via a network structure, often forming temporary networks that give them flexibility and reduces the ability of governments to address the threats posed by these organizations. Most importantly, these organizational structures resemble those of legitimate business enterprises.

The Al Qaeda manual is another example of the similarities between organized crime and terrorist groups. The rules and oaths of groups such as La Cosa Nostra (LCN) and the Yakuza are intended to achieve the same goals of efficiency and effectiveness as the Al Qaeda manual.

Corruption of public officials by both entities results in their ability to operate in many areas with almost impunity. Moscow, the Golden Triangle (Laos, Burma, and Thailand), the Philippines, southern China, Laos, Myanmar, the Fukian province in China, and Thailand are examples of regions where corruption thrives due to weak law enforcement or governments (Shelley, 2002, 2004).

When examining the differences between terrorist groups and organized crime, a major difference in motivations becomes apparent. Terrorist motivations include religious fanaticism, anti-Israeli actions, economic distress, the presence or existence of democracy, and postwar developments. In a much earlier time, John Stuart Mill argued that tensions in a multiethnic society are often the basis for distress and anger. Terrorists are opposed to democratic principles that often leave minority groups with a feeling of inadequacy or a state of under-representation or marginalization. Events such as the Oklahoma City bombing (an example of home-grown terrorism in the United States) serve as examples of the power of terrorist acts to change government policy and procedures, even in democratic societies. Research by William Eubank and Leonard Weinberg of the University of Nevada–Reno concluded that terrorist groups are four times as likely to develop in democratic states as opposed to nondemocratic states. Other groups that are often inspired to act against democratic governments include anti-abortionists, Christian militants, animal rights groups, and environmental extremists. According to this view, the growth of these far-right and far-left groups is attributable to the spread of democracy.

Three types of terrorist motivations have been identified in the past:

- Rational motivation occurs when the terrorist thinks through the goals and options, including completion of a cost–benefit analysis or examination of the ability to succeed against the target.

- Psychological motivation occurs when terrorists have a personal dissatisfaction with their lives or accomplishments or become what is called "true believers."

- Cultural motivation involves the identification with a family, clan, or tribe with a willingness of self-sacrifice. Such a group fears the values of others, and this fear results in a perceived threat to the group's survival. Values deemed worthy of protection may include the group's language, homeland territory, religion, and group membership.

For example, some terrorists are motivated by the prospect of achieving the martyr status that guarantees entrance into paradise. When a terrorist act is committed to avenge the deaths of other terrorists, it is not considered as committing suicide, but rather is justified as being part of a religious war designed to resist secularization.

In recent years, there has been a dramatic increase in the number of religious terrorist groups that have political goals. Groups such as Hezbollah and Hamas, for example, operate from a religious ideology. Religion-motivated terrorists are considered the most dangerous and produce the violent outcomes to which the world has become accustomed ("What Motivates Terrorists?," 2000).

Terrorism also often flourishes in countries or environments where youth have limited opportunities for success. There is a growing concern by many U.S. correction administrators that prisons—where inmates are often from impoverished backgrounds and face bleak employment prospects upon their release — will be fertile recruiting ground for potential U.S. home-grown terrorists for this reason.

Overall, the conclusion is that organized crime and terrorism should not be viewed as totally separate phenomena, but rather as linked by activities, goals, structures, and networks. Dishman (2001, 2002) makes the observation that terrorists vary in terms of their reliance on crime, but are moving progressively toward a greater involvement in both conventional and organized crime activities. Although their motivations may differ, it is easy to understand why the two groups would develop links, associations, or common networks.

Comparison of the Structure of Terrorist Groups and Transnational Organized Crime

The structure of both terrorist organizations and transnational organized crime varies with the size of the group. Larger organizations can create complex branches that provide methods for acquiring resources, administrative support, and operational control. Both groups may incorporate loose networks formed for specific operations; alternatively, they may develop hierarchical rigid structures that comprise well-defined vertical chains of command, control, and responsibility. Dandurand and Chin (2004) and Dandurand and Prefontaine (2004) suggest that the structure of terrorist groups can be compared with major economic enterprises that have extensive logistical infrastructure. They describe these groups as nontemporarily structured, powerful, anonymous, and discreet organizations that specialize in diverse unlawful activity.

Both large and small terrorist groups are concerned with security as a means of survival. The primary method of achieving this level of protection is the clandestine cell. Normally, only the cell leader has knowledge of other contacts or cells, and only the top leadership has knowledge of the entire organization. Groups vary in size from those with 20 to 50 members to groups as large as several hundred strong. This variation has also been noted with many transnational organized crime groups, such as the Cali drug cartel. The elements of the terrorist cell are command and control, followed by (in order of importance) tactical, and logistical support. Smaller groups typically have 40 to 50 members, who are organized into two- to three-cell units consisting of two to five persons each (**Figure 14-1**).

Larger or medium-sized groups add levels to leadership beyond this structure, and sometimes resemble the business model adopted by many transnational organized crime

Command element

Intelligence section   Support section   Tactical units

Source: Intelligence in Terrorism, the U.S. Army Institute for Professional Development
Correspondence Course (Newport News, Va: 1989).

Figure 14-1   Elements of a terrorist cell.

groups. Leaders provide vision and policy for the group; they are often religious extremists and intellectuals. Of course, there are some exceptions to this model in which leadership is neither educated nor intellectual. The second level in the organizational structure consists of individuals who perform missions or assignments. The cell structure of this second level insulates the command and support components, thereby enhancing the organization's security—the same principle that is practiced in organized crime. With this structure (as depicted in **Figure 14-2**), one cell cannot reveal the identity, location, or mission of other cells or the leadership of other cells.

Each subcommand has an intelligence section, a support section, and tactical units. As the groups expand, more subcommands can be added, and eventually a third level of command may be necessary. The subcommands carry out attacks or missions. The structure consists of the following elements:

- Members of the active cadre perform missions depending on their skills and resources. These individuals are often the most dangerous and active members of the terrorist organization.

- Active supporters provide vital logistical networks consisting of safe houses and communication technology; they also provide intelligence for the organization.

- Passive supporters help maintain political support and try to win credibility or legitimacy for the organization.

- The command element provides leadership and training that often results in military precision supported by intelligence, surveillance/reconnaissance, security, and realistic training exercises.

The terrorist planning cycle consists of a preincident phase, an initiation phase, a climax phase, a postincident phase, an after-action briefing, and finally a new planning phase based on lessons learned or the success and failure of missions. This structure and the long-term planning are consistent with that of most transnational organized crime and help to explain why these two groups can network and work together. Terrorism, like transnational organized crime, can be a local, national, transnational, or international problem (Baker, 2005).

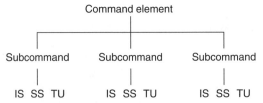

Source: Intelligence in Terrorism, the U.S. Army Institute for Professional Development Correspondence Course (Newport News, Va: 1989).

Figure 14-2 Terrorist group structure.

Possible structures for such groups have been described by the U.S. military as the chain, hub, and all-channel network — structures that bear a remarkable resemblance to the structures described in conspiracies. In the chain network, each cell links only to those cells on each of its sides (A − B − C − D − E). Communication is passed along the line. In hub and star networks, cells communicate with one central element, like the spokes of a wheel, with the center of the wheel comprising the command element. The chain and wheel structures may be combined to form a more complex organization. In what is described as the all-channel network, all nodes or cells are connected to one another with no hierarchical command being present. Command and control is distributed throughout the network, which can pose a security risk to the cells if the links can be identified and traced. These three structures (chain, hub, and all-channel network) may be used by both organized crime and terrorists during large operations.

The blurring of crime and terror presents a difficulty when it comes to distinguishing between terrorist and transnational organized crime. Tamara Makarenko (2003) developed a diagram that views the intersection of transnational organized crime and terrorism as a continuum of activity that results in the crime–terror nexus (**Figure 14-3**). On the left side of the diagram, transnational organized groups are shown as forming alliances with terrorists, using terror tactics in their operations, and blurring the line between political crime and commercial terrorism. The right side of the diagram illustrates the transformation of terrorist groups from purely ideological terrorists to criminals. The structure of both groups results in a dynamic and flexible organization through the transformation of both criminal groups. The groups lose their individual attributes and become similar entities that are both violent and enterprising, driven by greed and power.

The structure of transnational organized crime often mirrors that of the terrorist structures described earlier. Organized crime enterprises, however, are still localized, often fragmented, and ephemeral entities, but have adapted effectively to changes in the global community. The structure of these groups evolves to promote cohesiveness, with vertical

Figure 14-3　The nexus of transnational organized crime and terrorism.

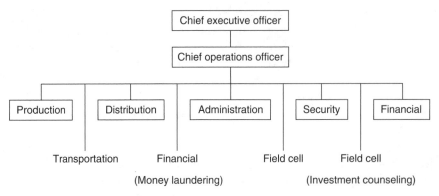

Figure 14-4 Cali cartel cell structure.

integration, numerous sources of supply, and, much like the terrorist structure, the ability to exploit social and political conditions while insulating leaders from culpability.

The Cali cartel used a cell structure much like that employed by many terrorist groups. This structure, which is depicted in **Figure 14-4**, was very successful for the world's largest drug trafficking group in the 1980s. The chief executive officer and chief operations officer resided in Cali, Colombia, isolated from the activity of each cell, but remained in control of these cells. This is very similar to that of Al Qaeda structure in which leaders remain hidden and isolated from the activity of their cells. Such a structure allows criminal organizations to be dynamic and flexible in adapting to market demand and political change and enables them to form symbiotic relationships with any entity—whether businesses, governments, or other crime groups—to achieve their goals and objectives. Thus it seems clear that structure does play a role in the nexus of transnational crime and terrorism.

Early History of Networking and Common Criminal Activity by Organized Crime and Terrorists

The criminal activity of terrorist groups dates back to at least the 1960s and 1970s, and perhaps even earlier depending on the definition used:

- Pancho Villa and his Mexican rebel group engaged in the criminal activity of horse theft.
- Mexican groups engaged in smuggling of people and illegal whiskey.
- The Bakunin and the Narodnaya Vovya enlisted criminals in their efforts.
- A number of groups ran protection rackets or taxed illegal goods.
- Russian terrorists robbed banks.
- Anarchist groups in the United States robbed banks (Laqueur, 1999).

The most infamous link between organized crime and terrorist may be the alliance formed by the Colombian drug cartel, the Mexican drug trafficking organizations (DTOs), and La Cosa Nostra with the National Liberation Army (ELN) and the Revolutionary Armed Forces of Colombia (FARC). FARC's connection to Hezbollah is also well documented. In the early years of the 1970s, FARC was linked to the terrorist group Sendero Luminoso as well. FARC is known to have used profits from its cocaine operation to purchase weapons; in fact, two of the members of FARC were arrested in 2006 for exchanging arms for illegal drugs (Jimenez, 2006). An attack executed by the terrorist group M19 at the instruction of the Medellín cartel on the Colombian Supreme Court in 1984 killed 115 civilians and 9 Supreme Court justices. The 1970s became known as the age of "narco-terrorism"; Laqueur (1999), for example, describes these events as the beginning of a new type of terrorism.

In the past, the United Self-Defense Forces (AUC), a right-wing terrorist group in Colombia, was involved in drug trafficking as well. The U.S. Department of Justice indicted the leader of AUC for transporting 17 tons of cocaine into the United States and Europe (Liddick, 2004).

Terrorist groups such as the Sunni Taliban in Afghanistan and the Shiite groups in Lebanon at one time in their history did not allow the consumption or sale/production of illegal drugs such as heroin; now, however, they are engaged in a variety of criminal activities. On the other side of this terrorist–organized crime nexus, Moscow has seen a pattern in which criminal gangs from Azerbaijan, Dagestan, Chechnya, Armenia, North Ossetia, and Ingushetia have become more political in their goals (Laqueur, 1999). This trend has been observed in Asia as well. Louise Shelley (2004) of the Transnational Crime and Corruption Center has identified several areas in the Pacific region where the nexus of organized crime and terrorism is especially prominent:

- Russian Far East
- Southern Philippines
- Sri Lanka
- The Golden Triangle
- Parts of Indonesia

Another early example of the link between terrorist and organized crime is the case (prosecuted in 1983) in which Jeff Fort and the El Rukins, an alleged Muslim religious street gang, were tied to terrorist activities in conjunction with the country of Libya. Testimony by gang members revealed that the Libyan government agreed to pay $2.5 million to the gang to plant bombs on U.S. aircraft (Lyman & Potter, 2004). At the time of this investigation, the author of this book was assigned to this case; Fort was eventually convicted in Mississippi of drug trafficking as result of a two-year investigation into his activities. Gangs like El Rukins may offer an avenue for either the recruitment of "home-grown terrorists" or international terrorists. Gang members who have a tremendous dissatisfaction with authority and government, are extremely violent, and perceive themselves as victims of the lack of opportunities are all too well suited to the mission of terrorism.

Corruption also played a vital role in the early history of organized crime and terrorist groups. In the early years, for the most part, terrorism and organized crime had no common ground or interest, but did have common enemies and methods. As Shelley (2004) notes, collusion of government officials was and is central to operations such as smuggling. The Colombian and Mexican drug cartels, for example, have a long history of corruption of government, business, and law enforcement. The same was certainly true of the early development of LCN in the United States; this group's history is well known for the merging of political machines and gangs, as are the documented cases of the Tammany Hall machine in New York and the Pendergast machine in Kansas City.

Other examples that illustrate the early nexus of organized crime and terrorism include the Basque Fatherland and Liberty organization (ETA) and the Irish Republican Army (IRA) of Northern Ireland, both of whose members have been involved in arms and narcotics dealing. Both groups have done business with FARC and other narco-terrorist organizations in Latin America. The Kurdistan Workers Party (PKK) is currently involved in narcotics and arms trafficking in Turkey and Western Europe. Yugoslavia arms traffickers are active suppliers of terrorist groups in Western Europe and other countries. The result of such liaisons is a more flexible, multinational relationship between terrorist and transnational crime groups (Curtis & Karacan, 2002).

The history of the diverse criminal activity of both terrorists and organized crime has been a factor in the growth of the links between these two groups. Illegal arms trafficking and drug trafficking have expanded throughout the world, thanks to the stockpiles of arms in Eastern Europe and the former Soviet Union and the tons of illegal drugs being produced in a number of countries. Treverton et al. (2009) concluded that a number of terrorist organizations have sizeable criminal operations and gave the following partial list:

- Hezbollah
- FARC
- Egyptian Islamic Jihad
- Kosovo Liberation Army (KLA)
- Kurdistan Workers Party
- Islamic Movement of Uzbekistan (IMU)
- Provisional IRA
- Liberation Tigers of Tamil Eelam (LTTE)

Hezbollah was formed by a group of radical clerics in late 1982 and backed by the Islamic Republic of Iran. The "Party of God" was formed with three primary goals: to resist the Israeli occupation, to reject Lebanon's sectarian political system, and to support the establishment of an Islamic state in Lebanon (Ayoob, 2008; Blanford, 2007).

Hezbollah is integrated into the Lebanese government, supported by the Lebanese Shiite population, and has a paramilitary wing that engages Israeli forces while promoting its anti-Western and anti-Zionist platform. The 1983 attacks on the U.S. embassy and U.S, Marine barracks in Lebanon have been attributed to Hezbollah. In addition to their terrorist activity, members of this group have engaged in criminal activity—specifically, drug trafficking, human smuggling, money laundering, counterfeiting, and extortion (Dishman, 2005). Smuggling and drug trafficking operations by Hezbollah have been documented at the U.S.–Canadian and the U.S.–Mexican borders and represent a major concern for homeland security and regional stability (Carter, 2009; Dishman, 2005). The same group has also been active in the tri-border region of Paraguay, Argentina, and Brazil, smuggling both narcotics and humans (Carter). Dishman (2005) estimates that Hezbollah's profits from narcotics and human trafficking in this tri-border area may be in the range of $50 billion to $100 billion. According to Asman (2007), Hezbollah cells within the United States have engaged in credit card schemes, arranged illegal "green card" marriages, and scammed the government out of $1.7 million in the form of a loan from the Small Business Administration.

The history of Al Qaeda, the group led by Osama bin Laden, indicates that this organization has engaged in criminal operations that are considered the equal of those carried out by the organized crime syndicates. Founded based on hatred of the Saudi regime and Western influence in the region (e.g., the stationing of U.S. forces in Saudi Arabia during the Gulf War in 1991), bin Laden's stated goal for Al Qaeda was to remove all "corrupt" governments and Western influence from the Middle East. The attacks by Al Qaeda have been extremely violent, including the attacks on the U.S. embassies in Kenya and Tanzania in 1998, the attack on the *USS Cole* in 2000, and the 2001 attacks on the World Trade Center and the Pentagon. Al Qaeda has established smuggling networks for heroin and hashish that move these drugs to buyers in the Middle East, Asia, and Europe; it uses the profits to purchase weapons and explosives. Group members have purchased illegitimate diamonds from rebels in Africa to finance their operations as well (Dishman, 2005).

The obvious conclusion from this brief history is that both organized crime and terrorists are willing to use their extensive worldwide networks to engage in both terrorism and criminal activity, and that criminal groups will sell to and do business with anyone who has enough money.

Types, Links, and Methods of Cooperation Between Organized Crime and Terrorists

Louise Shelley (2003) has identified the following links between organized crime and terrorist organizations:

- Organized crime activity is a means of financial support for terrorists.
- Both terrorists and organized crime operate in areas where there are weak governments or law enforcement and open borders.

- Both groups launder money using similar methods and operators to transfer their money.
- Both groups use corruption as a means to achieve their goals and objectives.
- Terrorists and organized crime operate using networks that often intersect.
- Both groups use similar means to communicate and take advantage of developing technology.

Terrorist groups do vary in terms of their reliance on crime and alliances with other crime groups, but there appears to be an emerging trend toward greater involvement by terrorists in both conventional and organized crime (Dishman, 2001, 2002, 2005).

Dandurand and Chin's (2004) research examined the links between terrorism and other forms of crime, including organized crime. These authors surveyed members of the United Nations through this institution's Office on Drug and Crime. The survey presented respondents with five choices regarding types of cooperation or linkages between terrorist groups and organized crime groups that might potentially occur in their respective countries:

- Operational
- Logistical
- Financial
- Political
- Ideological

The results of their survey were as follows:

- Seven countries responded that operational cooperation was observed.
- Nine countries observed a logistical cooperation.
- Twelve countries observed a financial link.
- Four countries observed a political connection.
- Six countries observed an ideological link between terrorist and organized crime groups
- Twenty-five respondents did not report the presence of cooperation in their country.

Traughber (2007) developed a terror–crime continuum as a mechanism to study the link between terrorism and arms, drug, and human trafficking in Georgia (the country formed through the breakup of the former Soviet Union). Rather than use the terms of "nexus" or "hybrid," the methodology known as Preparation of the Investigative Environment (PIE) was used in this research. The terror–crime interaction spectrum included the following methods of demonstrating the links between terrorism and crime groups:

- Activity appropriation: Terrorist and crime groups use similar methods without working together.

- Nexus: Each group relies on the support and expertise of the other group.

- Symbiotic relationship: The groups develop cooperative relationships of mutual benefit or dependence.

- Hybrid: The groups share methods and motives.

- Transformation: The terrorists abandon their ideological/political motives in favor of criminal objectives, or the criminal groups become terrorist groups.

The research indicated that terrorists are using the same routes as arms, drug, and human traffickers in organized crime and are benefiting from the same environment in which organized crime groups operate. Terrorists may use arms and drug trafficking to finance their activities, which establishes a nexus to organized crime and creates a hybrid organization. The researchers concluded that both a nexus and a symbiotic relationship between terrorists and drug and arms traffickers exist.

Curtis and Karacan's (2002) research indicated that overlapping and cooperation of activities of organized crime and terrorists increased during 2001 and 2002. Their research described the two groups cooperating using three broad patterns:

- In an alliance for mutual benefit, the terrorists enter into agreements with transnational criminals to gain funding, without engaging directly in commercial activities or giving up their ideologically base mission.

- Terrorists become directly involved in organized crime, thereby removing the middlemen while maintaining the ideological mission.

- The terrorists replace their ideology with the profit and greed motive.

These researchers concluded that most terrorist groups follow the second pattern; that is, they engage in the direct sale of commodities such as arms, narcotics, and people, and are involved in money laundering their profits. Curtis and Karacan (2002) found that in a terrorist organization, a natural progression frequently occurs from the first pattern toward the third. Over time, their association with transnational criminals may result in the terrorists thinking like businesspeople engaged in criminal activity. The terrorists may diversify their activities by engaging in a variety of criminal activities so as to develop more profitable business ventures.

This transformation is described by Makarenko (2002) as "fighters turned felons." Examples of groups that have followed this progression include the Revolutionary Armed Forces of Colombia, the Kurdistan Workers' Party, and the Real Irish Republican Army. Some terrorist organizations have actually preserved the environment of instability in a country simply to protect the group's criminal activity.

Integration of legitimate and illegitimate funds—a common activity of organized crime—is now characteristic of both organized crime and terrorist groups. Al Qaeda, for example, has used charities to move its funds. The complexity of this type of operation makes identifying and tracking illicit funds difficult, as illustrated in the highly publicized Bank of New York case, in which the integration of millions of dollars in illicit funds with legitimate accounts occurred.

Al Qaeda has also employed the Italian Mafia's network and expertise to forge documents and used the same transportation route that the Camorra organized crime group of Italy uses to traffic drugs and contraband. Chepesiuk (2007), a journalist and Fulbright Scholar, has quoted security experts as being highly concerned about this type of growing connection between terrorism and organized crime. For example, in 2002, members of a Hezbollah cell in Charlotte, North Carolina, were arrested and charged with involvement in credit card fraud and cigarette smuggling to finance a Lebanon-based group. In another case, Dawood Ibrahim, a major crime figure in India, was reported to have shared smuggling routes with terrorists who were involved in the 1993 Mumbai bombing.

Research by Schweitzer (2005) has shown a clear overlap between terrorist and organized crime networks, in that both rely on the same global transportation, communication, and financial infrastructures, and both take advantage of the breakdowns in authority and enforcement in weak and strong states alike. This author predicts that in the future transnational organized crime groups will collaborate in spawning high-tech attacks on Western countries based on the following rationale:

- Membership of terrorist groups is growing, and the groups are successfully recruiting technically skilled members.

- Terrorist are emboldened by the successful operation of groups in the United States, Europe, and Russia.

- Money laundering networks are expanding and becoming more complex.

- Terrorists are using the Internet in growing numbers and in more operations.

- Drug trafficking with a clear link to terrorist organizations in the Middle East and Asia is expanding.

Schweitzer's concern is that radiological terrorism will become a present and future danger; this author cited 85 other experts as reaching the same conclusion. The radioactive material needed to build a "dirty bomb" can be found in most countries, and many of those countries have inadequate control and monitoring programs for their nuclear programs. Schweitzer has given the following examples of how this lax control allows radioactive materials to fall into terrorist and organized crime hands:

- Russian and Ukrainian forces' arrest of an international criminal group for possession of osmium-187

- Ukrainian security's arrest of an organized crime group in possession of six containers of cesium-137

- Ukrainian police's arrest of three or four members of a criminal gang for possession of strontium-90 along with a large number of arms

These and other incidents are clear indications of the interest of terrorist and transnational organized crime in the profits and results from the use and sale of dirty bombs. As noted previously, transnational organized crime and terrorists are willing to use any type of force, violence, and intimidation necessary to achieve their goals, whether those goals focus on political, religious, ideological, or power and greed needs.

White-collar crime is another criminal activity that connects transnational organized crime and terrorists. White-collar crime is commonly defined as illegal acts characterized by guile, deceit, and concealment, which are not dependent upon application of force or violence. Often committed by means of conspiracy, the objective of these activities is to obtain money, property, or services. Such crimes include avoiding the payment or loss of money, property, or services and seeking to gain business or personal advantage.

It is evident from the preceding discussion that terrorist and transnational organized crime groups not only share structure, methods of operations, and the criminal environment, but also frequently engage in the same types of criminal activity.

Recent Developments in Networking and Criminal Activity of Terrorists and Transnational Crime

The DEA has reported that more than 14 groups designated as "Foreign Terrorist Organizations" have been engaged in drug trafficking. The agency has identified FARC and AUC in Colombia; PKK in Turkey; IMU in Uzbekistan; the Islamic Jihad of Palestine; LTTE in Spain; Hezbollah in Lebanon; PIRA in Northern Ireland; the tri-border Islamic Group in Argentina, Paraguay, and Brazil; Shining Path in Peru; and Al Qaeda as having ties to drug trafficking. It has also reported a nexus between terrorism and other criminal offenses such as medical insurance fraud, visa fraud, mail and wire fraud, and human and cigarette smuggling (Casteel, 2003). These examples serve as an indication that terrorists around the world are finding that crime pays—and pays well enough to support their operations.

The arrest of Monzer al Kassar by the DEA in 2007 revealed the existence of a massive network of transnational organized crime that supplied terrorist organizations. This organization was selling rocket-propelled grenade launchers, surface-to-air weapon systems, automatic weapons, and ammunition to terrorist factions in Somalia, the United Kingdom, Spain, Romania, Iran, Iraq, Nicaragua, Brazil, Cyprus, Bosnia, and Croatia. In addition, Kassar sold millions in weapons to FARC in Colombia. Arms trafficking is a major source of income for both transnational organized crime and terrorists, and a business that presents a major challenge for law enforcement worldwide. According to Traughber's (2007) research, the end of the Cold War with the Soviet Union and the breakup of the Soviet bloc have served as an impetus to the growth of both transnational organized crime and terrorism. The profits from arms, human, and drug trafficking are enormous—a fact that has not escaped the attention of emerging criminal groups. Kouri's (2009) research, for example, found that Albanian transnational clans are involved in arms trafficking, loan sharking, human smuggling, stock market manipulation, and drug trafficking, and that these criminal activities were a major source of funding for the terrorist groups.

Ralf Mutschke (2000), Assistant Director of the Criminal Intelligence Directorate of the International Criminal Police Organization, cited the following examples of other links between terrorism and criminal organizations:

- Algerian terrorists in Montreal and Moudjahidin groups (Groupe Islamique trafficking Arme [GIA]) specialize in computer theft.

- Albanian organized crime and terrorist groups have worked with Italian organized crime in drug trafficking.

- Drug trafficking links exist between Albanians and the Sacra Corona Unita and Ndrangheta.

The Executive Director of the United Nations Office on Drugs and Crime (UNODC), Antonio Maria Costa, outlined his concerns about the nexus between drugs, crime, and terrorism to an international audience in Rome in October 2004. Costa concluded that drug trafficking is the source of the financing of terrorism. He indicated that there is sufficient evidence to conclude that terrorist organizations are increasingly relying on revenues from arms, human, and drug trafficking. He described the nexus of organized crime and terrorist by listing three examples:

- The production of opium in Afghanistan (approximately 3600 tons in 2003) has resulted in terrorist and warlords in Afghanistan, insurgents in Central Asia, the Russian Federation, and traffickers in the Balkans sharing the estimated $30 billion world heroin market.

- Coca cultivation by insurgents and paramilitary groups has allowed the ELN, FARC, and AUC to benefit from billions of dollars generated by the coca industry.

- Drug trafficking in Morocco, amounting to more than $12.5 billion, was a major source of funding for three major terrorist events: the March 2004 attack on rail passengers in Madrid, the bombing of several sites in Casablanca in May 2003, and the aborted attack on a U.S. Navy vessel in Gibraltar in 2002.

Both Berry (2002, 2003) and Shelley (2001) have noted that terrorist groups are involved in many aspects of the drug trafficking business, including the cultivation, manufacture, distribution, and sale of the controlled substances. According to these authors, terrorists use many of the same corrupt government officials to protect their criminal operations and neutralize law enforcement efforts. Organizations such as the PKK of Turkey and the Georgian crime organizations are involved in production and trafficking illegal drugs and extorting a tax from other drug traffickers.

The most serious threat posed by the alliances of terrorist and organized crime or criminal groups relates to the availability of nuclear, chemical, and biological materials on the black market. A number of reports indicate that organized crime groups have acquired nuclear material and are willing to sell them to the highest bidders (Lilly, 2003; Rosenbaum, 1977; Schweitzer, 2005; Zaitseva, 2007). Al Qaeda has been reported by military and government agency intelligence to be very determined to obtain weapons of mass destruction.

The trend toward forging alliances or links between terrorists and organized or transnational organized crime appears to be escalating. For example, Basque Homeland and Liberty (ETA), a separatist terrorist group that operates in Spain, has been reported to be connected to FARC of Colombia and has been cited as having Venezuelan governmental cooperation. Spain's anti-terrorism court has indicted 12 members of the ETA for terrorist training, making sophisticated bombs, and plotting to assassinate Colombian President Alvaro Uribe with the support of Venezuelan officials. Venezuela is also accused of state sponsorship of terrorism against Spain and Colombia (Arostegui, 2010).

The first American indictment in this area serves as substantial evidence of the alliances between organized crime and terrorists. The complaint charges three Al Qaeda associates with conspiring to smuggle cocaine through northwest Africa. Al Qaeda in the Magreb — an ally of Osama bin Laden's organization — has exploited the weak state of West Africa, a nation that is known for corruption, poverty, and violence. The terrorist organization finances part of its operations by smuggling drugs and illegal immigrants through Morocco into Spain and through Libya and Algeria into Italy. This group was cited as being involved in the Madrid train bombings that killed 190 people in 2004 — an operation financed by the sale of hashish and Ecstasy. Reports suggest that there is an alliance between Al Qaeda, Mexican DTOs, Colombian guerrillas, and Lebanese militant groups as well. The former chief of DEA operations, Michael Braun, has confirmed that terrorist and organized crime groups are doing business and will become operational allies in the future. According to Braun, Moroccan officials have warned that Al Qaeda in the Magreb is involved in illegal drug trafficking.

Guinea Bissau was described as the first "narco-state" in Africa in one article. Investigators have also been quoted as saying that Lebanese mafia groups with a long-time presence in West Africa have ties to Hezbollah and play a role in the smuggling of illegal drugs for Latin American drug lords. Morocco's Interior Minister has indicated that Al Qaeda in the Magreb is involved in taxing cocaine smuggling routes in Mali and Mauritania (Rotella, 2010). This information was verified by Jay Bergman, DEA director for the Andean region of South America. He reports an alliance between American narco-terrorists and Islamic extremists; three al Qaeda members were arrested in December 2009 for plotting to smuggle drugs to raise money for jihad. Colombian cartels are believed to be using Africa to smuggle their illegal drugs to Europe, with Venezuela as the preferred shipping point from South America (Nagraj, 2010).

The U.S. Border Patrol reports that it is facing a growing problem with the Mara Salvatrucha (MS 13) gang in the Tucson sector; this group controls much of the arms, human, and illegal alien movement into the United States. Evidence also indicates that special-interest aliens, such those from Saudi Arabia, Syria, Iran, Pakistan, Afghanistan, Egypt, Somalia, Yemen, Jordan, Lebanon, and Iraq, are entering the United States with the help of MS 13. There are reports of entry points along the southwest border of the United States being littered with discarded Muslim prayer blankets, pages from Islamic texts, and Arabic newspapers (Williams, 2009). Hezbollah has been using the U.S.–Mexican border as a route to enter the United States for some time. According to Fox News (2008), Mexican courts convicted Salim Boughjader Mucharrafille in 2002 for human smuggling; he was involved in smuggling sympathizers of Hezbollah into the United States. Mucharrafille is a Mexican of Lebanese descent who ran a cafe in the city of Tijuana, Mexico.

Conclusions

There can be little doubt that the trend of alliances between terrorist and organized crime groups is escalating. Although state-sponsored terrorism continues, its scale has declined in the past decade. Faced with the loss of this support, terrorists have found that profits from criminal activity can fund their operations and provide for a luxurious lifestyle. Such alliances have made transnational criminal activity more efficient and effective, while presenting a major challenge for law enforcement and governments. Even when these groups are not formal allies, they often share the same criminal environment, corrupt officials, criminal activities, structure, and method of operations.

No matter what it is called — nexus, association, symbiotic relationship, or link — there is a connection between these two criminal groups. The long-time differences in motivations for criminal activity are becoming blurred. To deal with this changing environment, governments should focus on the criminal activity of both groups, applying the same strategies against international groups that have been successful against organized crime in the United States. The threat is clear: It comes from weapons of mass destruction and criminal activity that can destroy entire economies or countries. Transnational criminal and terrorist groups have the ability to transport anything, anywhere, at any time, with immunity owing to the diminished threat from detection, arrest, and prosecution created by their increasing complexity and unholy alliances. These conclusions should serve as an impetus to governments and law enforcement to establish alliances and pass international laws that can be as effective as the criminal organizations themselves. If the trends are allowed to continue, the world will become exceedingly more violent and corrupt than it is today.

Discussion Questions

1. Discuss the similarities of and differences between terrorist groups and organized crime.

2. Explain why there appears to be a blurring of the lines between terrorism and organized crime so as to create a crime–terror nexus.

3. List and discuss the events in history where links between organized crime and terrorism are evident.

4. List and discuss current examples that confirm the existence of a nexus of organized crime and terrorism.

5. Discuss the types and methods of cooperation between organized crime groups and terrorists.

6. Discuss how cooperation and links between terrorist and transnational organized groups have affected law enforcement and governments.

References

Arostegui, M. (2010). Venezuela Linked to Terror Groups. *Washington Times*. Retrieved March 10, 2010, from http://www.washingtontimes.com/news/2010/march/09venezuuuuuuela-linke

Asman, D. (2007, January 18). Hezbollah Inside America: Fox News Tells All in Documentary. Retrieved March 8, 2010, from http://www.foxnews.com/printer_friendly_story/03266,244002,00.html

Ayoob, M. (2008). *The Many Faces of Political Islam: Religion and Politics in the Muslim World*. Ann Arbor: University of Michigan Press.

Baker, T. (2005). *Introductory Criminal Analysis*. Upper Saddle River, NJ: Pearson Prentice Hall.

Berry, L. C. (2002, May). *A Global Overview of Narcotics-Funded Terrorist and Other Extremist Groups*. Washington, DC: Federal Research Division, Library of Congress.

Berry, L. C. (2003, October). *Nations Hospitable to Organized Crime and Terrorism*. Washington, DC: Federal Research Division, Library of Congress.

Blanford, N. (2007). Introduction. In N. Noe (Ed.), *Voice of Hezbollah: The Statements of Sayyed Hassan Nasrallah* (pp. 1–13). (E. Khouri, trans.). New York: Verso.

Burke. R. (2000). *Counter-terrorism for Emergency Responders*. Boca Raton, FL: Lewis.

Carter, S. A. (2009, March 27). Exclusive: Hezbollah Uses Mexican Drug Routes into U.S. *The Washington Times*. Retrieved March 20, 2010, from http://www.washingtontimes.com/news/2009/mar/27/hezbollah-uses-mexican-drug-routes-into-us/

Casteel, S. (2003, May 20). Narco-Terrorism: International Drug Trafficking and Terrorism — A Dangerous Mix. Testimony of Assistant Administrator for Intelligence, U.S. Drug Enforcement Administration, before the U.S. Senate Judiciary Committee.

Chepesiuk, R. (2007, September 11). Dangerous Alliances: Terrorism and Organized Crime. *Global Politician*. Retrieved January 12, 2009, from http://www.globalpolitician.com/23435-crime

Congressional Statement of Ralph Mutschke, Assistant Director, Criminal Intelligence Directorate, International Criminal Police Organization. (2000, December 13). American Russian Law Institute. Retrieved January 20, 2009, from http://www.russianlaw.org/mutschke.htm

Curtis, G. (2002, October). *Involvement of Russian Organized Crime Syndicates, Criminal Elements in the Russian Military, and Regional Terrorist Groups in Narcotics Trafficking in Central Asia, the Caucus, and Chechnya*. Washington, DC: Federal Research Division, Library of Congress.

Curtis, G. E., & Karacan, T. (2002, December). *The Nexus Among Terrorists, Narcotics, Traffickers, Weapons Proliferations, and Organized Crime Networks in Western Europe*. Washington, DC: Federal Research Division, Library of Congress.

Dandurand, Y., & Chin, V. (2004, April). *Links Between Terrorism and Other Forms of Crime*. Report submitted to Foreign Affairs, and the United Nations Office on Drugs and Crime. Vancouver, Canada: International Centre for Criminal Law Reform and Criminal Justice Policy.

Dandurand, Y., & Prefontaine, D. C. (2004). *Terrorism and Organized Crime: Reflections on an Illusive Link and Its Implication for Criminal Law Reform*. Annual Meeting International Society for Criminal Law Reform. Retrieved March 20, 2010, from http://www.iccir.law.ubc.ca/Publications/Reports/International%20SocietyPaper%20of%20Terrorism.pdf

Dishman, C. (2001). Terrorism, Crime, and Transformation. *Studies in Conflict & Terrorism, 24,* 43–58.

Dishman, C. (2002). Terrorism, Crime and Transformation. In P. L. Griset & S. Mahan (Eds.). Thousand Oaks, CA: Sage.

Dishman, C. (2005). The Leaderless Nexus: When Crime and Terror Converge. In R. D. Howard, R. L. Sawyer, & N. E. Bajema (Eds.), *Terrorism and Counterterrorism: Understanding the New Security Environment* (3rd ed., pp. 295–310). New York: McGraw-Hill.

FoxNews.com. (2008, December). Mexico Sentences Migrant Smuggler to 60 Years. Retrieved May 20, 2010, from http://www.foxnews.com/wires/2008Dec28/0,4670,LTMexicoUSSmuggler,00.html

Hoffman, B. (2006). Defining Terrorism. In R. D. Howard, R. L. Sawyer, & N. E. Bajema (Eds.), *Terrorism and Counterterrorism: Understanding the New Security Environment* (3rd ed., pp. 4–33). New York: McGraw-Hill.

Jimenez, M. (2006, August 10). Costa Rica Arrest Suspected Guerilla. *Fox News*. Retrieved July 3, 2007, from http://www.foxnews.com/wires/2006Aug10/0,4670,CostaRicaSuspect,00.html

Kouri, J. (2009, January 21). The Transformation of Organized Crime. *American Chronicle*. Retrieved January 30, 2009, from http://www.americanchronicle.com/articles/view/88515

Laqueur, W. (1999). *The New Terrorism: Fanaticism and the Arms of Mass Destruction*. Oxford, UK: Oxford University Press.

Liddick, D. R. Jr. (2004). *The Global Underworld: Transnational Crime and the United States*. Westport, CT: Praeger.

Lilley, P. (2003). *Dirty Dealing: The Untold Truth about Global Money Laundering, International Crime and Terrorism* (2nd ed.). London: Kogan Page.

Lyman, M. D., & Potter, G. (2004). *Organized Crime* (3rd ed.). Upper Saddle River, NJ: Pearson Prentice Hall.

Makarenko, T. (2003). "The Ties That Bind": Uncovering the Relationship Between Organized Crime and Terrorism. In *Global Organized Crime: Trends and Developments*. The Hague: Kluwer Law International.

Nagraj, N. (2010, January 5). Colombian FARC Rebels, Al-Qeda Joining Forces to Smuggle Cocaine into Europe, Says DEA. Retrieved March 20, 2010, from file:///C:Users?Mlri3/AppData/Local/Temp/Temp2_attachments%

National Institute of Justice. (2007). *Asian Transnational Organized Crime and Its Impact on the United States*. Washington, DC: U.S. Department of Justice. Retrieved March 15, 2010, from http://www.ncjrs.gov/pdffiles2/nij/214186.pdf

Rosenbaum, D. (1977). Nuclear Terror. *International Security, 1*(3), 140–161.

Rotella, S. (2010). Associates of Al Qaeda Group Charged with Drug Trafficking. *Baltimore Sun*. Retrieved May 12, 2010, from http://www.baltimoresun.com/health/sns-dc-alqaeda-drugs,0,3983033,print.st

Schweitzer, G. E. (2005). The Nexus of International Organized Crime and Terrorism: The Case of Dirty Bombs. Testimony to the Subcommittee on Prevention of Nuclear and Biological Attacks of the Committee on Homeland Security, U.S. House of Representatives. Retrieved May 20, 2010, from www.nti.org/e_research/official_docs/congress/congress092250Schweitzer.pdf

Shelley, L. (2001). *The Nexus of Organized International Criminals and Terrorist*. Transnational Crime and Corruption Center.

Shelley, L. (2002). The Nexus of Organized International Criminals and Terrorism. *International Annals of Criminology, 20*(1/2), 85–92.

Shelley, L (2003, June 25). Statement to the House Committee on International Relations, Subcommittee on International Terrorism, Nonproliferation and Human Rights. *American. edu.* Retrieved January 12, 2009, from http://www.american.edu/tracc/resources/publications/shelle18.pdf

Shelley, L. (2004, September 27). Organized Crime, Terrorism and Cybercrime. Computer Crime Research Center. Retrieved January 12, 2009, from http://www.crime-research.org/articles/Terrorism_Cybercrime/

Swanson, C. R., Territo, L., & Taylor, R. W. (2008). *Police Administration: Structures, processes, and behavior* (7th ed.). Upper Saddle River, NJ: Pearson Prentice Hall.

Terrorist Research and Analytical Center, Counter-Terrorism Section Intelligence Division. (1993). *Terrorism in the United States 1982–1992.* Washington, DC: U.S. Department of Justice, Federal Bureau of Investigation.

Traughber, C.M. (2007, Spring). Terror–Crime Nexus? Terrorism and Arms, Drug, and Human Trafficking in the Caucasus. *All Academic Research,* Retrieved January 12, 2009, from http://www.allacademic.com//meta/p_mla_apa_research_citation/1/8/0/1/4/pages180143/p180143-1.php

Treverton, G. F., Matthies, C., Cunningham, K. J., Goulka, J., Ridgeway, G., & Wong, A. (2009). *Film Piracy, Organized Crime, and Terrorism.* Santa Monica, CA: RAND Corporation. Retrieved May 10, 2010, from http://www.rand.org/pubs/monographs/2009/RAND_MG742.sum.pdf

What Motivates Terrorists? (2000). In *Terrorism.* San Diego: Greenhave.

Williams, P. (2009, August 3). MS-13 Smuggles Muslim Terrorist into U.S. Retrieved May 12, 2010, from file:///C:Users/Mlri3/AppData/Local/Temp?Temp2_attachments%

Zaitseva, L. (August, 2007). Organized Crime, Terrorism and Nuclear Trafficking. Center for Contemporary Conflict. Retrieved May 20, 2010, from http://www.ccc.nps.lnavy.mil/si/2007/Aug/zaitseveAug07.asp

Chapter 15

Where Do We Go from Here?

Personal excellence can be achieved by a visionary goal, thorough planning, dedicated execution, and total follow-through.

— Gerald R. Ford, 38th U.S. President

Law Enforcement Response to Organized Crime

When it comes to organized crime, law enforcement agencies have accumulated a significant amount of information regarding the history, structure, activities, and methods of operation of these sophisticated criminal organizations. Even so, perhaps what is most disturbing about these groups is the lack of knowledge about the extent of their current corruption and other criminal activities in the United States and abroad. Gaps in information also exist concerning the alliances that may have been forged among the many diverse organized crime groups. If the past is any indication of what the present and the future hold, we must assume that these groups will continue to become more efficient and effective in their ability to gain power and reap huge profits by means of both violence and corruption. Given their history of successfully corrupting governments, businesses, and the community, why would we not assume that such activity is occurring on an unprecedented scale today and is certain to continue into the future?

Twenty-first-century criminal enterprises will be more educated, high-tech, and computer-literate organizations that will benefit from the growth of a global community and the information age. Certainly, one of the major targets of modern organized crime continues to be financial institutions—a focus that is likely to give rise to international conglomerates and corporations controlled through the wealth and power of organized crime groups. Major investments in legitimate avenues have been a trend among organized crime groups since gangsters like Meyer Lansky first began to see their potential for profit. Profits from drug trafficking; theft of high-tech information, systems, and equipment; trafficking in human body parts and slave labor; global Internet sports betting; waste disposal—all will contribute to an ever-increasing international market for organized crime's goods and services, both illicit and legitimate. Most of the providers of these revenue streams are the organized crime groups discussed in this book.

A variety of evolving groups, such as MS 13 (Mara Salvatrucha 13), will undoubtedly rise and fall in the future. MS 13's roots are in the revolution-torn countries of El Salvador and Honduras of the 1980s. This gang appeared in Los Angeles in the late 1980s, and its operations spread as Central American migrant workers and illegal aliens moved throughout the United States. Now documented by the FBI to be present in more than 30 states and to have an estimated 20,000 members, MS 13 has seen more than 200 of its members arrested by U.S. task forces established to develop cases on this gang. Known for their brutal ruthlessness, group members committed more than 1200 murders between 2000 and 2005, and their involvement in racketeering activity classifies them as an organized crime group. In the future, they will almost certainly be joined by new groups and transnational organized groups that continue to evolve.

Before money laundering sites and safe havens for the leaders of these complex criminal organizations can be eliminated, the entire global community must adopt more effective legislation and other strategies that can trace the flow of money more accurately. To do so, the power of regulatory agencies must be increased. Repealing bank security laws, establishing an international financial intelligence unit, criminalizing the act of money laundering, and developing RICO, conspiracy, CCE, and forfeiture laws in all nations are essential if law enforcement hopes to have any chance to significantly impact these powerful organizations. If these organizations remain untouched until they reach the U.S. border, they will never be defeated.

Holding the thin line that separates professional law enforcement from the ever more sophisticated organized crime alliances is a formidable task. The disparity between the vast resources of organized crime and the relatively small resources devoted to law enforcement must be addressed. Using satellites, telecommunications, and computers to complement their effective use of violence and corruption, organized crime enjoys distinct advantages over today's law enforcement.

Organized crime's state-of-the-art equipment, its use of the best experts that money can buy in all professions, and its advanced communication systems put much of law enforcement resources to shame. In the future, these organizations may well operate with more efficacy, efficiency, and impunity from arrest and prosecution.

Three factors have permitted organized crime to take advantage of opportunities to become even more powerful: the growth of new organized crime groups; the diversion of U.S. resources away from fighting organized crime and into homeland security; and the enforcement culture of not sharing information and resources. RICO statutes may have started the decline of some groups such as La Cosa Nostra, but others such as the Japanese Yakuza have increased their holdings in both private companies (e.g., through the stock market) and real estate in America and other countries worldwide. The questions remain: Who will manage the multinational corporations of the future? Who will use any means to be successful?

With the fall of the Soviet Union, powerful nuclear, biological, and chemical weapons became available on the black market. Adding to the danger of this development are alliances of Russian organized crime with both Mexican and Colombian organized crime groups. Currently, numerous foreign terrorist organizations, such as FARC, ELN, and AUC, among others, are engaging in organized crime activities, including narcotics trafficking with the DTOs of Colombia and Mexico. Hamas and Hezbollah members located in Paraguay, Argentina, and Brazil are known to generate income from drug, weapon, and liquor trafficking that support their respective organizations in Lebanon, Palestine, and elsewhere in the Middle East. The Peruvian Shining Path group is yet another terrorist organization engaged in drug trafficking. Other groups in southwest Asia, including organizations in Afghanistan and Uzbekistan, are connected to Al Qaeda, a group that derives significant income from heroin and opium trafficking. Likewise, the Southeast Asian Tamil Tigers group uses drug trafficking to support its terrorist activities. Also found in Southeast Asia is the United Wa State Army, a major producer of both methamphetamines and heroin. The Philippines is home to the New People's Army, which supports its terrorist activities by cultivating and trafficking marijuana. Other Filipino groups that support terrorist activity by narcotics trafficking include the Moro National Front, Moro Islamic Liberation Front, and Abu Sayyaf groups. Financing terrorist networks and activities through drug trafficking has a decades-long history, with narco-terrorist groups in Colombia having generated billions of dollars in profits from their illicit trade.

There are strong indications that alliances have been formed between many organized crime and terrorist organizations, including the terrorists groups listed in the preceding paragraph. These alliances present problems for law enforcement that are likely to escalate in the future. Operations such as the U.S. Attorney General's Money Laundering Operation (a 1999-initiated task force focusing on undercover sting operations that was designed to seize laundered drug proceeds) are necessary to legally capture and coerce organized crime groups to forfeit their assets and cash, thereby eliminating organizations' major sources of income to support their terrorist activity.

The links between terrorism and organized crime include state-sponsored entities such as Afghanistan's opium and heroin operations (which have increased under U.S. occupation) and the narco-terrorist groups existing in Colombia. The war on drugs and the war on terrorism are inextricably linked, it seems. International effort and cooperation are needed now to prevent such events as the September 11, 2001, attacks from being repeated.

Transnational organized crime is the most significant development in the organized crime environment of our time. The number of alliances that have allowed these groups to collaborate and cooperate to deliver illicit goods and services on a global scale are unprecedented. These enterprises have incorporated technological advancements and exploited changes in the economic and political environments in their fluid schemes of operation. Globalization of organized crime has allowed these groups to deliver their goods and services anywhere, anytime, to anyone. They have no problem with violating international borders—in fact, they find it easy to do so.

The basics of organized crime today remain the same as those that have existed for centuries. These groups are still a local problem that relies on corruption for its continued existence. However, the combination of crime organizations with terrorist groups has greatly added to the challenge for law enforcement in combating their crimes. The new face of organized crime is the alliance between traditional and nontraditional organized crime groups and international terrorists.

The historical evolution of a variety of organized crime groups and their leaders is sketchy and debatable, as is the structure of these groups. Much of what we think we know about organized crime comes from law enforcement or government sources. Media speculation, confessions of organized criminals, and other questionable sources contribute to our knowledge of organized crime. Nevertheless, little sound research by academia into organized crime has occurred, despite numerous publications and books on this subject. It is very difficult to conduct research into secretive and dangerous organizations that depend on codes of conduct such as omerta and murderous retribution for their survival.

Many of the leaders of organized crime groups began their criminal careers by committing petty crimes as they tried to imitate a criminal role model. Over time, they committed more serious crimes, became gang members, and eventually worked their way up the ladder to become trusted members of the organization. Leaders may have turned into legitimate businesspeople late in their careers as the profits of their illegal activities were invested into reputable legal enterprises. By examining the rise and fall of these leaders, law enforcement can develop strategies for the future. Leaders and bosses of organized crime share many similarities, as demonstrated in this book. Understanding this pattern can be used to help direct future law enforcement strategies.

Criminal leaders and their organizations will always be part of our future. They have proven to be very adept at managing a dynamic environment, as they quickly adjust to new legislation and law enforcement strategies. As they seek to avoid arrest and prosecution and continue to survive, their criminal organizations will become more sophisticated, structured, and even more of a threat than in the past. For example, as the United States and other countries move toward becoming cashless and paperless societies, organized crime will be prepared for this change with high-tech electronics as well as financial and legal experts who can exploit opportunities for profit in this new milieu. This willingness to evolve on the part of organized crime requires law enforcement and its investigators to be equally proactive in the training of their own experts on current technologies.

A different type of investigator—one who is trained in cutting-edge technology, computers, and financial investigations—is necessary to meet this challenge. Preparation for this role will require substantial formal education in the areas of business, accounting, computer science, and market dynamics in addition to the criminal justice field. Task forces comprised of highly specialized personnel are required, as is continuous training in both market dynamics and technology as they relate to organized crime activity. Investigators of the future may well be multilingual and possess advanced degrees in a variety of fields. In-service training involving case studies and an ability to take advantage of technology to advance skills and knowledge are essential elements if investigators want to keep pace with the dynamic nature of these criminal groups.

Governments will always have prohibitions on items such as drugs and alcohol, so the problem of corruption will continue to plague law enforcement efforts. While past efforts against organized crime members have been impressive, as explained in the preceding chapters, the war is far from won. Allegations of mob influence at the U.S. presidential level spanning the administrations of at least four presidents are a worrisome omen for the future. If these criminals have reached the presidential level in the past, what prevents them from achieving the same level of influence in the future?

The government efforts of the past are not sufficient to face an allied global organized crime community. Given these criminal syndicates' ability to corrupt the U.S. government at the local, state, and federal levels, combined with their mergers with major corporations, a new level of corporate crime is becoming apparent.

Demands for illegal services and goods by the public are continuing and probably will increase in the future. If the global alliances between major organized crime groups are successful (i.e., if they are not already established), then organized crime will become the largest business in the world, attracting large numbers of recruits who desire power and wealth no matter what the actual cost.

The early strategies of organized crime to neutralize law enforcement and politicians through bribery, control of the source of supply by monopoly, and development of unity by structuring the organization and dividing the geographic areas among smaller affiliated groups will continue, except that they will be deployed on a global scale, not just within a single country. Theories, history, and definitions of organized crime are starting points for the investigator's understanding of this evolving phenomenon.

The concepts underlying organized crime and the methods used to address these complex groups will always be controversial. Because of the lack of accurate intelligence, one problem is that much of the information concerning organized crime derives from journalistic sources. Many in academia disagree with or are suspicious of information from law enforcement sources. Informants and personal experiences serve as other sources of information about these crime enterprises.

Controversies in this area begin with the variety of definitions for organized crime that are used in different countries and in academia. If consensus on a comprehensive definition cannot be reached among experts, how can research be validated and how can meaningful discussions occur? How much organization and structure do these groups have? These questions are areas of discussion within academia, but are far less controversial among those in law enforcement who are coping with the destruction left in the wake of these criminals.

Much debate surrounds the effectiveness and appropriateness of U.S. statutes and legislation, such as the RICO Act, the Patriot Act, and narcotic laws. Invasion of privacy and individual rights are issues raised by critics of the Patriot Act and RICO. Considered by many people to be too broad and invasive, these statutes have been suggested to violate constitutional freedoms; critics also argue that they might potentially be used against individuals who do not belong to a criminal or terrorist group. Just the threat of RICO charges can lead to guilty pleas from executives whose business assets are frozen, even when the company is innocent of RICO violations. The prospect of paying triple damages in civil suits, freezing personal assets, and being labeled a "racketeer" can be very intimidating to innocent individuals.

The sunset clauses of the Patriot Act that expired in March 2006 were being debated in Congress at the time of this book's writing. Key arguments focused on the following issues: the need for such extreme measures to address terrorism; the effectiveness of the broad money laundering statutes; the involvement of the National Security Agency and CIA in domestic intelligence and surveillance collection; and the legitimacy of roving wiretaps. Some abuse of forfeiture regulations has fueled controversy surrounding precisely what is subject to forfeiture under which conditions. Policies such as "zero tolerance" (seizure of large assets when even small amounts of drugs are discovered) have been a subject of concern and debate.

The idea of legalizing drugs and prostitution has been presented as a solution to the problem of organized crime by some in law enforcement who join the political left wing in advocating this position. This concept also calls for spending more on prevention and education and less on law enforcement and corrections. Other proposals under debate include relaxing legal hurdles for illegal workers who live in the United States; these workers include many families who have evaded deportment and paying taxes for a decade or more, as well as criminal elements.

Some critics of current law enforcement policies suggest that the U.S. government created the concept of organized crime to obtain support and funding for law enforcement and the bureaucracy. Those holding this view do not believe that organized crime groups have developed global alliances or are allied with terrorists. They consider claims of the terrorist–organized crime nexus to be part of a plot to allow known government invasion of individual rights, and as an excuse to use the military and other government powers.

The vast majority of the law enforcement establishment—including this author—does not support these extreme views.

Corruption is yet another subject of debate. How does corruption first occur? Do organized crime members corrupt people, businesses, and government, or are the criminals approached by those entities in their pursuit of power and profit? Has corruption become more frequent and simply moved underground, or have efforts against organized crime truly reduced the level of corruption? Despite these and other questions, it remains clear that less coordination and sharing of information occurs among international, national, state, and local law enforcement agencies because of the threat of corruption.

Organized crime is controversial and will continue to generate much discussion. As it expands further into our society, becoming more opaque, complex, and diverse, new issues will arise for those law enforcement and governments charged with developing new laws and strategies to combat these groups' membership and crimes.

It is often said that if we fail to study and know the past, we are doomed to repeat our failures. The deeper the understanding and the more accurate the concepts of organized crime that the investigator develops, the more effective he or she will become. As described throughout this book, the future of organized crime in the United States is likely to include an ever more diverse line-up, featuring groups such as Triads, drug cartels, the Red Mafia, and the Yakuza. All of these organizations depend primarily on corruption and public demand for their services and goods. Just as the rising demand for drugs created an unprecedented number of sophisticated international and transnational criminal networks, so the information-age takeovers of financial institutions and terrorist demands will serve as an impetus for the continued growth of organized crime.

At this writing, an international commission may not have been established among the many organized crime groups; undoubtedly, however, increased cooperation among these groups is occurring. The market potential for such a new global crime community is unlimited. Despite numerous successes realized by law enforcement, all prior efforts have failed to stop the growth of organized crime. Investigators of the future must understand market dynamics to examine how these criminal enterprises have emerged, survived, and continue to profit by supplying the public demand for illegal services and goods. Putting a halt to this pattern calls for multiple strategies to address corruption, money laundering, and market demand, all of which require enormous improvements in developing intelligence on an international scale.

Emerging trends, emerging activities, and emerging groups as well as old problems have created a dynamic atmosphere for organized crime, and they certainly make investigating transnational organized crime a major challenge for law enforcement. The activity of Mexican border drug trafficking continues to escalate, in tandem with ever more serious security threats and violence. For example, authorities uncovered and halted a plot by the Zeta that posed a threat to the Falcon Dam. This group planned to blow up the dam and unleash billions of gallons of water to get back at a key rival, the Gulf cartel, which controls smuggling in the Falcon Dam area. This plan required access, means, knowledge, and motivation—all characteristics that are exhibited by organized crime. These kinds of threats have prompted the introduction of major legislation and additional funding to address organized crime on the southwestern border of the United States and cost taxpayers millions of dollars, thereby affecting the economy of both Mexico and the United States.

Organized crime's influence over politics and the business world must be targeted if we are to derail the growth of alliances, power, and wealth of these complex criminal organizations. Clearly, future investigators must view organized crime as a dynamic phenomenon and stay on top of these changes by developing accurate and timely intelligence. New strategies must be developed to ensure that adequate resources are available to support the very best and brightest investigators America has to offer.

Author Index

A

Abadinsky, H., 43, 94–95
Acacio, Negro, 102
Accardo, Tony, 120, 121
Albanese, J., 36–37, 40, 42
Albini, J. L., 43, 45
Amuso, Vittorio, 119
Anastasia, Albert, 23
Anslinger, Harry, 151
Arellano Felix, Francisco Rafael, 74–75
Arellano Felix, Javier, 74–75
Arena, Andy, 98

B

Bagley, Bruce, 64, 71, 78, 82
Barger, Ralph Hubert (Sonny), 184
Barksdale, David "King", 214–215
Barnes, Leroy "Nicky", 217
Beccaria, Marchese de, 38
Bell, D., 35
Bentham, Jeremy, 38
Bergman, Jay, 273
Berry, L. C., 272
Berry, William, 183
Bin Laden, Osama, 267
Blakey, G. Robert, 7, 225
Bonanno, Joseph, 118–119
Bruno, Angelo, 121
Buchalter, Lepke, 115
Burke, Jimmy, 128
Bush, George H. W., 153
Bush, Prescott, Jr., 153

C

Calderón, Felipe, 69, 71, 73, 83, 84
Capone, Al, 21, 22, 120, 229
Caracas, Tomas Medina, 102
Cardenas Guillen, Osiel, 75
Carolla, Anthony, 122
Carrillo Fuentes, Amando "Lord of the Skies", 56, 76–78
Carrillo Fuentes, Vicente, 77
Casso, Anthony, 128
Casteel, Steven, 97

Castellano, Paul, 113, 114, 133
Castro, Fidel, 121
Cavazos, Ruben, 192, 194
Chabat, Jorge, 78
Chambers, Donald Eugene, 186
Chepesiuk, Ron, 52, 55–56, 270
Chiang Kai Shek, 163
Chin, Ko-lin, 160
Chin, V., 268
Choitner, Murray, 29
Chong, Peter, 168
Cirillo, Dominick "Quiet Don", 119
Clinard, M., 18–19
Coke, Christopher, 218
Colombo, Joseph, 119
Colucci, Joey, 133
Corallo, Anthony "Ducks", 119
Costa, Antonio Maria, 272
Costello, Frank, 29, 115, 122
Cressey, Donald, 9, 19, 37–38
Curtis, G. E., 269

D

D'Alfonso, Frank "Flowers", 122
Daly, Richard, 121
Danduran, Y., 268
Davis, John, 185
Defede, Joe, 119
Dewey, Thomas, 117
Diamond, Eddie, 115
Diamond, Jack "Legs", 115
Dobkin, Lou, 186
Dobovšek, B., 9
Donovan, Raymond, 29
Drug Enforcement Agency (DEA), 60
Durkheim, E., 38

E

Eaton, Tracey, 77
Escobar, Pablo, 54–55, 59
Espinoza Barron, Alberto "La Fresa", 79
Eubank, William, 260
Exner, Judith, 121

F

Fainberg, Ludwig "Tarzan", 102–103
Fein, Bennie "Dopey", 112
Finckenauer, J., 45
Fort, Jeff, 214, 265
Fox, Vicente, 70, 78, 83, 84
Fratianno, Jimmy "The Weasel", 113, 133

G

Gagliano, Frank, 122
Galante, Carmine, 118
Gallardo, Miguel Angel Felix "El Padrino", 69
Gambino, Carlo, 113, 119
Genovese, Vito, 23, 113, 119
Giancana, Sam, 120, 121
Gigante, Vincent "The Chin", 119, 133
Gillich, Mike, Jr., 24
Goldberg, Boris, 97
Gonzales, Alberto, 60
Gottfredson, M., 36
Gotti, John, Jr., 114, 133
Gotti, John III, 119
Gotti, Peter, 119
Gravano, Salvatore "The Bull", 113, 128, 133
Grayson, G. W., 81
Guzman Loera, Joaquin "El Chapo", 75, 76, 78

H

Halat, Pete, 24
Hancock, John, 25
Hauser, Joseph, 134
Hennessey, David, 112
Herrera, Pacho, 55
Herrnstein, R., 36
Hill, Henry, 127–128
Hirschi, T., 36
Hodge, Ronald Jerome, 186
Hoff, "Boo-Boo", 122
Hoffa, Jimmy, 132

Hoover, J. Edgar, 1, 114
Hoover, Larry, 214–215

I

Ianni, F. A., 35
Ibrahim, Dawood, 270
Inagawa, Kakuji, 142
Ishizuka, Takashi, 145
Ito, Iccho, 145
Ivankov, Vyacheslav K., 100–101

J

Johnson, Junior, 26
Johnson, Lyndon B., 27
Jones, Edward, 120
Jones, George, 120
Jones, McKissack, 120

K

Karacan, T., 269
Al Kassar, Monzer, 271
Kefauver, Carey Estes, 113
Kennedy, John F., 121, 132
Kennedy, Joseph, 121, 122
Kennedy, Robert, 121, 122
Kenny, D., 45
Kharabadze, Nikolai, 96
Kiang Hsi, 162
King, Martin Luther, Jr., 122
Kirillov, Oleg, 23
Klebnikov, Paul, 105
Kodama, Yoshio, 142
Konanykhine, Alexander, 100
Kot Siu Wong, 164
Kramer, Rudy, 202

L

Lamb, Peter, 154
Lansky, Meyer, 29, 116, 117
Laxalt, Paul, 29
Lazcano, Heriberto, 80
Leo, Daniel "The Lion", 123
Leyva, Beltrand "El Barbas", 73
Lombardo, Joseph "The Clown", 121
Lombroso, Cesare, 38–39

Long, Huey P., 29, 122
Lo Piccolo, Salvatore, 124
Lo Presti, Gaetano, 124
Lucas, Charles, 217
Lucas, Frank, 216
Lucchese, Gretano, 119
Luciano, Charles "Lucky", 115–118, 127
Lyman, M., 129

M

Maas, Peter, 133
Macko, Steve, 161
Maggaddino, Stefano, 118
Makarenko, Tamara, 263, 269
Maranzano, Salvatore, 116, 118
Marcello, Carlos, 29, 122, 132, 134
Marcello, Joe, Jr., 122
Marino, Daniel, 124
Marron, John "Satan", 187
Masseria, Giueppe "Joe the Boss", 116
Massina, Joseph, 119
Matranga, Antonio, 112, 122
Matranga, Carlo, 112, 122
Matthews, Frank, 216–217
McClure, Gwen, 100
McDonald, Big Michael, 22, 112, 120
McFeely, R. A., 41
McGuire, Phyllis, 121
Medina, Carlos, 61
Merlino, Joey, 200
Merton, R., 38
Michii, Hisayuki, 142
Mill, John Stuart, 260
Mogilevich, Semion, 99–100
Montague, Larry, 134
Montoya Sanchez, Diego, 60
Moreno Gonzales, Nazario "The Craziest One", 79
Mucharrafille, Salim Boughjader, 274
Muskalel, Meyer, 96
Mutschke, Ralf, 272

N

Natale, Ralph, 123
Nekrasov, Vladimir, 99

Nitti, Frank, 120
Nixon, Richard, 29
Noel, Joey, 115

O

Ochoa-Soto, Albert, 77
Orgen, "Little Augie", 115

P

Pankau, Edmund J., 249–250
Peckler, Margarita, 96
Pecora, Norfio, 122
Pendergast, Thomas, 21
Pileggi, Nicholas, 128
Pistone, Joe, 127
Poretto, Joe, 122
Potter, G. W., 129
Presser, Jackie, 29
Profaci, Joseph, 113

Q

Queen, William, 192

R

Reagan, Ronald, 28, 29
Ricca, Paul, 120
Rodríguez, Gilberto, 55, 60
Rodríguez, Miguel, 55, 60, 77
Rosen, Nig, 122
Rothstein, Arnold, 22, 114–115
Russo, Andrew, 119

S

Sabella, Salvatore, 121
Safiev, Georgy, 96
Samper, Ernesto, 28
Santacruz, Jose, 55
Santoro, Salvatore, 119
Sasakawa, Ryoichi, 153
Sasakawa, Takashi, 153
Savela, Joe, 132
Scarfo, Nicodemo, "Little Nicky", 122, 123
Schultz, Dutch, 115
Schweitzer, G. E., 270–271

Segal, Benjamin "Bugsy", 116, 117
Shapiro, Jacob "Gurrah", 115
Shelley, Louise, 7, 265, 266, 267–268, 272
Sherry, Margaret, 24
Sherry, Vincent, 24
Shiroo, Tetsuya, 145
Sinatra, Frank, 121
Smith, D., 45
Stanfa, John, 122
Sun Tzu, 12
Susumu, Ishii, 153
Sutherland, E. H., 19, 37–38

T
Taoka, Kazuo, 142
Tate, Christian, 200
Taylor, Frederick W., 114
Testa, Philip, 122
Thrasher, Frederick, 208
Tieri, Frank, 133
Tolson, Clyde, 114

Torrio, Johnny, 120
Trafficante, Santo, 132
Traughber, C. M., 268–269, 271–272
Trevino, Miguel "El Cuarenta", 80
Tweed, William March "Boss", 21, 112

U
Umansky, Alexander, 96
Uribe, Alvano, 64

V
Valachi, Joseph "The Rat", 27, 110, 113, 118, 128, 133
Valdes Villarreal, Edgar "La Barbie", 76
Vario, Paul, 128
Vickers, Stephen, 171
Volkov, Alexander, 101

Vollmer, August, 247
Voloshin, Vladimir, 101

W
Wagner, Angie, 200
Walters, John, 61
Washington, George, 25
Watanabe, Yoshinori, 142–143
Weber, Max, 2, 114
Weinberg, Leonard, 260
Weiss, Hymie, 120
Wilson, J. Q., 36, 42
Wilson, O. W., 247

Y
Yamamoto, Hiroshi, 142

Z
Zakone, Vory V., 90
Zambada Garica, Ismael, 76

SUBJECT INDEX

A

Administrative program
    evaluations, 246
AFO (Arellano-Felix organization)
    cartel, 68, 69, 74–75
African American gangs
    Barnes profile, 217
    Black P. Stone Nation, 214
    Bloods and Crips, 212–213
    Charles Lucas profile, 217
    Frank Lucas profile, 216
    Gangster Disciples, 214–216
    Matthews profile, 216–217
Agency personnel structure and
    responsibilities, intelligence
    gathering, 251–252
Aida-ikka criminal group, 144
Aizu Kotetsu criminal group, 144
Alcoholic beverage trafficking, 22,
    24–27, 102, 112–113
Alien conspiracy theory, 35–36
All-channel network, terrorism,
    263
Al Qaeda
    cell structure, 264
    connections to organized
        crime, 244
    legitimate businesses as fronts
        for, 269–270
    use of organized crime
        funding methods, 267
    weapons of mass destruction
        and, 273
AMA (American Motorcycle
    Association), 181
Amalgamation-based organized
    crime, 10
"American Dream" expectations
    and motivation to crime,
    38, 45
American Mafia
    activities and methods
        gambling, 129–130
        illicit goods and services
            provision, 129
        labor racketeering,
            130–131, 237
        new partnerships, 131–132
    Chicago, 22, 120–121

conclusions, 135–136
corruption as tool for, 29
current activities, 123–124
drug trafficking debate in,
    22–23
historical perspective, 21, 28,
    110–114
Hobbs Act extortion
    prosecutions, 225
introduction, 109–110
investigative strategies
    exposure—informants and
        witnesses, 132–133
    government oversight, 134
    grand juries and
        legislation, 134–135
    sting operations, 133–134
Las Vegas, 120–121
membership as assumption of
    criminality, 11
New Orleans, 122–123
New York Mafia, 114, 115–119
OMGs and, 199–200
Philadelphia/Atlantic City,
    121–122
resiliency of, 43–44
structure, 125–129
American Motorcycle Association
    (AMA), 181
Amezcua-Contreras cartel, 68
Amphetamine trafficking, Yakuza,
    151
Annunzio-Wylie Money
    Laundering Act (1992), 230
Anomie, 38, 45, 46
Anti-Drug Abuse Act (1986), 233
Anti-Gang Youth and Violence Act
    (1997), 220
Anti-insurgency in Colombia, 62
Apalachin incident, 113, 114, 121
Arellano-Felix organization (AFO)
    cartel, 68, 69, 74–75
Armenian group in Russian Mafia,
    96
Arms trafficking. *See* Weapons
    smuggling
The Art of War (Sun Tzu), 12
Aryan Brotherhood prison gang,
    219

Asano-gumi criminal group, 144
Assets, attacking organized
    crime, 155, 227–228. *See also*
    Financial analysis
Atlantic City/Philadelphia Mafia,
    121–122
AUC (United Self-Defense Groups
    of Colombia), 62, 244, 265

B

"Baby" drug cartels, 61
Bakuto criminal group, 141, 148
Banana Wars, 118
Bandidos OMG, 180, 186, 196
Bank fraud schemes, 100. *See also*
    Money laundering
Bank Secrecy Act (1970), 229
Barrio Azteca gang, 69, 78
Barrio/varrio, 209
Basque Fatherland and Liberty
    organization (ETA), 266, 273
Bell's "queer ladder of mobility",
    35
Beltran Leyva organization (BLO),
    75–76
BGF (Black Guerilla Family)
    prison gang, 213, 219
Big Circle gang, 164, 174
Big Four OMGs, 184–191
Biker women, 194, 196
Binding and reciprocal obligation,
    35, 161, 177. *See also*
    Membership
Biological theories, 39
Black Belt, Chicago, 120
Black Biscuit OMG, 202
Black Disciples gang, 214
Black gangs. *See* African American
    gangs
Black Guerilla Family (BGF)
    prison gang, 213, 219
Black Hand organization, 111–113
Black Liberation Army (BLA)
    prison gang, 213
Blackmail, 225. *See also* Extortion
    and protection
Black market
    drug trafficking and, 70

Black market (*Continued*)
   investigative strategies, 34
   peso exchange, 58, 232
   Russian Mafia and, 90, 91–92,
      101
   Yakuza and post-WWII, 141
Black P. Stone Nation, 214
BLA (Black Liberation Army)
   prison gang, 213
BLO (Beltran Leyva organization),
   75–76
Bloods gang, 212–213
Bootlegging, 22, 24–27, 102,
   112–113
Born to Kill (BTK) gang, 174
Boryokudan. See Yakuza
Boryokudan Countermeasures
   Law (1992), 153–154
Boxer Rebellion (1896–1900), 163
Brighton Beach, 93, 101
BTK (Born to Kill) gang, 174
Bureaucratic/corporate model of
   crime, 2, 43
Burn company, 96
Business principles, 2, 43. *See also*
   Legitimate business

C
Cali cartel
   cell structure, 264
   development and operations,
      55–59
   Mexican DTO associations, 77
   as shadow government, 28
Caló, 209
Canada
   Hells Angels, 185
   intelligence gathering strategy,
      254
   Russian Mafia infiltration, 100
Caporegime, 125, 126
Caro-Quintero cartel, 68
Carrillo-Fuentes cartel. *See* Juárez
   cartel
Cartel, definition of, 4. *See also*
   individual cartels
Castellammarse Wars, 115, 116
CCE (Continuing Criminal
   Enterprise) statute (1970),
   6, 202, 224, 236
Cell structure
   Colombian cartels, 57–58
   intelligence gathering, 235

Mexican DTOs, 80
Russian Mafia, 93
terrorism/organized crime
   nexus, 235, 261–264
Central Intelligence Agency (CIA),
   121, 245
Chain and wheel network, 263
Chain network, 234, 263
Check It Out (Pankau), 249–250
Chemical Diversion and
   Trafficking Act (1988),
   232
Chicago Commission (1915), 27
Chicago Mafia (the Outfit), 22,
   120–121
Chinese Green Dragons' gang, 174
Chinese organized crime
   activities and methods of
      operations
      business investments, 174
      gangs, 172–173, 174
      human smuggling, 172,
         174
      Tongs, 171–172
      Triads, 170–171
      violence and intimidation,
         173–174, 175
   conclusions, 176–177
   historical perspective, 160–164
   introduction, 159
   investigative strategies,
      174–176, 177
   structure
      Tongs, 167–168, 169
      Triads, 164–167, 168–169
Chiu Chau Triad group, 169
Chuen Triad group, 169
CIA (Central Intelligence Agency),
   121, 245
CIs (confidential informants), 202
Civil property forfeiture, 227, 228
Class conflict and crime
   motivation, 37
Classical theories, 36, 38–39
Cliques/*clicas,* 80, 210
CMIR (Currency and Monetary
   Instrument Report), 229
Cocaine trafficking
   Colombia as producer, 62
   historical perspective, 22, 23
   Jamaican Posse, 218
   Mexican DTOs, 68, 69, 70, 82
   rise of, 52–54
   Russian Mafia, 97, 98

smuggling operations, 58
Yakuza, 151
Codes of conduct
   American Mafia, 2, 35,
      113–114, 126, 127
   OMGs, 188–191, 197–198, 199
   Russian Mafia, 91, 95
   three "Rs", 5, 210–211
   Triad societies, 165, 170–171
   Yakuza, 147–149
Colima cartel, 68, 78
Colombian drug cartels
   American Mafia connections,
      132
   Cali, 28, 55–59, 77, 264
   conclusions, 63–65
   current activities, 60–63
      "baby" cartels, 61
      FARC, 61
      Norte del Valle, 60
      paramilitary groups, 61–62
      Plan Colombia, 62–63
      threat assessment, 63
   decline of major cartels,
      59–60
   historical perspective, 52–54
   introduction, 51–52
   Medellín, 54–55, 59
   Mexican DTOs as successors
      to, 54, 56, 69, 70, 77
Colonial-era piracy, 17–18
Color of official right, 225
Colors
   gang, 213
   OMG, 183, 185, 186, 187, 192
Combination wheel and chain
   conspiracy, 235
Combined Task Force 151, U.S.
   Navy, 18
The Commission, 116–118, 126,
   127
"Commission" trial, 110, 114
Commodity flow analysis,
   intelligence gathering, 252,
   253
Communication methods
   American gangs, 213
   colors. *See* Colors
   Hispanic/Latino gangs, 209
   tattoos. *See* Tattoos
   Triads, 167
   Yakuza, 149, 156
Comprehensive Crime Control Act
   (1984), 233

Comprehensive Drug Abuse
    Prevention and Control Act
    (1970), 6, 232
Comprehensive theory for
    organized crime, 45–47
Confidential informants (CIs),
    202
Consigliere, 125
Consortium, 4
Conspiracy. *See also* RICO
    alien conspiracy theory, 35–36
    overview, 6
    statutes addressing
        case development and,
            233–234, 235
        CCE, 6, 202, 224, 236
        electronic surveillance
            usage, 237–239
        grand juries and witness
            immunity, 239
        Kingpin act, 224, 236
        labor racketeering,
            236–237
    theoretical perspective, 41–42,
        45
    types of, 234–235
Continuing Criminal Enterprise
    (CCE) statute (1970), 6, 202,
    224, 236
Controlled substances acts. *See*
    Drug control statutes
Convention Against Transnational
    Organized Crime (2000), 16
Corporate corruption, 18–19,
    28–29, 48
Corporate crime, 16, 18–19, 34
Corruption
    in Colombia, 63
    controversy surrounding, 285
    corporate, 18–19, 28–29, 48
    decline in American cities,
        131–132
    definition of, 7
    Dixie Mafia, 24
    drug trafficking and, 21–22
    effect on investigation, 30, 283
    historical perspective, 19, 21,
        28–29
    importance for organized
        crime, 6, 11, 28–29, 48
    importance of knowledge
        concerning, 34
    international problem of, 44
    in Japan, 144

of law enforcement, 16
Medellín cartel, 55
Mexico's battle against, 71
moonshine and, 26
piracy's success with, 17, 18
Prohibition era, 25, 113
in Russia, 91, 105
terrorism/organized crime
    nexus, 259–260, 266
Yakuza, 141
Country Boys, 216
Crews in American Mafia, 43,
    125–126
Crime by association, 252–253
Criminal–community relationship
    American gangs, 218
    American Mafia, 117
    Chinese organized crime, 163
    cultivation of, 46
    OMGs, 201
    Russian Mafia, 90
    Yakuza, 142, 143, 147, 153
Crips gang, 212–213
CTR (Currency Transaction
    Report), 229
Culture and language
    American gangs, 209–211, 213
    Chinese organized crime
        investigation, 175
    ethnic succession
        American Mafia, 123
        in former Soviet Union
            regions, 91
        Russian Mafia, 95
        theoretical perspective,
            35, 45
        transmission of criminal
            behavior, 37–38
Culture conflict, 38
Currency and Monetary
    Instrument Report (CMIR),
    229
Currency Transaction Report
    (CTR), 229
Cybercrime, Russian Mafia, 96–97

D

Dai Dai Lo, 168
Daisy chain, 96
Data analysis, intelligence
    gathering, 251
Demand for illegal goods and
    services

American Mafia's meeting
    of, 129
colonial era, 17
as continued threat to
    investigation, 283
enterprise theory and,
    40–41
importance for organized
    crime, 11, 34, 47, 48
increases in, 23, 258
Mexican DTO expansion and,
    69–70
moonshine, 27
Derivative use immunity, 239
Deterrence theory, 42
Diablos OMG, 191
Differential association, 37–38
Differential opportunity, 38
Dinero anti-money laundering
    program, 59
Dion-O'Banion battles, 120
Dirty bombs, 270–271
Disciple Nation (Folks), 212
Dixie Mafia, 23–24
Dojin-kai criminal group, 144
Dragon syndicates, 170. *See also*
    Triads
Dress code
    OMGs, 183, 185, 186, 187, 192
    street gangs, 209, 213
Drug Abuse Act (1988), 230
Drug control statutes
    controlled substances acts, 6,
        230, 232–233
    expansion in early 20th
        century, 21–23
    impacts and consequences
        on Mexican DTOs, 70,
        83–84
    as opportunity for organized
        crime, 10, 83–84
*Drug Lords: The Rise and Fall of the
    Cali Cartel* (Chepsiuk), 55
Drug trafficking. *See also individual
    substances*
    American and Sicilian Mafia
        cooperation, 117
    American gangs, 216–217
    Chinese organized crime, 164
    Colombian drug cartels. *See*
        Colombian drug cartels
    as conspiracy, 224, 236
    corruption and, 21–22
    Jamaican Posses, 218

Drug trafficking (*Continued*)
  as major income source, 10–11,
    22–23
  Mexican DTOs. *See* Mexican
    drug trafficking
    organizations
  OMGs, 180, 185, 200, 202,
    203–204
  Russian Mafia's role, 23, 82,
    97, 102
  for terrorism, 265, 267, 272, 273
  Yakuza, 151
DTOs. *See* Mexican drug
  trafficking organizations
Durango cartel, 68

E

Eastman gang, New York, 21
Economic factors in organized
  crime activity, 40, 45
Ecstasy, 23
Electronic Communications
  Privacy Act (1986), 238
Electronic surveillance
  Chinese organized crime, 176
  OMGs, 202–203
  statutes related to, 224,
    237–239, 245
  Yakuza, 156
El Paso Intelligence Center (EPIC),
  232
El Rukins gang, 214, 265–266
EME (Mexican Mafia) prison
  gang, 219
Enforcers
  American Mafia, 125
  Mexican DTOs, 68, 72, 75, 76,
    80–81
  OMGs, 194, 197
  Russian Mafia, 93–94
Enterprise, RICO definition,
  225–226
Enterprise groups *vs.* power
  syndicates, 47
Enterprise model of crime, 42
Enterprise syndicates, 47
Enterprise theory in law
  enforcement, 40–42
Entrepreneurial organized crime.
  See Russian Mafia; Triads;
  Yakuza
Environmental factors
  criminal motivation, 34, 36,
    37–38, 39, 45–46

organized crime activity,
  40
EPOC (El Paso Intelligence
  Center), 232
ETA (Basque Fatherland and
  Liberty organization), 266
Ethical perspective on crime
  motivation, 37
Ethnic succession
  American Mafia, 123
  in former Soviet Union
    regions, 91
  Russian Mafia, 95
  theoretical perspective, 35, 45
ETI (enterprise theory of
  investigation), 41–42
Event flow analysis, intelligence
  gathering, 252
Evolution of organized crime
  colonial-era piracy, 17–18
  corruption's contribution to,
    28–29
  disparity in resources *vs.* law
    enforcement, 29–31, 34
  expansion in early 20th
    century, 21–23
  illegal whiskey trade, 22,
    24–27, 112–113
  immigrant crime groups, 19,
    21
  introduction, 15–17
  modern developments
    overview, 27–28
  Robber Barons, 18–19
  Southern organized crime,
    23–24
Exposure strategy against
  American Mafia, 132–133.
  See also Informants and
  witnesses
Extortion and protection
  definition of, 225
  Hobbs Act, 224–225
  labor racketeering, 131, 237
  as origin of American Mafia,
    111, 112
  Russian Mafia, 96–97, 101
  Yakuza, 150–151, 153

F

La Familia Michoacan, 76, 78–79
The family. *See* American Mafia
FARC (Revolutionary Armed
  Forces of Colombia)

Brazilian expansion, 64
  drug trafficking income for,
    244
  profile of, 61
  Russian Mafia and, 102
  terrorist group connections,
    265
FBI (Federal Bureau of
  Investigation)
  American Mafia history, 114
  definition of organized
    crime, 5
  sharing of intelligence
    information, 245
Federal Comprehensive Forfeiture
  Act (1984), 228
Federal government, U.S. *See also*
  Legislation
  corruption influences in, 29,
    121, 122
  definitions of organized crime,
    7–9
  FBI, 5, 114, 245
The Federation, 69, 76, 78
Fifth Amendment right to avoid
  self-incrimination, 134–135
Financial analysis. *See also* Money
  laundering
  Chinese organized crime
    challenge, 177
  intelligence gathering, 251,
    252
  money trail's importance to
    investigation, 41
  need for international
    coordination, 280
  OMG investigations, 202, 203
  Yakuza, 156
Financial Crimes Enforcement
  Network (FinCEN), 130,
    202, 231
Firearms violations and OMGs,
  202
FISA (Foreign Intelligence
  Surveillance Act), 245
Five families of New York,
  118–119
Five Points gang, 21, 116
Flamingo casino, 120–121
Folks (Disciple Nation), 212
Following the money. *See*
  Financial analysis
Foot soldier, 126
Foreign Intelligence Surveillance
  Act (FISA), 245

Foreign Narcotics Kingpin
    Designation Act (1999), 224,
    236
14K Triad group, 164, 169
Fraud schemes. *See also* Money
    laundering
    banking, 100
    fuel frauds, 96
    Nigerian, 217
Freudian explanation for criminal
    behavior, 39
Fuel frauds, 96
Fukching gang, 164
Fukien American Association
    Tongs, 164, 168

G
Gambino crime family,
    prosecution of, 123–124
Gambling
    American Mafia, 129–130
    in Japan, 141
    Las Vegas Mafia, 120–121
    Yakuza, 150–151
Gaming Devices Act (1951), 130
Gangs
    American
        Barnes profile, 217
        Black P. Stone Nation, 214
        Bloods and Crips, 212–213
        Charles Lucas profile, 217
        conclusions, 221
        culture, 209–211, 213
        evolution of, 112
        Frank Lucas profile, 216
        Gangster Disciples, 208,
            214–216
        Hispanic/Latino gangs,
            192, 194, 209–210,
            219
        historical perspective, 21,
            26, 116, 207–208
        introduction, 207–208
        investigative strategies and
            laws, 220
        Jamaican organized crime,
            217–218
        Matthews profile, 216–217
        Nigerian organized crime,
            217
        OMGs. *See* Outlaw
            motorcycle gangs
        prison gangs, 213, 218–220
        structure, 211–212

Barrio Azteca, 69, 78
Chinese organized crime,
    163–164, 168, 172–173,
    174
    definition of, 5
    as Mexican DTO agents, 71
    prison. *See* Prison gangs
    Russian, 90–93
Gangster Disciples, 208, 214–216
Garcia-Abrego/Cardenas-Guillen
    cartel. *See* Gulf cartel
Genetics/biological theories for
    criminal motivation, 39
Giri, ethics of, 148
Globalization. *See also*
    International environment
    advantages for organized
        crime, 44, 244, 285
    investigative adaptation to, 250
Goodfellas (film), 128
Goodfellow, 125–126, 127, 128
Government. *See also* Corruption;
    Legislation
    conditions in organized crime
        activity, 40
    corruption influences in, 29,
        121, 122
    definitions of organized crime,
        5, 7–9
    organized crime as shadow, 16,
        28, 126, 143
    oversight of American Mafia,
        134
Graffiti, 209
Grand juries, 134–135, 203–204,
    239
Greed as primary motivator, 35
Grim Reapers Motorcycle Club
    (GRMC), 191–192, 193
Guadalajara cartel, 69
Guanxi (mutual obligation), 35,
    161, 177
Guatemalan Kaibiles, 75, 81
Guilt by association, 235
Gulf cartel
    enforcers, 68
    operations of, 75–76
    vs. Sinaloa cartel, 72, 75
    territory of, 69
Gurentai, 141–142, 149

H
Hamas, 244
Harrison Narcotics Act (1914), 21

Hatchet men, 173
Hells Angels Motorcycle Club
    (HAMC)
    historical development,
        180–181, 184
    vs. Mongols, 200
    vs. Outlaws, 185
    structure, 184–185, 196,
        197–198, 199
Heroin trafficking
    African American gangs,
        216–217
    Chinese organized crime, 169,
        172
    from Colombia, 54, 61
    historical perspective, 23
    Mexican DTOs, 67–68, 71
    Russian Mafia, 98
    Yakuza, 151
Herra family, 68
Herrera cartel, 68
Hezbollah, 84, 244, 265, 266–267
Hierarchical model in law
    enforcement, 42
Hierarchical model of crime, 42
Hing Ah Kee Kwan, 164
Hip Sing Association, 168,
    173–174
Hispanic/Latino gangs (American)
    clicas, 210
    communication methods, 209
    Mongols Motorcycle Club,
        192, 194
    prison gangs, 219
Historical conspiracy, 234
Hobbs Act on extortion, 224–225
"Hollister riot", 181
Homeboys, 213
Homeland security *vs.* organized
    crime busting, 30, 280
Hong Kong as base for Triad
    operations, 160, 165
Honorary OMG club members,
    198
Honored Society of the Mafia,
    125
*Honor Few, Fear None: The Life and
    Times of a Mongol* (Cavazos),
    194
The Hoodlums, 54
Hotel and Restaurant Employees
    Union (HRE), 237
"Hotspot theory", 37–38
House Assassination Committee
    (1979), 132

Human sources of intelligence, 249

Human trafficking
Chinese organized crime, 172, 174
Russian Mafia, 226
by terrorist groups, 267
Yakuza, 152

Hung Gar Kung Fu, 163

I

IBT (International Brotherhood of Teamsters), 237

Ichiwa-Kai syndicate, 142

Ikka traditions and rituals, 148

ILA (International Longshoremen's Association), 237

Illegal enterprise. *See* Organized crime

Illegal goods and services. *See* Demand for illegal goods and services

Illegal whiskey trade, 22, 24–27, 112–113

Immigrant crime groups. *See also* Culture and language; Tongs
alien conspiracy theory, 35–36
American Mafia history, 111–113
Chinese gangs, 172–173, 174
Hispanic/Latino gangs, 192, 194, 209–211, 219
political machines and, 19, 21
Russian Mafia as, 92

Immigration, special-interest aliens on Mexico border, 274

Inagawa-Kai criminal group, 142, 144

Individual motivation for criminal behavior, 38–39, 46, 47–48

Informants and witnesses
American Mafia, 132–133
Chinese organized crime, 176
grand jury immunity, 239
OMG investigations, 202
Russian Mafia, 105–106
WITSEC, 133, 239
Yakuza, 156

Initiations
American Mafia, 128–129
OMGs, 198
Tongs, 172

Triads, 164–165
Yakuza, 147

Innovation, 38, 46

Institutional crime, 27. *See also* Organized crime

Intelligence gathering
activities overview, 47
analytical models
agency personnel structure and responsibilities, 251–252
commodity flow analysis, 252, 253
crime by association, 252–253
data analysis, 251
event flow analysis, 252
financial analysis, 251, 252
unit activities within intelligence division, 253–254
cell structure and, 235
Chinese organized crime challenge, 176
conclusions, 254–255
defining intelligence, 245–246
evaluation of information, 248–249
historical perspective, 246–248
improvements in, 30
introduction, 243–244
on OMGs, 201–202
sources of intelligence, 249–250
statutes addressing, 245
terrorist group connections, 244–245
on Yakuza, 156

International Asian Organized Crime conferences, 176

International Brotherhood of Teamsters (IBT), 237

International Crime Control strategy, 105

International environment. *See also* Transnational organized crime
Chinese organized crime presence, 161
definitions of organized crime, 4, 6–7, 8, 10
intelligence gathering coordination, 248, 250

investigation cooperation, 16, 44, 106, 155–156, 176, 280
Russian Mafia's activities, 92, 99–100, 104
safe havens in, 34–35
Yakuza's operations, 145

International law enforcement academy, Bangkok, 176

International Longshoremen's Association (ILA), 237

Intimidation. *See* Violence and intimidation

Investigation. *See also* Evolution of organized crime
Albanese's models as guide for, 42
American gangs, 220
American Mafia, 132–135
Cali cartel, 58–59
Chinese organized crime, 174–176, 177
corruption effect on, 30, 283
ETI approach, 41–42
globalization adaptation, 250
historical perspective, 27–28
importance of interagency coordination, 30–31
intelligence. *See* Intelligence gathering
international cooperation imperative, 16, 44, 106, 155–156, 176, 280
investigator knowledge base, 283
NAFTA as challenge to, 70
OMGs, 201–204
resources issue, 3, 29–31, 34–35, 44, 280
results of Colombian cartel repression, 63
Russian Mafia, 95, 104–106
statutes. *See* Legislation
Tongs' opaqueness, 172
working definitions of organized crime, 1–5
Yakuza, 153–156

Irish immigrants and political machines, 19–20

Irish Republican Army (IRA), 266

Ishikawa-ikka criminal group, 144

Italy and Mafia origins, 110–111. *See also* American Mafia

J

Jackson-Vanik Amendment, 92
Jamaican organized crime, 217–218
Japanese Mafia. *See* Yakuza
Jewish leaders in American Mafia, 22, 114–115
Joints (gambling halls), 24
Juárez cartel
  Carrillo and, 76–78
  enforcers, 68
  prison gang connection, 69
  Sinaloa cartel and, 76, 78
  turf wars, 72–73, 75
"Jurassic Park" (Sinaloa, Mexico), 77

K

Kabuki-mono, 140
Kanto-Kai criminal group, 142
Kazuo-Taoka criminal group, 142
Kefauver Committee, 9, 27, 113
KGB agents in Russian Mafia, 94
Kidnapping, Russian Mafia, 95–96
Kingpin act, 224, 236
Kingpin strategy, 58–59
Koiki-Boryokudan faction, 145
Kozakura-ikka criminal group, 144
Kryshas, 94
Kudo-rengo Kusano-ikka criminal group, 144
Kurdistan Workers Party (PKK), 266
Kyokyryu-kai criminal group, 144
Kyosei-kai criminal group, 144

L

Laborers International Union of North America, 237
Labor OIG (Office of the Inspector General in the U.S. Department of Labor), 130, 131
Labor racketeering, 130–131, 236–237
La Cosa Nostra (LCN). *See* American Mafia
La Familia Michoacan (LFM), 76, 78–79
La Linea, 75, 78

Las Vegas mafia, 120–121
Latino gangs. *See* Hispanic/Latino gangs
La Violenca (1947–1953), 52
Law-abiding behavior, motivations for, 46
Law enforcement. *See also* Evolution of organized crime; Investigation
  controversy surrounding motivation and methods, 284–285
  Dixie Mafia effect on, 24
  future challenges from organized crime, 279–286
  impact of organized crime on, 16, 40
  Mexican DTOs' challenges to, 72, 83–84
  military as agent of in Mexico, 83
  vs. organized crime in resources, 29–31, 34, 280
  theoretical perspectives on role of, 40–43
LCN (La Cosa Nostra). *See* American Mafia
Leftist guerillas in Colombia, 52, 61, 64
Legislation
  American gangs, 220
  conclusions, 240
  conspiracy. *See also* RICO
    case development and, 233–234, 235
    CCE, 6, 202, 224, 236
    electronic surveillance usage, 237–239
    grand juries and witness immunity, 239
    Kingpin act, 224, 236
    labor racketeering, 236–237
  controlled substances. *See* Drug control statutes
  controversy surrounding, 225, 284
  definitions of organized crime from, 5–6
  grand juries, 134–135, 203–204, 239
  Hobbs Act on extortion, 224–225

improvement in crime control, 30
intelligence gathering, 245
introduction, 223–224
money laundering, 6, 105, 130, 224, 229–232
OMGs, 202–203
Patriot Act. *See* USA Patriot Act
property forfeiture, 227–228
summary of other statutes, 240
tax violations, 228–229
Yakuza, 153–154, 156
Legitimate business
  American Mafia's influence, 110
  Chinese organized crime influence, 174
  Jamaican Posses' infiltration of, 218
  labor racketeering as control tool, 131, 237
  OMG participation in, 198–199
  organized crime's infiltration of, 22, 39, 280
  terrorist use of, 269–270
  Triads and Tongs influence, 169–170, 174
  Yakuza influence, 145, 150–151, 153, 155, 156
LFM (La Familia Michoacana), 76, 78–79
Local-ethnic model in law enforcement, 42
"Los Pepes", 59
Los Zetas, 72, 75–76, 80–81
LSD (lysergic acid diethylamide), 23
Luan Triad group, 169
Lucchese crime family, 131

M

Machi-Yakko, 140
Made man, 125–126, 127, 128
Mafia, origins of term, 111
MAFIC (Multi-Agency Financial Investigative Center), 232
Mafioso, 111
Mala in se, 3
Mala prohibita, 3
Mamas, OMG, 194

Mann Act (1910), 226
Mara Salvatrucha 13 (MS 13) gang, 75, 221, 273–274, 280
Marijuana trafficking
historical perspective, 23
Mexican DTOs, 68, 71, 78, 79, 82
Martial arts, Triad origins in, 162–163
MBN (Mississippi Bureau of Narcotics), 248
McClellan Committee (1963), 27, 132, 133
MDMA trafficking, Mexican DTOs, 71
Medellín cartel, 54–55, 59
Membership
American gangs, 211–212
American Mafia, 11, 127–128
Chinese organized crime entities, 164–165
OMGs, 194–199
Russian Mafia, 93–95
Yakuza, 146, 147–149
Mental deficiency and criminal activity, 39, 46
Merida Initiative, 84
Methamphetamine trafficking
Mexican DTOs, 71, 78, 79, 82
OMGs, 180
Russian Mafia, 102
Yakuza, 151
Mexican drug highway, 54
Mexican drug trafficking organizations (DTOs)
American Mafia connections, 132
cartels, 73–78
Colombian cartels and, 54, 56, 61, 63
conclusions, 84–85
current activities, 81–83
development and expansion, 69–71
drug policy consequences, 70, 83–84
historical perspective, 67–69
OMGs and, 180
Russian Mafia's role in, 82, 97, 102
as shadow government, 28
subsidiary and emerging organizations, 78–81
violence among, 70, 71–73, 75, 76, 79, 81

Mexican Mafia (EME) prison gang, 219
Mikaelian organization, 96
Military, loyalty issues for Colombian, 64
Millennium cartel, 78
Mississippi Bureau of Narcotics (MBN), 248
The Mob. See American Mafia
Modus operandi files, 247
Money laundering
definition of, 58
Dinero anti-money laundering program, 59
international resources for, 34–35
Russian Mafia, 99
statutes addressing, 6, 105, 130, 224, 229–232
Yakuza, 145, 152–153, 155–156
Money Laundering Control Act (1986), 6, 105, 130, 224, 230
Money Laundering Prosecution Improvement Act (1988), 230
Money Laundering Suppression Act (1994), 230
Money trail, following. See Financial analysis
Mongols Motorcycle Club, 192, 194, 200
Monikers, gang, 209
Moonshine and moonshiners, 25, 26–27
Motivations for criminal behavior
vs. avoiding criminal activity, 36
biological, 39
environmental, 34, 36, 37–38, 39, 45–46
importance of discerning, 34
individual, 38–39, 46, 47–48
overview, 2
vs. terrorist motives, 260–261
Motorcycle gangs. See Outlaw motorcycle gangs
MS 13 (Mara Salvatrucha 13) gang, 75, 221, 273–274, 280
Mules (in drug smuggling), 54
Multi-Agency Financial Investigative Center (MAFIC), 232
Multi-jurisdictional task and strike forces, 30
Murder Inc., 116

N
NAFTA (North American Free Trade Agreement), 54, 70
Narco-terrorism, 265
Narcotics trafficking. See Drug trafficking
NASCAR (National Association for Stock Car Auto Racing), 26
Nationalist Chinese government, 163
National Liberation Army (NLA), 244
National Security Act (1947), 245
National Task Force on Organized Crime (1976), 28
Ndragheta, 111
The Negros, 76
New Federation, 75–76
New Orleans Mafia, 122–123
New York Mafia
Commission, 116–118, 126
crime families, 118–119
Luciano, 115–116
Rothstein, 22, 114–115
NF (Nuestra Familia) prison gang, 219
Nigerian organized crime, 217
Ninkyo-do, 140, 148
NLA (National Liberation Army), 244
Nomenklatura, 90, 91, 94
Norte del Valle cartel, 60
North American Free Trade Agreement (NAFTA), 54, 70
Nuestra Familia (NF) prison gang, 219
Nueva Federacion, 75–76
Nuevo Laredo, violence in, 72

O
Oaths. See Codes of conduct
OCDETF (Organized Crime Drug Enforcement Task Forces), 201
The Office. See American Mafia
Office of Foreign Assets Control (OFAC), 60
Office of the Inspector General in the U.S. Department of Labor (Labor OIG), 130, 131
Okinawa Kyokurya-kai criminal group, 144
Old ladies, OMG, 194

Omerta, 2, 35, 113–114, 126
Omnibus Crime Control Act
(1968), 224
One percenters, OMGs as, 183
Ongoing conspiracy, 234
On Leong Association, 168,
173–174
Open sources of intelligence, 249
Operation Black Rain, 192
Operation BRILAB (bribery and
labor), 134
Operation Green Ice, 59
Operation Java, 98
Opiates, 21, 22
Opportunity factors in organized
crime activity, 40
Organization, definition of, 2, 4
Organizatsiya. See Russian Mafia
Organized crime. *See also*
Evolution of organized crime
controversial aspects, 283–284
definitions, 1–12
dynamic leadership in,
282–283
Organized Crime Control Act
(1970), 6, 224, 226
Organized Crime Drug
Enforcement Task Forces
(OCDETF), 201
Organized Crime Strike Force
Unit, 105
Organizing *vs.* organized crime, 10
The Outfit (Chicago Mafia), 22,
120–121
Outlaw motorcycle gangs (OMGs)
activities and methods,
199–201
Big Four
Bandidos, 186
Hells Angels, 184–185
Outlaws, 185
Pagans, 186–191
conclusions, 204
Grim Reapers, 191–192, 193
historical perspective,
180–183
introduction, 179–180
investigative strategies,
201–204
Mongols, 192, 194
structure, 194–199
Outlaws, 185, 196
Overt act, 233
Oyabun-Kobun (father–child)
relationship, 146, 147–148

Oyster Bay Conferences
(1965–1966), 27

P
Pagans OMG, 180, 186–191, 196,
199–200
Paramilitary groups
Colombian drug cartels,
61–62, 64
La Familia Michoacan, 79
OMGs as, 194
Patent medicines, 21
Patrimonial/patron–client model
of crime, 43
Patriot Act (2001). *See* USA Patriot
Act (2001)
PCP (phencyclidine) trafficking,
23
The Pelones, 76
Pendergast Machine, Kansas City,
19, 21
People (Vice Lord Nation), 212
Personam, 228
Peso exchange method in money
laundering, 58
Pharmaceutical drugs, diverted, 23
Philadelphia/Atlantic City Mafia,
121–122
Picciotto, 125
PIE (Preparation of the
Investigative Environment),
268
Piracy, colonial-era, 17–18
Piru Boys, 213
Pissed Off Bastards of
Bloomington (POBOB), 181
PKK (Kurdistan Workers Party),
266
Plan Colombia, 52, 62–63, 84
Plaquesos/placas, 209
"Plazas," Mexican DTO, 69
Pleasure/pain guide and crime
motivation, 36
POBOB (Pissed Off Bastards of
Bloomington), 181
Police Administration (Vollmer), 247
Political activities and influence.
See also Corruption
American Mafia's continued
influence, 132
American political machines,
19–20, 21
Black P. Stone Nation, 214
Gangster Disciples, 215

leftist guerillas in Colombia,
52, 61
Political ideologies
prison gangs, 220
Triads, 164
Yakuza, 149
Political machines, 19–20, 21
Pornography, Yakuza operations
in, 152
Positivism (positive theory), 36,
38–39
Posses, Jamaican, 217–218
Poverty and motivation to crime,
46
Power syndicates, 47
Predicate offenses under RICO,
226
Preparation of the Investigative
Environment (PIE), 268
President's Commission on
Law Enforcement and
Administration of Justice
(1965 to 1967), 27–28
President's Commission on
Organized Crime (1983), 28
President's Commission on
Organized Crime (1984),
150
President's Commission on
Organized Crime (1986), 9
President's Commission on
Organized Crime, 11
President's Task Force on Crime
(1967 and 1976), 9
Prison gangs
Bloods and Crips in, 213
drug trafficking by, 69
elements and structure,
218–220
El Rukins, 214, 265–266
Gangster Disciples, 216
as Mexican DTO agents, 71
OMGs and, 180
in Soviet Russia, 90–91
Privateers, 17
Profiling, 39
Prohibition era, 22, 25–26,
112–113
Project Coronado, 79
Property forfeiture, 227–228
Prospects, OMG, 198
Protection rackets. *See* Extortion
and protection
Psychoanalytic explanation for
criminal behavior, 39

Public perception of organized
crime. *See* Criminal-
community relationship
Puppet clubs, OMG, 180
Purple Gang, Detroit, 21, 26

Q

Qingqing, 161, 177

R

Racketeer and Corrupt
Organization Statute.
See RICO
Racketeering. *See* Conspiracy
Rational choice theories, 36,
38–39
Reciprocal obligation, 35, 161,
177. *See also* Membership
Red Command, Brazil, 64
Red Mafia. *See* Russian Mafia
Regulatory initiatives, 135
Rem, 228
Reputation, 5, 210
Respect, 5, 43, 126, 211
Retaliation, 5, 211. *See also*
Violence and intimidation
Retirement bylaws, OMGs, 199
Revolutionary Armed Forces of
Colombia. *See* FARC
RICO (Racketeer and Corrupt
Organization Statute)
controversy surrounding,
284
definition of organized
crime, 6
effectiveness against organized
crime, 105, 133, 134, 202
federal and state versions, 7
provisions and impact of,
225–227
Right to Privacy Act (1978),
229–230
Roaming wiretap, 238
Robber Barons, 18–19
Rockers, OMG, 183
Rondan Doyukai, 145,
150–151
Rural crime opportunities, 44
Russian Mafia
activities and methods
cybercrime, 96–97
expansion of, 97–104

violent crimes, 93, 94,
95–96, 101
alien conspiracy theory, 36
American Mafia connections,
132
conclusions, 106
drug trafficking, 23, 82, 97,
102
historical perspective, 89–93
human trafficking, 226
investigative strategies, 95,
104–106
Mexican DTOs and, 82, 97,
102
as shadow government, 28
structure, 93–95
weapons smuggling, 97–98,
102–103

S

Samurai origins of Yakuza, 140
Sendero Luminoso, 265
Sgarrista, 126
Shadow governments
American Mafia as, 126
Mexican DTOs as, 28
Russian Mafia as, 28
Yakuza as, 16, 28, 143
Shan Chu, 165, 167
Shang Hai Green Gang, 163
Shaolin monks, 162–163
Sheep, OMG, 194
Shinwa-kai criminal group, 144
Shower Posse, 218
Sicarios, 68
Sicilian gangs in America, 111
Sicilian Mafia
American Mafia and, 117
crackdown on operations, 124
historical perspective, 35,
110–111
Sinaloa cartel
alliance forming, 76
development of, 69
vs. Gulf cartel, 72, 75
Juárez cartel and, 76, 78
Smuggling
bootleg liquor, 22, 24–27, 102,
112–113
drugs. *See* Drug trafficking
human slaves. *See* Human
trafficking
origins of, 17–18

weapons. *See* Weapons
smuggling
Smurfing and smurfs, 58, 229
Snakeheads, 174
Soai-kai criminal group, 144
Social conditions and crime
motivation, 34, 36, 37–38,
39, 45–46
Social control theory, 36, 46
Sokaiya, 150–151, 153
Somalian pirates, 18
Sonora cartel, 68
Southeast Asian gangs, 174, 212
Southern organized crime, 23–24
Soviet Union and origins of
Russian Mafia, 90
Spangler Posse, 218
Speakeasies, 25
Specified unlawful activities
(SUAs), 230
Sports betting, 129–130
Sports event fixing, 103
State governments
alcohol prohibitions, 25
corrupt influences in, 29
definitions of organized crime,
7–8
drug control laws, 23
Statutes. *See* Legislation
Sting operations
American Mafia, 133–134
Cali cartel, 59
Chinese organized crime, 176
OMGs, 201–202
Yakuza, 155
Strain theory, 38
Strasburg Convention (1990), 155
Strategic intelligence analysis
functions, 246
Street gangs, 5, 69, 71. *See also*
Gangs
Strike insurance, 237
Structural approach to crime
motivation, 37
Sturgis Rally, 181
SUAs (specified unlawful
activities), 230
Sumiyoshi-Kai criminal group,
144, 146
Sun Yee On Triad group, 170
Surveillance. *See* Electronic
surveillance
Sweetheart contracts, 237
Syndicate, 4

T

Tactical intelligence analysis functions, 246
Taliban, 244
Tammany Hall Machine, 19, 21
Tattoos
    American street gangs, 210
    Bakuto criminal group, 148
    Chinese street gangs, 173
    OMGs, 183
    Russian gangs, 90
Tax violations, 228–229
Technical intelligence, 249
Technological resources for organized crime, 40, 77, 123
Tekiya criminal group, 140–141
Terrorism
    cell structure, 235, 261–264
    definition of, 259
    in Medellín and Cali cartel war, 59
    Mexican DTO connections to, 84
    vs. organized crime as target of investigative resources, 29–30, 44
    organized crime connections to, 16–17, 244–245, 281
    transnational organized crime and
        comparison of, 258–264
        conclusions, 274
        cooperation methods, 267–271
        current activities and cooperation, 271–274
        group connections, 244–245
        historical perspective, 264–267
        introduction, 257–258
Texas Syndicates prison gang, 219
Theoretical perspectives
    Albanese's typologies, 36–37
    alien conspiracy, 35–36
    anomie, 38
    Bell's "queer ladder of mobility", 35
    biological theories, 39
    classical theories (rational choice), 36, 38–39
    conclusions, 47–48
    differential association, 37–38
    ethnic succession, 35, 45

introduction, 33–35
law enforcement role
    bureaucratic/corporate model, 43
    deterrence theory, 42
    enterprise theory, 40–42
    hierarchical and local-ethnic models, 42
    patrimonial/patron–client model, 43
    nontheoretical explanations and, 43–47
    social control, 36, 46
    strain theory, 38
    summary, 39
Three Mountain Association, 168
"Three Rs" in organized crime, 5
Tijuana cartel, 68, 69, 74–75
Tongs
    activities and methods of operations, 171–172
    historical perspective, 160, 162
    initiations, 172
    investigative challenge, 172
    legitimate business influence, 169–170, 174
    structure, 167–168, 169
    Triad connections, 164
Torrio-Capone battles, 120
Tosei-Kai criminal group, 142
Traditional organized crime, 10.
    See also individual groups
Tranquil Happiness Triad, 164
Transactional immunity, 239
Transnational organized crime
    Cali cartel, 56–57
    definitions, 10
    importance of developments in, 282
    overview, 16
    terrorism and
        comparison of, 258–264
        conclusions, 274
        cooperation methods, 267–271
        current activities and cooperation, 271–274
        group connections, 244–245
        historical perspective, 264–267
        introduction, 257–258
    Triads, 163–164, 170, 171
    UN convention against, 231

Trap and trace records, 238
Treaty of Mutual Assistance in Criminal Matters (1973), 7
Triads
    activities and methods of operations, 170–171
    global dispersal, 163–164, 170, 171
    historical perspective, 160–164
    introduction, 159
    legitimate business influence, 169–170, 174
    structure, 164–167, 168–169
Tribute, Mafia, 132
Tung On Association, 168
Tung Triad group, 169
Typologies, Albanese's, 36–37

U

Under and Alone (Queen), 192
Underboss (Maas), 133
Uniform Narcotic Drug Act (1932), 23
Unions and labor racketeering, 130–131, 236–237
United Nations, 16
United Nations Convention against Transnational Organized Crime (2000), 231
United Self-Defense Groups of Colombia (AUC), 62, 244, 265
USA Patriot Act (2001)
    controversy surrounding, 225, 284
    intelligence gathering consequences, 245
    money laundering, 202, 230–231
    surveillance expansion, 224, 238
Utilitarianism, 39
Uyoku right-wing group, 141

V

The Valachi Papers (Maas), 133
Valencia cartel, 69
Vendetta, 127
Vice Lord Nation (People), 212
Vietnamese gangs, 174
La Violenca (1947-1953), 52

Violence and intimidation
   American gangs, 213
   American Mafia power
      struggles, 116, 120
   Cali cartel, 58
   Chicago Mafia, 120
   Chinese organized crime,
      173–174, 175
   definition of organized crime
      and, 6
   Jamaican Posses, 218
   Medellín cartel, 55
   Mexican DTOs, 70, 71–73, 75,
      76, 79, 81
   OMGs, 181, 185, 186, 200
   piracy, 18
   political machines and, 21
   Russian Mafia, 93, 94, 95–96,
      101
   Uyoku, 141
   Yakuza, 142, 143, 145
Violent Crime Control and Law
   Enforcement Act (1994), 220
Voroskoy Zakon, 91
Vory V. Zakone (thief-in-law),
   90–91

W

Wah Ching gang, 172–173
Weapons of mass destruction, 258,
   270–271, 273

Weapons smuggling
   Russian Mafia, 97–98, 102–103
   terrorism/organized crime
      nexus, 17, 266, 271
   Yakuza, 152
Wheel network, 235, 263
Whiskey Rebellion, 25
White-collar crime, terrorist
   participation in, 271
White Lotus Society, 163
White Slave Act (Mann Act)
   (1910), 226
White supremacy philosophy
   among OMGs, 183, 191
Wickersham Committee (1931),
   27
Wiretap, 238
Wiseguy, 125–126, 127, 128
Wiseguy: Life Inside a Mafia Family
   (Pileggi), 128
Witnesses and informants. *See*
   Informants and witnesses
Witness Security and Protection
   Program (WITSEC), 133, 239
Wo Hop gang, 172–173
Working definition, 2–3
Wo Triad group, 169

Y

Yakuza
   activities and methods

      business influence, 145,
         150–151, 153, 155,
         156
      drug trafficking, 151
      gambling, 150–151
      money laundering, 145,
         152–153, 155–156
      pornography, 152
      protection and extortion,
         150–151, 153
      weapons smuggling, 152
   conclusions, 156–157
   current activities, 144–146
   historical perspective, 28,
      140–144
   introduction, 139–140
   investigative strategies,
      153–156
   as shadow government, 16,
      28, 143
   structure, 146–149
   Triads' WWII work for,
      163–164
   violence and intimidation,
      142, 143, 145
Yamaguchi-gumi criminal group,
   142–144
Yamano-kai criminal group, 144

Z

Los Zetas, 72, 75–76, 80–81

Photo Credits

Chapter 5
page 73 © meraklitasarim/ShutterStock, Inc.; page 74 Courtesy of DEA

Chapter 6
page 90 © ITAR-TASS/Landov

Chapter 7
page 115 © Everett Collection Inc./Alamy Images; page 119 © Daniel Sheehan/AP Photos

Chapter 8
page 148 © Chris Wilson/Alamy Images

Chapter 9
page 173 © Str Old/REUTERS

Chapter 10
page 187 © POOL New/REUTERS

Chapter 11
page 219 © Tomas Bravo/REUTERS